I AM HARMONY

A BOOK ABOUT BABAJI

by Radhe Shyam

The American Haidakhan Samaj
P.O. Box 9
Crestone, Colorado 81131
www.BabajiSamaj.org

The American Haidkhand Samaj
P.O. Box 9
Crestone, Colorado 81131 U.S.A.
www.BabajiSamaj.org

Cover design and composition by
Kailash and Ramloti

ISBN: 0-9626421-1-8

First Printing 1990
Second Printing 2006

"I bow to Thee, O Lord, Image of mercy;
To Shiva, Who is affectionate to His disciples, Doer of Goodness,
The Destroyer of sins and suffering;
To Thee, the incarnation of compassion, I surrender always."

CONTENTS

ACKNOWLEDGEMENTS

On the (1990) publication of this book, I need to make a number of acknowledgements for help without which this book might never have seen the light of day.

First and foremost, I acknowledge Shri Shri Haidakhan Wale Baba, Mahavatar Babaji, Who, in 1981, instructed me to write this book and Who has, I think, inspired many of its pages.

I thank "Om Shanti Devi" and Sheila Devi Singh for a vast quantity of translation of Babaji's words from Hindi into English, without which I would have missed even more of the kaleidoscopic activity which took place in Babaji's presence. I am grateful to the many people who shared with me significant personal experiences which illustrate Babaji's teachings and His methods of teaching. Their experiences, the written experiences of people of 'Old Haidakhan Baba,' and my own experiences with Him form the major part of this book.

I owe many thanks to the generous hosts who arranged travel for Babaji and His followers to many cities in India, who housed and fed us, and whose functions provided opportunities to share experiences of Babaji, as well as stimulating new experiences. I thank the many devotees who lived in Haidakhan and acted their roles in Babaji's earthly play and to those who maintain some semblance of His presence there still.

I thank Swami Fakiranand for encouraging my use of his voluminous files and stories about Haidakhan Baba. I thank Vishnu Dutt Shastriji again and again for his comprehensive knowledge of the Vedic scriptures and of Babaji's message and teachings, for the beauty and clarity of his explanations and exhortations, and for his generous sharing of his knowledge and wisdom. And I thank Shri Trilok Singh - whom Babaji called "Muniraj," King of the Sages - for his steady and uplifting example, and for his constancy in service to The Divine.

In the United States, where this book was completed and published, I want to acknowledge and thank Brad Bunnin for sharing his comprehensive knowledge of copyright and publishing law; Bill Bowman, for his assistance in establishing the Spanish Creek

Press; and Richard Baltzell for excellent advice on publishing and distribution of the book. I thank Elizabeth Weisiger for finding the Ringier America printing firm and brokering the contract for the printing of this book, and Virginia Masi for executing J.D. Marston's book cover design.

I am deeply obliged to friends for providing photographs which illustrate the chapters: to Robert Linn for the painting of Shri Babaji on the cover of the 1990 edition; to Paramananda for the photograph on page iv; to Anton Waelti for the photograph on page 1; to Rajendra Kumar Sharma for the photograph on page 25; to Deborah Wood for the photograph on page 85; to Ram Singh Sammal for the photograph on page 97; to Arun Vora for the photograph on page 117; to Roland and Gertraud Reichel for the photographs on pages 149, 239, and 279; to Lisetta Carmi for the photographs on pages 195 and 261; and to Balbir Singh Sethi for the photograph on page 217. I regret that I do not know who took the other photographs.

I bless Jackie for buying the book that gave us our first knowledge of Babaji. I thank my brother Arthur Swan for reading the manuscript several times and especially for a thorough and helpful critique of a near-final draft of the book. I thank Sita Rami for leading me to Babaji and for her constant support of this project. I acknowledge a great debt to Ram Dass (J.D. Marston) and Ramloti (Deborah Wood) for the growing experiences we shared in establishing an ashram in Crestone, Colorado, based on Shri Babaji's teachings, schedule and methods. And I thank all the members of the American Haidakhan Samaj and the Loving Relationships Training who participated to any degree in that experience.

Crestone, Colorado, July 1990

FORWORD TO THE SECOND EDITION

Since the first publication of "I Am Harmony", in 1990, the book has gone around the world with its account of Shri Babaji's most recent ministries and teachings on Earth. "I Am Harmony" has been translated and published in Bulgarian, Croatian, German, Italian, Japanese, Korean, Polish, Russian, Slovenian and Swedish; it has been translated into Dutch and is awaiting publication; and it is in process of translation into Latvian and Serbian.

With the original printing exhausted, the American Haidakhandi Samaj has authorized and supported the republication of the book in a new format. The new format allows the inclusion of additional and different photographs from many people, most of whom are mentioned in the earlier forward or are unknown. I would like to thank Emam and Ramloti for their contribution of several of the color images in this new edition. The 2006 reprinting of "I Am Harmony" contains few other changes: the story of Shri Babaji's ministries in the past two centuries has not changed since "I Am Harmony" was published in 1990. For this edition, the first chapter of the 1990 edition was trimmed and moved to the last chapter in the current printing, and a few typographical and other errors have been corrected.

Thought was given to up-dating this edition to reflect what has been accomplished by Shri Babaji's followers since His Mahasamadhi, but that is a whole new story. You can learn some of that story by going to the listing of Babaji ashrams and centers around the world, which has been added to the information sections at the end of the book. Their websites offer a good deal of information.

FOREWORD TO THE FIRST EDITION

Paramahansa Yogananda called Mahavatar Babaji the "Yogi-Christ of modern India." The Haidakhan worship service describes Babaji as "Supreme Guru, Lord of mercy", "King of sages" and "Lord of the universe."

This book is about Babaji[1], a great manifestation of The Divine Who has a history of appearing in a flesh-and-blood human form throughout the course of human civilization to help humankind understand, experience and achieve its relationship to The Divine. The tradition of Babaji's manifestations is that He appears in remote places at varying intervals in time - especially when humanity is undergoing major changes and challenges that have a potential for purification and the elevation of the whole human race - and, by example and teaching, helps transform a few people who may be inspired to share the teachings and help humanity take a few more steps forward on the path toward conscious reunion with the Divine Source of this whole Creation.

His teaching is not sectarian, but is supportive of all religions that guide human beings toward a life lived in harmony with The Divine. The practitioner of any of the major religions of the world today can find inspiration and support in the life and teachings of Babaji. Babaji taught from the basis of the ancient, eternal truths, but He focused the teachings on present-day problems.

The experience of Divinity seems a rather rare thing in human lives these days. Many people believe that a relationship or communication with an aware Creator is impossible. But, unless we totally discredit the experiences and statements of thousands of saints and holy men and women of all ages and all religions, it must be acknowledged that some people have seen, heard, or otherwise experienced The Divine in some way.

There is a mythology of Babaji in the Himalayan regions that reaches back into very early human civilizations. Paramahansa Yogananda's "Autobiography of a Yogi"[2], published in 1946, introduced the stories and experiences of Mahavatar Babaji to the West in a book which dealt mainly with people's experiences of Him between 1861 and 1920, in India. There are books written about a manifestation of Babaji as Haidakhan Baba in the period of about 1890 to 1922. And now there are books written about the manifestation of Babaji which was experienced by many thousands of people in the period from June 1970 to February 14, 1984. This book collects and shares some of the stories from the long history and focuses on the experiences people had of this latest manifestation of Babaji. People still encounter Babaji in various ways all over the world. These experiences are by no means limited to India or to that physical manifestation of Babaji which 'died' on February 14, 1984.

Babaji is a spiritual being who serves constantly as a link between the Formless Divine and the physical creation, between God and humankind. He states that He is a manifestation of Lord Shiva, one of the names India gives to The Divine - a form of God known as a renunciate, a helper, and the greatest of Teachers. There are a number of stories (some of them in this book) which attest to His ability to create forms - either astral or flesh-and-blood human - at will. On one occasion, He told a devotee who had knowledge of His having been seen and experienced in three widely-separated places in India on the same day, that He could be seen in as many as eight forms at the same time. Some people who have experienced one or more of the forms of Babaji have come to the belief that there are five forms of Shiva (see the frontispiece which gives one commonly-pictured form of the five-faced Lord Shiva) involved with Earth at any given time. One is usually to be found in Nepal in an "old" form and another in a "young" form; one is often present as Haidakhan Baba; one may be elsewhere in India; and a fifth may be in a spirit or astral form. And all of these forms come and go at will. Such is the experience and belief of many people in the Kumaon Hills.

Each of the forms, when encountered in the flesh, in dream, or in vision, has divine attributes. Always, Babaji appears to give some form of blessing or teaching. There are many experiences of people (some are related in this book) which give evidence of what we would call miraculous powers exhibited by Babaji. Even if you wish to discount or discredit such experiences, He remains an unusual and unusually powerful character who fulfills the predictions and declarations that He comes into human society to serve and to teach. He does not make an issue of His divinity. It helps in the transmission of His teachings if the disciple acknowledges that divinity, but He accepts any honest seeker of Truth who is ready and open to learning and spiritual growth.

People saw Him in many roles - as Lord Shiva, the Supreme Guru, purifier, friend, the Divine Child, the Divine Mother, Divine Father, Supreme Yogi, a healer, an Immortal. He is all of those things and we see in Him that for which we look. We also see ourselves in Him, for He mirrored each of us, so we could see where we were on our Paths and gain insight into ourselves and what we needed to work on. He is a great Teacher and Guide, working on each individual who is open to Him, while still managing to give a cohesive program to all who come to Him.

His chief concern is with the human spirit or soul - that in humankind which is closest to The Divine, which carries the spark of The Divine. He teaches that the Creator and all of the Creation is One: He sees the whole Creation as the Manifestation of The Divine. Gods, demons, humans, animals, plants, rocks - all are 'built' with the building blocks of the divine Creative Energy. The Divine at rest is formless, chaotic Energy; when It is moved to create forms, the Conscious Energy moves in accordance with Divine Law to shape sub-atomic particles, which combine to make atoms, which combine over and over to create, over aeons of time, the universes we humans eventually see. All created forms, then, are aspects of The Divine, Which experiences Itself in action through all of these forms throughout the whole period of Creation.

Babaji taught that these myriad forms which make up the Creation function best when they function in harmony with The Divine and with each other. Because the times require it and have prepared the way for this knowledge, Babaji extended Christ's message of "love thy neighbor" to a message of concern for harmony among *all* created forms. All forms - human and other - are so tightly interrelated that we cannot abuse one form without disrupting the rest. That interrelationship is so close that beneficial actions offered by one created being to another have beneficial results throughout the whole universe. The very vibrations of our emotions or being have effects throughout the Creation.[3]

To be in Babaji's presence was an opportunity to gain an understanding of this principle. His Presence transformed and uplifted the atmosphere of any room or area into which He walked, and each person in His Presence felt the enlivening of the spark of The Divine within him/herself and a quickened sense of harmony with the people and other life around them. Babaji seemed to literally vibrate a feeling of love and harmony with a force that brought those around Him into a sympathetic, harmonious level of vibration. The concept of unity and the need for harmony within the Creation has a very profound effect on human responsibility for the Earth on which we live, and for the universe beyond Earth's atmosphere.

Babaji seeks to bring humankind back to an awareness of its unity with The Divine and with all other created forms in the universe. Both His words and His actions focus on the need for harmony among all elements of Creation. He pointed to human abuses of Nature and warned of coming catastrophic reactions of Nature, which can be mitigated by focused, conscious, disciplined human action taken in harmony with the Divine Law.

Babaji comes not to espouse any particular religion (He says all religions lead to The Divine), but to show and teach a *way of life*. Babaji called this way of life *Sanatan Dharma* - the Eternal Way (or Law or Truth). He indicated that the Creation was manifested and is extended and maintained in accordance with the Sanatan Dharma; that humanity's deviations from this Law of Life create imbalances and disruptions in the harmonious operation of the Universe; and that He comes - again and again - to help restore balance and the Sanatan Dharma. He teaches people - and shows by His example - that leading lives based on Truth, Simplicity and Love can restore to the individual, to societies, and to our whole world the inner peace and balance on which alone world peace and social justice can be established.

The great spiritual Masters throughout the ages of human civilizations have all shown a valid Way to different peoples at different ages in different cultures, emphasizing what their people needed to learn at that time to advance them on the Way and bring them into closer harmony with The Divine. Each way has been tested and has led people to "God-realization" and each has developed great saints. The important thing is for a person to focus on and *follow* a path that is suitable and inspiring for him or her. To wander aimlessly, tasting the fruits of this and that interesting philosophy or ritual is likely only to lead one in circles, rather than to a clear goal. Discipline - of mind and body - is an essential element of Babaji's teaching; without discipline and hard work, nothing valuable is achieved.

Following a Path of discipline is no easy thing for a human being distracted by the lure of many pleasures, as we particularly are in this age. The <u>Bhagavad-Gita,</u> a truly inspired Indian scripture, describes one's mind and senses as a team of twelve strong horses hitched to a chariot. If the charioteer (the individual soul) cannot tame and control his team, he is off for a wild ride through life; but if he can exercise control over his team, he controls great power and speed in action. One's religion or philosophy- whatever shapes one's way of living -is the most important factor in life; but that factor is useless if it leads to no practical end or output. Babaji looked not only to one's inner spirit but to the results, the products, of people's lives. He looked for beneficial action performed in harmony with the Divine Will and all of Creation.

We human beings tend to become like those we choose as role models; we become what we focus on, or like the people with whom we most associate. Babaji, like most Teachers, urged His followers to "go to the wise and learn." The Katha Upanishad, another early and inspired Indian scriptural work, helps in the definition of "the wise" whom we should seek out.

"The good is one thing; the pleasant is another. These two, differing in their ends, both prompt to action. Blessed are they that choose the good; they that choose the pleasant miss the goal.

"Both the good and the pleasant present themselves to man. The wise, having examined both, distinguish the one from the other. The wise prefer the good to the pleasant; the foolish, driven by fleshly desires, prefer the pleasant to the good."[4]

Babaji taught by His own example and by guiding people into experiences they needed for growth. He *showed* people how to live in harmony with The Divine and Its Creation. He put people into situations where they could experience The Divine, however briefly. He sought practical results from His followers - even as they struggled toward purification and enlightenment. On one day, Babaji admonished: "You monkeys and bears! Only wagging your tails won't be enough! You will have to do something practical, something useful. Babaji says you must work hard and put [the teachings] into practice. First, be inspired yourselves; then inspire others with this message of <u>karma yoga</u> [work]."[5] He urged His followers to spend some time in His ashrams, with their monastic schedule and style, to experience and practice a pure, focused life in harmony with The Divine and all of Nature. Then go out to serve, as "householders" living in the real world, or to create ashrams "as islands in a sea of materialism" to serve in whatever capacities our countries need.

Babaji lived and taught squarely against the Western quip of "you only live once." He taught from the position that the human soul, like its Source and Goal, is eternal and that the experience of millions of lifetimes in various forms of the soul proceeds in a continuum from life to life. Each life in human form is an opportunity and challenge to build toward perfection of the soul, which returns again and again (through reincarnation) until the soul attains perfection. The soul's goal is to return to a state of unity with the Divine Perfection from which it came and from whence it has strayed in its experiencing itself and life's pleasures through constantly expanding senses and the concept of itself as an individual *body*, rather than as a manifestation of the Supreme Soul. Each lifetime *can* take the soul and its temporary human body closer to the goal of reunion, or we can throw away a lifetime's opportunity through ignorance or willfulness.

In His teaching and life, Babaji used miraculous powers, but indicated (as have other Masters} that they are attainable by anyone who can exercise the discipline to focus his or her mind and follow their Path to unity with The Divine. The powers come from thinking, working, living in harmony with the Creative Energy of the Universe. Babaji, for example, knew - even before they arrived or spoke to Him - who was coming to His ashram, whether they were ready for the experience of Haidakhan, whether they should stay or go. He read people's minds, healed their ailments, guided them into experiences they needed. And it has been people's experience that He comes and goes in human form, at will, through the course of human history.

His Message is not sectarian, but for all human beings of whatever religious or philosophical leaning. Hindus, Moslems, Christians,

Jews, Sikhs, Parsis, agnostics, animists, atheists, and others came to live and learn in His presence. His teachings and actions express the best in all religions and can challenge, enrich and expand spiritual knowledge, wisdom and experience within the framework of any of them. Krishna, Moses, Jesus, Mohammed, all stated that their highest and best followers can be identified by how they *live* - how they put into practice the religion they profess. Jesus, when asked "Which is the first commandment of all?", answered, "...thou shalt love the Lord thy God with all thy heart, and with all thy soul, and with all thy mind, and with all thy strength: this is the first commandment. And the second is like, namely this, Thou shalt love thy neighbour as thyself." Babaji's teachings are focused on *living* in harmony with The Divine, and loving the whole of Creation as thyself, more than on worshiping The Divine by any particular ritual or belief. He would surely agree with a statement attributed to His old friend, Neemkaroli Baba, "It is better to see God in everything than to try to figure it out."

When He had given His message, through example, experience and teaching, Babaji left, in order that people might absorb the Message and learn to live in Truth, Simplicity and Love, rather than to blindly follow His charming and beautiful Presence like so many sheep.

This book is a collection of people's experiences of Babaji; it is something of a biography of Babaji based on personal stories and recollections of people in whose veracity I have reason to believe. No one person and no one book can possibly "capture" this Being in print: The Divine in Its manifest forms is beyond human capacity to understand or to relate. Still, I invite you to read this book about Babaji as I and others have experienced Him. He does not come to create a new religion or to establish a "new God"; He comes to remind and teach humankind of a harmonious way of life. Whether you experience Babaji as divine or as a stimulating, challenging, unusual human being, His life and message (which are really the same thing) have much to offer to people in this era of change and possible growth.

NOTES

[1]   Babaji is also known as Bhole Baba (the Simple Father), Haidakhan

Wale Baba (the Baba from Haidakhan), Mahavatar Babaji (Babaji, the Great Avatar), Manmunindra Maharaj, and hundreds of other names. "Baba" is a Hindi word meaning Father (generally used in the sense one refers to a priest) and the suffix "-ji" is a term of added respect. Babaji can be translated as Revered Father.

[2] "Autobiography of a Yogi," Paramahansa Yogananda, page 345; 11th edition, 1987; published by Self-Realization Fellowship, 3880 San Rafael Avenue, Los Angeles, California 90065, U.S.A. N.B. Self-Realization Fellowship, the society founded by Paramahansa Yogananda, maintains that the Mahavatar Babaji about whom Yogananda wrote in his autobiography and other incarnations such as Haidakhan Baba are not one and the same. Readers of this book are invited to weigh the evidence presented here and come to their own conclusions.

[3] "Space and time are now dynamic quantities: when a body moves, or a force acts, it affects the curvature of space and time - and in turn the structure of space-time affects the way in which bodies move and forces act. Space and time not only affect but also are affected by everything that happens in the universe." Stephen W. Hawking, "A Brief History of Time from the Big Bang to Black Holes" ; Bantam Books, 1988, page 34. Itzhak Bentov's book, "Stalking the Wild Pendulum, On the Mechanics of Consciousness," (Destiny Books, 1988; first copyrighted and published by Bentov in 1977), provides a well-reasoned, enjoyable effort at presenting a scientific hypothesis of the creation and operation of the universes which relates closely to what Shri Babaji and others teach about the created universe.

[4] "The Upanishads, Breath of the Eternal," selected and translated by Swami Prabavananda and Frederick Manchester; a Mentor Book, New American Library, 1948 (copyright renewed 1975 by Swami Prabavananda); page 16.

[5] All the quoted remarks of Shri Babaji in this book (except for those contained in an experience quoted from some other source) come from the three little volumes of "Teachings of Babaji," published in India. These volumes are cited in the bibliography section at the back of this book.

"I surrender to Thee, O Lord; Thou alone art my refuge;
Thou alone art my mother, my father, my kin, my all;
Thou art my Lord in the world and in the scriptures.
Hail, hail, O King of Sages, Remover of the pain of Thy devotees!"
From the Haidakhan Aarati (worship service)

CHAPTER I

WE MEET HAIDAKHAN BABA

Margaret met me in New Delhi on February 21, 1980, and insisted we go the very next morning to meet Babaji, despite an unconfirmed business meeting I had requested at the Indian Ministry of External Affairs. We arranged for a car and driver and rode for two and a half hours south, to Vrindaban, where there is a Babaji ashram.

We rode across the flat plains of central India, sharing the sometimes divided highway with forms of transportation that reflected thousands of years of human existence - cars, smoke-belching trucks, crowded buses, two-wheeled, horse-drawn carts, four-wheeled, rubber-tired ox carts, a few camels, one or two laden elephants, and hundreds of people walking along the side, carrying everything from children to bundles of firewood and jugs of water. It was a lovely scene (and a slow ride), similar to what I had experienced in other third-world countries during my just-completed career in the Department of State in Washington, D.C.

What was more unusual, in my experience, was the peaceful repose of a sari-clad Margaret sitting beside me as we drove to meet Babaji. In the United States, Margaret Gold was a lawyer and teacher of law, a dynamo of energy directed at relieving the problems of all who came into her sphere. For much of the time as we drove, she was content to sit quietly, repeating a mantra[1] as she moved the beads of her <u>mala</u> (rosary) through her fingers, and occasionally pointing out to me the timeless beauties of the Indian landscape. It was clear that the seven weeks she had spent in Babaji's presence in India had made a profound change in Margaret.

When we reached Vrindaban, our driver slowly and carefully threaded his way through the crowded, narrow streets of the ancient town, famed as the childhood home of the great Lord Krishna. The rivers of people, rickshaws, hand carts, ox carts, cows, pigs and other cars parted gently to allow our progress to the winding, narrow lane on which Babaji's Vrindaban ashram is located. Our driver parked in a wide spot in the street and Margaret led me toward the

3

door of the ashram.

We left our shoes on a porch outside the entrance, along with a hundred other pairs of shoes and sandals, and walked into Babaji's ashram. The temple, which occupies two-thirds of the ground floor area of the ashram, was jammed with perhaps four hundred devotees who were sitting cross-legged on the floor, singing and chanting rhythmically, with harmonium, drums and bells playing. Margaret and I got into the long line of people who were going to where Babaji sat, yogi-fashion, on a raised dais, blessing devotees, receiving their gifts of flower garlands, candies, nuts, fruits, etc., and Himself giving out gifts. Margaret and I both had gifts for Babaji. Margaret had a mobile of hearts from Finland and I had a golden, heart-shaped locket that I had bought in Paris for $300 and on which I had paid another $100 in customs duties at the airport in Bombay.

It took perhaps fifteen minutes for us to reach Babaji, so I had a chance to see how people knelt before Him and touched His feet, handed Him a gift, or just raised up for His touch of blessing. When my turn came, I felt awkward in kneeling and touching my forehead to the floor before Him, but I did that and looked up at Him. Babaji was older - looking like someone in his early 30's - and chubbier than the photographs of Him that I had seen. He looked intently into my eyes as I reached to hand Him my little jewel box with its locket and chain. Babaji took the box, gave it a puzzled look and handed it back to me to open. I opened the box and gave it back to Babaji, who glanced casually at my gift - apparently far less impressed by it than I - and gave it to the devotee standing at His left who was handling the gifts which Babaji did not immediately give away.

I stood up to go, but Babaji motioned for me to sit down before Him at His right. So I sat on the floor, legs crossed, and watched Babaji for five or ten minutes. He sat soberly, with His hand raised in blessing, for some devotees. Others He received with a smile or laughter and a touch of blessing, perhaps exchanging a few words in Hindi. With an impish grin on His face, He threw apples, oranges, and candies into the laps of the ladies and children sitting directly in front of Him. There was constant hustle, noise, and activity swirling around Babaji, and yet an atmosphere of peace and serenity. I

4

remembered the many "little miracles" of my European trip on my way to India and I chuckled to myself as I inwardly asked, "Is this God on earth?"

After a few minutes, the mustachioed Indian devotee standing at Shri Babaji's left came to me and said Babaji had told him to take me to see "Swamiji," who could answer my questions in English. I wondered if Babaji had been reading my mind, as people said He did. We picked our way through the crowded temple to the far corner where Swami Fakiranand[2], a 70-year-old devotee who administered Babaji's ashram at Haidakhan, sat selling English and Hindi literature about Babaji. We talked for a few minutes about Babaji as the present physical manifestation of the scriptural Lord Shiva; then Swamiji was called away to a meeting. I stood up in that corner farthest from Babaji and watched the scene, so foreign to anything that even my Foreign Service travels had prepared me for.

Soon I saw Babaji beckoning for someone to come to Him. The man next to me said Babaji was telling me to come, so I walked back through the crowd, feeling that four hundred pairs of eyes were on me. As I knelt before Babaji, He opened a cardboard box and took out two big round pieces of sugar-and-milk candy and placed them in my right hand. I sat at His feet, eating the candy and looking up into His face. He was full of kindness and love, beyond anything I recollect having seen in any person's face and form; He seemed to literally radiate that love, like a measurable energy force. Suddenly, Babaji moved to get up; He leaned forward, put both His hands on my back and raised Himself to His feet, then hurried along the path through the crowd and out of the temple area. It was time for lunch. Margaret and her American and European friends came to tell me that Babaji had honored me greatly in His welcome and that I had been greatly blessed. I had no experience of how Babaji greeted other newcomers, but my mind and body held the 'charge' of His blessing for a long time. Even through the great confusion of entering into a culture that was very strange to me, I felt that I had been pulled to Babaji by His will and in His time.

In typical ashram fashion, we sat cross-legged on the floor of the temple for our noon meal, about a hundred people at each sitting.

Plates made of broad leaves sewn together were placed before each person and devotees served us, from steaming buckets, with rice, lentils, vegetables, fried bread (chapatis), a sweet, and tea in stainless steel 'glasses.' The food we ate had been offered first to Babaji and blessed by Him. This blessed food is called prasad: all the meals served to Babaji's devotees, wherever He went, were blessed and served as prasad. We ate with our right hands. As I ate, Shri Babaji came back into the temple, stood before me, and asked my name.

After prasad, there was a period for rest and household activities before Babaji's late afternoon darshan - the time in which a saint sits with devotees to share his or her radiance, advice and uplifting energy - and the evening aarati (a sung worship service). Margaret and I went to a guesthouse and napped and bathed before starting back to Babaji's ashram.

Vrindaban is the town where Lord Krishna, a great manifestation of The Divine as Lord Vishnu, and the central character of the Indian epic, *The Mahabharata,* lived as a child with his cow-herding tribe. Scriptural tradition places Lord Krishna's time in Vrindaban about 6700 years ago, but many historians guess the time to be much closer to the birth of Christ. Recent archaeological finds push the date back toward the traditional dates. Under any circumstances, Vrindaban is an old town and its narrow, winding, crowded streets, even though paved now with asphalt, provide the many religious pilgrims and tourists with a setting more conducive to spiritual search than the bustling, aggressive commercial cities of India. Vrindaban is still famous for its milk and milk products and there are many street-side stalls and shops where delicious hot milk or milky tea, called *chai,* is served, and we could buy milk-and-sugar sweets to offer to Shri Babaji. Outside the many temples, street vendors offered flower garlands at a rupee or so each, to be offered to The Divine during the evening worship services. The streets were full of activity - shoppers, vendors, strollers, rickshaws, bicycles, horse-drawn carts, ox carts, a few cars, many cows, some pigs and piglets. As the afternoon came to a close, Vrindaban's thousand temples offered up the sounds of bells and gongs and chanting and the sweet scent of incense.

Babaji's ashram also filled and again people waited in long

lines to touch His feet with reverence and offer their gifts and themselves, while Om Namah Shivaya[3] was sung to many tunes. That evening, after aarati, when I placed a flower garland on Babaji's knees and knelt before Him, He put the garland around my neck. On my way back to my place, I stopped in a darkened area behind and to the left of Babaji to talk with an Indian devotee. I happened to look away from the devotee to look at Babaji: I saw He had turned just at that second to look over His left shoulder at me, and before I could even smile at Him, I was aware of an orange flying past a column and over the outstretched hands of three or four devotees - a left-handed, sideways shot that hit me square in the chest, as if to say, "Who else but God could make a shot like that?" Babaji laughed and turned back to the devotees in front of Him.

For two days Margaret and I were caught up in the excitement and joy of being with Babaji. We were up at 3:30 a.m. to bathe and make our way to the temple before 5 for the first activity of the day. Hours were spent in the temple, singing and chanting and being bathed in the waves of love, peace and joy emanating from Babaji and His devotees. We talked with devotees from many parts of India, Europe and North America, hearing tales of their experiences with Babaji.

After two days, Margaret and I went back to Delhi to tend to my business with the Ministry of External Affairs; then we drove back to Vrindaban. We arrived at the temple late in the evening; the service was over, the temple nearly empty and scantily lit. We feared we had missed Babaji, who was about to leave for Bombay. But Babaji appeared out of the dark shadows in the temple and, through interpreters, told Margaret and me to join Swamiji and a party of mostly Western devotees who were going to the ashram in Haidakhan that night.

We rode through the night on the narrow-gauge train to Haldwani, at the edge of the plains where the foothills of the Himalayas begin to rise. Pedal rickshaws carried us, two by two, with baggage behind, through busy shopping streets to the modest shop of Trilok Singh, a grain and vegetable dealer and strong devotee of Babaji, from which place most of the last 'legs' of people's trips to Haidakhan depart. On this occasion, there was a jeep to take Swamiji and some of his party to the end of the road up the river valley, to what is known as "the dam site."

As the jeep wound its way through the hills overlooking the river, I was amazed at the beauty of the area. Most of the hills are covered with trees - lots of pine - and, here and there, families had cleared, over the years, terraces along the hillside which were, at that season, richly green with corn, wheat, or vegetables. On the edges of some of the fields were stone houses with red tin roofs and barns, outside of which oxen and buffaloes stood or lay. Overhead, eagles flew; a family of monkeys fled through the trees as the jeep rolled by. Down in the wide, stony valley a chastened river flowed quietly in one or more channels down a largely dry bed; the river's time to howl is from July through September, when the monsoon turns the quiet stream into a raging demon and cuts off easy access between the Haidakhan valley and the plains.

In the mid-70's, the Indian Government decided to build a dam near the mouth of 'Babaji's' Gautam Ganga (the river which flows through Babaji's ashram at Haidakhan) in order to supply water to plains cities and farms. A road was built to the dam site, which greatly benefited the farmers of the valley. But despite work crews at the site every year and a dedication speech by Prime Minister Indira Gandhi, the dam has never gotten under way. Nor is it likely to, since engineers note that the rock at the site is too crumbly, too likely to shift, to support a dam; and the monsoon erosion would fill the reservoir with mud within ten or fifteen years, anyway. But the project has supplied needed jobs in the valley, brought buses to the mouth of the valley, and created tea shops where travelers to and from Haidakhan and other villages can sit while they wait for the infrequent buses.

Our jeep stopped at the dam site and we got out to walk the remaining three or four miles up the riverbed to Haidakhan. Village men carried our baggage for ten rupees (about one dollar) - a price then set and enforced by Babaji to provide villagers with a fair income and to keep villagers from gouging naive foreigners who would pay almost anything asked. On our hike up the river on that trip, I counted twenty-one river crossings, some ankle-deep, some knee-deep. As our party walked, we met valley dwellers going to the bus, dogs barked at us from their hillside stations, and as we neared the houses on the hillsides, children came out to shout "Bhole Baba ki jai!" - "Hail to the Simple Father!" -one of Shri Babaji's many names. There was a strong sense of coming home, despite the strangeness of the whole scene and culture.

Within sight of the ashram, about a quarter mile downstream, there is an island in the riverbed on which a tree grows. Legend has it that Lord Shiva brought His consort to the mount known locally as Mount Kailash, which rises above the island, and that Sati used to bathe in the river by the island. The crown of this Mount Kailash and the cave at its feet are associated with Lord Shiva's doing thousands of years of *tapas* (meditation and other spiritual practices) here for the benefit of humankind. There is now an orange-painted statue of Shri Hanuman - a god[4] with the form of a monkey, who came to earth to serve Lord Ram and His consort, Sita - stationed on this island to greet and bless travelers and pilgrims.

I was confused by the numbers of gods and holy figures I was being 'introduced to' in the Hindu culture and I asked what to make of Hanuman. I learned then (and over and over in later experience) that despite the hundreds of identifiable, storied gods, goddesses, and demons in the Hindu culture and religion, the scriptures and thoughtful Hindus firmly declare that "The Lord is One, without a second."[5] The multiplicity of gods and goddesses arises from human efforts to demonstrate and give form to the many aspects of the One, Formless God, to illustrate and personalize the laws which make the universe operate in harmony and the principles which underlie the creation, maintenance and 'destruction' (or purification) of the universe. Adherents worship that form - or those forms - of The Divine which are most attractive to them, or whose qualities they wish to attain. And, if one gives credence to statements from past and present, The Divine appears to sincere devotees in the forms that they worship and expect to encounter. Hanuman, noted for his strength and his wholehearted devotion and service to God (as Lord Ram), is a great favorite all over India. Hanuman is also a great favorite of Shri Babaji and His devotees.

9

Our journey up the valley ended with a climb up what is called "The 108 Steps." (There are actually a few more than 108 steps from the riverbed to the ashram's temple garden, but 108 has a spiritual and numerological significance.) Near the top of the steps is a one-story building housing an office and tiny bedroom for Swami Fakiranand, facing the steps, and, facing the other direction, a small room in which Babaji slept and received visitors. Outside Babaji's room was a concrete terrace which contained an ancient pipal tree and a sacred fire pit, at which Babaji performed a dawn fire ceremony every day He was in Haidakhan. The terrace, shaded by the sacred pipal tree, looks out over the valley and the little village of Haidakhan. Margaret and I spent ten days in the Haidakhan ashram, living very simply and following the schedule which Babaji had established. We got up at 4 a.m. and went to the river to bathe, in pre-dawn temperatures hovering around 40 degrees Fahrenheit. There was an hour or so for meditation and a hot cup of chai before the hour-long aarati service at sun-up. The ashram did not serve breakfast. The concept was that one meal a day, at noon, is sufficient for simple living, but Babaji also provided an evening supper and frequently distributed fruits, nuts and candies, or gave tea parties, so no one felt hunger. But Western devotees, used to breakfast, found cereals and buffalo milk or cheese and biscuits and chai at the village tea shops. Then we went to work.

Shri Babaji taught that work done without selfish, personal motive, dedicated to The Divine as service performed in harmony with all of Creation, is the highest form of worship. It is also a means of purification for a devotee, transforming inner negativity and hostility and opening the individual to spiritual growth. This is karma yoga. So there were work sessions both morning and afternoon. Our work at that time was enlarging the terrace on the right bank of the Gautam Ganga, where four small temples had been built and two more were under construction. Both men and women tackled the slopes of the hillside with pickaxes and shovels, carrying the dirt away in wheelbarrows and (mostly) in metal pans which Indian laborers carry on their heads. "Moving the mountain" seemed an impossible task with those simple tools, but progress was noticeable week by week, if not day by day. Patience was one of the virtues which Babaji taught

10

through experiences.

At noon, we stopped and washed in the river and sat in the warm sun on the cemented terrace outside the ashram kitchen to eat. There was half an hour or so to rest, then back to work until just before sundown. We washed or bathed and went to the evening aarati service. After the service, the kitchen crew served supper, generally left-overs from the noon prasad, but occasionally something freshly cooked. The ashram rule was that lights go out at 10 p.m., but there were many conversations held after supper until weariness put an end to them.

Margaret had come to my house in Washington shortly after the sudden death, from a bee sting, of my wife Jackie at the end of October 1978. Margaret was a teacher of Transcendental Meditation, looking for a job and a place to stay. I was then part of a State Department team negotiating the contract for construction of the new American Embassy compound in Moscow and I needed someone to house-and-cat-sit while I traveled back and forth before and after Christmas, 1978. By the time my travels were over, I found Margaret so charming and supportive that I had asked her to marry me. She didn't say "yes," but she stayed on in the house. Margaret, like Jackie and me, had read Paramahansa Yogananda's "Autobiography of a Yogi" and had been fascinated by the tales of Mahavatar Babaji. When she learned, in the summer of 1979, of Babaji's presence in Haidakhan, Margaret had decided to travel with Leonard Orr and a group of Rebirthers to meet Babaji in January 1980. I had helped her make the trip and Margaret was to have joined me on a post-retirement business trip through Europe and Israel to test the possibilities of establishing an international consulting firm. But when I got to London to meet Margaret on her return from Haidakhan, I found two letters from her saying that all she wanted to do was to spend the rest of her life in Babaji's presence; and thanks for everything. After a night of pondering what to do, I extended my airline ticket from Tel Aviv to New Delhi and cabled for an interview in the Ministry of External Affairs. It was in this way that I met Babaji somewhat earlier than my Capricornian schedule had contemplated.

In New Delhi, in Vrindaban, and during the ten days in Haidakhan, I tried to talk Margaret into returning to the United States and marriage, but she was firm in her desire to stay with Babaji. I grew more and more concerned with my need to pursue my consulting business proposal and, finally, headed back to the U.S.A. Margaret went with me to Delhi to see me off, but she would not go back to the United States with me.

In Washington, D.C., I sat at my desk to prepare a report to my prospective clients on my findings on the business trip, but nothing came. Day after day I went to my desk, then wandered off, stymied and bewildered. I read through the Haidakhan aarati service morning and evening and almost always ended up teary and in confusion. I could not understand what had happened to me. After about ten days of this, words began to flow from my pen and in another ten days I had a good report in the mail to my prospective clients. I had a contractual obligation to my former office and I sat to complete work on that project and went through the same process of "nothingness," followed by a burst of work.

Margaret called from India to tell me that when Babaji returned to Haidakhan, His first question to her was, "Why did your friend leave without My permission?" A few days later, Babaji sent Margaret out of the ashram (for the third time in her three-month stay) and told her to "go to your home." She considered her home was with Babaji, so she went to another of His ashrams.

I was so upset, so 'incomplete' in my relationships with both Margaret and Babaji, that six weeks after my return from India I was back on a plane, bound for New Delhi and Haidakhan.

When I reached the top of the "108 Steps" at the Haidakhan Ashram, Margaret was standing in the door of Swami Fakiranand's office, cleaning a rug. I had left Washington so precipitously that I had not sent a telegram. Margaret almost fainted from surprise, but she recovered quickly and told me that Babaji was giving darshan by the temple and that I should wash before going to see Him.

Shri Babaji was sitting on His dais in the kirtan hall, the three-walled room whose open side faced the temple which housed the marble statue of 'Old Haidakhan Baba.' Babaji was talking with an Indian devotee, so I knelt and touched His feet and sat down. When Babaji finished His conversation, He turned to me and asked, "Why did you leave without My permission?" (I learned later that ashram protocol required that one have Babaji's permission to stay in the ashram and that one was expected to clear things with Babaji before leaving the ashram.) I told Him that I had needed to work on my new business proposal, and told Him how the work had gone and why I had returned. After a few minutes more of giving darshan, Babaji left His dais and took me to the bottom of the stairs leading to guestrooms in the largest building in the ashram. He told an Indian devotee to give me one of those rooms, and we took my luggage upstairs.

When I came back down, people were sitting down to eat the noon meal. Margaret started to sit apart from me and Babaji came over to us, told the person between us to move, and firmly sat us down together. He told me, "You can have her in your room, if you like," and walked away. Margaret was appalled and annoyed; ashram rules separated male and female sleeping arrangements. Before Margaret had finished telling me I should not ask her to stay in my room, Babaji came back to us and said to me, "You can marry her, if you like," and then He went off to the room where He ate a few morsels of the food offered to Him. Margaret's indignation was great, but, even then, she recognized that she had surrendered her will to His; she would not deny anything He required of her. But, lawyer-like, she noted that in both statements Babaji had left the choice to me and she started working to make certain that I would not "exercise my option."

Babaji played with us for a week. We did share the guest-room, and we worked together, ate together, went together to talk to Babaji. On one occasion, at the temple near the hillside work project, as we knelt before Babaji, He took our right hands in His, pressed them together, and laughingly said, in English, "You're married! You're married!" and then quickly walked away, leaving us wondering if He were serious. We knew that He 'threw' people into situations to test them and help them grow through their problems and desires; but there was also the possibility that He really willed our marriage. So we began asking Babaji, "Is this marriage Your Will?," or was it my desire that Babaji was fulfilling? When Margaret asked that question of Him one day, Babaji responded that He was supporting my desire. When I asked on another occasion, I got a non-committal response.

After a few days of this, I agreed with Margaret that I had no desire to be wedded to a woman who didn't want to be married. I went to Babaji to tell Him so. I knelt before Him, touched His feet, and raised my head to speak. And Babaji got up and hurried away. Because He stopped talking about the marriage, we concluded He had stopped playing the marriage game with us. We decided that if He asked again, I would tell Babaji that there would be no marriage.

Early in this visit to Haidakhan, I had gotten a case of diarrhea and Shri Babaji had told me to rest and eat carefully. Late one morning, a week after my arrival, I had taken a nap and I was awakened by the sound of the temple bells welcoming Babaji back from the work sites across the river. I heard Babaji's laughter and felt pulled to go to His presence. When I got to Him, He was seated on the wall outside His room and about twenty devotees, including Margaret, were standing and sitting around Him. I knelt before Him and as I rose up, Babaji asked, "What do you want to say?" With my mind stilled by sleep, I had nothing to say; but what came out of my lips was, "Baba, we just want to do Your Will." And Babaji replied, "It is My Will that you marry." And, without further ado, Babaji married us on the spot - literally tied our hands together, sent us to the temple to make our pranams, had rings produced for us to exchange, and told us to arrange a wedding feast for the next day!

The next day I had a <u>mundan</u> - a complete head shave, hair and mustache gone. Shri Babaji sometimes recommended mundans for healing, or for helping a person work through a spiritual block (like attachment to one's established looks and identity), or simply as a symbol of one's submission to his or her guru. I think it was the latter thought that prompted my request to Moti Bhagwan, the ashram barber, for the mundan.

In the late afternoon, Margaret and I went to the garden where Shri Babaji was directing the evening's work. He tenderly led us to a log and sat us on it so we could look down the lovely

14

valley. A few days before, Babaji had given Margaret the name Sita Rami. Ram was the first of the great "human" forms of The Divine in the Hindu experience, and Sita was His wife, so perfect and so devoted to Lord Ram that she is still held up to Indian girls and women as the ideal of womanhood. The name Sita Rami combines both the male and female energies and aspects of God. Babaji asked if I had any other desire. I laughed and said that now that I had a new wife and a mundan, I would like a new name. Without hesitation, Babaji said my name was Radhe Shyam (or Radheyshyam). A devotee explained to me that Shyam is one of the many names of Lord Krishna and Radha was His most devoted female follower; in stories and pictures, Krishna and Radha are linked. So Babaji gave both of us powerful names that link the male and female energies of The Divine.

We stayed in the ashram for about a week after our marriage. Babaji blessed us in so many ways that we were dizzy with it. We came from heaven. We were made for each other in heaven. The gods smiled on our marriage; even the birds of the valley were rejoicing. He had never seen a more perfect couple. We began to think that maybe He was serious about this marriage.

Early in May, Babaji sent us back to the United States. We asked when we could return to Haidakhan. He gave us the charge of sending money for three more temples to be built on the right bank of the river; that would cost "three or four lakhs of rupees" - about $50,000 at that time. When the money had been sent, we could return, "if you wish."

As we left the ashram, Shri Babaji told us that our names, repeated together - Sita Ram, Radhe Shyam - constitute a mantra. And His last words to us, as we started down the 108 steps from the ashram to the riverbed, were "Be happy, children!"

By coincidence or otherwise, everything we turned to in the United States went well. We sold our house very well in an awful real estate market. Mortgage rates fell from 18-19% in May to 11% in July, and after our contract was signed on July 4, rates climbed again to 18% by the end of the year. We were able to send Babaji $50,000 for the three new temples in less than four months after our return. In four more weeks, we managed to give away the rest of the proceeds and officially terminate my stalled effort to start the consulting business. At the end of August, we applied for visas to return to India.

Our lives had been totally changed by our encounters with Shri Babaji. Our thoughts were very much focused on The Divine and on service to the whole of Creation. Religion, or spirituality, had an immediate, practical, moment-to-moment relationship to our lives. We felt the 'pull' of Babaji's love, joy and wisdom and wanted further to experience His presence and teaching. We had much to learn and wanted to have Him be our guru, wanted Him to accept us as His disciples. So, late in December, 1980, when our visas came, we went back to India to be with Babaji again, to sit at the feet of the Master and learn about and from Him.

NOTES

1   A mantra is a sacred Sanskrit phrase or statement which, by frequent or constant repetition, focuses the mind of a devotee on some aspect of The Divine.
2   Formerly known as Chandra Singh Rana, of Dhanyan, Almora District, Uttar Pradesh. "Swamiji" is a retired Indian civil servant.
3   The mantra Om Namah Shivaya, which Babaji recommends to all, means "I surrender to (or take refuge in) Shiva [one of the names of God]." The Sanskrit word "Om" is said to be the sound the Formless Divine utters to start the vibrations which initiate the process of Creation. Worshippers of Lord Shiva say that Om Namah Shivaya was the first mantra that The Divine uttered.
4   The Shiva Puranas say that Hanuman is a manifestation of Shiva.
5   Svetasvatara Upanishad, from The Upanishads, Breath of the Eternal, translations by Swami Prabhavananda and Frederick Manchester; a Mentor Book, New York and Scarborough, Ontario, Canada; 1948; page 121.

17

"There is a great saint, an ocean of all qualities,
Whose beginning and end nobody knows,"
From the Haidakhan Aarati.

"In the beginning was the Word, and the word was with God,
and the Word was God. The same was in the beginning with God.
All things were made by him;
and without him was not anything made that was made."
John 1: 1-3 (King James translation)

"Creating all things, he entered into everything. Entering all things,
he became that which has shape and that which is shapeless;
he became that which is conscious and that which is not conscious;
he became that which is gross and that which is subtle.
He became all things whatsoever; therefore the wise call him the Real."
From the Taittiriya Upanishad

CHAPTER II

PREVIOUS MANIFESTATIONS OF BABAJI

Some Experiences of Yogananda's Line

There is a belief in, a tradition of, and there are published reports of earlier manifestations of Babaji. The traditions extend back to prehistory; the written reports start with the second half of the 19th century - or go back to the early centuries A.D., depending on how you choose to interpret a scriptural prophesy.

Millions of people all over the world have read about Mahavatar Babaji in Paramahansa Yogananda's *Autobiography of a Yogi*[1], which was first published in the United States of America in 1946. Yogananda's guru's guru, Lahiri Mahasaya, began talking and teaching about Babaji in the 1860's and his disciple Shri Yukteswar - Yogananda's guru - wrote a book in 1894, under Babaji's instructions, which gave some information about Babaji.

Yogananda, passing on information obtained by Lahiri Mahasaya, Shri Yukteswar, and himself, in conversations with Shri Babaji, stated that Mahavatar Babaji gave yoga initiation to the great Shaivite teacher, Shri Shankara (788-820 A.D.) and to the poet-saint Kabir (1440-1518), as well as to Lahiri Mahasaya.[2] There are no facts relating to birth or family in any of His manifestations.[3]

Yogananda's spiritual line's experience of Babaji began in the autumn of 1861, when Shyama Charan Lahiri was 33 years old.[4] He was then an accountant in the Military Engineering Department of the British Raj in India, a married man with four children. A telegram from the head office directed his transfer from his post in Danapur, a town near Benares, to Ranikhet, in the Almora District of the Kumaon Hills in modern Uttar Pradesh state (renamed Uttaranchal in 2000). After thirty days of travel by horse and buggy, Lahiri reached his new office. His duties were not demanding and he was able to spend many hours roaming the hillsides. The area has been known, since before written history, for the saints who live and wander there, and Lahiri felt a strong desire to see them.

One afternoon, on Dronagiri Mountain, he heard a distant

voice calling his name. He followed the voice and found a smiling young man who welcomed him and took him to a cave which contained some woolen blankets and some water bowls. The young man asked Lahiri if he remembered these things. In English, the young man said that it was apparent that his telegram had taken effect. When a baffled Lahiri asked what he meant, the young man said that he referred to the telegram that directed Lahiri to transfer to Ranikhet. He himself had put the suggestion into the mind of Lahiri's superior officer. The young man said that when a person feels unity with all of humanity, he or she can work through anyone's mind.

Since Lahiri remained bewildered by all this, the young man tapped him lightly on the forehead and suddenly Lahiri began remembering his previous life. He recognized Babaji, the cave, the blankets and water bowls and recalled the years he had spent in this cave in his last incarnation.

That night Shri Babaji initiated Lahiri into kriya yoga in a spectacular palace created by Babaji to satisfy a desire of Lahiri, from some long past life, since all desires must be attained and fulfilled before one embarks on this last high spiritual climb. When the initiation rites were completed, the palace disappeared, but Babaji and the disciples who accompanied Him remained with Lahiri on Dronagiri Mountain. During another seven days, Lahiri, in an unbroken state of bliss, attained Self-knowledge.

On the eighth day, Lahiri fell at Babaji's feet and implored Him to let him stay always in the wilderness with Shri Babaji. Babaji told Lahiri his duty was to serve in the city as an example of the ideal yogi-householder; people burdened by ties to work and family would take inspiration from him. Babaji said the family man is not barred from attaining the highest yogic growth; one who faithfully pursues a spiritual path can attain enlightenment.

The next morning, when Lahiri knelt at Shri Babaji's feet for blessing, Babaji told Lahiri that there was no separation between them; that whenever Lahiri called on Him, wherever Lahiri was, Babaji would come to him.

Soon after Lahiri's return to his office in Ranikhet, a letter came from the head office saying that his transfer to Ranikhet had occurred by error and that he should return to Danapur. On his way back to his post, Lahiri stopped to visit friends in Moradabad. His high spirits compelled him to share the tale of his miraculous experiences and his friends were incredulous. In his enthusiasm, Lahiri said that if he called Him, his guru would appear. He was immediately put to the test. Lahiri went into a windowless, quiet room and told his friends to wait outside until he called. Lahiri went into meditation and asked Babaji to appear. The room filled with a glow from which a luminous figure of Babaji appeared.

Babaji sternly rebuked Lahiri for calling Him for a trifle. Truth, He said, is not for the person of idle curiosity. Spiritual truths are discovered by people who overcome their skepticism. Babaji agreed to remain, but told Lahiri that from then on He would appear to Lahiri only when he needed Him, not always when he called.

The door was opened and the friends stared in disbelief. One laughed; saying this was a case of mass hypnotism, since no one could possibly have entered the room without their knowledge. Babaji smiled and let each one touch his warm, solid flesh, and they all prostrated before him. Babaji asked that a simple, sweet dish - halva - be prepared and talked pleasantly with them while it was being made. After they had eaten, Babaji blessed each one, then disappeared in a sudden flash of light.

Lahiri Mahasaya, after his initiation by Shri Babaji, became a great teacher and saint. There are recorded incidents of miraculous healings attributed to him; of restoring at least one person to life the day after his death; healing the blind; disappearing from sight in the presence of people; simultaneous appearances in two places; and, the day after his death, appearing to three disciples in three different cities at the same hour, in the flesh.

After his initiation, Lahiri Mahasaya met Babaji several times in unexpected circumstances. One of these incidents illustrates a point which seems to run through all of Shri Babaji's manifestations. At a <u>khumba mela</u>[5] in Allahabad, Lahiri was astounded to find Babaji kneeling before a matted-haired renunciate. Lahiri asked Babaji what He was doing. Babaji replied that he was washing the feet of a renunciate, that he would then clean his cooking utensils; He said that He was practicing the virtue of humility.

Shri Yukteswar, who was Yogananda's guru, was perhaps the greatest of Lahiri Mahasaya's disciples. He, too, was a miracle-worker. During his lifetime, he met Shri Babaji three times. On the first of these occasions, Shri Babaji set Yukteswar on another of the themes which Babaji has pressed in recent times. Babaji said that East and West must establish a middle path of activity and spirituality. India had much to learn from the West in material development and India could teach the methods by which the West would be able to place its religious beliefs on the foundations of yogic science. Babaji said there were potential saints in America and Europe who were waiting to be enlivened.[6]

On a later occasion, Shri Babaji instructed Yukteswar to write a book showing the underlying unity between the Christian and Hindu scriptures. This work resulted in Yukteswar's "The Holy Science."[7]

Shri Yukteswar's outstanding and most beloved disciple was Paramahansa Yogananda. While Yogananda was a babe in arms, Babaji informed Yukteswar that He would send him a disciple to train for dissemination of yogic knowledge in the West. In 1920, when Yogananda was committed to going to the United States of America to start this work, but experienced concern about leaving his native land for the materialistic West, Shri Babaji, in answer to hours of Yogananda's prayers, knocked on his door and came to confirm to Yogananda that he was the disciple sent to Yukteswar for this task, and to give His blessings on the venture.

Scriptural References

There are indications of Shri Babaji's manifestations long before the events described above. There are two books of religious prophesy - one ancient and one modern - which 'foretell' the appearance of Lord Shiva in a 'human' form during Lord Krishna's incarnation, at the end of the Dvapara Yuga and the beginning of the Kali Yuga, with the implication that this form will continue to assist mankind through the Kali Yuga (the Iron Age; also translated as the Age of Strife, Conflict or Darkness).

The older book is the <u>Shiva Purana</u>, which was put into its present form in (perhaps) the fourth or fifth century A.D., but which contains written and oral material from a far more distant past. There is the following statement concerning one of the many incarnations of Lord Shiva to carry out His worldly activities.

> "In the twenty-eighth aeon of Dvapara, there will be... born...Krishna...as the foremost of the sons of Vasudeva.
>
> "Then I [Shiva] too shall be born with the body of a Brahmacarin and the soul of a Yogin by means of Yogic Maya to the great surprise of the worlds.
>
> "On seeing a dead body forsaken in the cremation ground I shall enter into it and make it free from ailments by means of Yogic Maya... Then I will enter the holy divine cavern of Meru along with you [Lord Brahma] and Visnu. O Brahma, I shall then be known as Lakulin.
>
> "The physical incarnation thus and the holy Siddha centre will be greatly renowned as long as the earth lasts."[8]

It is an historical fact that there was a great religious figure in India named Lakulish (a form of the name Lakulin, which means "one who carries a staff"). Tradition states that he lived at the time of Lord Krishna.[9] Lakulish settled in a place called Kayavarohan, in modern Gujarat state, which is said to have been established as a religious teaching center by Maharshi Vishwamitra in the still earlier era of Lord Ram. Lakulish is credited with formulating and propagating the Pashupatmat form of Shaivism and establishing twelve "Jyotirlingams" (special phallic forms symbolic of Lord Shiva's creative energy) around India. The administration of these jyotirlingams and the learning centers associated with them lasted for about a thousand years. The lingams and their temples still exist. Haidakhan Baba frequently walked with a heavy staff, and Mount Meru is another name for Mount Kailash, where Lord Shiva has performed thousands of years of *tapas*. When Babaji visited Kayavarohan in 1980, He was greeted and worshipped as Lakulish and Lord Shiva.

The present text of the <u>Shiva Purana</u> was compiled some time later than Lakulish's era and it is now impossible to determine whether the prophesy in the <u>Shiva Purana</u> was contained in the earlier written versions or oral traditions, or was written at a later time to exalt Lakulish's Pashupatmat sect. Whether Lakulish represents the first appearance of Shri Babaji in a human form or not, a tradition among Shri Babaji's followers is that He has been in and out of physical worldly activities in an identifiable 'human' form (but not limited to one form only) at least since the end of the Dvapara Yuga, the time of Lord Krishna.

The modern book referred to is "Shrisadashiv Charitamrit"[10], a divinely inspired book published by Shri Vishnu Dutt Shastri in 1959. The first chapter of this book relates the visions given to Shri Vishnu Dutt of a discussion among the ancient, fabled sage Narada and the gods, concerning the need to send someone to the earth to help and guide humankind. All concerned agreed that only Lord Samba Sadashiv (a subtle form of The Divine as Shiva, Who is believed to have interacted with the created universe since the beginning of Time) has the qualities needed for this task. Therefore, they went to Lord Samba Sadashiv and prayed that He go to the world and help it in its miseries. The Lord responded with this statement:

> "I will very soon come to the world. In the Treta Yuga, I will come with Rama as a brahmachari and clean the world of non-knowledge. In the Dvapara Yuga, I will enter and give knowledge to all those who will open their hearts to me. Vishnu then will enter into me as a swan and the people of Kumaon will begin to call me Paramhansa [the Supreme Swan; the swan is a symbol of knowledge] and Brahmachari [a brahmachari is a dedicated, celibate student, a seeker of knowledge]."[11]

Vishnu Dutt Shastri understood this prophesy to have reference to Babaji. Babaji is believed by many to be a manifestation of the earliest forms of the Formless Divine (like "the Word" used in the gospel of John) and, in early and recent manifestations, is associated with the Kumaon Hills of Uttar Pradesh, where one of His many names is Brahmachari Baba.

"Shrisadashiv Charitamrit" also contains chapters relating to

24

other earthly manifestations of Shri Babaji. Chapters V and VI deal with the period of Lord Ram. In a later chapter, Lord Shiva glorifies Ram to Lord Vishnu and concludes with the statement, "My heart is always filled with Ram's glory. As an incarnation of devotion, Ram is everything."

Another chapter deals with Lord Samba Sadashiv's appearance in Vrindaban in Lord Krishna's time. It describes Samba Sadashiv having darshan of the baby Krishna and the later worship of Shiva by Lord Krishna. Shri Babaji, in His recent incarnation, mentioned on a few occasions that He was one of the teachers of Jesus Christ during His years between the ages of twelve and thirty, on which the New Testament is silent. And, as stated above, Shri Babaji said that, some centuries later, He also had initiated Shri Shankara and the great religious poet Kabir into yogic practices. He told others that He lived in Tibet as the great Buddhist saint Milarepa in the eleventh and twelfth centuries AD.

A Dream Confirmed

There is evidence from two or three sources of an incarnation of Shri Babaji in Tibet about six hundred years ago. Swami Fakiranand, the man who administered Babaji's ashram at Haidakhan, wrote in the early 1970's of the following experience:

"In 1972, Babaji gave me a drawing of His previous physical manifestation of a long time ago. This drawing showed Him with four arms...a typical feature of divinity. In one hand, He is holding a coudi shell (a conch); in the second a trishul (trident); in the third, a kamandalu (water pot); and in the fourth a chakra (symbol of a spiritual center). [These are all traditional symbols of Lord Shiva.] Somehow, I always forgot to ask Babaji when and where this drawing was made.

"In October, 1972, during the time of Navratri, the Shri Jagadamba Yagna ceremony was performed at my native village of Dhanyan, District Almora, U.P. The ceremony was being held in the presence of [Babaji].

"On the fourth day of Navratri, on 11th October,

at about 3 a.m., I dreamt I was in Tibet and in the company of a group of lamas. The picture of Babaji with four arms I had with me, and in the dream I showed it to everyone present, asking them whether they knew when it was made and where it came from.

"Then I met...a lama by the name of Jaukshu Lama, and it was he who told me that he himself had drawn the picture about 600 years ago and that its place of origin is Tibet. At that time, Baba Haidakhan had assumed the divine body of a lama and was well known as Lama Baba, and Jaukshu Lama was one of His ardent devotees. Jaukshu Lama proceeded to tell me:

"'I was a very devoted worshipper of Lord Shiva and it was the great longing of my life to be blessed with the darshan of my adored deity. This was my constant request of my master. Little did I know then that my master Himself was Lord Shiva.

"'It was in the middle of a severe winter and I kept on pestering my great master to wear a chola (a long shirt worn by sadhus), since it was bitterly cold; but my master would never wear anything except wrap His body with a sheet. However, one day He did give me permission to make a chola for Him.

"'I was overjoyed and bought a piece of cloth for the purpose, but when I started to make it at night, I suddenly remembered that I had forgotten to take His measurements. So I went straightway to His hut.

"'The door was covered with a straw mat, so I peeped through its chinks. What I now saw struck me dumb with amazement. Lord Shiva was sitting there in deep meditation. In one hand, He was holding a coudi shell, in the second a trishul, in the third a kamandalu, and in the fourth a chakra. I pinched myself to see whether I was awake or asleep, for I could not make out whether what I saw was real or whether I was just imagining it. Then it occurred to me that my

Lord might think I was spying on Him, so I ran back to where I was staying. Now I realized for certain that my master (Babaji) was Lord Shiva Himself.

"'You may imagine my immense joy at the fulfillment of my life-long prayer. The fact was that I had been living with my Lord Shiva all those years without realizing it.

"'The next day, I had a chola made for Him with four sleeves, and took it to my master. When He saw it, He was furious with me, saying, 'What is this? Do you take Me for a juggler? Or are you playing games with Me?' Then I told Him what I had seen the previous night - which, of course, He knew all along; it was just His lila [God's 'play'] - and He continued to speak, softly, to me: 'Since it was your life-long desire, I had to fulfill it, and so I showed you what you saw last night.'

"Jaukshu Lama finished his narrative by saying, 'This was when I made the drawing of what I had seen.'

"In the same year [1972]...when Babaji was at Haidakhan ...five or six lamas came there to have the darshan of Prabhu [the Lord]. Babaji conversed with them in their own language, telling them about His having been a lama in Tibet. This was the first time He had mentioned this to anyone. In reply, the lamas hailed Him with 'Lama Baba ki jai!' [Hail to Lama Baba.]

"This whole incident has also been confirmed by the present day, well-known saint, Gangotri Baba, also known as Swami Akhananda, who, on instruction of Bhagwan Haidakhan, has been living in the Himalayas... for the last fifty years. This covers the period of Bhagwan Haidakhan's disappearance [after] 1922.

"When Gangotri Baba came to Vrindaban in February 1973, I had a satsang [religious discussion] with him. During our conversation, he told me that Jaukshu Lama, he himself, and I had all been devotees

27

of Bhagwan Haidakhan in Tibet during the time of His being Lama Baba, and that we all have been His disciples for many lifetimes "[12]

Stories of 'Old Haidakhan Baba'

The manifestation of Shri Babaji in the 19th century and into the 20th century is well documented and remembered by living persons. There are several books in print (mostly in Hindi) which relate the stories of people's experiences of this incarnation, which, for the sake of easy differentiation, Babaji's present devotees call 'Old Haidakhan Baba.'

Mahendra Baba and Baba Hari Das wrote that this incarnation of Babaji, in the Kumaon Hills area, began around the year 1890[13] in an unnamed village in the hills east of Nainital. The residents of this village saw, on several consecutive days, a bright light (jyoti) which appeared on a nearby hill, stayed for some time, and then vanished. The villagers concluded this was a divine sign and assembled one day, before the usual time of this appearance, and began to sing bhajans - devotional songs. This time, when the light appeared, a divine youth emerged from it. The people begged him to come to their village. He stayed in the house of the forest guard, Shri Dhansingh. Dhansingh, afraid that this divine youth might leave, locked him in his room every day when he (Dhansingh) went off to his work. One day during Dhansingh's absence, the curious and enchanted villagers broke open the lock and discovered that Babaji had disappeared.

Some time later, Shri Babaji appeared in the village of Haidakhan (closer to Nainital), on the banks of the Gautam Ganga. (In its lower stretches, above and below Haldwani, this river is known as the Gola River.) He stayed in Haidakhan for some time and returned there often when He traveled around northern India and through the Himalayas. This gave Him the name - among many other names - of Haidakhan Baba. He built a small ashram in Haidakhan and in the mid-1890's He designed and helped construct a unique octagonal temple in the ashram.[14] An interesting feature of this temple is that the stone slabs used in this small temple are not available anywhere near the locality. Elders of Haidakhan village in the 1970' s recalled their parents telling them that Babaji took workers to a hill and, after putting a mark on the rocks, asked them to take out the slabs. These rocks changed into entirely different nature.[15]

Babaji was well known throughout the Kumaon area and the Himalayas, which He covered on foot many times, traveling with a small band of devotees. His miracles and His more 'normal' routine of living were unusual even in this area where miracle-working saints were numerous. His food habits were also unusual. It is said that He never ate cereal foods. Occasionally, when a devotee insisted, He would eat fruits or milk. Shri Shiromani Pathak, of Sheetlakhet in the Almora District, where the Siddhashram was built for Babaji, stayed with Babaji for a period of six months and did not see Him take food or water during that time. Neither was Babaji ever found asleep.[16]

> "One day in February some saints who had heard of the fame of Shri Munindra Baba [one of Haidakhan Baba's names] went to see him. During their conversation with him, they began to talk about kaphal fruit. Some local people noted that kaphal was available in the hills only in May and June, and never in the winter. The desire arose in them that Babaji would give them kaphal as prasad. Responding to their thoughts, Shri Babaji went a little distance away and brought back - from who knows where - some ripe kaphal fruits still on the branch, and distributed the fruits to them as prasad."[17]

Babaji daily used to perform <u>yagya</u>, or <u>hawan</u>, a religious fire ceremony in which offerings of Earth's bounty are made to the fire which is viewed as a symbol of the mouth of the Divine. When ghee (purified butter), which is used as an oil, was not available, Babaji used water, instead. Once, in Ranikhet, the son of Shri Ram Datt told the Christian principal of his college about this practice of Babaji. The principal was curious and went to see Babaji, who was doing hawan on the flat roof of a devotee's house. Whenever Babaji poured water into the hawan pit, the fire flared up to a height of eight to ten meters.

The principal became an ardent devotee of Shri Babaji.[18]

Another of the widely-observed miracles of Babaji was to sit in the center of four or five fires, for hours at a time. Elderly people in Haidakhan still tell their grandchildren of seeing Babaji sit in the midst of fire - or of gathering wood for these fires. Giridhari Lal Mishra wrote of this practice.

"Nobody has ever seen another incarnation or saint who has such a complete and clear control over the five fires as Munindra Bhagwan had. Wonderful was his <u>tapasya</u> with five fires; it gave evidence that he was the form of Lord Sadashiv.

"Shri Moti Singh, who is about 100 years old and lives near Devguru, described with moving words in his hill dialect the fire tapasya of Prabhu [God]. When he was a child, Moti Singh used to go with his mother to see the fire tapasya of the Lord.

"In the summer, Shri Babaji would collect heaps of wood and cow dung, each heap being only a short distance from the others. He would sit in the middle of the heaps and the fires would ignite themselves by his yogic powers. At that time, Babaji used to wear just a sheet of light cloth. Intense fires burned all around him. He would sit in the middle of the fires for many days. When the fires burned low, more wood was added.

"The people who saw this used to fear that his body would burn to ashes. Shri Moti Singh used to tell his mother, with tears flowing from his eyes: 'Mother, look! The yogi must have been burned by now.'

"After the intensity of the fire subsided, the great Yogi's body used to shine like the rising sun; it was almost impossible to look at him. When he stood up and removed the sheet from his body, water dripped from the cloth.

"Once he sat amid the fires continuously for 45 days. He came out of it only because of the intense prayers of his devotees.

"Wonderful is the Lord and limitless are his yogic powers."[20]

*　　*　　*　　*　　*　　*　　*　　*

"Shri Jwaladatt Joshi was a great devotee of Shri Babaji. He was a high-ranking officer in the service of the rajah (king) of Gwalior. The king of Gwalior was a great devotee of God and habitually served saints.

"Once at the court, Shri Jwaladatt described the divine leelas of Shri Babaji and from that day on, the king had a great desire to have Babaji's darshan. As Shri Bhagwan did not have a fixed place to stay, Jwaladattji said he was unable to help the king meet Babaji.

"After some time, Shri Babaji unexpectedly came to Jwaladattji's house. Jwaladattji was very pleased to have Babaji's darshan, and he immediately sent word to the king.

"The king went immediately to Jwaladattji's house and requested Babaji to go to the palace and give his darshan. Touched by the king's feelings, Babaji consented and went to the palace in the evening. There the queen and the rest of the royal company had their lives blessed by having Shri Babaji's darshan.

"After Babaji had left the palace, the king asked the queen, 'How old do you think Shri Munindra Maharaj is?' The queen answered, 'He is not less than 80 years old.'

The king was astonished by her answer, because he had seen Babaji as an eleven-year-old boy."[21]

*　　*　　*　　*　　*　　*　　*　　*

One summer, Shri Munindra Bhagwan [Babaji] was in the Khurpatal Ashram in Nainital. One day an educated young man heard about Babaji's leelas from

31

people who had seen him. He also learned that Babaji wore a cap which covered his ears, and from this the young man guessed that maybe Babaji was Ashvatthama [one of the immortal warriors who fought in the battle at Kurukshetra in the Mahabharata epic], because people said Babaji had some wounds dating back to the Mahabharata war. The young man thought that maybe Babaji wore such a cap to hide the head wound that Ashwatthama received after the battle at Kurukshetra. The young man went to the Khurpatal Ashram to check into this.

"As soon as the young man reached the ashram, Shri Babaji told him that he wanted to have a bath, because it was so hot. Hearing this, the young man pressed to be allowed to bring water from the lake for Babaji's bath. He thought that Babaji would take off his cap to have his bath, which would give an opportunity to see the wound.

"Babaji asked the young man to carry his lunghoti and towel and go to the lake for the bath. The young man was very happy, thinking that at the lake he would have enough time to check for the wound.

"When they reached the lake, Babaji told the man to take off his (Babaji's) kurta (shirt) and cap and give him a bath. Strangely enough, before removing Babaji's cap, the young man forgot his desire to check on Babaji's wound. After removing Babaji's kurta and cap, the young man gave Babaji his bath with much faith, and dried his body. He dressed Babaji again with lunghoti, kurta and cap.

"The whole process took almost half an hour, but the thought of checking Babaji's wounds did not come to the young man's mind until Babaji was completely dressed again; only then did he remember and regretted having forgotten to check.

"Shri Babaji then said to the young man,

with great love: 'When one goes to a great soul, one should go with faith, compassion and love; and if one has some doubts, one should pray to God Himself to remove them. By the Lord's Grace only, the knowledge of a saint's greatness comes. Only a saint can test a saint - or one on whom the saint's grace falls, whose heart is simple and who is without ego. When a human being does not even know himself, how can he test a great saint? A saint is a form of God, and to judge a saint is as difficult as judging God 'Himself'."[22]

*   *   *   *   *   *   *   *

Yogi Jalendar Nath, a third-generation Babaji devotee, relates the following experiences of his grandfather, Shri Birshan Singh Gusain, with Shri Babaji. Yogiji heard these stories from his grandmother as a child, and from his 90-year-old uncle, who was a child when some of these incidents occurred. Most of these stories are well known throughout the area where Birshan Singh lived.

Near the village of Barrechina in the Almora District of Uttar Pradesh is a locally famous temple called Shakteshwar Mahadev Temple. It and its predecessors are believed to have existed on this spot for three thousand years or more. Shri Babaji used to visit the ancient ashram here quite frequently. Babaji used a very old dhuni (sacred fire pit) and stayed in a hut with an open side from which He could talk to people who came to see Him.

Birshan Singh Gusain met Shri Babaji there in the 1890's. Birshan Singh was then in his mid-60's, a widower with a mostly-grown-up family. Babaji told Birshan Singh that he should marry again, and Birshan was married to a thirty-year-old woman. After the marriage, the bride declared she wanted nothing to do with this old man and she refused to leave her father's house. Several times Birshan Singh went to the bride's father's house to ask her to come to his home, but he was rudely rebuffed.

The old man was a great devotee of Shri Babaji and he decided to live and travel with Babaji, serving Him in any possible way. Leaving family matters in the hands of his mature eldest son, Birshan Singh stayed with Babaji for seven years, walking through the Himalayas - to Nepal, Tibet, and China - and here and there in northern India.

At the end of those seven years, when Birshan was about 74, he and Shri Babaji were in Haldwani. Babaji told Birshan it was time for him to establish a home again and raise more children. The old man protested that he had tried several times to set up his marriage but he had always been harassed and refused. Babaji told him to try again. Birshan walked for four or five days to reach his village of Chhani, beyond Almora. As he entered the town, friends greeted him with the news that his wife had been washing and cleaning her belongings for the past three days, getting ready to move into her husband's house. Birshan was warmly welcomed by his wife and her family, and he took her to live with him. When Birshan Singh was 75, a daughter was born. Yogiji's father was born the next year, and another son followed. Birshan's wife, who also became a great devotee of Shri Babaji, always considered these children as gifts of God.

Even with a new young family, old Birshan used to spend a great deal of time with Shri Babaji, serving Him when He was at Shakteshwar Mahadev Temple or occasionally traveling with Him. One summer Birshan had been around home enough to plow his rice fields and plant the paddy, but he had not been there when the hillside streams were directed into the fields to irrigate the young rice; the neighbors' fields had been irrigated, but Birshan's had not, and his rice crop was threatened with ruin. The critical neighbors began to whisper, "Let us see what Birshan's children will eat this winter."

Babaji came to visit at Shakteshwar Mahadev Temple. He asked Birshan what his neighbors were saying, and Birshan tried to pass it off by saying, "It is nothing." But Babaji made Birshan Singh tell Him that the neighbors were saying Birshan spent so much time with Babaji that his children would have nothing to eat that winter. Babaji told Birshan not to worry.

As they sat and talked, Birshan noted that it was getting cloudy. Soon it began to rain heavily all around them. Babaji commented that it was "a nice rain" After thirty minutes or so, when the rain stopped, Babaji sent Birshan out to check the fields and see how much it had rained. As Birshan walked past his neighbors' fields, he was amazed to see no evidence of rain; but when he came to his fields, they were knee-deep in water

The rice crop that year from Birshan's fields was many times greater than normal. The family had so much rice that they ate from that harvest for more than two years; Birshan did not even plant rice in the second year.

Once Birshan singh suffered a fall from a great height. The fall broke his back and left him unconscious and bleeding from cuts in many places. Villagers carried his unconscious form to his home. Everyone thought he was either dead or dying; his wife started to weep and mourn.

All night Birshan lay unconscious and unmoving. The next morning, his wife, restless and upset, arose at 3 a.m. and went to open the big, front, double doors of the house. Babaji was standing outside. Birshan's wife burst into tears and made pranam to Babaji. Babaji asked why she was crying and she replied that Birshan was almost dead. She led Babaji to Birshan's side.

Babaji told her not to worry. He sent her out to the fields to find a special herb. When she returned with the herb, Babaji made a paste of it and told Birshan's wife to apply the paste to the place where the back was broken. Some time after this had been done, Babaji put His hand under Birshan Singh's back and lifted the unconscious body to a sitting position

As he was propped up, Birshan Singh regained consciousness. He was delighted to see his guru and Lord sitting beside him and Birshan got up and knelt and made his pranam to Shri Babaji, with no expression of or comment about pain: he was completely healed. He asked what had happened, then sent his wife to the barn to get cow's milk for Babaji to drink.

Babaji said He would not take anything; He had just come from Jaganath, where he was about to perform a yagya (fire ceremony), and He must return quickly to the people who were waiting. (There is a Jaganath temple about eighteen kilometers from Shakteshwar Mahadev

35

Temple; not quite close enough for a walk back for an early morning ceremony.) Birshan's wife came in from her kitchen with a plate of flour, rice, sugar, and other things traditionally offered to saints in the Kumaon Hills, and Babaji took just a pinch of each and put them into His shoulder bag. The wife then ran to the barn to get the milk for Babaji.

Babaji told Birshan Singh that He really must go quickly, but that He would stop at the temple to make a morning offering. Birshan made his pranam and Babaji hurried out. Birshan's wife came running from the barn with a container of milk for Babaji. He was two or three hundred yards ahead of her, crossing the fields toward the temple. She lost sight of Babaji, but she heard a conch blown and the temple bells rung. When she ran into the temple, the lingam (symbol of Lord Shiva) had been watered (water is one of the traditional offerings to God), but there was no Babaji in the temple or anywhere in sight.

*   *   *   *   *   *   *   *

Dr. Hem Chand Joshi was a widely known language scholar who reportedly was able to read, write, speak and teach in fifty-two languages. He was also a great devotee of Shri Babaji. During his lifetime, he collected stories about Haidakhan Baba and wrote the manuscript of a book about Him. The book was not published during his lifetime but was set aside to be published when Babaji would return. The book was found and published by Dr. Joshi's widow at Shri Haidakhan Baba's instruction after His return in 1970. The following is a story from this book.

"Dr. Joshi's father-in-law, Shri G.N. Joshi, had been suffering from tuberculosis for three or four years and had on this day succumbed to the dreaded disease. A pall of gloom descended on the family and the household, and heart-rending cries rent the skies. The dead body was brought outside the house and placed under a lemon tree.

"People from the village came to join the family in lamenting the loss, and preparations were under way to make the cortege to carry the body to the cre-

36

mation grounds. As the last holy bath was being given to the body, Babaji suddenly appeared on the scene

"Shri G.N. Joshi's mother fell at Baba's feet and prayed thus: 'My Lord, now that You have come to me in my time of crisis, please give me Your Grace and somehow grant another lease of life to my dead son. I am worried to death regarding my young daughter-in-law (G.N. Joshi's wife). How will she bear this irreparable loss and go through her life all by herself? I have three other sons, but my heart weeps for this young, 24-year-old girl. Please, Lord, please...'

"The Lord smiled and said, 'Don't worry; your son will be all right.'

"Everyone who was present got a very sly look about him and a murmur broke out, as if to ask how can anything be done to a dead body at this stage, when all was over bar the shouting? But, obviously, Babaji had other ideas.

"Suddenly Babaji became seriousness personified and broke a branch from the very tree under which the dead body lay, and He started to do the now-familiar 'jhara'.[23] Barely a minute had passed when He told the lamenting mother, 'Don't worry; warmth seems to be returning to the body.' One more minute and He said, 'I can even feel his pulse returning.'

"The entire crowd stood bewildered: what was Bhagwan Haidakhandi up to? G.N. Joshi is dead and how and from where is He calling him back? It seemed that everybody who heard Babaji's proclamations had lost his power of comprehension. But anybody would do so, seeing this kind of spectacle.

"A little later, Shri Babaji asked if it was possible to get some milk from a woman's breast. It was possible and a cup or so was brought to Babaji. Sip by sip, He fed this milk to G.N. Joshi and then, with His hands, He opened Joshi's eyes.

"Everyone saw that Shri G.N. Joshi had come alive and was looking around in total surprise. Practically everyone had heard that Baba Haidakhan was God incarnate, but now they had actually witnessed it.

"Now Babaji ordered them to take Joshiji into the house; but superstitions are hard to get over and even now everyone was afraid to lift the body back into the house, for fear that this ghostly spirit might take possession of them should they touch the body.

"Babaji once again smiled and said, 'Don't worry. This man is alive and not dead, as you think. Take him inside; nothing will go wrong.'

"Shri G.N. Joshi was subsequently taken to his bed in the house where slowly but surely he began to recover. By and by he started drinking milk and taking food, etc.

"Babaji left thereafter, but came back to the house after eight days and told the family members to take Shri G.N . Joshi to the nearby river (Ramganga). There the Lord took a few dips in the river Himself and asked people to give a few dips to Shri G.N. Joshi, also. After that, He asked them to lay him on his stomach and cover him with a blanket. After half an hour or so, people saw that a lot of filthy, foul-smelling water ran out of Joshi's nose.

"The Lord then asked Joshi to accompany Him and, lo and behold!, Joshiji got up and walked up the hill for a distance of two and a half miles, quite comfortably, back to the house.

"This happened in 1910 or 1911 and after being given this fresh lease on life he eventually died in 1950 or 1951, a 40-year lease renewal."[24]

*   *   *   *   *   *   *   *

There are many stories of Shri Babaji raising people from the dead. There are even a few examples of the following variant of the resurrection story. This story is written by Shri Giridhari Lal Mishra.

"Once Haidakhan Baba was traveling with a devotee (Jeevan-chand Joshi) to Badrinath [a religious pilgrim center in the Indian Himalayas]. En route, the devotee was struck by cholera. After a violent but short period of vomiting and profuse dysentery, he was very close to breathing his last.

"Babaji, compassionate as ever, felt sorry for him and said, 'I shall leave My body instead of you, as there is no one to mourn My loss.' The attack of cholera subsided immediately, as far as the devotee was concerned, but Babaji, on the other hand, was hit by the same disease very quickly and He told the devotee, 'When I leave My body, consign the lifeless form to the flames and the ashes to the Ganga.' Shortly afterwards, He left the human body. The devotee, grief-stricken though he was, did as he had been instructed by Babaji.

"Shortly thereafter, the devotee returned to his home town of Almora. On arrival at his house, he was informed that Shri Babaji was staying, for the last few days, at another devotee's house. It was impossible to believe that this could be true, as he had himself done the last rites. Nevertheless, he hastened to this devotee's house. Lo and behold! Babaji was sitting there in person! He did not even believe his eyes until he had felt Babaji's body.

"The entire episode so shocked the devotee that he was practically insane for about six months."[25]

*   *   *   *   *   *   *   *

Shri Mahendra Baba spent many years looking for Bab-aji. Just before he found Babaji, Mahendra Baba met an old man named Shiromani Pathak in a small village named Sheetlakhet, in the Almora District of Uttar Pradesh. Shiromani had known 'Old Haidakhan Baba' (Babaji had left the scene over twenty-five years before Mahendra Baba met Shiromani) and had helped create the Siddhashram for Babaji, just outside of Sheetlakhet. The old man took a great liking to Mahendra Baba and the two sat and talked for hours through the night about Babaji. Whenever Mahendra Baba

39

asked Shiromani about Babaji, Shiromani would burst into tears and Mahendra Baba would wait for him to get quiet again. Mahendra finally got this story of Babaji from Shiromani.

"An hour before my uncle died, he said, 'Just see how gracious He is! Give Him something to sit on. Worship Him!' Those present around him thought he was delirious, but, actually, Shri Sadashiv was giving him liberation by showing Himself to him in His glorious body. From that very moment [Shiromani] said, he, too, felt a great desire to obtain a sight of Him. It became an over-whelming wish, but how to meet Him? He had heard tales of His wonderful appearance, but had never been blessed by a sight of His form.

"One day, unexpectedly, 200 to 250 men came to his house, and with them were some palanquins. In one beautiful palanquin, ceremoniously surrounded by many rich and respectful people with folded hands, was a great and merciful Sage, wearing a shirt and cap, and with a loving smile on His face, shedding grace on all animate and inanimate things around Him. Shiromanji, at that time, was suffering from a very septic wound. As soon as he heard of Shri Bhagwan's arrival, he ran toward Him with joy. He slipped on the wooden steps and a splinter of wood pricked his foot, and he fell down in a faint. The people surrounding him were anxious about him, but Shiromanji was lying with his head resting on the merciful Master's lap in a trance which would put to shame the trance of great Brahma Rishis, and was experiencing a nectar-like peace, fully gratified.

"After resting at this place for some time, Shri Maharaj, with all His worshippers, whose number had swelled to thousands within a short time, left to proceed onwards.

"There was no fixed programme for Shri Maharaj; wherever He went, there, without any effort or call, thousands of men and women collected. Hearing of His coming, there was seldom anyone who could stay at home. There were no questions and answers, but people experienced peace at the mere sight of His presence.

"Many learned Sanskrit scholars, ministers, social reformers and social workers, and rajas and nawabs came to see Him. In the presence of this Great One - the final goal of all teachings, the solution of the existence of the Self - the natural practice of mutual intercourse and the tranquility of those who realized Brahman was available to all in equal measure.

"Always of sweet countenance, compassionate eyes, benevolent behaviour, slender of body, with child-like gestures, dressed only in shirt (kurta) and cap - these physical features were a source of supernatural attraction for all. Of food, He took very little; He drank a lot of buttermilk. When He opened His palms, the group of devotees around Him got intoxicated with their divine fragrance. His hair never grew longer. He never slept. Shiromanji lived with Him for six months but he never saw Him sleep. If someone clothed Him, He allowed Himself to be clothed, but He never asked for clothes and, even if there were clothes available, He never used them. His devotees presented Him with costly clothes, gold coins and many precious things, but He did not even glance at these uninteresting things. Yes, to entertain His devotees, He sometimes used to play with the things, like a child, for ten or fifteen minutes; then anything could happen - anyone could take the things; He made no arrangements about their disposal. To Him, dust and precious things were all alike. To Him, friend and foe, detractor and admirer, sinner and saint, in His compassionate sight, all had rights to His mercy.

"[Shiromani] recounted to me great, wonderful, and unheard-of stories of His supernatural acts, seen by himself. Due to my doubtful nature, sometimes I used to wonder at his stories and then Shiromanji used to swear on his faith, his own self, his son, and on everything, that whatever he told me was perfectly true.

"At that time, even though my heart had not much faith, I was forced to believe in these supernatural happenings. We talked together for hours. At that time I also thought to myself that though I had no inclination for prayers, repetitions of religious verses, and discourses on religious subjects, yet how interesting I found these talks! They drew me forcibly. The whole purport of [Shiromani's] talk was that Shri Haidakhan Baba was Ishwara Himself! This personification of God was extraordinary!

"[Shiromani] had seen many instances with his own eyes when the dead were made alive, when the illiterate were given instant eloquence to compose, the childless were given sons, those with financial troubles were given the boon of patrons. Devotees in search of divine qualities had all their desires fulfilled and gained power over occult phenomena. Those in search of salvation, not only from India but from Europe, and the holy men from Tibet, by taking refuge under His fearless and generous protection, gained illumination. People of diverse views and religions and great devotees had their hopes fulfilled by coming to the feet of the Lord. The long and the short of Shiromanji's good company and talk was to prove this. He swore repeatedly under oath, and greatly agitated, about these phenomena."[26]

*   *   *   *   *   *   *   *

In 1921 or 1922, Shri Babaji made some preparations for ending the incarnation. Gangotri Baba, who became a widely-known saint, was then about fifty years old; he had retired from his profession as a school teacher. On his return from a pilgrimage to the Tibetan Mount Kailash, Gangotri Baba met Sombhari Baba in the town of Haldwani. Sombhari Baba (a great siddha yogi) told Gangotri Baba that Haidakhan Baba wanted to see him in His ashram at Kathgharia, about three miles outside of Haldwani.

Gangotri Baba went straight to the Kathgharia Ashram and sat with Haidakhan Baba. Haidakhan Baba said that He was about to leave the material world and go to the astral plane to do other work. He told Gangotri Baba to take up the work He was leaving behind. Haidakhan Baba instructed Gangotri Baba to go to live near the mountain village of Gangotri, from which he later received his name. Babaji also instructed Gangotri Baba to take special care of Dr. Hem Chand Joshi, the linguist, and his wife, Durga Devi. Then Babaji handed to Gangotri Baba a tulsi mala (a necklace or rosary made of tulsi wood beads) in a cotton mala bag and told him to keep it safely, saying, "I will take it back when I come next time."[27]

In the autumn of 1922, Haidakhan Baba traveled again to Tibet and ended this trip with a stop in the town of Ashkot, just inside the Indian border with western Nepal. Babaji stayed in Ashkot for a few days as a guest of the local rajah (king). When Babaji left the town, the rajah himself helped carry the palanquin in which Shri Babaji sat. A few miles out of Ashkot, Babaji sent the rajah back to Ashkot and continued His journey with some devotees and some of the rajah's attendants.

When the party came to the junction of the Kali and Gori Rivers, Shri Babaji told the party that He would return again for the benefit of all human beings. Then He stepped onto the waters of the river, which is deep and swift at that point, walked to the center of the river and sat yogi-fashion and changed into Light and disappeared.[28]

NOTES

1   Copyright by the Self-Realization Fellowship, 3880 San Rafael Avenue, Los Angeles, California 90065, U.S.A.
    I sought SRF permission to quote parts of Yogananda's chapters on Mahavatar Babaji, but they withheld that permission for reasons stated in Note 2 of the Introduction. This section paraphrases these few stories in my own words.

2   Yogananda, "Autobiography of a Yogi," page 347; 1979 edition.

3   Ibid., page 348.

4   Ibid., pages 356-370. This whole relating of Lahiri's initiation comes from these pages.

5   Every twelve years, for millennia past, there has been a gathering of saints, yogis, sadhus, other holy persons and millions of seekers at Allahabad. These gatherings are called khumba melas. They also occur in three other cities of India at different twelve-year intervals.

6   Yogananda, op. cit., pages 389-390.

7   Ibid., pages 390-393. "The Holy Science" is also published by the Self-Realization Fellowship of Los Angeles, California, U.S.A. In India, it is published by the Yogoda Satsang Society, Ranchi, Bihar.

8   Shiva Purana, Vol. III, of the "Ancient Indian Tradition & Mythology Series," published by Motilal Banarsidass, Delhi; 1978 reprint; page 1085. A similar statement is found in the Linga Purana.

9   See "The Age of Imperial Unity," Vol. II of "The History and Culture of the Indian People," published by Bharatiya Vidya Bhawan, Bombay, 1954; pages 453 and 454.

10 This book is written in Sanskrit and Hindi verse, in the same meter as "The Ramayana." It is now being translated into English.

11 As translated from "Shrisadashiv Charitamrit" in the June 1984 issue of Haidakhan News, Delhi.

12 As this book goes to press, Swami Fakiranand writes that a marble murti of Lama Baba is being prepared for installation at the Babaji Ashram in Dhanyan. This ashram will then have a murti of each of three 'recent' manifestations of Shri Babaji.

13 Dr. V.V.S. Rao's book, <u>Baba Ji</u>, (now out of print), states that 'Old Haidakhan Baba' first appeared in 1800. He used this date after Swami Fakiranand changed the 1890 date Dr. Rao first used, after Babaji and Swamiji reviewed Dr. Rao's manuscript. There are some other possible scraps of evidence which may support an earlier date for 'Old Haidakhan Baba's' appearance, but I was unable to track them down in archives in India. One intriguing hint is to be found in Moti Singh's story on pages 30 and 31.

14 Dr. Rao's book states the temple was built by Babaji in 1840.

15 Rao, <u>op. cit.</u>.

16 <u>Ibid.</u>, pages 7 and 8.

17 Translated from Giridhari Lal Mishra's "Bhagwan Shri Haidakhan Wale Baba"; published in 1959 by Samba Sadashiva Kunj, Vrindaban (Mathura), U.P.; printed (in Hindi) by Pallika Printers, Valasan, Dist. Khera, Gujarat. Giridhari Lal Mishra was Vishnu Dutt Mishra's brother, a highly respected judge in the Rajasthan Judicial Service.

18 Rao, <u>op. cit.</u>, page 8.

20 From Giridhari Lal Mishra's book.

21 <u>Ibid</u>.

22 <u>Ibid</u>.

23 'Jhara' is a 'sweeping,' cleansing of the aura, usually with a 'broom' of peacock feathers. The healer repeats a mantra as he or she 'sweeps.'

24 From Dr. Hem Chand Joshi's "Haidakhandi Leelas." This incident was translated into English by Col. Bhupendra Lal Sharma, Retired.

25 Translated by Col. B. L. Sharma. I have been in Jeevanchand Joshi's house in Almora. His grandson showed me the closet in which Shri Joshi shut himself for much of those six months.

26 From an incomplete and unpublished, anonymous English translation of Mahendra Baba's book (in Hindi), <u>Anupam Kripa</u> ("Amazing Grace").

27 This incident reported by Gangotri Baba to Swami Fakiranand in 1973.

28 Dr. V. V. S. Rao, <u>op. cit.</u>, page 8.

"Whenever there is a decline of righteousness in the world,
Then Thou comest in the world to save righteousness;
O Destroyer of sins, cleanse us of all our defects!
Hail, hail, O King of Sages,
Remover of the pain of Thy devotees."
From the Haidakhan Aarati

CHAPTER III

PREDICTIONS AND PREPARATIONS
FOR BABAJI'S RETURN:
MAHENDRA MAHARAJ AND
VISHNU DUTT MISHRA

Mahendra Baba finds Babaji

During the years of Shri Babaji's physical absence, from 1922 to 1970, a great siddha yogi[1] came on the scene to tell people about Babaji and to foretell and prepare for His return.

The man who became known as Mahendra Baba, or Mahendra Maharaj, was born on March 4, 1908, in the home of his maternal grandfather in a village called Manika, near Mithila, Bihar. Mithila is the reputed birthplace of Lord Ram's wife, Sita. His childhood and boyhood were spent in this grandfather's home.

Mahendra's grandfather was a staunch devotee of the Goddess Durga - one of the names and aspects of The Divine Mother, the Creatrix and Nurturer. The family was well-to-do and well-educated. Mahendra attended the local school and when he came home from school he was taught Sanskrit by learned teachers. He also studied several other languages, including English.

The grandfather was learned in Sanskrit, astrology, and the ritualistic worship of God. He had a room separate from the rest of the household where he could do his <u>pujas</u> (ritual worship). He also read <u>Durga Saptshati</u> ("Seventy Verses in Praise of Goddess Durga") in Sanskrit several times a day. Young Mahendra soon learned to read it, too.[2]

In his childhood and youth, Mahendra had several experiences of Babaji. He said that, as a very young child, he was healed of a near-fatal illness by a vision of Babaji and the Divine Mother, Goddess Durga. On his fifth birthday, Mahendra went to a sweet shop to buy candy and was given sweets by Shri Babaji. A man in Bombay, whom Mahendra Baba insisted on treating as a friend, rather than as a devotee, says that Mahendra Baba told him that when he graduated from high school, Mahendra went to buy sweets to celebrate the

47

event and that, at the sweet shop, he was embarrassed by the stare of a tall, old saint. When Mahendra received his sweets, he offered some to this saint. The saint refused the sweets but said he wanted to go to Mahendra's home. Mahendra led the saint to his home and for the next six days and nights the saint taught Mahendra yogic knowledge. Then the saint walked out of the house and did not return. Mahendra had asked this guru where he came from (he replied that he had come from the Himalayas), but he had not asked his name. It is customary to call religious men "Baba" or "Maharaj," so Mahendra had needed no other name in his conversations with the saint.

Mahendra told other devotees that as soon as he reached boyhood he developed a desire to go to Vrindaban and meditate; he had a great love and respect for Lord Krishna. One day, when still a young boy, he asked his mother's permission to go to Vrindaban and repeat Krishna's name and 'find God.' His mother wept and begged him not to go until he had more education and understood spirituality better.

Mahendra went to college in Patna, Bihar. He told his friend in Bombay that while he was in Patna he saw his saintly teacher again. On a cold December day, Mahendra and a number of other college students saw and were intrigued by a 'mahatma' (great soul) and followed him through the city streets. The mahatma went to the bank of the Ganges River, threw off his outer clothes, waded out to an island in the river, and sat yogi-fashion. As he sat, the whole area around him became warm; the boys on the river bank took off their winter wraps as they stood and watched the saint. The saint shouted out to them, "Do not try to test a yogi's powers!" and the boys quickly left the area.

Mahendra capped his formal education with a Master of Arts degree in philosophy from Bhagalpur University in Bihar. His writings indicate a high degree of learning; they are so full of Sanskrit quotations and allusions to scriptural and literary incidents that they often make heavy reading for educated readers and they are extremely difficult to translate. Mahendra Maharaj told people that after he completed his education, he took part in Mahatma Gandhi's political movement for a while and visited many cities while involved in this work.

Mahendra said he decided to leave his home in 1928. One day, while out for a walk, he decided to go to Benares, so he just kept on walking - a distance of at least two hundred miles from his home. He spent some time in the Vishwanath Temple in Benares and then started a school. After a few days, his grandfather, learning where Mahendra was, sent him some money and said he would come to see Mahendra. On hearing this, Mahendra used the money his grandfather sent to move on to Vrindaban, where he "fell at the feet of Mother Radhaji."[3]

He settled down for a long stay for 'sadhana' (religious practices for spiritual growth) in the village of Lohban, some miles from Vrindaban and close to Mathura, where Lord Krishna was born. His stay there lasted about twenty years, during which time he traveled a good deal and spent much time also in the Datta District of Gujarat, near the town of Ambaji, an area closely associated with the Divine Mother Amba. He never again visited his family in Bihar. While in Lohban, Mahendra Baba organized sessions for japa (repetition of God's names), for singing devotional songs, and for reading of scriptures like the Ramanaya. Many people came to him and were benefited by their association with him.[4] He is still well remembered in Lohban. In 1984, the people of the village gave land and began collecting funds to build a temple and a small ashram in honor of Mahendra Maharaj and Shri Haidakhan Baba.

Though Mahendra Baba went to Vrindaban and Lohban to be with Lord Krishna and Mother Radha, he did not forget his great desire to find his guru. He walked through the Himalayas - in India, Nepal, and Tibet - searching for the guru who had come from the Himalayas to teach him yogic knowledge. It is said of Mahendra Baba that he never begged for food or other things - as most religious wanderers do - and that he often went hungry and in want, though usually people brought him food and gave him things he needed, without his asking. He spent much time in long fasts and meditated for long periods, wearing little, eating little, and speaking little. He was known for his severe penance. His growing number of devotees, including the rajah (king) of the Datta area, used to offer him food and sweets to ease his penance and preserve his health, but he rarely accepted these things.

For years, Mahendra Baba prayed that he might find his guru from the Himalayas, but he continued to be in ignorance of who he was. We are told that in 1949 Mahendra Baba had a vision at the Ambaji Temple in Datta in which the Goddess Durga came to him and told Mahendra Baba to go to the Almora District of Uttar Pradesh to look for his guru. His search in the Almora District is the first major theme in Mahendra Baba's book, "Anupam Kripa."

Early in the summer of 1949, he went to a temple in the town of Almora and stayed there for three or four days, but since he did not find his guru there he became restless and walked to Kosi, five or six miles away The next day he walked to a Surya Devi temple a mile above Kosi. In the evening, a villager offered to lead Mahendra Baba to another temple farther into the mountains. In the dark of early night, they walked along a path about a foot wide, high above a stream. Tired and hungry though Mahendra Baba was, there was no room to sit on the path and rest. After two hours, the villager pointed out the path to the temple and disappeared into the darkness to go home to his sick son. Mahendra Baba groped his way to a tiny village, but was stopped by barking dogs. He called out names of God and was heard by some women in the village temple, who sent a man to help him. The man offered to feed him, but Mahendra Maharaj asked only that he be led to the Shatrudra temple and, after midnight, they reached the Shiva Bolenath temple at Shatrudra.

As soon as Mahendra Maharaj drank the water of the stream that flows near the temple, his hunger and thirst vanished and he went to sleep on the porch of the temple. Very soon he was awakened by the priest of the temple, who, in great agitation, said, "Maharaj, tell me quickly what food I should bring for you. Tell me quickly, for the Lord Himself has told me sternly that an ascetic is hungry, and I am to feed him. See how, even now, my heart is beating!" Mahendra Baba protested he wanted nothing and he was so obviously tired that the priest told him to go to sleep. As Mahendra Baba settled down to sleep again, the priest went into the temple and stumbled against a bundle in the darkness. It contained flour, so he insisted on making bread and a vegetable in great quantities and fed Mahendra Maharaj well.

From place to place, like this, for eleven days, Mahendra Baba was led across the Almora District to Sheetlakhet where he met Shiromani Pathak, who, after an all-night talk[5], sent Mahendra Maharaj on to the Siddhashram, just half a mile or so below Sheetlakhet.

"I came to the Ashram with [its] priest. Even a poet would be unable to describe the beauty of the place. In the Ashram is a bungalow type of travelers' rest house, a Laxmi Devi temple, with a stream constantly flowing by, and a hermitage. On the highest point is another hut from which one gets a view of the snow-covered peaks of Nandakot, Badrinarayan, Nilkanth, and many others.

"At some distance from the hut there are two deodar trees known by the names of 'Nar' and 'Narayan.' The priest told me to seat myself there - though neither any sadhu nor pilgrim usually is allowed to stay in this hut. In it are kept only Shri Maharaj's pictures, His mala [rosary], some books on Durga, Vishnu, the Gita, and certain other things pertaining to religious observances. No one has any right to use it. But, by the Lord's Grace, the priest opened the lock as soon as we reached the hut.

"I saluted the pictures and made obeisance [pranam]. My mind became exhilarated at once. What was this? These pictures were of my Gurudev[6] who had long ago made me His own when I was a student!"[7]

Immediately, Mahendra Maharaj was overwhelmed with doubt, confusion, and conflict. Joy and the pains of doubt chased each other through his mind. He thought of fasting, but when he slept, the Goddess Mother appeared in his dreams and said, "Brother, I am hungry." He woke up crying and offered food and sweets to the goddess, and then ate from the offerings. He could not concentrate on jap (repetition of God's names) or meditation.

For three days Mahendra Baba lived in this inner confusion.

"I used to ask myself, 'What is the use of passing my time this way? Even after meeting Him, He forgets me; I cannot live without Him. Oh, mind of mine!, either forget Him completely and get immersed in worldly wealth and ease, or, by the might of your soul-force, lay your head at your Beloved's feet.' I made up my mind that I would fast unto death from the following day or until Shri Maharaj would root out this doubt of mine...

"Due to the cold, I had a late bath, and said my prayers, did my meditation and jap, and read a part of the scriptures; then I closed my door carefully from the inside and chained it. There was a small window on one side of the room, but it was closed with an iron grille; even so, I closed the shutters carefully and pushed the bolt shut... Making my obeisance to Shri Maharaj, I intended to sleep, never expecting that His Grace would descend so soon on me.

"In Shri Bhagwat I had read of Dhruva and had also read the lives of modern saints, such as Narasingh Mehta and others. These great rishis had attained salvation after great trials borne with strength and devotion. I was inexperienced, not a devotee, with neither faith nor love, and did not expect to meet the Lord so soon - though I knew His Grace would descend on me, for, if He did not intend to bestow it on me, why should He have called me to His holy temple? I knew for a certainty that He would pour His Grace on me. Such thoughts ran through my mind for some time; then I felt sleepy, for I was not afflicted with such great love for Him as to drive away sleep. I did not want to eat or drink, my mind was not directed toward ceremonies or singing sacred verses, so I decided to pass my time in sleep.

"Unthinkingly, whilst going to sleep, I looked toward the door while stretching out my legs - and I *saw Shri Bhagwan standing there!* From where He had come, and when, these things are unknown. Due to lack of space, the suddenness of His appearance, over-

52

whelming reverence, and weakness of body and mind, I could not get up, but sat up and put both my weak and sinful hands on His holy feet - speechless; I was struck dumb!

"Even though my eyes were directed at His holy feet, I tried to catch a glimpse of His lotus-like face. For some time, He kept looking at me affectionately, as if making me His own by His Grace. I was oblivious of all external things. I was not aware of anything, except the intoxicating nectar of His Presence. Only that day did I realize my complete merging in Him - a true state of oneness with Lord Shiva Himself.

"Breaking my trance-like condition, Shri Bhagwan asked, 'Baba, what do you want?' That sweet voice of Shri Bhagwan was indescribable. Saints like Shri Valmiki, Vaidvyas, and others, on such occasions, have thought silence the best speech. In His generous and compassionate presence, I became whole. He was as happy to call an orphan under His fearless protection as a nursing cow feels on seeing her weak and wobbly child! The beauty of His revered body, its fragrance, the delicacy of His skin and His gentleness were beyond not only my vision but my knowledge, also. Then, putting His hands on my head, He asked, 'Baba, what do you want?'

"Hearing these words from His lotus-like appearance, and at the sight of His holy feet, I felt in my heart as if a royal father, seeing his son's pitiful condition, was instantly ready to give away everything to relieve him; so also was Shri Bhagwan eager to help me by bestowing on me the boon of all worldly and supernatural powers. Shri Bhagwan, Sambasadashiva, Lord of the Three Worlds and of all living creatures, was bestowing on me the great boon of salvation!

"I was filled with ecstasy! To appear before His child like this! To grant my wish by His Grace!

With delight and great happiness, keeping my hands pressed to His holy feet, in a low voice I said, 'Your blessings.' The compassionate Lord's eyes filled with tears; His strong heart melted. Putting both His holy hands again on my head, and saying, 'Baba, this way has been closed: He disappeared from my sight."[8]

It took some time for the overwhelmed Mahendra Baba to calm down. After a while, he unlatched his door and went out onto the verandah, looking everywhere in amazement and happiness, to see if he could see Lord Shiva again. The ashram priest came by and Mahendra Baba asked him to go and ask Shiromani to come to him, and to bring food from the shops in Sheetlakhet. Mahendra Baba stood confused as to whether what he had seen was a reality or a delusion.

"...There were a number of reasons for my doubt. First of all, I have a doubting nature; secondly, Maharaj was not dressed in a cap and kurta [the long shirt] when He appeared to me; a short length of cloth was wrapped around His waist, and half of it was tied lower down. The cloth was very bright and attractive. In a semi-conscious condition, thinking of Shri Prabhu's compassion and power, again and again I was overpowered with the joy of His Presence.

"Meanwhile, [Shiromani] arrived. The priest came a bit later with his purchases. I asked [Shiromani] what sort of clothes Shri Baba wore. In a grave voice, he explained that He had no special type of apparel. We sometimes made Him wear a kurta and cap, he said; sometimes a jacket and turban, and for a short time Shri Prabhu would accept whatever we gave. Generally, He had a dhoti [a long length of cloth], half of which was wrapped round the upper part of His body, and the rest around the lower part.

"As soon as I heard this, my doubts vanished. Then, pointing to the side of the room Shri Bhagwan had glanced at just before He left, I asked him, '[Shiromani], was there ever a door on this side of the room?'

54

[Shiromani] was greatly astonished at this question. Falling at my feet, he asked, 'Are you deluding me? Are you yourself Shri Haidakhan Wale Baba? He, also, did not have any fixed likeness! The All-powerful Lord, putting on all sorts of forms; He was in the habit of appearing in various forms; He was God!' Saying this, he started weeping.

"Now Shiromanji regained his composure and, holding me by the hand, took me into the room. He pointed out to me certain signs showing where a door-frame had been formerly, in the direction toward which Shri Maharaj had pointed. It was only a mark of where the door had been. I could not fully understand the significance of the door and so I requested [Shiromani] to explain it fully to me. He told me that Shri Maharaj's room had a door on that side, but one of the devotees had it blocked and opened another, for his own convenience. This was enough for me; I had been granted what I longed for, and my heart said that even if I died now, I had, by His great blessing, attained peace in this world.

"For the next five or six days there was no will to do anything. Then a strong desire arose that the world should hear the blessed and compassionate message of Lord Shiva. Only He could save humanity in these dark days in the world. I examined and searched my heart minutely to see whether there was any lurking desire hidden in my heart to achieve greatness or fame for myself, which sought to be gratified in this way. But it is useless to write more about that, for by the Lord's blessing, such a motive was not there, and is not now present. The prompting of this wish was for the good of humanity only, and especially for those who believed in me as their spiritual teacher, and wished to attain salvation through my help - though often then, and even now, I explain my inability to give them this aid. I explained to them that this is all Bhagwan's Lila [God's activity or 'play'] and I was a mere messenger of His. But I felt I should give to humanity this blessed message of the Lord. So be it!"[9]

After leaving Siddhashram, Mahendra Maharaj made a visit to Haidakhan - the first of many visits there. He spent about a week in the cave where 'Old Haidakhan Baba' used to sit. During the third or fourth night of his stay, he was awakened by a rattling sound, which was repeated two or three times. When he fell asleep again, the noise woke him again and he jumped up in alarm. He was amazed at his fright; he had slept in fearful forests and on mountains without such fear. Thinking that whatever God sent him was for his good, "not out of faith or fear, but just to pass the time"[10] he started reciting prayers. He lost consciousness and in this state he composed prayers to Shri Munindra (one of the names of The Divine) through the power of divine Grace. Repeating the verses gave him great joy. But after saying them once, he started to forget them. He thought that if he had a pencil and a light he could have written them down. Then he thought that if they were inspired by God, God would not forget them but would bring them back to Mahendra Baba's memory in the morning, whereas if they were of his own making, there was no harm in forgetting them. So he went peacefully to sleep.

A teacher from the village used to pass by the cave and bring milk to Mahendra Baba. At 8 a.m., the teacher found Mahendra Baba still asleep and awakened him, saying, "I think you are an educated person; take this pencil and paper in case you wish to write something."

Before drinking the milk, Mahendra Baba sat on a stone near the river, in front of the cave, and, after saying a short prayer, he began writing the verses which had come to him in the night. "Ah! At that time each word of the invocations appeared as if illumined. With extreme joy I wrote down the mantric illuminated words with hands trembling with emotion; then, thanking God for His boundless grace and greatness, I drank the milk."[11]

Mahendra Maharaj stayed in the cave another three or four days and composed poetic invocations and prayers without any effort. Some gave teachings; others gave explanations of beautiful but difficult Sanskrit verses. The thought came to him that since child-hood he had prayed that he did not want wealth, acclaim, beautiful women, or poetry, but here, by God's grace, he had acquired this po-etic power which he was using with joy. He concluded this gift was an enticement, a test [12] - and Mahendra Maharaj tore up all his own compositions, saving the divinely given one, and left Haidakhan.

Shri Manherlal K. Vora of Bombay states that soon after the experiences at Siddhashram and Haidakhan, Mahendra Baba came to the Vora home, still pondering his experiences, still wavering be-tween faith and doubt. Mahendra Baba had Mr. Vora take him to Ra-mana Maharshi's ashram[13] at Tam Vana Malali near Madras. There Mahendra Maharaj was reassured that Haidakhan Baba was great, and was a reality, and that he (Mahendra Baba) was in good hands.

Mahendra Baba wrote to many friends and acquaintances about his experiences; he began to teach and preach more urgently the Message of God; he assembled the Haidakhan Aarati (the sung wor-ship service), writing parts of it himself and incorporating hymns from other traditional aaratis; he went to the several ashrams established by 'Old Haidakhan Baba' and repaired and maintained those which had decayed, and united the devotees 'Old Haidakhan Baba' had left with those who learned of Him through Mahendra Baba's efforts.

Some Experiences with Babaji

As you may remember, Mahendra Baba went to Vrindaban and its vicinity because of his great devotion to and love for Lord Krishna. One day he was bathing in the Ganges River and thinking of returning to Vrindaban after his bath.

"Reciting the mantra to my Guru whilst bathing, I prayed to the compassionate Lord, Shri Haidakhan:

"Prabhu [God] You are Ishwara, the Refuge of all creation, .the embodied Guardian and ever-ex-isting, compassionate Lord. It has been said, 'O Lord, Your supremely effulgent Form is the complete form of God; O Changeless God, there is none to equal Thee in the universe.' Therefore, I pray for a vision of You at

Vrindaban in the form of Shri Krishna.'

"I made this prayer and then forgot it. There is
no doubt of the fact that Shri Prabhu, Manmunindra
Shri Haidakhan Baba, and the Great Lover, the happy
Lord Shyam of Vrindaban, are one and the same."[14]

Back in Vrindaban, one morning Mahendra Baba came upon a
place associated with Krishna, where a play was being presented under a banyan tree, with Krishna playing His flute to Radha. Mahendra
Baba remembered his desire to see Krishna and prayed to Him for a
vision. Hardly had he completed the thought than he 'saw' the Yamuna River flowing near a banyan tree. Under the banyan tree, surrounded by growing wild flowers, stood Shri Krishna, as a beautiful
young boy, smiling gently, looking at Mahendra Baba from the corners of His eyes, and playing His flute, softly and sweetly, like Pan.
"I felt as if my sight - reaching up to glance at His eyes, found their
brilliance so great that it forgot its natural function and became a fish,
swimming in that ocean of love - became unconscious with joy." After
quite some time, he 'awoke' from this vision and saw again the play
going on under another banyan tree, with the same actors as before,
the same audience; and Mahendra Baba became his old self again. But
he was filled with wonder and joy and found himself repeating, "The
Great Guru Shri Haidakhandi Himself is Krishna! It is Shri Krishna
dressed in a gown and cap appearing as Shri Haidakhan Baba!"[15]

*   *   *   *   *   *   *

The year 1957 was a year of great significance for Mahendra
Maharaj and Shri Babaji's devotees. Mahendra Maharaj spent a good
deal of time at the Kathgharia Ashram, about three miles from Haldwani - a place established by 'Old Haidakhan Baba,' in which He used
to stay for fairly long periods of time. A statue (murti) of Shri Babaji
was installed at the temple in this ashram on Sunday, February 24,
1957. Prior to the installation, a festival was held for four or five days,
which was attended by thousands of people, many of them from distant places. Although neither devotees nor police made any effort to
enforce discipline, there was no disorder - and no stealing; in fact, lost

58

items - even items of jewelry - were returned to their owners.

On Saturday night, a large throng of people, including great sages and saints, learned men and philosophers, people from East and West, gathered to hear the <u>Ramayana</u> being read and to sing kirtan (religious songs) through the night prior to the installation on Sunday morning. Mahendra Baba, Vishnu Dutt and Giridhari Lal Mishra, and a tailor named Ram Chandra were locked in a room in the ashram with the murti, to provide space and time to make a kurta for the murti, and they were happily talking about Shri Babaji. At about eleven o'clock, at the height of the celebration, when the compound was filled with happiness, love and worship, some ladies sitting under the banyan tree, singing songs, saw a Divine Light. For a moment or two they did not understand its significance and were frightened. Then, as it moved here and there in human form, they understood it to be the vision of Shri Babaji for which they had been praying. Some of them ran to tell others and hundreds came running to see, amid a great clamor of rejoicing voices. A devotee ran to the room where Mahendra Maharaj and the others worked, and shouted, "Baba, Shri Haidakhan Baba has come!" Instantly, the four dropped their work and ran out and shared in this experience. After a few more minutes, the Light entered the room where the murti was and disappeared.

"This Light was about ten feet away from the gathering and Maharaj walked about there for some time along a straight line of about 125 feet, about two feet above the ground. Everyone saw it merely in the form of Light.

"The description of this Light is given in almost all religious books. Wherever there is a description of Him, it is always in the form of Light. In the great Vedic Gayatri Mantra, the word 'Bharg' has this significance. In the New Testament, the Light mentioned is in no way different from that written of in Hindu scriptures. In the Buddhist, Jain, Islamic - in fact, in all religions - there is this written reference to 'the Light.' But in such a collective form, during a sacrificial ceremony, for such a long time, walking about before all, showing His Glorious Image to all - such an event is almost unheard of in history."[16]

Some people reported that they saw, in the Light, the form of 'Old Haidakhan Baba,' clad in kurta (long shirt) and cap; Vishnu Dutt Shastriji says that he saw in the Light, which passed him at a distance of about ten feet, the young form of Shri Babaji. Shri Laxmi Narayan Mittal of Gwalior told me that the Light was so bright and pulsating that it was impossible to distinguish the features of the Form within the Light.

Later in the year 1957, Mahendra Maharaj wrote the book "Anupam Kripa," to share with others the experiences of Shri Babaji's Grace in the form of these appearances to him and others. The next year, Mahendra Baba wrote "Divya Kathamrit," which, like the Hindu Puranic texts, relates discussions among the gods, with guidance for humankind, and foretells the coming of Shri Babaji and activities which He would undertake.

In 1958, Mahendra Baba, who had been spending more and more time in Vrindaban, living with devotees on his visits there, persuaded his devotees to acquire property in Vrindaban to build an ashram. Devotees (mostly from Bombay) raised about 55,000 rupees and bought land and built the first rooms of the present ashram. Although Mahendra Baba had precise ideas for a fitting marble temple to Babaji on this site, it was not built in his lifetime. However, in 1958, when the first rooms were inaugurated, Mahendra Baba brought the murti of 'Old Haidakhan Baba' that was installed at Kathgharia in 1957, to this new ashram, where it remains today.

Mahendra Baba's Teachings

Mahendra Baba's teachings anticipated Shri Babaji's message in many respects; he communed deeply and often with Shri Babaji. He wrote of the essential unity of all of Creation and the necessity of harmony among all the elements of Creation. In a pamphlet entitled "Blessings and Precepts,"[17] Mahendra Baba had this to say on these concepts:
"The human body and the infinite Brahman are similar in their creational structure. The materials

60

for formation of both are the same. The resemblance is not in the physical body of the five elements only, but also in the subtle and causal bodies...

"If any part of the body is broken, one feels pain and consequential want. So also it is an indubitable fact that *if there be any injury in any part of the universe, its effect* - whether we know it or not - *is sure to fall on the entire Brahman, in the natural course of events.* [Italics mine.] Just as our affairs in our short lives are to some extent hereditary, in the same way actions in the vast universe are also determined and well organized. In the activity of our bodies, the cooperation of the sense organs is necessary; it is the same in the operation of the cosmos through the basic elements of Creation."[18]

Mahendra Baba wrote about the 'Jivatma' (the individual soul, or atma) and the 'Parmatma' (the universal Soul, or Brahman), noting that "the nature of both Jivatma and Parmatma is wholly identical. They are the manifested states of the same Being, just as the limited intelligence of childhood and the experience of old age are of the same person."

"Whether separately or unitedly - that is, individually or in association - a harmonious and genial cordiality is beneficial for all. If the literary man assigns to harmony a proper place in his realm; the administrator and politician conform to a harmonious way of thinking; the religious preceptor - keeping in view one truth in all religions - on seeing the same ideal in the infinite number of practices, preaches a religion of harmony to mankind throughout the entire world; then, surely, all demoniac and evil propensities, like man-made worries, envy, and vindictiveness, will very soon be banished from our society.

"We should begin this harmonious practice of general usefulness in our homes. We should regard all members of our family as parts of our body. We should entertain the same pure feeling of affinity toward our families as we have toward the organs of our bodies. Just as our pleasure and pain affect our minds and we feel worried and uneasy under those circumstances, we should be moved similarly in their weal and woe.

"From this stage, we shall learn to do service to the whole universal brotherhood. Mean selfishness has kept us dissociated from the universal fraternity: in reality, we are children of the same parents. *Our wants are the same; we are inhabitants of the same earth; and the same God is the object of worship by us all.*"[19] [Italics mine.]

Mahendra Maharaj, following Lord Shiva's counsel, urged people to follow the path of Truth, Simplicity and Love (Satya, Saralta, and Prem). Mahendra Baba described Truth as "Whatever the mind thinks, the voice should tell and the organs should do." In "Blessings and Precepts," he stated it this way:

"In all the religious books of the world, Truth has been given the highest veneration for the reason that there is most excellent harmony in it. Whatever the mind thinks, the eye should see the same, the ear should hear the same, speech should speak the same; in other words, perfect harmony and cooperation are necessary in mind, speech and action. That all these should remain in their proper place as complementary to each other is conducive to good."

Leading a simple, natural life develops the 'simplicity' that is helpful to walking this Path. To be 'simple,' in this context, requires a clear conscience and detachment toward (not rejection of) the materialistic world. The practice of Truth, as defined above, helps in the development of Simplicity. Greed and lust and resultant anger, hostility, sorrow, and the strengthening of feelings of separateness are not compatible with Simplicity. To lead a simple life, one should consider practicing voluntary poverty. This is not a directive to renounce activity or wealth (which often comes to those who practice Truth, Simplicity and Love), but a standard against which to consider one's personal demands or one's criteria for personal "needs" in life.

Love is the basis of devotion. According to the Hindu scriptures, physical or sexual love does not lead beyond itself; but when the same love, or passionate desire, is directed toward God alone, it becomes devotion.

Mahendra Baba taught that will power supports Truth; physical power is involved in the control of Simplicity; the power of the heart controls Love and devotion. By practicing Truth, Simplicity and Love, one can gain control over mind, body and the feelings of the heart. By the harmonious use of these 'controls' and by practicing tolerance and the remembrance of God's name, one can reach God. Walking this Path leads to a happy, useful, and contented life in the material world in which we live, based on realization of what life is all about.[20]

Vishnu Dutt and Giridhari Lal Mishra

Vishnu Dutt Mishra -"Shastriji"

Vishnu Dutt Mishra and Giridhari Lal Mishra were two brothers from the present Indian state of Rajasthan. Their father and father's fathers before them were the <u>raj gurus</u> (gurus of the kings) of the Alwar state, and Vishnu Dutt has also held this title. Vishnu Dutt is a "shastri" - a scholar with an "acharya" degree in Sanskrit from

Benares University (the equivalent of a Ph. D.) - who taught Hindi and Sanskrit in the secondary school at Rajgarh, District Alwar, in Rajasthan. His younger brother, Giridhari Lal, was a highly respected judge in the Rajasthan Judicial Service.

In 1951 or 1952, when Vishnu Dutt was about 43 and Giridhari Lal was about 37 years old, and when Giridhari Lal was performing his duties and living in Bandikui (not far from Rajgarh), Mahendra Baba visited Bandikui. Giridhari Lal met Mahendra Baba during that visit. On the same day, Vishnu Dutt felt called to go to Bandikui and he also met Mahendra Baba, through Giridhari Lal, at the railroad station, as Mahendra Baba was leaving Bandikui. As the train was about to move, Mahendra Baba told Vishnu Dutt that when the two brothers lived in the same town, he would come to them. After about one month, Giridhari Lal was transferred from Bandikui to Rajgarh, and Mahendra Baba started visiting them frequently.

Vishnu Dutt (known as "Shastriji") had a remarkable memory for the scriptures, in both Sanskrit and Hindi, and could recite long passages from memory. Mahendra Maharaj used to ask Shastriji to recite various scriptures to him. One day, in 1954, Mahendra Baba remarked, "You recite so well; why can't you *write* some literature?"

The next day, Mahendra Baba had Giridhari Lal take him to a place outside of Rajgarh for his bath. When Shastriji, at home, took *his* bath, as he poured the first pitcher of water, an original <u>sloka</u> (a religious verse of praise) came into his mind, and he spoke it as he bathed. He wrote it down and when Mahendra Baba returned, Shastriji showed him the sloka. Mahendra Baba was delighted and said that a gift of 10,000 rupees could not make him so happy. He told Shastriji the sloka - and the ability to compose it - was the blessing of the Divine Mother and that he now had Her full blessings.

The next day, when Shastriji went to school, in a free period he started writing slokas -and they flowed easily, almost automatically. When he showed them to Mahendra Maharaj that evening, Mahendra Maharaj was so excited that he literally jumped for joy, and then put his hand on Shastriji's head in blessing. Ever since this time, Shastriji has been able to compose easily whatever he wishes. He had never written anything for publication before, nor had any thought of doing so.

The following day Mahendra Maharaj left for Vrindaban. As he was sitting in the bus, he blessed Shastriji again and assured him that he could write whatever he wanted. This started Shastriji on his first book, "Sadguru Stuti Kusmanjali," a book of prayers to and verses about Shri Babaji. The whole book was written in seven or eight days. It was written in Sanskrit verse and translated into Hindi, also in verse form. When it was completed, Giridhari Lal read it and became very excited, asking how such an excellent book could be written in such a short time. He insisted that he and Shastriji take the manuscript to Mahendra Maharaj, so they went to Vrindaban the next day.

They found Mahendra Maharaj sitting by a small pond, in meditation. They sat down before him and after two or three minutes he opened his eyes. Immediately, he asked what they had brought, and Shastriji handed the manuscript to Mahendra Baba. Mahendra Baba had Shastriji read the book to him as they sat there. Shastriji read until about 3 p.m., when Mahendra Baba interrupted and apologized for not having given them tea, even yet, but this day was closing day for shops in this part of Vrindaban and what could he do? "Well," he said, "you go on reciting and we'll see about food later." Shastriji continued to read. About twenty minutes later, a young girl, carrying a tray of sweets and tea, came up and put the tray before them and went away.

After he heard the whole book read to him, Mahendra Maharaj commented that Shastriji wrote excellent Sanskrit verse, but that his Hindi verse should equal that of Tulsidas, Kabir, and other great poets. That time will come, he said; but, until then, you should write only in Sanskrit.

About six weeks after this, Mahendra Baba sent word to Shastriji that he should take leave from his teaching duties and come to Vrindaban immediately. Shastriji found Mahendra Baba in a small room at Shyamji's house, above a sweet shop. Mahendra Baba was sitting in front of a photograph of 'Old Haidakhan Baba.' Shastriji made a pranam to the photograph and told Mahendra Baba that he had never before seen a photograph of Haidakhan Baba but that he had seen that form in his dreams. In 1940, in the temple to Laxman in his home in Rajgarh, Shri Laxmanji had given Shastriji a vision, or dream, of Babaji in the same form as he now saw in the photograph, and told Shastriji that "He [Babaji] can give you everything."

Mahendra Maharaj then told Shastriji that the time had come when he could write such beautiful compositions that they would excel those of Tulsidas, Kabir, and everyone. Shastriji made a pranam to Mahendra Baba and asked him how to proceed with the writing. Mahendra Baba protested, "How can I give these blessings?" He removed the jasmine garland that was hung on Babaji's photograph. He gave the garland to Shastriji, saying, "Your daughter is the incarnation of Saraswati [the Goddess of Knowledge and artistic inspiration]. You give this mala to her and she will give you the outline of what has to be written." (At that time, Shastriji's daughter was four years old.)

When Shastriji returned home from Vrindaban, the whole family came to greet him and to inquire what Mahendra Maharaj had wanted. The four-year-old daughter came, too, so Shastriji took the garland and put it on her, as directed by Mahendra Maharaj. The girl took the pen from Shastriji's pocket, found a piece of paper and started scribbling on the paper. Each day, the little girl scribbled on a number of pages, and each day Shastriji wrote exactly the same number of pages of poetry (slokas). If she scribbled on ten pages, he wrote ten pages of slokas; if she scribbled on twenty-five pages, he wrote twenty-five pages of slokas. Occasionally, she would return for a second session of scribbling and Shastriji wrote more pages of poetry.

The book Shastriji was beginning to write was "Shrisadashiv Charitamrit," the book which chronicles the "Babaji leela" from discussions among the gods, through His manifestations in the eras of Lord Ram and Lord Krishna, and on up through that of 'Old Haidakhan Baba' (and now - as of December 1983 - the latest manifestation of Shri Babaji). While Shastriji was writing this book, Mahendra Maharaj used to come to Shastriji's home every week or ten days to check on the progress of the writing.

One evening, as Shastriji was reciting to Mahendra Baba what had been written recently, he came to a description of the Divine Mother. As Shastriji recited this, he saw Mahendra Maharaj's body turn into that form of the Divine Mother that his slokas described. Suddenly, there was 'Ma,' wearing a red sari, with a big red spot of kum-kum in the middle of her forehead, wearing a jeweled nose-ring - altogether a beautiful form beautifully adorned. Shastriji was greatly frightened, but he could not stop his recitation. This experience continued for a full twenty-five minutes, while Shastriji recited, by the end of which he was drenched in sweat from his nervousness. When the recitation ceased, the familiar form of Mahendra Maharaj was straightening out his beard and mustache; he slapped his right thigh and said to Shastriji, "You got scared by just *this* much?"

The following day Mahendra Maharaj enriched Shastriji's powerful spiritual experience by directing the family to a Hanuman temple some miles outside of Rajgarh where Mahendra Maharaj sat, with Shastriji at his side, and sang a religious song to Lord Hanuman three times. By the time Mahendra Maharaj had repeated the song the third time, Shastriji saw the statue of Hanuman come alive and begin to expand immensely. Shastriji was so frightened that he fainted. When Mahendra Baba brought Shastriji out of his faint, Mahendra took the family on to an ancient and particularly holy Shiva temple. There, both Mahendra Baba and Shastriji took ritual baths and then Mahendra Baba directed Shastriji in giving the Shiva lingam at the temple a ritual bath.

The result of this series of powerful experiences was to put Shastriji into such a trance that for a full six months thereafter he had no feelings: he did not experience hunger or thirst; he did not feel like temple worship because if he went to a temple or to a Shivalingam he saw only Babaji standing there blinking His eyes.

Shastriji had no desire to speak and he remained silent. His wife became quite worried about Shastriji and called some doctors to examine him; they reported that he was perfectly all right, he was just not speaking.

Throughout this six months, Shastriji 'saw things' - "like a whole show, going on and on." He watched these 'visions' and wrote what he saw - whatever passed before his eyes. He had never gone to Haldwani or been in that area, but, during this period, he had visions of how Haidakhan started (early in Creation), how it changed and grew. He saw the Haidakhan Cave formed, saw the trees as they grew. He saw the similar growth of each of Shri Babaji's ashrams. He 'saw' Lord Shiva and other gods and 'listened' to their conversations; he saw Shiva/Babaji play His role in Lord Ram's time and in Krishna's time. And what he saw, he wrote - in Sanskrit verse, in the same meter in which the <u>Ramayana</u> was written. And when, years later, he went to Haidakhan, Siddhashram, Kathgharia, and other Babaji ashrams, he saw that his descriptions were accurate.[21]

The visions were received by Vishnu Dutt Mishra in 1954 and 1955, and he wrote then the Sanskrit slokas which describe what he saw. In the following two years, Shastriji composed Hindi verse translations of the Sanskrit slokas and added commentary in Hindi. The book, with eight chapters, was published in 1959, and the Rajah of Alwar had a limited edition printed in gold leaf.

The second chapter of "Shrisadashiv Charitamrit" relates a number of conversations between Lord Shiva and other gods and goddesses. One of these conversations, between Lord Shiva and His Shakti (called Jagadamba, the Universal Mother, in this instance) contains the following statements.

Jagadamba requested Lord Shiva to go to the world to help mankind, and Shiva replied:

"To make You happy, I will go to the world as Sadguru Mahavatar Shri Haidakhandi Baba."

Jagadamba responded:

"As I am the other half of Your body, I should be Your first disciple. I would like to precede You in the world and tell Your world about Your Glory. I will be instrumental in bringing all the people of the world to You. As Your disciple, I want always to remain with You. My name should be Shri Charanashrit Shri Paramguru Mahendra Maharaj."[22]

Lord Shiva granted Jagadamba's request and continued:

"When I come to the world, I will first go to the Kumaon and appear in a cave at the base of Mount Kailash. Although I will go around the world as an immortal saint, I will come for some time to the caves of Kumaon.

"In that place there is an herb called 'Haira'; the Gautam Ganga flows there twenty-four hours a day; nearby there is a beautiful cave. This place will become famous in the world as 'Haidakhan Vishwa Mahadham.'[23] This place I love. I will become known as 'Haidakhan Baba.' People of the area will have My first darshan in the form of a divine, pure, peaceful sadhu."

"Whoever reaches this place will not be touched by the evils of the Kali Yuga. I shall grant the wishes of all who come. I shall perform great yagyas [fire ceremonies] there and people from all over the world can have My darshan there. I Myself shall tell people how they are to worship Lord Shiva. I will give the greatest mantra to the people - Om Namah Shivaya - and I will go from house to house, telling them to repeat this mantra."[24]

The fourth chapter of "Shrisadashiv Charitamrit" records, among other things, teachings of Shri Babaji as He spoke (in Shastriji's visions) to saints and siddhas who came to Him and asked Him to teach them. One of the basic teachings of Shri Babaji in these visions centered on the repetition of God's Names. Babaji is quoted as saying:

"To realize the Universal Soul - the Soul of men and of Nature - only the Name of the Lord can help. There is no difference between Name and Form. By practicing the repetition of the Lord's Name, the devotee becomes the Name Itself - the Name of the Lord. His Form and the one reciting the Name unite: the Name is the Lord. To reach the Ultimate, the practice of the repetition of the Lord's Name is the best practice."

"The Lord Himself resides in the heart of him who recites His Name."

"The mixing of Truth, Simplicity, and Love with the Lord's Name gives 'tasty food'; then the Lord is happy. The best and easiest religious practice (sadhana) in the world is nama japa [repetition of the Name]. Its recitation with faith leads to the ultimate happiness.

To recite the Lord's Name with every breath is the way to work properly; it creates a divine atmosphere.

"All material wealth, all attachments will pass; the one thing that is permanent is the Word of the Lord. Awake, and forget your worries!"

Shri Sambasadashiv is quoted in this Chapter as saying:

"I Myself always recite the Name of the Lord; that is why I am happy. Only those reciting the Name of the Lord with every breath are true karma yogis.[25] There is no knowledge without the Name of the Lord. You speak so many words, but not the Name of the Lord."

"Have faith! Reciting the Name of the Lord is not the first, but the last stage of spiritual practice."

"When lions enter the forest, the other animals run away. Likewise, all evil thoughts will vanish with the recitation of the Lord's Name. Reciting the Name of the Lord will bring you the company of good people and you will be near saints. Blessed are the few who will discard the kingdom of the world for the Lord's Name. Such a devotee always resides in My heart;"

Chapter Four also contains these comments about human activity and aspirations for those who seek God-realization:

"Without knowledge, karma [activity or work] is useless. Without love and devotion, karma is useless. Plain karmas bring miseries. Karma, japa, and knowledge together bring happiness and simplicity. Good character and detachment are necessary for the realization of the Lord.

"In the womb, you take a vow not to get attached; but as soon as you come out, you get entangled. Abandon attachment! Your mind plays tricks on you! That is why you are after pleasures! All worldly things - including the desire for liberation - are obstacles to which you are attached. If you want divine peace, leave behind ignorant karmas."

While Vishnu Dutt Mishra was working on "Shrisadashiv Charitamrit," his brother Giridhari Lal - having had visions of and 'talks' with 'Old Haidakhan Baba' - gathered stories of 'Old Haidakhan Baba' and published them in a book called "Bhagwan Shri Haidakhan Wale Baba." Mahendra Baba, Giridhari Lal and Vishnu Dutt Mishra all came to the conclusion, on the basis of their research, visions, and spiritual insight, that 'Old Haidakhan Baba,' the Babaji of whom Shri Yogananda and Shri Yukteswar wrote, and the (then-coming, or foretold) Haidakhan Babaji of recent manifestation are all manifestations of Lord Shiva and all are the same Entity.

Mahendra Maharaj spent twenty years after his experience of Shri Babaji at Siddhashram telling people of this Babaji, developing a degree of unity among them, caring for the ashrams, creating and teaching people a sung service of worship of Babaji as the manifestation of Lord Shiva, and telling people that Shri Babaji would re-appear, and that they could hasten that appearance with their prayers. Many miracles are attributed to Mahendra Maharaj, which he always insisted were the blessings of Haidakhan Baba - not his. Illiterate people, with his blessing, became learned scholars or composers; the literate Vishnu Dutt Mishra became a powerful and widely recognized religious poet and prophet; dying devotees were restored to health; poor people attained riches; childless couples had children. And he continued to predict Shri Babaji's return in physical form; in 1968 or 1969, he is said to have told some people that Babaji would come in 1970; others say he told a few people Babaji would come "soon."

In the summer of 1969, Mahendra Maharaj felt somewhat unwell and decided to go to hill stations (the 5000 -7000-foot, cool resorts in the foothills of the Himalayas) for his health. He left Vrindaban with two devotees and went to Haldwani, then on to Almora for about twelve days. There was nothing particularly wrong with him and the cooler weather restored his good feelings. He came back to warmer Haldwani, on the plains, and stayed at the home of his devotee Mistrilal.

Giridhari Lal Mishra died, in Rajgarh, unexpectedly, of a heart attack, on June 11, 1969. Shastriji wrote a letter to Mahendra Maharaj telling him of Giridhari Lal's death. The letter took twelve days to catch up with Mahendra Maharaj. When he received it, in Haldwani, Mahendra Maharaj commented to disciples around him that when his best disciple has departed, "What is the point in my staying here?" Mahendra Baba then sent one of his devotees to deliver his condolences to Vishnu Dutt. That evening, at about 8 p.m., Mahendra Maharaj became very sick. Doctors were called to Mistrilal's house, but they could do nothing; at 8:30 Mahendra Maharaj had left his body.

A decision was made to take his body to Vrindaban for cremation, and telegrams were sent to devotees in Bombay, Gwalior, and Gujarat. A wooden carrier was made; Mahendra Maharaj's body was given its ritual bath and dressed, and chandan (sandalwood paste) was applied to his forehead. The body was put on blocks of ice and covered with flower garlands and driven off to Vrindaban in a truck.

When the truck and the devotees reached Vrindaban, they drove all around the town so that all who knew him could have Mahendra Maharaj's last darshan and pay their respects. At about twelve noon, the body of Mahendra Maharaj was cremated on the banks of the Yamuna River in the town that he had loved all his life. With hundreds of weeping devotees gathered, soon after the fire was lit, Mahendra Maharaj's hand lifted up and gave his final blessing to his mourning friends and devotees.

NOTES

1   A siddha yogi is a spiritually advanced person who has attained special, 'miraculous' powers, which are called 'siddhis.'
2   This and much of the information in this section comes from <u>Shri Mahendra Maharaj Smriti Granth</u>. Vol.I, compiled by his disciples and published by Shri Mahendra Maharaj Smriti-Granth Samati, at Samba Sadashiv Kunj, Brahmakund, Gopinath Bazar, Vrindaban, U.P., India; 644 pages; published in 1983, in Hindi.
3   <u>Ibid</u>. Radha was Lord Krishna's most devoted female devotee and is considered His "Shakti" (Energy form).
4   In 1984, when I visited Lohban, a resident of the village told me that, as a result of their connection with Mahendra Maharaj, an

unusually high percentage of people in the village were teachers.
5	See pages, 39-42.
6	A "gurudev" is a guru who is worshipped as God or the guru who leads the devotee to surrender to and unity with The Divine.
7	From the unpublished, anonymous English translation of Mahendra Baba's "Anupam Kripa" ("Amazing Grace").
8	Ibid.
9	Ibid.
10	Ibid.
11	Ibid.
12	Most of the teachers of higher yoga warn their students to be wary of - be cautious of - the 'siddhis,' the supernatural powers which come to the successful practitioner of yoga. They are so beautiful, so fascinating, that they, more often than not, tempt the aspirant to stay at this level of growth. The 'siddha' can even drift from The Path, caught in the mayic fascination and enjoyment of these powers.
13	Ramana Maharshi was a "realized" saint and a great devotee of Lord Shiva.
14	From "Anupam Kripa."
15	Ibid.
16	Ibid.
17	A Hindi pamphlet translated into English by retired professor B.C. Das of Allahabad University; first published in 1963 by Shri Bankelal Pathak, Samba Sadashiv Kunj, Gopinath Bazar, Brahmakund, Vrindaban, U.P. (the ashram which Mahendra Baba established).
18	From "Blessings and Precepts"; edited somewhat to make the English clearer.
19	Ibid.
20	From V.V.S. Rao's "Baba Ji."
21	Shastriji recited this account of his experiences with Mahendra Baba in October, 1984.
22	This is one of the names of Mahendra Maharaj.
23	This means "Haidakhan, the Most Wonderful Place in the Universe."
24	From Chapter II of "Shrisadashiv Charitamrit."
25	A karma yogi is a spiritually advanced person who works constantly, without ego, for the benefit of all, in harmony with Creation.

"Hail, hail to Lord Haidakhan,
Who incarnated for the liberation of the world!"
From the Haidakhan Aarati

74

CHAPTER IV

BABAJI'S RETURN TO HAIDAKHAN

Ram Singh Makes a Murti

Master Ram Singh Sammal has taught in the school in Okhaldunga since the 1956-57 school year. He was born a few miles down the path from Okhaldunga to Haldwani, in a village called Himatpur-Lachampur, in 1937. Tradition has it that the Sammal ancestors came from the Punjab after some now-forgotten disaster in a time before the English moved into the Kumaon area (1815). Now Sammals occupy much of the land in this area.

Ram Singh's family is a family of farmers, and he still walks down the hill toward Haldwani on Sundays and school holidays to tend his farm in his native village. His mother was very devoted to God. Siddha-like, what she told people - or foretold - came to pass, and because her statements of future events were so consistently accurate, people from the whole area came to her for guidance, though she did not encourage this or set herself up as a special person. She and her family used to pay special respect to Nantin Baba, a saint who was widely known and revered.

When he was still a very young child, Ram Singh heard from his family the stories of 'Old Haidakhan Baba' and the miracles He performed. Early in his life, Ram Singh developed a very strong desire to see Babaji. This desire was fanned by his meeting Mahendra Baba in 1955, as he walked the Okhaldunga route from Haldwani to Haidakhan. After that, Mahendra Baba stopped occasionally to visit Ram Singh.

In 1962, Ram Singh had a series of dreams about 'Old Haidakhan Baba.' One night, at 2:30 a.m., Babaji came to Ram Singh in a dream and said, "Make My murti."[1] Babaji repeated His words and the dream ended. During the day, Ram Singh told his mother of the dream, but she said there was no hurry to make a murti; it was nice that he had had Babaji's darshan. The next night, again at 2:30 a.m., Ram Singh had the same dream. This time, his mother said there must be something to this dream. On the third night, the same dream came at the same time. Both mother and son decided Ram

Singh should make a murti.

On the fourth day, in the evening, as Ram Singh was saying his evening prayers, his mind became concentrated on making the murti; he had no idea how to go about making a murti. He drifted into meditation and, in his meditation, Ram Singh 'saw' several instruments useful in sculpting. He made drawings of what he had seen, then went to a blacksmith and asked if he could make those instruments for him. When they were made, on the first following school holiday Ram Singh and some of his students went into the jungle and brought back some special 'holy' clay.

On the next holy day, Ram Singh took his clay and made a pile of it which he expected he could scrape and shape into a murti about eighteen to twenty inches tall. He sketched into the clay lines to delineate hands, feet, legs, etc. As he looked at the clay and wondered what to do next, the school master came to tell Ram Singh that Nantin Baba was in Haldwani and wanted Ram Singh to come to him; if Ram Singh came to him in Haldwani, Nantin Baba would return with him to Ram Singh's house. With some feelings of relief, Ram Singh put his clay away (covering it with wet cloths to keep it workable) and left quickly.

Ram Singh stayed with Nantin Baba in Haldwani for three days, basking in his powerful presence, finding answers to spiritual questions just by looking into his eyes with love and faith. Then Nantin Baba came with Ram Singh to his house in Okhaldunga, and Nantin Baba stayed there for nine days.

The first three days, Ram Singh said nothing about the dreams of Babaji and the murti project, but then he related the whole story. Nantin Baba looked at what Ram Singh had done, said it was a nice project, and encouraged Ram Singh to work on it.

On the ninth day, Nantin Baba said he wanted to go to the Surya Devi temple, in the jungle a few miles from Okhaldunga. Seven other people joined them for the walk. When they reached the temple, late in the afternoon, they found Surya Devi Baba - a middle-aged renunciate who took care of the temple and usually stayed there - in residence. Whether for this reason or some other, Nantin Baba decided not to spend the night there, but to walk on; so the whole party left.

The jungle was very dense and it soon became very dark. Nantin Baba selected a big, spreading tree and sat down under it. Everyone but Nantin Baba was very much afraid of the animals known to roam in the jungle, so they quickly built and lit a fire. Nantin Baba told Ram Singh to go to the nearby stream and get water. They could hear the sounds of a large animal coming their way, and Nantin Baba cautioned Ram Singh about tigers in the jungle. Ram Singh was very much afraid and he went to wake up a friend who had drifted off to sleep, in order to have company in the jungle; but Nantin Baba shouted at him not to disturb his friend. So Ram Singh gathered all his courage and walked into the dark jungle, toward the water and the noise of the approaching animal. But, before he had taken many steps, Nantin Baba sent someone to accompany him. Together, they got the water and brought it back, in complete safety. Nantin Baba then cooked kitcheri (a moist rice dish, with whatever vegetables are available, and spices) and fed all the group.

As they sat near the fire after their meal, a tiger walked into their midst; everyone - except Nantin Baba - was scared almost to death. Someone picked up a stone to throw; Nantin Baba told the company to sit still. The tiger walked up to Nantin Baba and lay down before him, put his great head on his paws and looked steadily at Nantin Baba. The tiger lay there, focused and looking, for five or six minutes, then got up and quietly walked away. The company around Nantin Baba, who had been terribly frightened by the tiger's presence, experienced a great sense of bliss when the tiger left, and all through the night in the jungle.

The next day, Nantin Baba sent Ram Singh back to his home with the instruction that his most important work was to complete the murti of Haidakhan Baba. When he got to his home, Ram Singh found the pile of clay too hard, too dry, to shape, so he started all over again with a new pile of clay.

As he worked on the new pile of clay, Ram Singh talked to Babaji as he would if he had seen Babaji sitting in the room with him. He said he didn't know how to shape the hands or feet, how to show the legs, how to give the impression of a kurta hanging over His body; or anything else. He told Babaji that he had heard that Baba had a scar on

His head from the Mahabharata War, and he asked what he should do.

Every night, for twenty-two nights in a row, at 2:30 a.m., Shri Babaji appeared to Ram Singh in dreams. Each night Babaji helped Ram Singh with the next day's problem on the murti. Babaji would sit yogi-fashion and tell Ram Singh to observe how and where His legs crossed, let Ram Singh measure lengths and breadths of His body by his hands or by finger-widths. Then during the day, Ram Singh wrote the dream in his diary and followed Babaji's guidance to shape the clay. When they were working on the head of the murti, during one dream Shri Babaji bent His head toward Ram Singh, told Ram Singh to part His hair and locate the scar on His head, and to measure it with his fingers. (The scar measured five or six finger-widths.) In this fashion, with very practical help from Shri Babaji, the murti was finished in twenty-two or twenty-three days.

Two or three days after the murti was finished, a ninety-year-old man of the village, a disciple of Nantin Baba, came to Ram Singh's house and told him to go and get Nantin Baba, who was then just about half a mile away. It was a hot mid-day, so Ram Singh found Nantin Baba lying down, resting. Ram Singh made a pranam to Nantin Baba and picked up his luggage, and Nantin Baba followed Ram Singh to his home without a word. At the house, Nantin Baba asked about the murti. Ram Singh showed the murti to Nantin Baba, who said that even a great artist could not have made such a fine murti of Shri Babaji.

Again Nantin Baba stayed with Ram Singh for nine days. During that time, Ram Singh (with help from the village) made a large, one-room hut of stone and mud-and-cow-dung mortar, with a thatched roof. Nantin Baba installed the murti with the proper Vedic ceremonies and he taught Ram Singh how to perform puja to the murti.

When all this was done, Ram Singh asked Nantin Baba if he would see Babaji in His physical form during this lifetime. ; Nantin Baba answered that *all* forms are one, the same; as the seed is and becomes the flower, so also God is in all forms. Then he added that Ram Singh would see Babaji in His physical form.

Very soon, people came to see Ram Singh's murti. Someone from Haidakhan village asked Ram Singh to give, or sell, the murti to him. Ram Singh refused to part with that very special murti, but he agreed to make a bigger murti for the Haidakhan temple. So he made a second murti of clay. But before the man from Haidakhan could get the murti, the murti cracked, then fell apart, at neck and legs, into three big pieces. Ram Singh was greatly disappointed; he had spent much time and effort on this murti. That night Babaji appeared to Ram Singh again, in a dream, and, looking sternly at Ram Singh, Babaji asked, "Do you want to start a *business* of making murtis?" Ram Singh's disappointment vanished with the dream.

Nantin Baba told Ram Singh to keep the door of the hut locked; not to make it common; to keep it only for his own worship and meditation. After many years, he said, people from all over India and from abroad would come to see it; *then* the hut should be open. He told Ram Singh that Shri Babaji would come to his house, and that Ram Singh would see Him, touch Him, and serve Him.

Ram Singh Meets the Oldest Man in Creation

Some weeks after the murti episode was completed, while Ram Singh was walking in the forest, he saw a beautiful young boy who seemed to be about twelve or thirteen years old, sitting straight, in meditation, with closed eyes. Ram Singh walked up to the boy, who opened his eyes and smiled. Spontaneously, Ram Singh said, "You look like the Absolute God in human form."

Ram Singh says that this young boy stayed in the hill area around Haidakhan and throughout the Kumaon region thereafter, but no one recalls seeing him earlier than 1961 or 1962. He lived alone, with no home, but often would spend some days, even a few weeks, outside someone's house yard or on village common land. He moved here and there around the area, often organizing and performing ya-gyas (fire ceremonies with all-day readings from scriptures). He was often found sitting in deep meditation. People enjoyed a strong sense of bliss in his presence.

Ram Singh walked through the hills with this young boy many times; so did others. He was fairly widely recognized in the area. People still recall seeing him in the hills and once or twice he came to Haidakhan, to the temple which 'Old Haidakhan Baba' had built. He performed fire ceremonies with Ram Singh in Ram Singh's hut with the murti of 'Old Haidakhan Baba.'

Ram Singh used to mention this boy to Nantin Baba, who told Ram Singh that one who has control over sitting, eating and sleeping is a Great Realized One; ordinary people, even 'ordinary' saints, do not have such control. Nantin Baba said, "You think he is a child? He is the oldest 'man' in Creation." Some time in 1968 or 1969, this young boy went to a banker in Almora and asked him for a donation of 100,000 rupees to build up the Haidakhan Ashram. His request was, of course, denied. Some time in the same period, a young hotel-keeper from Haldwani, who often spent time with the saints of this area, came upon this boy in the jungle and was so impressed by his beauty and purity that he spent several days with him in the jungle.

At this time, the young boy - now a young man in form - was also seen in Haldwani several times. Among other stops he made were two visits to Shri Trilok Singh, a wholesale vegetable and grain dealer. On one occasion, the young baba walked into Trilok Singh's shop and sat there for some time, quietly looking, then left without having said a word. On another occasion, he went to Trilok Singh's home, while a religious function was being celebrated there, and joined in the singing of the Hanuman Chalisa - a hymn of praise to the Shiva avatar Hanuman (the god with a monkey form who served Ram and Sita), who is a symbol and example of devotion and service to God.

In the second half of 1969, Surya Devi Baba - the keeper of the Surya Devi temple in the jungle - became ill and could not shake his illness. After a time, the young man came to the Surya Devi temple and stayed for some months nursing Surya Devi Baba. He made food for Surya Devi Baba, washed his clothes, kept the area clean, went into the jungle to collect medicinal herbs, and made herbal medicines for him; and at last Surya Devi Baba regained his health.

Surya Devi Baba thought this young sadhu was a wandering boy looking for a guru, so he took the young man on as a disciple. After a few more months, his 'disciple' told Surya Devi Baba that he was going to go to Haidakhan. For a moment, Surya Devi Baba had the idea that this young sadhu was "something very special," extraordinary, so he allowed him to go his way.

The young sadhu apparently went from the Surya Devi temple to a village called Kalichora (near Kathgodam, up-river from Haldwani) and stayed there, at a temple which 'Old Haidakhan Baba' and other saints used to frequent, for about three months. Robbers came and murdered a sadhu who was living there. A man who lived in the village of Kalichora told the young sadhu not to stay there because it was unsafe; he took him into his own home. The sadhu performed a nine-day yagya there and then, in June, 1970, the villager took the young sadhu to Haidakhan.

Babaji Returns

There are conflicting stories as to who saw Babaji first in Haidakhan when He returned to begin His recent teaching mission. In the light of subsequent experiences of Him, it is possible that *all* the stories are truthful, even if they appear to conflict: He was clearly capable of being in more than one place or one form at a time. Several people, including myself, have attempted to investigate the facts of His return to Haidakhan, and have only gotten deeper into confusion.

A man from Nepal, who spent months on this research, concluded that Babaji's first appearance was on top of Mount Kailash (the Kurmanchal or Kumaon Kailash, opposite the village of Haidakhan) and that after He had been there a few days, the priest of the temple up there brought Him down to the Haidakhan Cave.

A widely published and believed story was that of Chandramani, a man who lives a mile or so beyond Haidakhan village on the slopes of Mount Siddeshwar.[2] On a night in June, at about 3 a.m., he dreamed that his father, who had been dead for about twenty-five years, appeared to him and told him that Shri Haidakhan Baba had reappeared in a physical body and was staying in the Haidakhan Cave; he urged his son to go and have Haidakhan Baba's darshan. Chandramani awoke and went quickly down the hill and down the riverbed to the Cave. There he found an old man with a long white beard, wrapped in a white sheet. When the old man saw him, he told Chandramani, "My child, you should return home at once and come back only after three days." Chandramani went home, but he immediately put milk in a jar and returned to the Cave.

When he entered the cave the second time, Chandramani was amazed to find a young man - 20 or 22 years old, perhaps - who also had long hair, a long beard, and a big mustache. The young man drank a little of the milk and told Chandramani not to tell anyone what he had seen in the Cave. When Chandramani went back to the cave on the next two days, he could not find the man (young or old). Subsequently, Chandramani found Him sitting in the temple that 'Old Haidakhan Baba' had built, in a young form and without a beard or mustache.

Shri Shyam Behari Lal Gaur, a bank manager and an Ayurvedic doctor from Jaipur, states that he and several hundred devotees of Mahendra Maharaj had gathered at the Kathgharia Ashram on June 23, 1970, to observe the anniversary of Mahendra Baba's passing, and afterwards perhaps two hundred of those devotees walked into Haidakhan and spent a day or two there. On the night of the 25th or 26th of June, many of these people were sitting up late near the temple, meditating or singing kirtan. From about midnight to about 4 a.m., these people saw a divine light (jyoti). A big ball of white light appeared at the top of Mount Kailash, stayed there for a while, and then came slowly down the hillside (on the unclimbable slope of Kailash, which faces the ashram) and stopped for a time above the holy Haidakhan Cave. From there, the white light moved down the river three hundred meters or so to the island where Sati, Shiva's consort, is said to have bathed. From the ball of white light a ball of blue light emerged, and the two lights moved about a meter apart. They joined again, parted again, moved back upstream to the Cave, then down to the tree. This movement continued for three or three-and-a-half hours in full view of the people sitting by the ashram temple. At about 4 a.m. the light disappeared. The devotees left the ashram that day. Later, Shri Babaji told Dr. Gaur that if they had stayed on another day or two they would have met Him in His new physical form.

Dhan Singh, about seventy years old, who had a tea shop in the village of Haidakhan, used to go to the Haidakhan temple every morning to offer water to the shivalingam. Toward the end of June, the Forest Guard stationed in Haidakhan came to Dhan Singh's teashop in the afternoon and told Dhan Singh that there was a small, young sad-

82

hu sitting at the Haidakhan temple who looked like a "Great One."

The next morning, when Dhan Singh went to offer his water to the lingam, he took with him tea leaves, sugar, and milk and he went into the old hut in front of the temple, which 'Old Haidakhan Baba' had built, and made tea for the young baba. He continued this practice, when Babaji was in the ashram, for about two years. When Dhan Singh first saw Babaji, He had a very short beard; after two days it was gone.

Early Days in Haidakhan

Rather few villagers came to see or meet Babaji at that early time. One of those who came was Shri Dinesh Pant, the clerk at the Forest Ranger's office in Haidakhan. Pantaji had lost his right leg to a septic wound when he was about fifteen. Still, he had completed his education and, through his own strong determination and wit and with the help of God, he had 'forced' the Forest Department of Uttar Pradesh to acknowledge him as physically fit for clerical work and accept him on the rolls. They 'rewarded' his stubborn insistence by assigning Pantaji to the post in Haidakhan, a post which no one wanted because there was no road to Haidakhan, no electricity, none of the amenities of life. When he came to his post in October 1969, Pantaji had to walk on his crutches the eight miles or more up and down hill over the rough path through Okhaldunga to Haidakhan.

Pantaji met Shri Babaji at the end of June, 1970, in the old <u>dhuni</u> (the hut with the sacred fire) by the temple. Babaji wore only a lunghoti (two strips of cloth tied around the waist and the crotch) at that time. Babaji had some books with Him - a Bhagavad-Gita, one of Mahendra Baba's books, and Vishnu Dutt Shastriji's "Shrisadashiv Charitamrit." Babaji handed Pantaji His well-worn copy of "Shrisadashiv Charitamrit" and told Pantaji he was very fortunate: Pantaji had been called to Haidakhan where he could witness the divine leela of the return of Haidakhan Baba.

Pantaji turned the pages of one of the books and saw photographs of 'Old Haidakhan Baba' and he looked at the young Babaji before him and immediately saw them as the same. In those days, Pantaji did not meditate, but as he sat before Babaji he drifted into meditation.

In his mind's eye, Pantaji saw Babaji flying through the air and himself flying with Babaji. Then, on top of Mount Kailash, Pantaji saw Lord Shiva sitting yogi-fashion with Babaji in His lap. When Pantaji opened his eyes, he saw Babaji was looking at him intently, but with a smile on His face. Pantaji made no mention of his vision to Babaji or anyone; yet later in the day Babaji sent a man to Pantaji, with the statement that the man should ask Pantaji about his vision of Lord Shiva.

Another thing that Babaji gave Pantaji was a piece of charas, the local form of marijuana, harvested from the oil on the leaves of the plant and made into balls or thin rolls of black 'tar,' which is usually smoked with tobacco, but sometimes made into a 'bhang' drink. On one occasion soon after His coming to Haidakhan, Babaji prepared a chillum (a local pipe filled with tobacco and charas) for Pantaji. Babaji invited Pantaji to smoke the chillum, which he did. Thereafter, for two or three days, Pantaji saw Babaji *everywhere,* in everyone. When Pantaji looked at a person, he saw Babaji's eyes; when he closed his eyes, he saw Babaji's eyes staring at him. He could, by conscious effort, realize he was looking at someone else, but his immediate first impression was to see Babaji looking at him from everywhere; even the stones in the riverbed 'looked' at him with Babaji's eyes. Pantaji thought he was going mad; he became frightened. On the third day of this phenomenon, he went to Babaji and told Him he was afraid he had gone mad. Babaji asked Pantaji what was happening to him and Pantaji told Babaji what he was seeing. Babaji told Pantaji he was all right, he was not crazy; He patted Pantaji on the shoulder, and the 'sight' left Pantaji instantly.

Pantaji says that during these first weeks he never saw Babaji eat. He drank great quantities of tea, but no one ever saw Him urinate. And He smoked a good deal of charas at first - until He went up Mount Kailash for Navratri, at which time He seems to have stopped its use almost completely.

One Haidakhan villager reported that in June or early July (the hill people use an Indian calendar, based on lunar months - not the Western solar calendar; and most pay scant attention to either calendar) Babaji took him and two or three other villagers to an abandoned Shiva temple on Mount Siddeshwar - upstream and across the river from Haidakhan. The group opened the little temple and cleaned it

84

and sat before it to sing hymns for a while. Soon one of the men protested that he could not sing unless he had something to eat - he had not eaten in thirty-six hours. Babaji produced corn from somewhere and cooked it over a fire and fed everyone. By then it was too late and too dark to start back down the hill (its paths have a reputation for danger and accidents), so they sat and sang hymns. A heavy monsoon rainstorm came, but as the group sat outside the temple and sang only a few scattered drops fell on them.

At about 3 a.m., Babaji insisted that the men needed sleep and they all laid down to sleep except one who sat up to do japa for a while. After some time, this man became aware that someone was tending the fire. He opened his eyes and saw Babaji adding fuel to the fire. The villager called out to a friend to get up and help Babaji with the fire and his friend answered that Babaji could not be tending the fire because He was sleeping right there beside him. They both became alert and looked carefully - and saw one form of Babaji asleep on the ground and another at the fire.

Two villagers met Babaji on one of the paths in the village in June. Together, they talked to Him for a few minutes and then walked on. Later, telling someone else about their meeting with Babaji - describing Him to someone - they discovered that one man had seen Babaji as an old man with a long white beard and the other had seen Him as a young man with no facial hair.

Ram Singh Meets Babaji

On the tenth of July, Master Ram Singh set out from Okhaldunga to a village across the river from Haidakhan to buy a cow. When he reached Haidakhan, people at the teashop told him there was a sadhu-boy who did not eat or drink anything, sitting at the Haidakhan temple. They told Ram Singh to go to see him. So Ram Singh bought some incense and went to the temple to see the boy. It was 'his' Babaji - the boy who had been wandering in the hills these past eight years or so. Ram Singh made a pranam and Babaji welcomed him with a smile - and a chillum. Ram Singh soon forgot about his cow and stayed with Babaji.

Ram Singh's teaching service was 'broken' at that time; being unemployed, he was able to spend most of the next nine months at the ashram in Babaji's service. He would spend three days in the ashram, with Babaji, and then dash up the hill to Okhaldunga and spend a day or so at home, then return to Haidakhan. He was very close to Babaji at that time; they joked with each other, slept on the same mat sometimes, were 'best friends'; but Babaji was still the Master.

One day, Babaji led a group of people, including Ram Singh, up Mount Siddeshwar and back. When they returned, Ram Singh was tired and went to the thatched hut that served as a rest-house in those early days, to smoke a cigarette and rest. Suddenly he heard Babaji shouting, screaming at some villagers at the temple, scolding them. Ram Singh had never known Babaji in this mood. He threw away his cigarette and ran to Babaji's hut by the temple, made a pranam, and begged Babaji to forgive these people. Babaji quietly told Ram Singh to sit and watch, then returned to His shouting at the villagers. He yelled that they had stolen all the things out of His temple - the drum was gone; He named many items that 'Old Haidakhan Baba' had left in the temple and said they were gone: He would kill these thieves!, drown them! He was furious. The villagers prayed for forgiveness and begged Babaji not to curse them, and His anger cooled.

After some time, Babaji told the people to make a gate to the temple garden. Ram Singh offered to make it and he and several villagers got to work on it. Babaji picked out stones from the riverbed for the gate and laid the cornerstone; Ram Singh organized the little money and the labor that was needed, and what is now known as the Hanuman Gate (because, later, murtis of Hanuman were placed on each side of the gate) began to rise.

Babaji, in those first weeks, told Ram Singh that 152,000 rupees' worth of construction would be accomplished in the ashram that year. When the villagers heard this, most of them laughed; this young boy who did not have enough money to eat or drink was going to spend more money on construction in one year than they saw in a lifetime?

At that time, Shri Babaji also told Ram Singh that Haidakhan Vishwa Mahadham (Haidakhan, the Greatest Place in - or the Center of - the Universe) would be the highest pilgrim center in the world one day, because here all religions are welcomed and respected, whereas other religious pilgrimage places were dedicated to one religion. People would come from America, Germany, Africa - from everywhere. Ram Singh said, "Yes, yes," but he had doubts about that statement.

Ram Singh used to sit for hours in silence with Babaji. He notes there was never any 'childishness' about Babaji, even when He appeared to be only thirteen years old. During one such spell of silence, Babaji broke the silence with a quiet statement, "Master Sahib, in 1984 I will leave this place." Babaji repeated this two or three times, and Ram Singh responded, "You are the Master; You can do what You wish." Like so many things Babaji told people, Ram Singh did not know what to make of that statement.

Some of the villagers, talking about the impact of this young sadhu, discussing the miraculous events that took place in His presence, and noting that He handed them fruits and vegetables that were out-of-season, as prasad - as 'Old Haidakhan Baba' used to do - began to compare Him with 'Old Haidakhan Baba' and some few believed that He was, indeed, the returned Haidakhan Baba. Dhan Singh told me he concluded this was Haidakhan Baba because Mahendra Baba had said He would come 'soon' and because he had seen 'Old Haidakhan Baba' in his youth, and this Baba was very similar. Dhan Singh says he experienced no 'miracles' from Babaji, only strong feelings.

The word of Babaji's return spread wider.

On Top of Mount Kailash

On the first day of Navratri - the fall festival in honor of the Divine Mother - which fell early in October that year, Babaji climbed to the top of Mount Kailash. While He was preparing to go, Ram Singh, who was acting as a 'manager' of the ashram, in charge of construction work and other administrative details, wondered if he should go to Kailash or stay in the ashram. Babaji came to Ram Singh and told him that if he did not go to Mount Kailash, he should stay in the ashram, watch the work and make prasad daily to offer at the temple. Ram Singh decided to stay in the ashram, but he went up to the top of Mount Kailash for a day at a time several times during Shri Babaji's stay up there.

The monsoon rains lasted unusually long that year and there was rain both day and night during the first few days of Babaji's stay on Mount Kailash. Still, thirty or forty people went up to the top with Him and there were rarely fewer than twenty people with Babaji during the whole of His stay, which lasted forty-five to forty-eight days. By now, the word of the coming of this young baba had gone out to Haldwani and Nainital and the surrounding areas and these people came to see Him on Mount Kailash. During the nine-day Navratri ceremonies there were some hundreds of people at the top of Kailash - a stiff, three-hour climb from the Haidakhan Cave, which at that time was another good four-hour walk, for someone in good condition, from Haldwani.

Dhan Singh spent considerable time with Babaji on Mount Kailash. He says that, to his knowledge, Shri Babaji ate almost nothing the whole time - just a tiny bite of a fruit or vegetable cut up to pass around as prasad, because people considered the food more blessed if Babaji ate from the offering. Often people would present whole cucumbers or fruits to Babaji and He would cut them up for serving to all who sat around Him. Although He spent much time in deep meditation, Babaji also talked to people.

Dinesh Pant walked to the top of Mount Kailash on his crutches. Babaji was glad to see Pantaji; He smiled, spoke to him, and gave him a piece of charas. When Pantaji started his long walk back down the hill, Babaji went to the rim of the plateau on top and watched for some time as Pantaji made his way down.

One day, after Navratri, while Babaji was still on Mount Kailash, Master Ram Singh went up from Haidakhan to see Him. Ram Singh took his harmonium and his Brownie box camera with him. After some time spent in singing kirtan accompanied by the harmonium, Ram Singh took his camera and went to Babaji. Babaji was in deep meditation but, as Ram Singh approached, He opened His eyes. Ram Singh asked Babaji's permission to take a photograph and Babaji gave His consent. So far as is known, Ram Singh took the first photograph of Shri Babaji in this manifestation. (See page 74 .)

During that visit, Babaji told Ram Singh to send out an invitation to everyone for miles around to come to a meeting on Mount Kailash. Invitations were printed and distributed. Hundreds of people came back to Mount Kailash and heard Babaji tell them to constantly chant the mantra "Om Namah Shivaya," which is the fastest, surest, easiest way to salvation (moksha) in this Age of Darkness.

Babaji in the Haidakhan Cave

Shri Babaji came down from Mount Kailash in November, probably about the middle of the month. A feast was held in the Haidakhan Ashram (on the left bank of the river) and then Babaji crossed the river and took up residence in the Haidakhan Cave at the foot of Mount Kailash, where 'Old Haidakhan Baba' and Mahendra Baba - and, it is said, Lord Shiva Himself - had meditated and lived. He stayed there for about three months, apparently not eating anything more than morsels of offered food and drinking tea. Ram Singh and Chandramani, and perhaps one or two others, spent much time with Babaji in the cave; others came and went after brief visits. Chandramani stated that he slept in the cave with Babaji and sometimes they shared the same blanket, and Babaji would put Chandramani to sleep with the care and tenderness that a mother shows to her child.[3] Ram Singh tells of wakening Shri Babaji in the morning by singing a song that priests use in the temples to 'awaken' Lord Shiva in the murtis they are about to worship; and Babaji, all snuggled in sleep and the warmth of His blanket, would wake up and give darshan to those around Him in the cave.

When Babaji started living in the cave, people came from all over the area to see Him. Often there were lines of people waiting for His darshan or a word with Him. While they waited, both before and after meeting Babaji, the people sang kirtan, and some danced for joy. Dinesh Pant, looking down on the riverbed from the perfect vantage point of his quarters above the ashram and the cave, witnessing "the divine leela of the return of Haidakhan Baba," says that the kirtan continued night and day for weeks.

Mahendra Baba's Devotees Find Babaji

Many people were called to Haidakhan by unusual means.

Dr. Gaur, the banker from Jaipur, learned of Shri Babaji's return in this manner. After Mahendra Maharaj's mahasamadhi (a saint's conscious departure from the body), Shri Gaur had told his family that every time they remembered God's name they should ask Babaji to come. They had been doing this for more than a year. On November 30, 1970, the whole family awoke with the feeling that Babaji had returned or would come soon. They all decided to fast until Babaji appeared to them.

That evening, Shri Gaur's two young sons, then aged seven and nine, went to the family puja room (temple) to read from Mahendra Maharaj's "Divya Kathamrit." They spoke Babaji's name and asked Him to come; then they opened the book. When they had read eight or ten lines in the book, the boys became aware that light was coming out of a photograph of Haidakhan Baba, which was on the altar. The photograph was four by six inches and the light which emerged was the full size of the picture. The children called for their mother, shouting that light was coming out of a photograph. As they called, the light moved forward, out of the photograph and increased in size to about one foot square. Their mother and several other members of the household came running; they saw the light moving forward and back toward the photo. After a few moments of this movement, the light moved to the open book which the children had been reading and disappeared into it.

The whole family felt this was a certain sign that Shri Babaji was back on earth in human form. The next day Dr. Gaur wrote letters to many of his devotee friends, telling them of this wonderful happening; and he wrote a letter to Haidakhan to ask for information about Babaji's return. Babaji responded and invited the family to come to Haidakhan. On January 3, 1971, Shri Gaur met Babaji in Haidakhan.

*   *   *   *   *   *   *   *

Shri Ramesh Chandra Sharma, an assistant school teacher in Lohban, the village where Mahendra Baba had lived for many years, was still greatly saddened by the death of Mahendra Maharaj. One night he had a dream in which the dead body of Mahendra Maharaj turned into the live Haidakhan Babaji sitting in front of the Haida-khan Cave. Shri Sharma told this dream to a priest who took it very lightly. But the same priest, a few days later, came to Lohban to tell Mr. Sharma that he had received a letter telling him of Haidakhan Baba's reappearance in Haidakhan and that He was sitting in the Haidakhan Cave. Ramesh Sharma hurried to Haidakhan.

"We arrived there on a Sunday, at 7 p.m. I saw Him sitting in the Siddhasana pose on the third step, just as I had seen Him in my dream, when He rose from the dead; also He was wearing the same clothes as in my dream.

"The journey had made me feel very tired and, after taking some tea, I slept peacefully on the stones. Bhagwan [Babaji] had asked us to take our morning bath between 2:30 and 3 a.m. It was very cold, but I did have a dip in the river Gautami and actually enjoyed it. Then I sang some devotional songs and gradually people from the village started coming in crowds for Baba's darshan.

"At about 9 a.m., I again had Baba's darshan, but when I saw His new young body, I began to have grave doubts and wondered very seriously whether this young saint really was Baba Haidakhan. I was afraid lest we had come to the wrong saint and would thereby offend our Sadguru. I spoke of this to one of the devotees present, saying that since this saint has come to Baba's cave all those who are eager to see Baba Haidakhan again in their midst will start to imagine that He has reappeared; this young man, however, cannot be our Bhagwan [God]. At the same time, I began to pray very earnestly that if He had really reappeared He should give me some proof of His identity whereby I may believe in Him.

"As I was speaking in this manner with my fellow disciple, I saw Baba beckoning towards me. I went up to Him, bowed, and then stood near Him with folded hands. He asked me, 'Son, what books have you brought with you?' I told Him that I had a copy of <u>Divya Kathamrit</u> by Mahendra Maharaj and a copy of a collection of devotional songs. When He repeated His question, I suddenly remembered that I also had with me a copy of a book in which my father had written some verses in praise of Prabhu (God). I told Baba about this copy and He asked me to take it out of my bag. Without looking at it, Bhagwan leafed through it, then He suddenly stopped at one page, put His finger on one line, and asked me to read it. All this time, Prabhu had been smiling at me and had not once looked at the book; I, meanwhile, had been observing Prabhu's lila. The line He put His finger on read as follows: 'My heart, you have forgotten; your Sadguru is Shankar [a name of Shiva] Himself.'

"This line was written in my father's own handwriting. I prostrated before Him and decided that Bhagwan had taken me into His fold. All my doubts were dispelled in an instant by this indication of His omniscience."[4]

Babaji Leaves for Vrindaban

Many of the people who went to Babaji asked where He came from. He answered everyone differently, says Dhan Singh. To some, He answered Kathmandu, to others Almora, here, there. When He was confronted with these different replies, Babaji answered that He was a sadhu (a renunciate); where is a sadhu's home? When you pick up a sword to look at it carefully, do you concentrate on the sword or on its scabbard? Do not focus on the covers, or wrappers, of things.

Even during the cold of winter, Babaji continued to wear only a lunghoti and a cotton shawl. He used to take His bath in the river very early in the morning and sometimes would stay in the water for as long as an hour. During those times, Chandramani, sitting nearby on the edge of the river, saw a divine light on the water.[5]

In January: 1971, Shri Sher Singh, the Forest Ranger then stationed in Haidakhan, arranged for an all-night <u>Ramayana kirtan</u> (chanting of the Ramayana epic). Several hundred people gathered for this occasion outside the Haidakhan Cave. There was a heavy rain that night, but, to everyone's amazement, no one felt cold or uncomfortable in any way; nor was the sacred fire extinguished by the rain.[6] Dinesh Pant still recalls it as the most divine reading of the Ramayana that he ever heard.

Late in January, a large group of "people from the plains" came to Haidakhan. Among them were some trustees from the ashram that Mahendra Maharaj had created at Vrindaban, who came to see if this young baba was indeed the Bhagwan Haidakhan they had been waiting for, the One that Mahendra Maharaj had promised would come. They spent two or three days at Haidakhan and then, convinced that He was something very special, invited Shri Babaji to go with them to Vrindaban, where it would be easier for more of Mahendra Maharaj's devotees and disciples to meet Him.

Before they left Haidakhan, Babaji sent the priest of the Vrindaban temple to Rajgarh, to call Vishnu Dutt Shastri to Vrindaban. When the priest, Bankelal Pathak, reached Rajgarh he told Shastriji that Babaji had been thinking and talking about Shastriji, saying several times, "My Shastriji is in Rajgarh."

Early in February, a sizeable group of devotees walked with Babaji over the hill, through Okhaldunga, and down to the railroad station in Haldwani. A large throng of people saw them off on the overnight train to Mathura, on the way to Vrindaban.

NOTES

[1] A murti is a religious statue or idol.
[2] See K.L. Jand's "Baba Ji," pages 28-33.
[3] Rao, <u>op. cit.</u>, page 34.
[4] <u>Ibid</u>., pages 46-49.
[5] <u>Ibid</u>.

"Thou art great like the sun,
Dispelling the darkness of illusion;
The Soul of all beings,
Thou art the very life of Mahendra."
From the Haidakhan Aarati

"Unless you people see signs and wonders,
you will by no means believe."
Jesus - John 4:48

CHAPTER V

HOW BABAJI IDENTIFIED HIMSELF

Identification at Vrindaban

Following his brother's death in June 1969, Vishnu Dutt Mishra had been very sad and he could not bring himself to go to the ashram in Vrindaban where he and Giridhari Lal had spent so much time with Mahendra Maharaj. But when Bankelal Pathak, the priest at that temple, came to him with Shri Babaji's specific request to meet Him at Vrindaban, Shastriji decided to go to meet Babaji at the ashram. Shastriji arrived on the afternoon of February 22, 1971. He brought with him a heavy load of doubt and skepticism. Like many others among Mahendra Baba's devotees, Shastriji had concluded, from what he had heard, that this young baba was a cleverly-trained Nepali boy who was a member of a conspiracy to acquire title to the 'Old Haidakhan Baba' and the Mahendra Baba properties and sell them off for the benefit of the conspirators.

At that time, there was a wall enclosing the entire ashram property (an urban plot measuring roughly sixty feet on each side) and a row of small rooms on one side, larger rooms on the opposite side, with the center of the property open to the skies. When Shastriji walked into the ashram, about seventy devotees were sitting in the open, in front of Babaji, chanting "Om Namah Shivaya." Most of the leading disciples of Mahendra Baba were in this group. Shastriji made a pranam to Babaji - out of courtesy - and sat at His feet and waited.

After about five minutes, Babaji got up from His seat. He motioned to Pirji Bhatt, from the town of Bandikui, who was attending Babaji at that time, that Pirji should take Shastriji to the room where Mahendra Maharaj used to sit. As soon as they were all three in that room, Babaji asked Pirji to leave and, when he was out of the little room, Babaji bolted the door from the inside.

Before he left his body, Shri Mahendra Maharaj had given Shastriji a mantra. While passing this mantra on to Shastriji, Mahendra Baba had said:

"I am making you the Acharya [Teacher] of the

Haidakhandi Order.

"I made a mistake in building this temple, owing to the insistence of your brother and other devotees. I know that some day only donkeys will live here. So I will give you this mantra, which will give you these three powers.

"First, whenever there is some danger to the Order, you will be able to rescue the Order with the help of this mantra.

"Second, whenever there is a financial problem in continuing the tradition, this mantra will help you get the money.

"Third, any sadhu may come wearing a topi [the kind of cap 'Old Haidakhan Baba' wore] and kurta and claim to be Haidakhan Baba. The person who comes and says this mantra - accept *Him* as Haidakhan Baba."

As soon as the door was bolted, Shastriji heard the sound of this mantra from one side of the room to the other; it was so strong that it seemed to hammer itself into his brain. Shastriji immediately dropped to the floor and made a full pranam to Shri Babaji; he thanked Babaji and said that He had fulfilled Mahendra Baba's wish. Babaji told Shastriji to go out and opened the door, and Shastriji went out, shouting "Haidakhandi Bhagwan ki jai! [Hail, or honor, to the Lord of Haidakhan!] Paramguru [highest guru] Shri Mahendra Maharaj ki jai!"

Almost everyone rushed to make their pranams at Babaji's feet; they had been waiting for this signal.

*   *   *   *   *   *   *   *

Shri Ambalal Inamdar, the founder and owner of a private school in Bombay, and his close friend Shri Manherlal K. Vora, the owner of the publishing firm that had published all of Mahendra Maharaj's books, were two of the leading 'elders' of Mahendra Baba's order. They were among those who had been called by the Vrindaban trustees to pass judgment on the young Babaji. Shri Inamdar was the

96

devotee who had organized the purchase of the land for the Vrindaban temple.

Mahendra Maharaj had told Inamdar that he would leave and
that then Haidakhan Baba would appear again. Shri Inamdar was
very skeptical about this; he could not believe that a dead person
could return. Whenever Mahendra Baba talked about 'difficult' matters like this, Inamdar, the skeptic, just put them aside.

After Shri Inamdar and Shri Vora arrived at the temple in Vrindaban, Babaji was brought into the open courtyard and was seated
on a wooden table, covered with cloth. They saw a young, thin, gaunt
boy, with copper-red hair twisted in the braids which a renunciate often wears, wearing a rough, hand-woven, woolen shawl. And there
was fire in His eyes! Voraji's son, Arun, took the first two color photographs of Shri Babaji that we know of. (For one of them in black and
white, see page 94.)

Inamdar confirmed his belief that this was a young Nepali boy
– a fraud. He concluded that the trustees of the Vrindaban Ashram
were trying to get hold of the property in order to sell it: he was very
much opposed to this young baba. Still, his sense of manners and
courtesy led Inamdar to go to Babaji and make a formal pranam. Inamdar's wife went with him and also made a pranam. Babaji blessed
her strongly, reached out and touched her, and gave her prasad. That
forced Inamdar, who was as fair as he was skeptical, to decide that
perhaps Babaji's equanimity showed that He was "something special," but both he and Voraji left Vrindaban unconvinced of the boy's
identity as Haidakhan Baba. Inamdar put aside all further thought
about this young baba.

Travels in Central India

Many others who came to Vrindaban accepted Shri Babaji as
the One of whom Mahendra Baba had taught and for whose return
they had prayed. They pleaded with Babaji to come to their towns and
homes, and for over six months Shri Babaji traveled around central India. Everywhere He went, every day, He performed the ancient Vedic
fire ceremony known as <u>hawan</u>, or <u>yagya</u>; and everywhere He went

there were great feasts at which hundreds, often thousands, were fed.

From Vrindaban, in April, Babaji and a great party of devo-tees went to Vishnu Dutt Shastri's house in Rajgarh, District Alwar, in Rajasthan, south and east of Delhi. From there, the group went to Bharatpur and stayed with the family of Shiv Charan Lal Gupta, a railway employee of that city. Babaji stayed in Shiv Charan's house for three days.

Shiv Charan had a younger brother named Vijay, then about sixteen years old. On His first day in the house, Babaji – who looked to be only about eighteen Himself - called Vijay to Him and asked if he were Shiv Charan's brother, and then, while Vijay was standing before Him, Babaji flicked some vibhuti [1] into Vijay's eyes. The ashes pained Vijay's eyes and he was furious: ever since his childhood Vijay had a quick, angry temper. Babaji heard of Vijay's anger and the next day He called again for Vijay - and again threw vibhuti into Vijay's eyes. Worse yet, as Vijay was crying with pain and anger, Babaji sat and laughed gaily at him.

The third day, Babaji was to leave for Bandikui. In the morn-ing, the whole house seemed filled with beauty and sweetness; but as the departure time got closer, people lost their cheer and became sad. By the afternoon train time, everyone - including Vijay - was crying. At the train station, almost everyone was in tears, except for Babaji, who smilingly boarded the train and moved on to Bandikui. Vijay was uncomfortable the whole night and early the next morning he caught a train to Bandikui; he could not bear the separation from Shri Babaji any longer. Within a few days, he became Babaji's attendant and stayed with Him in that role for about three years, until Vijay's mother pleaded with Babaji to send Vijay home.[2]

*   *   *   *   *   *   *   *

The devotees in Bandikui had prepared for Shri Babaji's com-ing. Among other things, they had distributed a handbill throughout the town and district. The handbill warned of great destruction and loss of lives in the near future. As a farmer weeds his fields to save his crop from ruin, so God would clear out the 'weeds' from His harvest of living beings; man's failure to adopt Truth, Simplicity and Love as the basis for life would result in total destruction. "The Saint of Haidakhan is the incarnation of Shiva. Shiva is omnipresent in many forms. Be blessed by devotion to Him and please your eyes by seeing Him."

On the morning of Babaji's first day in Bandikui there was a great parade of welcome. Babaji rode on a conveyance decorated to look like a swan, a holy bird and symbol in Hindu mythology. All over the town people were chanting "Om Namah Shivaya" or shouting "Maharaj has come!" or other slogans in praise of Haidakhan Baba. The triumphal procession took Babaji to a place about a mile and a half outside of town where He was to stay during His visit to Bandikui.

The townspeople who had welcomed Babaji so warmly and eagerly in the morning began to question Him by afternoon. A little incident gave focus to the doubts, discontent and hostility and led to a riotous scene.

A saint respected in the district arrived at the place where Babaji was staying. He came with a lighted cigarette in his hand. Smoking was forbidden around Babaji, so a devotee stopped the saint. This enraged the saint and he loudly asked why so much respect was given to one saint and disrespect shown to another. He sat down outside the compound where Babaji stayed and stirred the fires of anger. Soon the crowd was split into two camps, and not long after, people began to throw rocks.

Babaji and the devotees who remained with Him in the late afternoon and evening were sitting on a verandah outside His room. They all continued to sit there while the stones were flying and, although many devotees were frightened, not a one was hit. The stone-throwers were afraid of the powers Babaji might have, so they stayed outside the compound walls to throw their stones. There were hundreds, perhaps thousands, of people throwing rocks and Shastriji swears that at least a ton of rocks was thrown during the long evening. The crowd cut the power line, so the compound was in darkness; still the stones flew, but it is said that the only people hit by stones were those outside the compound.

During the night a great snake was found in the room where

Babaji stayed. It was introduced into the room through a water drainage hole in the exterior wall, put there by the gardener of the place at the instigation of a number of people who were trying to test Babaji. Lord Shiva is shown in most representations of Him as wearing a snake, or more than one, around His neck, like a garland or necklace - as a symbol of His fearlessness and His wisdom. If Babaji is Lord Shiva, they reasoned, He will have no fear; if Babaji is a fraud, He and his devotees will scatter to the winds in fright, while we stand by and laugh.

Babaji and Shastriji had gone into Baba's room for meditation. It was Babaji who saw the snake first. It was the custom that once Babaji went into His room for meditation the door was not opened until His meditation was finished. Babaji told Shastriji He would not open the door and told Shastriji to come and sit on His bed. Shastriji refused to sit on the Lord's bed and said that if the snake bit him, he was ready to die at the Lord's feet. Babaji showed no concern for Himself, but He expressed concern for Shastriji; He seemed to be worried that Shastriji might die of fear. For several hours Babaji sat on the bed and stared at the snake; Shastriji sat on the floor, chanting "Om Namah Shivaya" as he had never chanted before; and the snake was coiled up in the middle of the room.

When Babaji's meditation time was over, He got up and opened the door. The gardener and his friends, waiting outside for their laughs, were puzzled to see no indications of panic. The gardener slipped into the room, found his snake alive, chanted some mantras and picked up the snake, put it into a big pot, and carried it away.

In the morning, after the devotees had their baths, they found the troublesome saint, whose cigarette had started all the fuss, weeping at Shri Babaji's feet. Babaji was laughing sweetly and told His devotees to give the saint a bath. From then on, this saint danced to the kirtan, morning and evening.

Soon after this, the gardener came back. This time, he was wailing and carrying his six-year-old son. Some people report the son was dead; others say he was only paralyzed; there was a good deal of noise, wailing, and confusion. When the boy was laid before Babaji, Babaji whispered to Shastriji that the gardener was an evil man, but the body was that of a child, and the child should be saved.

The gardener, through his cries, said that he had planted the snake in Babaji's room, and that while he had been outside waiting and watching for a reaction, at home his son had become paralyzed. The gardener had been told by people in his home that Babaji really *is* Lord Shiva and that He had been greatly displeased. The gardener pleaded with "Bhagwan" [God] to put his son right. Babaji smiled and replied that this was how the gardener had to pay for his 'karma.' But, after a moment or two, Shri Babaji got some vibhuti from the fire pit and put some in the boy's mouth, and within moments, the boy was on his feet again.

Many people had watched this happening, attracted by the gardener's wailing through the streets as he came carrying the boy. Many rushed to Babaji to beg forgiveness; then they went out to spread the word all over the district. Again people flocked to Babaji by the thousands - on foot, by car, bus, and train. Dignitaries and common folk came. They brought fruits, sweets, ghee, rice, and many delicacies. A nine-day <u>yagya</u> was celebrated with great pomp and thousands of people were fed. When the celebrations were finished, there was much food left for the poor.

From Bandikui, Shri Babaji went to Jaipur - at the invitation of Dr. Gaur and other devotees of Mahendra Baba and more recently won admirers. In each city there was an invitation to another, and Shri Babaji and His party went to several cities and towns in the states of Rajasthan and Gujarat. He visited Delhi and made several stops in Vrindaban. During this period, He made preparations for the construction of a marble temple in the undeveloped area of Mahendra Maharaj's ashram at Vrindaban. Everywhere that Babaji went, He performed the ancient Vedic fire ceremony and fed all who came to see Him. It was quite a triumphal tour for the 'young sadhu' who had appeared in Haidakhan only a year previously with no coins nor a pocket to carry them in.

At the Kathgharia Ashram

Late in August, 1971, Babaji and His party went from Delhi to the Kathgharia Ashram, a few miles outside of Haldwani. This ashram had been established by 'Old Haidakhan Baba,' and Mahendra Maharaj also had used it. When He arrived, Babaji made immediate arrangements to hold a yagya.

The Kathgharia Ashram was at that time the largest (in land area) of the Haidakhan Baba ashrams. It contains about twenty-five acres of land. A state legislator had his eye on the sizeable undeveloped portion of the land and it was to his interest that the ashram stayed vacant; but there was the young Babaji moving in with forty or fifty devotees. The legislator agitated an already divided town; he called Babaji a thief, robber, fraud, and he lodged a complaint with the police about the "anti-social element" which had moved into the ashram. The police went to the ashram several times, but Babaji paid no attention to them. The news of this kind of excitement spreads very quickly and scores, then hundreds, of people came to see Babaji. Apparently, most of those who saw Him concluded He was "very special"; some said "superhuman." Those who did not go to see Him inclined to the "anti-social" theory. And so tension grew.

One of those who came to see Babaji at that time was Shri Trilok Singh, the Haldwani grain dealer. As a young businessman, in 1960, Trilok Singh had been in a hospital, waiting for a thyroid operation. The night before the operation, 'Old Haidakhan Baba' had appeared to him, put something medicinal in his mouth, and left without saying a word. Through the years, Trilok Singh was a man who honored and worshipped God both in his home and in his business. By 1971, he was a trustee of several temple trusts and the head of a society which looked after the property of his former (deceased) guru. Trilok Singh had heard of Shri Babaji's return to Haidakhan, but had not gone there. When Shri Babaji came out of the Haidakhan Valley to go to Vrindaban, Trilok Singh had gone to the railroad station to catch a glimpse of Him, but he arrived after the train had left.

When he arrived at the Kathgharia Ashram, there were many people waiting to see Babaji - so many that Babaji sat in a room with two doors and had people enter by one door, make their pranam and go out by the other door. Trilok Singh got in the line, made his pranam, and got up to leave; but Babaji made a silent hand signal for Trilok

102

Singh to sit by His feet, so he remained there in the room at Babaji's feet. For twelve and a half years thereafter - often in Haidakhan, which he visited frequently, and almost always when Shri Babaji traveled - Trilok Singh was at or near Shri Babaji's feet, always serving Him.

Ram Prakash Bhasin, another Haldwani grain dealer, was not a 'saint-chaser' and never made pranam to a holy man, even when Shri Nantin Baba had come to his home. In September, 1971, Ram Prakash was one of those who went to the Kathgharia Ashram out of curiosity. Much to his own amazement, he found himself making a full pranam (body flat out on the ground, with hands joined above his head) before Shri Babaji. He liked what he saw of this young baba and Ram Prakash went back to the ashram several times. One afternoon, as Babaji headed to His bath in a crowd of people, Ram Prakash happened to look at Babaji's feet. As he looked, he saw that, for one or two steps, Babaji's feet did not touch the ground; then He walked on in normal fashion.

*   *   *   *   *   *   *   *

Because the Haldwani police failed to act decisively or quickly enough to suit him, the state legislator took his complaint to state officials in Nainital, the district headquarters. The District Magistrate in Nainital directed the Sub-District Magistrate (S.D.M.) in Haldwani to look into the matter officially.

Vijay Gupta, from Bharatpur, who was then serving Babaji, says the officials came late one Saturday afternoon in September, when Babaji was in meditation and Vijay was strolling in the ashram grounds. A jeep stopped outside and several policemen got out, followed by the Sub-District Magistrate, the District Superintendent of Police, and the local 'tehsildar,' a combination land records officer and tax official. The policemen moved to control the door to Babaji's room, removed the devotees from the room, and then asked for Vijay; they wanted permission to go into the room and ask Babaji some questions. Vijay took them into the room and sat them on a mat in front of the bed on which Babaji sat in meditation. When Babaji opened His eyes, the S.D.M. introduced himself and said he had come in connection with a case. Very politely he said, "Please don't think that I am insulting you; I am being compelled by many people to find out who you are." Babaji sat quietly; He spoke very infrequently in those days.

The S.D.M. asked more pointedly," Are you Haidakhan Baba?" and Babaji answered "Yes." The S.D.M. said that was difficult to believe because there was no proof. Babaji replied, "Time will tell." The S.D.M. said that he could not wait for time; Babaji would have to give certain statements. Babaji said He would make the statements. The S.D.M. asked if He would make His statements there and then, or in court; and Babaji replied, "In court." The S.D.M. said the time had been fixed for Monday at 10 a.m. Babaji said He would come the next day - Sunday. The S.D.M. said the court was closed on Sunday, but Babaji insisted He would go to the court the next day. Mystified and thwarted by the quiet strength of this young man who appeared to be less than twenty, the S.D.M. agreed to a Sunday hearing, subject to the approval of the District Magistrate. The S.D.M. assigned seven policemen "to provide security" at the ashram and left.

The next morning Babaji said everyone should go to the court and the devotees decided to hire a band and make a procession into Haldwani. At 10 a.m. a great number of people set out on the four-kilometer walk to Haldwani; Babaji was placed on an open Jeep and a band played as they all marched into town.

They reached the court at about 12:30 with a crowd of thousands. Police were everywhere; the courtroom doors were closed. Babaji was ushered into the room, along with two or three lawyers and Padma Datt Pant, the editor of a small weekly newspaper, Sundesh Sagar, and the doors were closed behind them.

The Sub-District Magistrate stepped down from his dais to greet Shri Babaji. Babaji took the courtroom oath on the Bhagavad-Gita. Then the S.D.M. told Babaji that he still did not know who He was, but he prayed that he would not reach a decision for which he would suffer all his life. Again, he said that he was not trying to insult Babaji, but people compelled him to ask if He were Haidakhan Baba. Babaji replied, "Yes."

The S.D.M.'s next question was, "What is your age?" Babaji

said He would answer that question the next day. The S.D.M. said He would have to answer today. Babaji repeated He would reply the next day. The S.D.M., aroused now, said, "I give you fifteen minutes; if you don't answer today, I will be forced to take legal action." Babaji replied, "You do what you wish, but I will reply tomorrow." Then He turned away from the magistrate.

The S.D.M. did not know what to do. He called for a glass of water for Babaji, and when He refused it, the S.D.M. drank two glasses. Then he stated that, because of the crowd, 'Maharaj' must be disturbed and would not answer today, but He would surely answer tomorrow. The S.D.M. adjourned the hearing and Babaji and His immediate devotees returned to the ashram.

After His bath and meditation, Babaji tested Vijay's courage. Vijay has written the following account of this incident.

"He said to me, 'Vijay, today we have been saved, but tomorrow *how* will we be saved? Let's run away!'

"I was astounded! I had never contemplated Baba's saying such a thing! I folded my hands and said, 'Maharaj, the time has come to show everyone.'

"He replied, 'What am I to show anyone? If *you* want to go to jail, that's fine: maybe you have too much work here?'

"I was quite amazed. I thought this was a testing time for me but I was in bad shape for a test. I asked, 'Baba, how will You run away? There are police all around.'

"He told me not to worry; we would go to the hills. I said that was fine with me, but 'Baba, what about all Your devotees who have come here from far and near?' He told me to go and find out what they thought.

"It was 11 p.m. and I ran around and told everyone what Baba had said. They all came into Baba's room with me; they all prayed to Babaji that He would show a miracle, or else things would be difficult: whenever any difficulty had arisen before, Baba had wiped it out.

"On seeing these anguished people, Baba was deeply touched and He asked, 'Why are you worrying?

105

If in this world there is a danger, Baba is the Danger of dangers. In this North India, there are many of Baba's devotees roaming around; and if anyone of them is ordered to do so, they will eat these people raw.[3] No power on this earth can do anything to Me. When a Great Soul comes, there is always opposition. Om shanti [peace], shanti, shanti; go and take rest.' All the disciples praised the Lord and went to bed. I slept near Baba, but I was restless the whole night and kept wondering what would happen if Baba left us."[4]

The next morning Babaji called for a jeep and went back to the court. On this day the crowd was thicker than before; there was great excitement and anticipation that the reality of this Babaji would come into the open on this day.

This time the magistrate arrived after Babaji. Babaji was sworn in and the S.D.M., in respectful tones, repeated his question of the previous day. There follows an unofficial translation of the court record.

"What is your age?

"One hundred thirty years.

"How many years have you been a saint?

"I don't know the exact year, but since the British rule came.

"Where is your birth place?

"Haidakhan, Nainital [District].

"How long did you stay with your mother and father?

"I never did.

"Who brought you up?

"A saint.

"What is the name of the saint?

"Siddha Bhairav Baba[5] raised me for six to ten years, and after that he taught me spiritual practices.

"Where is Bhairav Baba nowadays?

"He disappeared.

"Do you remember your parents?

"No.

"Has anyone ever asked you the mystery of how to reach Bhairav Baba?

"No.

"When did you attain this spiritual level?

"When I was ten.

"After that, where did you stay?

"Haidakhan, Nainital District.

"You went with somebody?

"I went alone.

"How long did you live there?

"One or two years.

"After that where did you go?

"Vasuka, Ranibagh.

"How long did you live there?

"Eight years; but I used to visit Haidakhan often.

"Did you go to the Gaura Surya Devi Temple and stay there?

"Yes.

"When were you there?

"A year ago.

"Did you ever study in any school?

"No.

"Which of the Indian scriptures do you know?

"I have knowledge of all the Vedas.

"...how many Vedas are there?

"Four Vedas. Rig Ved, Sama Ved, Gon Ved, Athar Ved.

"Have you ever read one of those Vedas?

"No.

"Then how did you get the knowledge of all the Vedas?

"Sombhari Baba, Bhaarav Baba, Mohan Baba. I stayed ten years with Sombhari Baba in the village of Padampur; at the same time I went back and forth to Mohan Baba; and had Bhairav Baba's satsang for ten years.

"Besides the Vedas, do you have any other knowledge?

"No.

"From whom did you learn your yoga and spiritual practice?

"From Bhairav Baba.

"What did you learn in your yoga and spiritual practice?

"Saririk practices and mind control.

107

"When you went to the Surya Devi Temple, was any saint present there?

"Yes.

"What is his name?

"I don't know.

"How much time did you spend with him?

"Two or three months.

"Was the baba ill?

"Yes.

"Who treated him?

"Don't know.

"Did you come to Haldwani, sometimes, for his medicine?

"No.

"Did any doctor come from Haldwani?

"Yes.

'What is his name?

"Don't know.

"Where is his clinic?

"Don't know.

"If the doctor is called here, will you recognize him?

"Yes.

"How many times did you go to his clinic to get medicine?

"Didn't go.

"Have you heard the name of Baba Mahendra Nath?[6]

"Yes.

"Have you seen him?

"No.

'When did you come to Haldwani?

"August 28.

"Where were you before that?

"Indrapuri, Delhi.

"Where were you there?

"With a Haidakhan 'satsang group.'

"When was this group started?

"This year.

"Who started it?

"The bhaktas [devotees] there.

"Where were you before that?

"Sambasadashiv Kund in Vrindaban.

"How long were you there?

"During the month of Maha [January-February].

"Where were you before that?

"Kathmandu Ashram, in Nepal.

"How long did you stay there?

"Twenty years.

"Where were you before that?

"Shiker in Almora.

"Did you ever stay in Fatepur?

"No.

"What is the total area of the Kathgharia Ashram?

"Fifty-five beedhas. [One beedha equals about half an acre, depending on the locality.]

"How did you get it?

"From one of the British Commissioners.

"When was it given?

"During the British rule.

"Do you understand and speak English?

"I understand, but I cannot speak it.

"In which year was the land given?

"I don't remember.

"To whom was the land given?

"It was given to Me.

"Did you go to the Commissioner or did he come to you?

"The Commissioner came to meet Me in Kathgharia.

"Why did he come?

"He came to see Me often.

"Why did he give you the land?

"For the ashram.

"How much did he give?

"Forty-five beedhas. The remaining ten beedhas were given by the villagers.

"Did you meet with the English Commissioner in Haidakhan?

"No.

"How many years ago did you come to Haldwani?

"I came here two years ago, but I had not come to Kathgharia.

"Then where did you go?

"I stayed in Haidakhan and Kailash.

"From where did you come to there?

"From Nepal.

"Before that, when had you come to Kathgharia?

"Forty years before.

"By chance, were there any devotees there at that time?

"Not out there.

"Until when did the British rule India?

"Until 1947.

"Where were you born?

"Haidakhan.

"When did you go from Haidakhan?

"After the age of thirty, I used to go and come from Haidakhan.

"Have you changed your form?

"Yes.

"How and when was your form different from this?

"Sixty years ago I was a little fat.

"Did you have hair at that time?

"Yes; I used to have hair and I wore a topi.

"Did you build any temple?

"I built a Shiva temple in Haidakhan.

"Is any devotee who was with you forty years ago still present?

"Yes. Govind Valabh Pant who is still living in Kathgharia. The wife of Dr. Hem Chand [Joshi] who lives in Nainital had come and gone away. The priest at Haidakhan, Shri Paramanandji is still a priest there, in Krishna Nand Gram [village], Nainital District.

"In Haldwani City, are there any old devotees of yours?

"Shri Anand Singh.

"Who is in charge of the land at Kathgharia and since when?

"It has been in the hands of Shri Ghovardhan for forty years.

"Was the committee established with your permission?

"No; it was formed later.

"Is it true that you are Haidakhan Baba?"

"Yes, I am Haidakhan Baba.

"Isn't it that you are a disciple of Haidakhan Baba?"

"No.

"Some people suspect that you are not Haidakhan Baba.

"That is their own belief. The people who think I am not Haidakhan Baba are wrong.

"Is it true that you are Haidakhan Baba?"

"Yes."

Babaji signed the transcript "Shri Yogi Raj 108 Baba Haidakhan." It appears that the Sub-District Magistrate managed to keep his decision and his signature off the record; at least, the transcript that was translated for me had neither the decision nor his name. Vijay Gupta reports that the S.D.M.'s decision favored Babaji - that the court believed Him to be Baba Haidakhan; those who did not so believe were invited to present their proofs. Others believe the court found it easier to come to no decision at all.

*   *   *   *   *   *   *   *

There were many who were still opposed and still unbelieving. Among them was the editor of <u>Sandesh</u> ~ Shri Padma Datt Pant. In his September 20, 1971 issue, he wrote this about the trial and its aftermath.

"... That day the court was filled with people and they were expecting Babaji to show some miracle and remove all the doubts and disputes from their minds. But nothing of that sort happened. Instead, Babaji simply answered all questions truthfully. There was nothing dishonest or untruthful about Babaji's testimony. But people still thought that Babaji was a hill boy and surrounded by wrong-thinking people and that his followers were taking advantage of and cheating the larger population. Similar thoughts were in the mind of the editor.

"The next day, Mr. Sharma of Jaipur came to

111

Haldwani and asked the editor to come to Kathgharia Ashram and be with Babaji for a time. Mr. Sharma
wanted the editor to publish in his paper the correct
picture of Babaji's court appearance and remove the
false rumors that Babaji was arrested by the police, etc.
Mr. Sharma invited two other journalists to accompany him to see Babaji.

"The next day, the editor reached Kathgharia
Ashram and was told that Babaji was resting. Both
the journalists were also waiting for Babaji. After half
an hour, Babaji received all of them in his room. They
told him that, after the court incident, the religious-
minded people had suffered a shock in their minds
and hearts. People have become indifferent toward
religion; what happened in the court was an insult
to Haidakhan Baba. An illusion had been created in
people's minds; if he was the famous old Haidakhan
Baba, known for his miracles, why did he not put a
stop to this whole thing? Why did he make a drama
out of the whole court episode? Many other, similar
questions were put by the journalists. Babaji replied
in a simple manner. 'Things have always happened
like this. *Everything depends on faith.*'"

Shri Pant told me that he asked Babaji many questions that
he later felt were "absurd" - because he had no belief in this young
boy. One of his taunts was, "Are you a real baba who has power to
punish those who are against you?" And Baba replied, "Who am I to
punish those men? Their own <u>karmas</u>[7] will punish them."

Pantaji kept hammering at the 'drama' that Babaji created. At
last, Babaji flashed angrily at Pantaji and asked, "Who are *you?* Why
do you come here? Why do *you* make a drama of the name of Haidakhan Baba and the Hindu dharma?" Immediately after this, Pantaji
had an experience which made a 'believer' out of him. Pantaji noticed
a shadow in Babaji's hair, by His ear. The 'shadow' spread over His
face. For a second, Babaji's head disappeared behind what seemed

to be protoplasm. On the surface of this 'screen,' or protoplasm, Shri Pant saw a 'sketch' of Babaji's body, as though it were drawn on a wall. The 'sketch' developed two faces of Babaji, of a light pink color, one above the other, with slit-like eyes. Pantaji was startled to see this sight and he turned his head from side to side to find what caused what he was seeing. When he returned his focus to Babaji's form, Pantaji saw Babaji 'sitting' a foot above His seat and smoke was pouring from His body; His head was surrounded by a halo of sparkling light. A beam of light came from Shri Babaji's third eye and rested on Pantaji. Pantaji could not stand this intensity of feeling and sight; he fell at Babaji's feet and begged Him, "Oh, Baba! Stop! Stop! Stop!"

Babaji pressed Pantaji's head with one hand and, crazed with fear, Pantaji pushed the hand away. He jumped up and dashed out of the room

As Pantaji looked for a rickshaw to take him back to Haldwani, the two journalists came to him. He asked them if they had seen anything, but they had shared nothing of Pantaji's experience. Several people asked him what he had seen, but he spoke of it to no one then.

That night, after his meal, Pantaji went to bed. He left the light on in his room until his wife came to bed. Pantaji shut his eyes and tried to sleep. Babaji came - physically, Pantaji says - and sat on Pantaji's bed. Pantaji jumped out of bed to welcome Babaji, but there was no one there. This happened several times. When his wife came into the room, Pantaji told her what was happening. Her answer was, "You taunted Babaji; this is the result."

The next morning, Pantaji went back to the Kathgharia Ashram. From a long distance, he saw Babaji; and from that long distance Pantaji made his pranam to Babaji and returned home.

Pantaji considered himself a devotee from that time on, but he puzzled over Babaji's identity. He knew that people considered Shri Babaji to be a manifestation of Lord Shiva; but Pantaji was no devotee of Shiva and had done no tapasya [spiritual discipline]. Why had he been given a sign of Shiva? Pantaji thought maybe Babaji was a tantric master and that, because he had teased or taunted the master, Babaji had used tantric powers to mesmerize him. The thought went through Pantaji's mind that Babaji might be truly divine, but he

113

was not comfortable with that thought until he heard it, some months later, from Shri Nantin Baba.

A Connection with 'Old Haidakhan Baba'

From Kathgharia, Shri Babaji returned to Haidakhan.

Some time after His return, a man named Jaman Singh, from the village of Udhwan, near Haidakhan, came to Babaji and related his personal troubles, which mostly revolved around his poverty. He had a very small piece of land, and water for irrigation of his crops or for his cattle was very far from his property.

Babaji told Jaman Singh, "My land is lying untilled," and He pointed to the first bend in the river, downstream from Haidakhan. "You may go and take it over."

This was a big surprise to everyone. The Babaji they knew had neither bought nor been given land in the valley. Jaman Singh was sent by Babaji to the court in Nainital to obtain the relevant document which showed the land belonged to 'Old Haidakhan Baba.' The documents involved were retrieved, after considerable search, and Jaman Singh came back to the Gautam Ganga Valley with a new document giving him the right, subject to payment to Baba Haidakhan, to till field No. 1421/1422, of three acres, which had been allotted to Baba Haidakhan in 1922.[8]

*　　*　　*　　*　　*　　*　　*　　*

Late in 1971, Babaji went to Haldwani and stayed in Ram Prakash Bhasin's house for three days. During all that time, He stayed in the room they provided Him, leaving only to take His bath, at which time He was served by members of the Bhasin family. During the whole time, Babaji did not eat enough to feed a child; He would eat perhaps one tiny piece of potato or fruit, and drink a few sips of milk or juice, apparently more as a method of blessing what was offered than from need or desire for food. He never once went to the toilet. He spoke only a few words during the whole three-day period. People did not touch Him in those days (as they did later), nor rub

114

His skin with scented oils - yet His body gave off a beautiful scent.

When the Bhasin family visited Shri Babaji in Haidakhan in December, they found Baba sitting in a mud-and-stone hut with half-walls (a gap of two or three feet between the top row of stones in the wall and the frame for the grass-thatched roof), clad only in a thin cotton kurta. There also, He ate almost nothing and did not go to the toilet. Most of the time, He sat in the hut in deep meditation, eyes either open or closed, sitting up all night in a perfect, upright, meditation pose. Occasionally, He took devotees for walks in the hills or along the river. He spoke rarely, but when He did speak, His statements were full of meaning.

Nantin Baba's Identification of Babaji

On the 12th of January, 1972, Shri Nantin Baba arrived in Haldwani and told his followers that he wanted to go to the Surya Devi Temple to meet Shri Babaji on the Sankranti holiday, January 14th - a day celebrating the start of the return of the sun toward the northern hemisphere. On the 13th, before he left for the Surya Devi Temple, Nantin Baba talked to some local journalists and told them that Baba Haidakhan had collected the complete Cosmic Energy within Himself and had appeared before the world to give Light. Now that many other people had seen Babaji, he (Nantin Baba) was also going to see Him.

Shri Nantin Baba arrived at the Surya Devi Temple several hours before Shri Babaji. When Babaji came, late in the winter afternoon, everyone present hailed Him. He walked right past Nantin Baba, without a glance, and Nantin Baba played with flowers and kept his back turned toward Babaji. The two babas played this game for several hours, while their baffled devotees made little efforts to get them together. Babaji told His devotees to feed Nantin Baba, and Nantin Baba ate the food that was sent to him. Late at night, after food had been served to all, Pantaji, the editor of <u>Sundesh-Sagar</u>, started asking Nantin Baba when he would go to meet Haidakhan Baba. Nantin Baba replied, "I would like to go, but I do not know where Babaji is."

Pantaji wrote in his newspaper that he himself led Shri Nantin Baba by the hand into Shri Babaji's presence, where Nantin Baba offered gifts at Babaji's feet and garlanded them with flowers. The two saints apparently spoke no words to each other at all, but communicated in deep meditation. Later, a woman asked Shri Nantin Baba what he had seen. He replied that he had seen Babaji as a very, very old man. The people standing around laughed and told Nantin Baba, "*You* are the old man and Babaji is a very young man!" Nantin Baba is reported to have said, "I am but a child and Babaji is an old man; He is immortal and the Controller of the Universe." He also said that after some years Babaji would leave His body and take the form of a five-year-old child.[9]

Old Haidakhan Baba's Mala Again

One day early in 1972, when Shri Babaji was again in the ashram at Vrindaban, a very old man in ragged clothing came into the ashram. Dr. Hem Chand Joshi's widow, Durga Devi, was there, and when she saw this man she prostrated herself before him. It was Gangotri Baba, who had been inspired to leave the Himalayas to come to have Shri Babaji's darshan. Someone ran to get Swami Fakiranand, who was the administrator of Babaji's ashram. Swamiji paid his respects, offered Gangotri Baba an asan, and returned to the room he used as an office.

Shri Babaji came out of His room and whispered to Swamiji that a great Himalayan saint had come; He told Swamiji to make a pranam to him. When Swamiji had made his pranam, Babaji told him to offer prasad - fruit and milk - to Gangotri Baba, which Swamiji did. Then Babaji sat and gave darshan, but there was no conversation between Babaji and Gangotri Baba that afternoon.

The next morning, Gangotri Baba returned for Babaji's darshan. After a little time, Babaji told Swami Fakiranand, "Get my mala from Gangotri Baba." Swamiji, thinking that Babaji must have given a mala to Gangotri Baba the previous day, went to him and said, "Baba is asking for the mala." Then Gangotri Baba smiled and told Swamiji the story of the mala which 'Old Haidakhan Baba' had given him.[10] He said he had brought the mala in its original cotton bag with him and he offered to get it from the place where he was staying. Babaji said he could wait until the afternoon darshan.

Late that afternoon, Gangotri Baba came. He said the bag had not been opened since Haidakhan Baba had given it to him in 1922. "Now, after about fifty years, I am returning it to Babaji, to Whom it belongs."

Swamiji took the bag to Shri Babaji. The bag was torn and dirty and the mala string was weak and thin, but it held together. Everyone present saw it with great interest and devotion. After two or three days, Babaji sent it to be re-strung, kept it for a few days, and gave it to a devotee.

Inamdar and Vora Make Their Pranams

In August, 1972, Shri Ambalal Inamdar[11] became disturbed by an inexplicable loss of concentration in his work; constantly he heard an inner voice saying, "Go to Vrindaban." He was greatly puzzled by this and talked about it with his friend Manherlal K. Vora. Voraji urged him to go to Vrindaban and find the answer to this puzzle, and Inamdar, being a man of action, took a train to Vrindaban. In Vrindaban, Inamdar met a man he knew from Ambaji, where they both used to meet Mahendra Maharaj. Inamdar asked about the temple at Mahendra Baba's ashram in Vrindaban. The man replied that he was in bliss: the temple was under construction just as Mahendra Baba had planned it.

Inamdar, who had raised the money for the purchase of the ashram land and had also helped in the preparation of the architectural drawings of the proposed temple, confesses that he had a great deal of ego wrapped up in that ashram. When he walked into the ashram and looked around the nearly completed temple, he felt his ego was deflated: everything was as Mahendra Maharaj had planned; his distrust was unfounded. Inamdar went to Mahendra Baba's old room and saw Mahendra Baba's photograph still hanging there Then Inamdar went to the place where Shri Babaji sat and gave Babaji a standing 'salute' with folded hands and sat down among the other devotees.

Babaji went into His room and signaled for Inamdar to come.

When they were settled, Inamdar asked Babaji a question he asked of all the saints he met and talked to: "Maharaj, when a devotee takes one step toward God, Mahamaya (Illusion, or the awareness of differences within Creation) comes and pushes him two steps back. Why is this?" Babaji's response was, "Inamdarji, why do you make a difference between God and God's Creation?" Inamdar was amazed at the response; he had had many different responses from many saints - mostly wise, old saints. This is a traditional question and there are traditional answers to it, but Inamdar thought the 'young' Babaji's response, going to the core of his question, was the best response he had ever heard or read: the whole of Creation is God manifested.

Inamdarji sat in silence for some minutes, pondering, while Babaji looked at him with grace. Then Inamdar got up and walked out to his place among the other people and sat down. Inamdarji had a back problem which made it difficult for him to sit for any length of time; now, all of a sudden, he did not feel that condition; he felt weightless. He sat on his hands in a tantric position. At that time, something happened that he had sought for years; he felt the sensation of peace which is supposed to allow kundalini[12] to begin to flow through the body from the lowest chakra upward. As Inamdar sat and experienced this wonderful, peaceful sensation, Babaji came from His room and walked toward Inamdar, and Inamdar found himself weeping copiously and long; he felt the tears washed away his ego and sin.

When Inamdar went back to Bombay, he saw his friend Vora and told Voraji not to be astonished if he saw Inamdar make a pranam to Babaji.

After this, Mr. Vora went to see Shri Babaji in the city of Amba-ji and obtained Babaji's promise to visit Bombay. In November, 1972, Voraji and Inamdarji went to Gwalior to meet Babaji and take Him to Bombay. On the plane to Bombay, Inamdar sat next to Shri Babaji. Through the noise of the plane's engines, Inamdar kept hearing "Om Namah Shivaya." He could not believe it; he focused his mind on the engine noise, but "Om Namah Shivaya" still rang in his ears. He tried reading a magazine to distract his mind. Finally, Inamdar turned to Babaji and asked if He were really Haidakhan Baba. Babaji only smiled. Inamdar then asked if Babaji had taken on someone else's

118

body or whether He had materialized a new body for Himself. Babaji took up the magazine Inamdar had been reading and asked Inamdar to read it. Inamdarji stood up and told Babaji he had read the magazine, now he was looking for Light from Baba; if Baba wants to answer, do so; otherwise, Inamdar would sit somewhere else.

Babaji motioned for Inamdar to sit down again and then He said, "Can you graft one tree onto another tree, or not?" Inamdar thought, inwardly, that only certain kinds of trees can be grafted onto each other. Babaji put His hand on Inamdar's knee and said, "You can only graft trees onto certain trees - not every tree will work." Then He added, "In this world, in this Yuga [Age], you can take electricity from place to place; you can even store it. In the same manner, *these* things can happen."

Shri Babaji was taken to Manherlal K. Vora's home in Bombay, where Mahendra Maharaj had often come for peace and quiet, to think through his problems and doubts. The Voras, who had by then accepted Babaji as Haidakhan Baba and Mahavatar Babaji, were naturally very curious about their unusual guest. He was still eating only very small morsels of food offerings - bits of fruit or a piece of cut fresh vegetable; all put together they would hardly make a tablespoon of food in a day. Despite the lack of food intake, He had boundless energy; He climbed the stairs to their third floor apartment two at a time - "like a monkey." He never went to the toilet in the ten days He was with them. He sat in meditation a great deal, spoke very infrequently, yet exuded peace and love. He participated in the nine-day yagya, with fire ceremonies and readings from the scriptures. And many people - devotees of Mahendra Baba and others - came to see Him.

The Lals Meet Babaji in Two Forms

Vimla Lal read Yogananda's autobiography in the early 1960's. She was particularly fascinated by the portions on Mahavatar Babaji, but this was something she felt she could not discuss with her husband, who was a medical doctor and scientist, very successful in the operation of a pathology laboratory in New Delhi, and well known and respected in medical science circles in India and the United States.

His scientific mind was just not open to tales of gurus' miracles and the devotion of their devotees.

Reading and re-reading the chapters on Babaji in Yogananda's book, Vimla Lal became convinced of Babaji's existence and decided that if she could only get to Dronagiri Mountain - where Lahiri Mahasaya had been initiated into kriya yoga - she, too, could find Babaji there. But how to get there?

In 1966, Dr. Lal asked Vimla if she would like to attend a medical conference in Nainital with him, and she saw her chance. She said she would go with him if, after the conference, he would take her to Ranikhet, about fifty miles from Nainital. Ranikhet is the town to which Mahavatar Babaji had called Lahiri Mahasaya.

They both went. In Ranikhet, while Dr. Lal played golf, Vimla read the 'Babaji chapters' and prayed and asked villagers where Dronagiri Mountain was; but no one could tell her. As the time approached for the Lals to return to Delhi, Vimla became upset; she cried and prayed through the night. She thought God had had a plan when He made this trip possible; would they go back to Delhi without seeing Babaji?

When Dr. Lal returned from his golf the next morning, he asked Vimla what she had been doing with her time. She said she had been reading, but her eyes were tired; would he read a chapter to her? She gave Dr. Lal the chapter about the palace on Dronagiri[13] and he read it to her and became intrigued. He wanted to investigate these phenomena, while they were in the area - to see whether great yogis like that can be immortal in this world. So they got into their car and went off to find Dronagiri Mountain.

After considerable difficulty, they finally were directed to the right road to Dronagiri and started driving through the hilly countryside. Near the last village on the road, they saw two sadhus standing by the side of Gangeshwar River. The elder of the two men, whom Mrs. Lal immediately thought was Babaji, strode into the middle of the road and tried to stop the car. As the doctor drove past him, Vimla excitedly told her husband to stop: "Babaji has come!"

Dr. Lal, grumbling that his wife had an obsession about Babaji and saw Him everywhere, pulled over to park. Mrs. Lal jumped out

120

of the car and ran back to the man, made a pranam, and asked if he were Babaji. He acknowledged that He was Babaji, blessed her, and told her that He was not visible to everyone, but, as she had come with such great devotion and faith, He had to appear to her. He offered to show the Lals the way to the temple on Dronagiri Mountain.

Mrs. Lal put the two sadhus in the back seat of the car and Dr. Lal grumbled, in English, that he didn't much like having those two village bums in the car. Babaji laughed.

The road to Dronagiri Mountain was then under construction. They drove as far as they could, then turned back to a village where they rented a jeep. When they reached the point nearest the temple, they got out and Babaji pointed up the side of the mountain to the then-unattended temple in honor of the Mother Goddess. The doctor immediately climbed over a four-foot wall and headed up the mountainside with his camera.

Mrs. Lal, left behind with Babaji and the other sadhu, felt anger toward her husband for walking away and leaving her to climb over the wall in a saree; but she said nothing. Babaji, reading her mind, told her not to worry about the wall; it would be no problem. She put her hand in His and, to this day, she has no idea whether they went through the wall, climbed it, or flew over it; but they were suddenly, and without any effort on her part, on the other side of the wall.

When they reached the temple, Babaji told Mrs. Lal to do puja, the formal worship service. She had brought nothing with her for a puja and Babaji sensed her embarrassment. He told her that He had known she was coming and had readied the temple for puja and, when they walked in, she found everything ready - flowers, incense, cloth, a food offering, and an aarati lamp. But she was embarrassed again; she had never done puja to the Goddess and did not know how to proceed. So Babaji stayed by her side and told her what to do, step by step.

After doing puja, they walked out of the temple. Close to the entrance was a big bell, hung too high for Mrs. Lal to reach. It is the Hindu custom to ring a bell when entering or leaving a temple and Mrs. Lal thought, "If I were a little taller, I would be able to ring that bell." As she had the thought, Babaji said, "You *can* do it. Ring it!" Mrs. Lal reached for the bell and began ringing it, aware that her feet were not touching the ground. After a few seconds, Baba said, "Come down now; it is very late and you have far to go."

With her feet on the ground again, Vimla Lal bent down and touched Babaji's feet and asked, "Baba, when do I see You again?" He replied very clearly, "My child, whenever you come with such devotion and faith, you will see Me here."

Dr Lal, who had been taking photographs most of this time, came over to them. He joined his wife in bowing, with respect, to Babaji - and when they looked up again, He was gone. At that point, Dr. Lal realized this old sadhu was no ordinary villager. He was not sure he had seen 'the Immortal Babaji', but he was open to that possibility.

In 1974, the Lals heard a rumor that a Shiva avatar had appeared in the form of Shri Haidakhan Wale Baba, also known simply as 'Babaji.' Dr. Lal did not give much credence to this claim until a friend came from Amritsar and said he had read a very holy book about Shiva coming as Shri Haidakhan Wale Baba and that this Babaji might be the Babaji they had met on Dronagiri Mountain. Hearing that Babaji was in Mathura, little more than a two-hour drive from New Delhi, the Lals drove off to meet Him.

They found a Babaji who looked nothing at all like the old man they had met at Dronagiri; this baba appeared to be a young man of twenty or so, healthy and strong - not much like the traditional pictures of Lord Shiva, either. He seemed very pleased to see the Lals before Him.

The Lals spent some days with Babaji in Mathura. It was too crowded and noisy there to talk privately and easily, so they followed Babaji to Vrindaban. Dr. Lal kept urging his wife to ask Babaji if He knew them, but it was not until the fourth or fifth day in Vrindaban that they found Babaji with only a few others present. Then Vimla Lal bowed and asked, "Baba, have You ever been to Dronagiri?" His response was, "Did *you* go there?" "Don't You know about it?" she asked. And Baba answered, "Yes, of course I do." Then He turned and asked Dr. Lal, "When will you go there again?" Mrs. Lal pressed again "Baba, when will *You* go there?" And He replied, "My child, whenever you go there with great devotion and faith, I will be there."

That reply convinced Mrs. Lal that this Babaji and the 'old' baba on the mountain were one and the same. But Dr. Lal had not heard that statement on Dronagiri Mountain, so Babaji turned to him and said, "Doctor, the last time you came to Dronagiri, I was with you for just three hours; now that you have come here, I will be with you for three days." That statement convinced Dr. Lal. He had never told Babaji of his profession. Also, he turned to Mrs. Lal and they did some quick calculations and realized that "the old Baba" had, indeed, been with them for about three hours at Dronagiri Mountain. With that, Dr. Lal touched Shri Babaji's feet and was an ardent devotee as long as he lived.

Some time later, when the Lals knew Babaji better, they drove Him in their car from Vrindaban to Delhi. Mrs. Lal asked about the other man who was with Him on Dronagiri Mountain. Babaji said the second man was Mahendra Baba, who is always with Him - in Him.

At the end of 1975, Shri Babaji rode from the ashram in Chilianaula to Haldwani with Dr. and Mrs. Lal and Vimla's sister, Kanta Sharma. As they neared the village of Garam Pani, Babaji pointed down - off the road, toward the riverbed - and said that down below there is a cave in which He had meditated for more than one hundred years. Dr. Lal blurted out, "Baba! One hundred years?" Babaji answered, "You are surprised because you don't think I am that old?"

Baba told the doctor to stop the car and told Vimla to walk down the hill toward the river and see that there is a pipal tree that has only thirteen leaves on it. Vimla started laughing at the thought, but they stopped the car and Dr. and Mrs. Lal started down the hillside. Soon they found two small, primitive temples on a built-up parapet overlooking the river. In one there was a small oil lamp burning, a murti covered with a woolen cloth against the cold, and a flower on it. Everything was in dilapidated condition. Vimla took the cloth off the statue and found it was a murti of 'Old Haidakhan Baba.' *That* was why He had sent them down, she thought. There was also a cave nearby, beside which was a pipal tree, mostly buried in a landslide. One branch only stuck out from the mound of earth - and it had thirteen leaves on it!

They climbed back up to the car and Shri Babaji said, "I am sure you never want to believe Me unless you see things with your own eyes."

Vimla asked Shri Babaji if He had meditated there as Lord Shiva Himself. Her sister asked, "Is Shiv 'adi' [the original, first Form of God]?" And Babaji answered, "No, Shiva is 'anadi' [from Time-without-a-beginning]." Babaji said He might look young, but you cannot imagine how old He is. "Don't go by appearances."

Shri Shri Sitaram Das Onkarnathji Meets Babaji

There are many, many tales of people's experiences of Shri Babaji as a Divine Being. When His devotees gather for religious festivals, there are many such stories exchanged. They were not limited to the early days of Shri Babaji's mission but continued to His last hours. People often caught glimpses of His divinity, despite the 'smokescreen' which He set up. Indians and foreigners, young and old, men and women, saints and sinners had sudden or unusual experiences of Babaji as Lord.

In February, 1981, after completing a nine-day yagya in Bombay, Shri Babaji and a small party flew to Calcutta for a brief stay, at the urgent request of Shri Sib Narayan Nandi. 'Nandi Baba,' as Shri Nandi was called, not only wanted Shri Babaji to bless his house and household and devotees in Calcutta by His visit, but he also wanted his long-time family guru, Shri Shri Sitaram Das Onkarnathji, to have Shri Babaji's darshan. Shri Shri Onkarnathji was then in his early 90's, an "established," miracle-working saint, and guru to tens - perhaps hundreds - of thousands of Indians and foreigners, with ashrams in fifty-five or sixty of India's holy places.

On the day after His arrival in Calcutta, a large hall was furnished to allow Shri Babaji to give darshan to His devotees. Shri Shri Onkarnathji was brought to this place in a car and carried on the shoulder of one of his devotees to the door of the reception hall where Shri Babaji sat. People were full of curiosity to see what would happen when the established, ninety-year-old saint met the young-looking Babaji.

At the door, Shri Shri Onkarnathji got down from the shoulder of his devotee and, with difficulty, walked up the aisle to Babaji's dais. There, Shri Shri Onkarnathji prostrated himself - lay flat on the floor - before Shri Babaji. Then, refusing the offered dais and still sitting on the floor, with folded hands and flowing tears, he told Shri Babaji that he had completed the work that Babaji had assigned to him. Then he stood and told the assembled people, "Shri Shri Babaji is God and I am His servant. He is Akhan Parambrahma Onkar Bhagwan [the Eternal Supreme Absolute (Formless) God, the Creator of everything]. I have seen Him as Lord Krishna." (Lord Krishna is the form of God whom Shri Shri Onkarnathji worshipped.) He went on to say that he was teaching the same <u>kriya yoga</u> that Babaji had given to Lahiri Mahasaya.

In the summer of 1982, Shri Shri Onkarnathji became ill and was hospitalized. For much of six months he was in a coma. Shri 'Nandi Baba' sent urgent messages to Shri Babaji to fly to Calcutta and give the old saint a last darshan. Shri Babaji said He would go, and made plans to go to Calcutta in October, and then cancelled them. At last He flew from Delhi to Calcutta on December 6, 1982. He was met at the airport by Shri Nandiji and taken directly to the apartment where Onkarnathji was being nursed. Shri Shri Onkarnathji had come out of his coma and consciously and gratefully received Shri Babaji's darshan, three tulsi leaves and a drink of juice from Shri Babaji. A few hours later, Shri Shri Onkarnathji left his body.

NOTES

1   Ashes from the sacred hawan or yagya fire.

2   This incident is taken from an unpublished manuscript, in Hindi, by Vijay Gupta.

3   Babaji seems to have referred here to spirit beings who, in the Hindu scriptures and tradition, are ready to fight Lord Shiva's battles with evil forces whenever He commands.

4   From Vijay Gupta's unpublished manuscript.

5   Bhairav is a spiritual energy of Lord Shiva. There are said to be 52 different manifestations of Bhairav in Hindu literature. Siddha Bhairav Baba is an enlightened teaching entity, master of all powers.

6   i.e., Mahendra Baba.

7   The fruits of ego actions.

8   Rao, op. cit., pages 38 and 39.

9   From the January 26, 1972 issue of Sundesh Sagar. This translated report is from Dr. Rao's book..

10 See bottom of page 42.

11 See bottom of page 96.

12 Kundalini is the spiritual life-force which is said to move up the spine as one's spirituality grows. It moves through centers called chakras, which are associated with areas of the body and functions of the mind. 1st chakra, at the base of the spine, deals with survival. The 2nd, behind the genital area, deals with sensual and sexual feelings; the 3rd, behind the solar plexus, deals with power and ego-power; 4th, at the center of the chest, relates to love; 5th, at the throat, relates to devotion and creativity; 6th, at the third eye, relates to wisdom and self-realization; and the 7th, at the crown of the head, relates to enlightenment.

13 See bottom of page 19 to page 20.

"I came to surrender to You, O Lord of Haidakhan,
Supreme Guru of true name;
Thou art the One who removes our sorrows."
From the Haidakhan Aarati.

"Abandoning all duties [dharmas], come unto Me alone
for shelter; sorrow not; I will liberate thee from all sins."
Lord Krishna to Arjun
The Bhagavad-Gita: 18th discourse, verse 66.

CHAPTER VI

HOW BABAJI CALLED PEOPLE TO HIM

Many times, in conversations with small groups or in speeches to devotees, Shri Babaji used to say that He had never called anyone or told anyone to come to Him. It may have been literally true that, in His physical form, He had not told anyone to come to Him until they had first met Him or written to Him, asking if they could come to see Him; but we all knew at least one tale of how people had been drawn to meet Shri Babaji.

A Lawyer Meets His Match

Hem Chand Bhatt is a lawyer who lives in Nainital, where the District Courts are located, except for the winter months when the courts and he move from Nainital's cold, sometimes snowy, heights to the lower, warmer plains area of Haldwani. During the Christmas and New Year period, the courts take a ten or twelve-day recess and during this time Shri Bhatt used to take his family to some place in the plains for a little holiday. During the 1971-72 recess, he decided to take the family to Varanasi (Benares) and Sarnath - not to see them as a pilgrim on a religious pilgrimage, because he was not much of a believer in God, but to tour them as places of historical interest. His wife, Savitri, had heard that Haidakhan Baba was going to have a yagya at the Surya Devi Temple during this period, and her curiosity about Babaji led her to insist on staying behind to go to the Surya Devi Temple with their younger daughter, then six or seven years old, while Bhattji went to Varanasi and Sarnath and other places with their older daughter and very young son.

When Bhattji returned home about a week later, he found the younger daughter, Shruti, was not at home. His wife told him that Babaji had insisted on taking Shruti to Haidakhan with Him and His party. Bhattji asked if Shruti had any spare clothes or money with her and was told she had neither. Two or three days later, on a Sunday, Bhattji heard that people were going to Haidakhan in a group

- going part way in Amar Singh's truck; so he packed a change of clothes for Shruti and went off with the group, intending to bring Shruti home on Monday.

When Bhattji reached Haidakhan, Shruti came running to him happily and told him that Babaji had told her, early in the morning, that her father would come to Haidakhan that day. When Bhattji met Babaji, he felt a strong attraction to Him, but he felt little religious faith in or reverence for Him. Late in the evening, Babaji asked Bhattji if he planned to stay a few days, and Bhattji replied that he did not believe in saints and babas and he had just come to pick up his daughter and take her home. Babaji said that on Monday there would be a trip to the top of Mount Kailash and Shruti had been staying just so she could make that trip. Bhattji said if that were so, he could stay another day. Babaji asked if he would like to go with the party and Bhattji replied that he would go for the sake of companionship, but not out of faith.

On the way up Mount Kailash, Babaji sent the rest of the party ahead and walked along with Bhattji, asking many things of him - personal matters and general matters. Bhattji answered everything truthfully but asked nothing of Babaji and did not initiate any conversation with Him.

There is no water on the top half of Mount Kailash and Bhattji got very thirsty. When they reached the top, he saw that Babaji had sent food and water - everything they needed - up ahead of the party. After rest and food, the party walked down, and again Babaji walked and talked with Bhattji most of the way.

About two kilometers out of Haidakhan, Babaji walked quickly ahead and a very tired Bhattji came in alone. As he neared the ashram temple, he thought that if he could just have some rotis (flat bread baked on coals) and potato-and-radish soup, he would go to sleep quickly. As he reached the temple gate, someone came to him and told him to come and have some food - and it was exactly what he had wished for.

Bhattji was so exhausted from his trek up Mount Kailash that he stayed Tuesday, as well - as he says, "...not out of reverence, but because I needed the rest." Still, he found Haidakhan and Babaji's

130

presence so enchanting that he did not really want to leave. But on Wednesday, he and Shruti returned to Haldwani.

A few weeks later, Bhattji was back in Haldwani on a Saturday evening. He had had two or three drinks of whiskey before someone in the bazaar told him that Shri Babaji had come to Amar Singh's house. Bhattji did not know where Amar Singh lived, nor did he have any intention of going to see Babaji; but when he met someone he knew who was riding on a motor scooter, Bhattji got on the back of the scooter and asked the man to take him to Babaji. Bhattji had heard that Babaji did not allow even tea in the Haidakhan ashram and that He turned out anyone who came to Him under the influence of liquor; but when he made his pranam to Babaji, Babaji asked Bhattji to stay at Amar Singh's house and sleep in His room.

The next day, Babaji was going to the ashram at Dhanyan and Bhattji planned to go back to Nainital. Bhattji casually asked Baba if he could go in Babaji's party as far as Bhowali, where a road splits off to Nainital. Babaji readily agreed and told Bhattji to get into the car He was riding in. At Bhowali, Bhattji asked if he could go on with Babaji to Dhanyan, and Babaji agreed easily.

When they reached the point in the road, beyond Almora, where a path marks the three-or-four-mile walk into Dhanyan, Babaji sent some of His party into Dhanyan and announced that He was going on to Jageshwar, site of an ancient temple, and would go in to Dhanyan the next day. Baba took Bhattji and a few others with Him.

It was still winter; Jageshwar nights are very cold, and no one had any bedding, or even very warm clothing. When they reached Jageshwar, it was quite dark and cold, and the few shops in the little town were all closed. Bhattji worried about getting something to eat and some bedding. Suddenly, a bus drove up and a sadhu got off the bus and walked directly to Babaji and asked Him and His party to be his guests that night. Within minutes, a tasty and bountiful meal was being prepared and comfortable bedding was arranged for everyone in the party.

The next day the party went back from Jageshwar and, where the path to Dhanyan starts, Bhattji again asked if he could go with Babaji to Dhanyan, and Babaji again agreed. As the party walked, again Babaji sent the others ahead and kept Bhattji back with Himself, putting His hand on Bhattji's shoulder and walking slowly through the forest. Bhattji became very frank and talked a lot; at one point, Babaji abruptly asked Bhattji why he hadn't come earlier to Him. Unthinkingly, Bhattji said his friendship with Babaji had just started; how *could* he have come any earlier to Babaji? Babaji had Bhattji repeat that statement. From then on, when Babaji and Bhattji were alone together, Babaji treated Bhattji on a friend-to-friend basis; even when Shri Bhatt had developed a strong belief in Babaji as an avatar of Shiva and was ready to accord Him that respect, when they were alone, Babaji behaved as a dear friend with Bhattji - not as his God.

Later on, when Babaji visited Bhattji at his apple orchard outside of Bhowali, Babaji sometimes took Bhattji for a walk. Several times Babaji sat on a big stone in a field of peas; He asked Bhattji to pick fresh peas and bring them to Him, and Babaji opened the pods and ate the peas and liked them very much. Then Babaji got up from the stone and made Bhattji sit while Babaji Himself went into the field, picked peas, and offered them to Bhattji.

A Diplomat Surrenders

In 1971 and 1972, the first foreign, non-Hindu devotees came to Babaji. The first that we know of was a diplomat in the Ghanaian Foreign Service, W.W.K. Vanderpuye.

Mr. Vanderpuye began searching for God as a young man. He read many books on religion, including Yogananda's "Autobiography of a Yogi." Eastern mysticism fascinated him; he wanted to go to India and find a 'Master.' In 1971, in his mid-40's, after several years in the Ghanaian Foreign Service, he managed to get an appointment to India as Ghana's Deputy High Commissioner. He learned meditation and made friends with an Indian who introduced him to many saints and spiritual people. He wanted to achieve 'liberation' and every saint he met he asked about liberation. When he asked the venerable Ananda Moi Ma, she made a sign to him that he would find his guru and gain liberation. He made a pilgrimage to Vrindaban and met Neem Karoli Baba[1], who gave him many gifts and the name of

Buthnath - King of all the creatures.

After Buthnath had seen Neem Karoli Baba, while walking through the streets, he came to Babaji's ashram. He asked about it and was told it was the ashram of a 'returned saint.' He immediately asked if the saint were Babaji and, on being told that He was indeed Babaji, Buthnath went into the ashram. It was Guru Purnima Day, the day on which disciples honor their gurus. Babaji was then sitting on His asan [a raised seat], but He got up and walked to Buthnath and stared into his eyes. Buthnath later learned that Babaji was recognizing a returning soul and welcoming him. Baba sat down again and Buthnath went and sat near Him. After introductions, Buthnath told Babaji he wanted liberation. Babaji told Buthnath he should visit Vrindaban often and he would get liberation: Babaji would teach him meditation. Babaji also told Buthnath that it was His plan to call all His former devotees from all over the world to India and that very soon there would be many foreigners coming to see Him.

When Buthnath went back to Delhi, he found his life changing quickly. Since he had come to India and started meditation, he had given up smoking; he had simply lost the desire to smoke and had stopped, despite having been a heavy smoker. Now he suddenly gave up chasing after women, quit drinking liquor, and became a vegetarian - changes which surprised him, as well as his friends. He spent more and more time 'inside,' in meditation and contemplation.

He went often to see Babaji in Vrindaban (Babaji stayed there for months on end in the first few years) or in other places, and every time he visited Babaji some 'little miracle' happened.

Once when Buthnath visited Babaji at Ambaji, in Gujarat, he was sitting alone in a room, reading Shri Aurobindo's "Life Divine:" when he felt a very heavy vibration in the room and a voice said, "God is real; He is closer to you than you think." Later, when Buthnath told Baba of this, He calmly replied, "Yes, God is real; He is closer to you than you think and if we forget Him for a minute, we are lost. We should try to remember God always."

On a later occasion, during his assignment to Pakistan as Ghana's High Commissioner [Ambassador], Buthnath traveled back to India to see Babaji, and he brought his housekeeper with him. On their return to Ghana, the housekeeper went to consult a spiritualist about some personal problem. The seer went into a trance and, surprisingly, began to describe Haidakhan. Then she told the housekeeper that the 'person' she had seen in Vrindaban was God Himself.

Tara Devi and Gaura Devi

Mary Opplinger, whom Babaji and His devotees called Tara Devi, met Babaji in the middle of February, 1972, at the Kathgharia Ashram. She was an American lady, born and raised in Baltimore, Maryland, who had come to India in the 1950's with her Swiss husband, who administered some Swiss and other aid programs in India. Babaji invited her to go to Vrindaban, where He was headed, and she felt drawn to Him as with the same power that Christ had called His disciples. She became a strong devotee of Babaji - a gentle but powerful example of a karma yogi, always serving others, until her death in July, 1982.

A month or so after Tara Devi first met Babaji, she went to visit Him in Haidakhan. He told her that He would soon be going to Almora (where she and her husband lived) and that she should gather all her friends. He was looking for someone among them who had been His disciple in a former life. So Tara Devi went back to Almora and invited her friends (mostly young, Westerners) to meet Babaji.

One of her friends was a young Italian woman who was searching for a spiritual guide. She had gone to India and Nepal without much of a clear idea of what she wanted, but she was attracted to the Himalayas and, with some friends, went to Almora and settled down for a long stay. One day she consulted the "I Ching," the Chinese book of oracles, about finding a guru. The response of the "I Ching" was that this was the right time to meet her spiritual master. The next day, through Tara Devi, she met Shri Babaji. When Tara Devi had said that Babaji was looking for a former disciple, she had the feeling that it was she. Babaji, later, told her that she had been His disciple in Almora in her previous life. Babaji gave her the name of Gaura Devi - one of the many names of Lord Shiva's consort. Gaura Devi recalled her meeting with Babaji in these words:

"Automatically, I sat down at His feet when I entered the room where He was sitting in meditation, and I looked into His eyes. They were so clear that I knew He had realized Truth.

"For two or three hours I gazed into His eyes. In my mind, I asked Him all the questions that had troubled me for years and felt that I received answers to all of them. For the first time in my life, I had met somebody who had internalized truth and wisdom. Silently, I prayed to Him to let me participate in His knowledge, to let me find Truth. When finally I rose to say 'farewell,' a voice inside me suddenly said, 'I'll meet you again.'

"That night I had a dream. Babaji was walking in a dark forest with a few disciples. He had a stick in His hand. And from the darkness of the woods, He emerged as Light and said, 'Yes, I will be your guru.' 'What will you teach me?' I asked, and He answered, 'I'll teach you to wash dishes well.'

"The washing of dishes symbolized humble tasks. Before I came to India, I had lived in a commune in Italy and nobody, including me, liked washing dishes... And, in fact, as soon as I arrived in Babaji's ashram, I had to clean and wash dishes for more than two years."

A Tea Salesman Learns a Higher Trade

In 1971, Jaimal heard that Baba Haidakhan had re-appeared; there was a group in his village of Lamachaur that talked favorably about Babaji. Jaimal earned his living by selling tea to shop owners in his area. He was a spiritually-minded man of 37, who read the Bhaga-vad-Gita and the Ramayana thoroughly, felt his religion strongly, and sometimes cried from his intense desire to see God. He knew the stories of 'Old Haidakhan Baba' well, so he talked several times with Sat Chiv and others in the group of Babaji devotees.

In 1972, Jaimal suddenly began to harbor doubts in his mind

that this baba could be the real Babaji. Because of the confusion in people's minds about Haidakhan Baba and the resulting divisions and hostilities that stirred up, Jaimal wondered whether this Babaji might be an American C.I.A. agent, sent to stir up trouble and division. Many times in that year Jaimal made plans to meet Babaji, but he never quite made it.

In September 1973, Jaimal heard that Babaji would visit a temple about one-and-a-half kilometers from his house. The temple and the surrounding grounds were very dirty and overgrown. Devotees of Babaji called a meeting to arrange to get the place cleaned up for Babaji's visit, and Jaimal felt he must cooperate in the work. Jaimal and a group of devotees worked for six or seven days; first, they cleaned up the area around the temple, then went inside. There was no room fit for a person to stay in. They could not find a carpenter, so Jaimal did that work, replacing rotted planks and door and window frames. On the morning of October 28, Jaimal painted the inside of the temple, then painted "Shri Shri 1008 Bhagwan Haidakhan Baba ki jai!"[2] on the walls. Many people were annoyed that Jaimal had painted that on the walls, but none dared tell him.

Late in the afternoon of the 28th, Shri Babaji and many disciples arrived at the temple. After His bath, people started making their pranams to Babaji and sitting in His presence. Jaimal also made his pranam, but he remembers that he could not see Babaji's face clearly. The next morning when Jaimal came back to see Babaji, he stood in line to make pranam to Babaji and he could see *only* Babaji.

The following day, Jaimal felt strongly that he must go to Haidakhan. He asked a friend to seek permission for his visit, but Babaji called directly to Jaimal and asked him what he would do in Haidakhan. Suddenly, Jaimal was inspired to reply, "If, Baba, You will bless me, I can do everything!" And Babaji said, "Yes, you may come." As soon as Jaimal left Babaji's presence, the idea came again that Babaji was an anti-government man and that he, Jaimal, should go to Haidakhan and watch Babaji's activities for a year or two - or three, or more.

When Babaji returned to Haidakhan from this trip, Jaimal went in His party. Trilok Singh's truck took them to Khera, just across the river from Haldwani, and then they all walked over the hills through

Okhaldunga. Jaimal arrived in Haidakhan before Babaji; he felt a strong, unexplained feeling, like shivering. He picked up a bucket and went to the river for a holy bath. Some time after Babaji and the rest of the party arrived, Babaji called for Jaimal and told him to look for a pick and shovel. When Jaimal returned with them, Babaji told him to take all the people down to the river and make a good place to bathe. A bit shy, Jaimal started down to the river alone, so Babaji told all the other people around Him to go down and work with Jaimal. When Jaimal reached the top of the stairs that go down the hillside to the river, Babaji was there. Babaji moved behind Jaimal and lightly touched Jaimal's right shoulder, then gently pushed one finger into the shoulder blade, as if activating a pressure point. Babaji said, quietly, "I would like to see many people coming here, but people don't want to come." Then Babaji headed down the stairs with Jaimal behind Him. Jaimal got the strong feeling that Babaji knew everything that was in Jaimal's heart. When they reached the bottom of the stairs, Jaimal moved ahead of Babaji, turned, and touched His feet; Jaimal thought that, in the future, he would not do anything without asking Babaji.

Two or three days after this, late in the evening, Babaji was sitting in his little hut near the ashram temple. Jaimal and other devotees were enjoying Babaji's darshan. Jaimal saw a very sharp, bright light, in a straight line, like a tube, going out from Babaji's right ear toward the West. Jaimal's thought was that this was Lord Shiva's destructive power, moving out to destroy evil influences. Jaimal wondered to himself, "Baba, why do You take so much trouble onto Yourself? If You give *me* the power, I will do this for You." Jaimal stood up and took four or five steps toward Babaji's hut and Babaji shouted at him, "Why are you coming here? Go away and go to sleep!"

For several years after that, Jaimal lived in the Haidakhan ashram almost continuously, except for about a year in 1974-75, and Babaji taught Jaimal much about survival in the hills: what uncultivated plants are good to eat, which ones are medicinal, how to plant trees and vegetables - very practical survival knowledge. Jaimal abandoned his thoughts of Babaji as a C.I.A. agent and experienced Him as The Supreme Power in human form. And, good to his word, with Babaji's blessings and training, Jaimal has done everything at Haidakhan, serving Babaji and His guests, from early morning until late at night, year after year.

A Film Star Meets Babaji

Sheila Devi, who, along with the rest of her family met Babaji at the Voras' home in Bombay in 1972, used to argue heatedly with her brother-in-law about Shri Babaji. She insisted that Babaji must be two thousand years old, or more; Shammiji said that was ridiculous. Shammi Kapoor was one of India's most dashing young movie stars from the mid-1950's to the late 1960's - a romantic hero and dominating figure both on-screen and off. He had been married to India's reigning movie queen and they had two children. His wife died suddenly, in 1964, of small pox, and in 1968 he married Sheila's sister Neela. Shammiji himself says he used to get disgusted with Sheila's frequent talk about Babaji and religion and shout at her, "Man has landed on the moon and you still sit and play with your beads doing jap!"

In 1974, Neela, who also met Babaji in 1972, asked Shammiji to meet Babaji, and he grudgingly agreed to meet Him - as a favor to her. It turned out that on the day set for Babaji to go to his father-in-law's house, Shammiji had a major shooting schedule, but he agreed to ask his director to let him go at 4 p.m.; if his director refused the request, he would not meet Babaji.

When Shammiji arrived at the location, he went to the director and asked if he could get off at 4 o'clock to meet his wife's baba. The director shouted in frustration: he had a whole constellation of stars lined up for this day's shooting and of course he could not let Shammi go. The only way he would let anyone go was if his mother-in-law died; she had been in a coma for six months, but if she chose this day to die he would cancel the shooting. Shammi told the director to calm down; he had made his request only to honor his commitment to his wife; he was perfectly content with a 'no.'

They filmed all morning, had lunch together on location, and went back to work at 2 o'clock. At 3:30, the director was called away to take an urgent telephone call. He came back in a few minutes and walked up to Shammiji and shouted, "Well, my mother-in-law just died - after six months in coma. Shooting is finished for today! You can go see your bloody baba!"

So Shammiji drove speedily to the Colonel's house and found Babaji there. Shammiji was unaccountably nervous. He made his pranam to this young Babaji and then retreated to the far corners of the room, even went behind curtains, and looked at Babaji through the telescopic lens of his camera - and took photographs. Every time he focused, he found Babaji looking at him with piercing, X-ray eyes. One of the photos Shammiji took has a clear Om symbol on Babaji's forehead.

A Doubting Priest Gets a Shock

Din Dayal, also known as 'Mahantaji,' was the chief priest (mahant) at a major downtown temple dedicated to Lord Hanuman, in New Delhi, just off Connaught Circus. It is believed there has been a Hanuman temple on this site for at least 2,500 years. According to tradition, Lord Krishna visited this temple to 'have Lord Hanuman's darshan.' Din Dayal's family has provided the chief priests for over eight hundred years; he was the 32nd generation of his family to be the chief priest.

In 1971, Mahantaji's married daughter, who then lived in Jaipur, tried to get Mahantaji to meet Babaji during His visit to Jaipur. Mahantaji got bathed and ready to go to the house where Babaji was staying, but a friend came along and insisted that Mahantaji go with him to a dinner in Mahantaji's honor, which several of his friends were presenting. So Mahantaji went to the dinner and did not meet Babaji.

Three years later, Mahantaji's friend, retired Wing Commander Srivastava, came to Mahantaji several times and urged him to meet Babaji. At last Mahantaji went with Srivastava to a place where Babaji was staying in New Delhi.

Mahantaji stood in the back of the tented 'hall' and looked at Babaji, whom he saw as a beautiful, smiling, young man. Mahantaji thought this baba would be just another little baba who would fleece his flock, take his money to Europe or America, and marry some Western woman. But Mahantaji saw people going to Babaji and making their pranams with devotion, so, at last, he too - his mind filled with suspicion - went to Babaji's dais. He knelt and touched Babaji's feet and received a strong, physical jolt like an electric shock. He jumped back and stared in amazement at Babaji. Then he tried again, somewhat tentatively - and got another shock. Mahantaji sat back on his heels, looked at Babaji, and prayed earnestly in his heart, "Forgive me, Baba, for my suspicious thoughts of You. Let me touch Your holy feet." Then he knelt again and touched Babaji's feet. This time there was no shock, only a sense of peace and acceptance.

A Photographer Gets the Picture

Lisetta Carmi is an Italian woman who was a concert pianist for a number of years, then decided that was too lonely a life; she resisted making the piano the central element of her life. She took up photography and became a free-lance photo-reporter, known for the sensitivity and artistry of her work. She won a European prize for a series of photographs she took of the aged Ezra Pound. Now she has formed and manages Shri Babaji's second Western ashram, in the heel of the 'boot' of Italy, in a town called Cisternino. She told this story of her being drawn to Shri Babaji.

"I was born into a Jewish family. We did not practice our religion; however, both my mother and father believed in God. My mother has a deep relationship with God. Furthermore, she 'knew' that during her last life she had lived in India. My father also had a lot of faith, but not in the various established religious conceptions. Naturally, these thoughts influenced me and since childhood I have been a seeker of God and truth.

"In 1974 I traveled to India. On a flight from Kathmandu to Delhi, I met a young Italian girl. It was Gaura Devi. We started a conversation in which she told me a lot about Babaji. There was no other theme; it was Babaji and Babaji again. When we arrived in Delhi, we spent four days together, at the end of which I had to return to Italy and Gaura Devi to Babaji.

140

"Two years later, Gaura Devi had a vision of me. At that time, she had been sent by Babaji to the jungle - to Dinapuri - for meditation. After three months there, she 'saw' me being called by Babaji. She mentioned this incident in a letter to me. As soon as I received the letter, I packed and flew to Delhi.

"Gaura Devi had given me a contact address in Almora, but when I arrived there the person who was supposed to guide me to her had left for Delhi. When I stepped out of the house, not knowing where to go, I met an elderly foreign lady. It was Tara Devi. I asked her if she knew Gaura Devi. Indeed she did, and she was able to tell me of her whereabouts. Tara Devi wanted to take me to Babaji, who was in Delhi, but I refused, saying, 'No, I have come for Gaura Devi.'

"For twelve days I lived with Gaura Devi in the jungle. She again told me a lot about Babaji and familiarized me with Indian life and traditions. We also meditated together a lot. On the twelfth day of my stay with her, a message arrived from Babaji. I was supposed to meet Him in Jaipur on March 12.

"Hearing His call, I was on my way immediately. With my luggage, I walked from Dinapuri to Almora; then I took a bus from Almora to Delhi, and from there to Jaipur, to the house of the Jain family, where Babaji was expected.

"When I arrived at the residence, garlands of green leaves had been prepared and hung, and I had the impression of living two thousand years ago and that I was waiting for Christ.

"When I finally faced Babaji, I had the intense feeling of His being God. I said to Him, 'I am Lisetta,' and immediately He replied, 'You are Janki Rani.' I felt Babaji's love intensely and I got the feeling that I had been expected.

"After some time, when I had sat down, an In-

141

dian came to me and said, 'Babaji has sent me to you; you should show me the way to God.' Spontaneously, I replied, 'God is love.' Thereupon, this man returned to Babaji and related what I had said. Babaji appeared to be satisfied.

"Then I had to give a speech. For a few minutes I was able to think about what to say, but then I just expressed my thoughts and feelings as they passed through my mind. I told everyone present how lucky they were to be able to seek Babaji's presence whenever they liked, whereas foreigners like me had to travel so far to have His darshan...

"For me, the path to Babaji was an easy one; no doubts or problems concerning His divinity entered my mind. From the first instant, I recognized God in Him."

An American Meets Babaji in his Orchard

An American named Michael Reynolds has felt, since childhood, that 'someone' was watching over him. When he got out of high school, Michael started up a small farm in Washington State, in order to 'live on the land.' At 18 or 19, he read "Autobiography of a Yogi." It opened up a completely new kind of religious experience for him; his life changed substantially; among other things, he became a total vegetarian.

In 1974, when Michael was twenty, Babaji began to come to him in visions, in the form of 'Old Haidakhan Baba,' complete with mustache and stern look. Michael accepted this form as his guru but he had no idea who He was.

Early in October, 1976, Michael was in his orchard and Babaji suddenly appeared before him and said, "Come!" Michael stared at Babaji's face, hardly aware of the lower body, other than that it was dressed in Indian garb. The voice was clear, but Michael did not know whether it was an 'inner voice' or whether it would have been audible to anyone else. He wanted to go to his guru, but he had no idea whose form this was or where to go. Babaji disappeared without any further speech.

A few days later, Michael picked up a magazine and idly flipped through its pages. He says he 'never' used to look at advertising, but this day he was attracted to read an ad about trekking in Nepal and attending a kumbha mela in India. He remembered, from Yogananda's autobiography, that a kumbha mela is a large gathering of saints, holy men, devotees and seekers. Michael decided he would find his guru at the kumbha mela. When his girlfriend came to the house, he told her that they were going to India. She was more interested in trekking in Nepal, but she was willing to help Michael find his guru at the kumbha mela. The next day, Michael mortgaged his farm truck and the following Monday he bought two airline tickets to India. He bought them without communicating with the organization that had advertised the trip, so they headed for India not knowing who his guru was, where to find him, or even where the kumbha mela was.

They left in November and spent three weeks in Hawaii because Michael had wanted to visit there. (Unwittingly, he found his next home there, where he later started the first Babaji ashram in the West.) Then they flew to Delhi. They arrived in the early hours of the morning. They went to a hotel but Michael was too excited to sleep, so he walked the streets of Delhi; he felt he had come home.

Early in the day, Michael found that the kumbha mela was in Allahabad; then he found that they could not go directly from Delhi to Allahabad because all those trains were full. (Newspapers estimated between thirteen and twenty million people attended this mela during the three weeks or more that it lasted.) They got on a train to Lucknow, then on another to Benares, and finally got on a bus from Benares back to Allahabad. In Benares, they left everything except money and bed rolls and went to the kumbha mela as pilgrims. Michael had read about austerities (<u>tapasya</u>) and, in Benares, he had made a vow not to eat or drink until his guru appeared to him.

They arrived in Allahabad late in the day. They took a quick walk through the great tent city which rises for these melas on the dry portions of the wide Ganges riverbed, but they did not find Michael's guru. When night came, they slipped under a tent flap and found themselves with a group of Westerners and their guru - but the guru wasn't Michael's guru.

The next day, Michael went from one tent or temporary building to the next, looking for his guru among the thousands of holy men and saints and the hundreds of thousands of visitors. He saw many wonderful men, but there was none with whom Michael felt the spark of a guru-disciple relationship. It was a very hot day and Michael developed a great thirst, but his stubborn resolve to honor his vow carried him through the day.

The second full day was a repeat of the first, except that Michael met an older Hindu saint for whom he felt respect and to whom he made his first pranam. This saint blessed Michael and seemed to be telling him to be patient in his search; and Michael left him feeling encouraged.

That evening, Michael found his girlfriend at the ISKCON (Hare Krishna) tent, talking to an American man who said he had just been with the Babaji of Yogananda's "Autobiography of a Yogi." Michael could not accept that at all; he was so abrupt and disbelieving that the man left. That night Michael found he was muttering to himself, wondering if that statement could be true; but still he made no connection between the guru of his visions and Yogananda's Babaji.

On the third day, still fasting, Michael tramped around the vast camp, searching even more thoroughly than before. His girlfriend was restless, wanting to head for the trekking in Nepal, so at one o'clock Michael headed back to the ISKCON tent to pick her up and leave. He was disappointed, but detached; he felt totally emptied out.

They headed for the train station; but when they came to the path that led to the center of the mela area, Michael felt drawn to make one last effort, and his girlfriend indulged his wish. They walked through the milling crowds, looked again in places Michael had been before. Suddenly, the 'river' of people parted and, perhaps fifteen feet ahead, they saw the man who had been with Babaji. This time, Michael felt a strong vibration on seeing the man and they ran to each other and gave each other a hug. The man told Michael he felt he was supposed to bring Michael to Babaji and that he had come to find Michael. He proposed to take them to meet Babaji after he had his bath in the Ganges.

They all went into the city of Allahabad, to the house where

144

Shri Babaji was to stay, but Babaji had not yet arrived in Allahabad. Michael, his new American friend, and Babaji's host - retired Wing Commander S.P. Srivastava - stood talking outside the puja room (temple) of the house, and Srivastava happened to flick open the shutters on one of the windows of the room. Michael glanced in and there he saw a photograph of the guru of his orchard vision - wearing the same clothes which Michael had seen in his orchard: he knew immediately that this was the guru he had been seeking.

Michael refused to budge from the house until he saw Babaji. He slept there that night, almost frozen because he had left his bedroll in his American guide's room. He broke his fast in the morning, because he felt he had already met his guru. But Babaji did not come that day.

The next morning, Babaji arrived. He came through the compound gate and walked toward the tent that had been set up for darshan and singing. His path brought Babaji to within twenty feet of Michael. Babaji stopped, looked at Michael, held up His hand in blessing, and said, "You come." Michael, understanding that to mean "You have come at last," replied, "Yes, Baba, I have come." Michael followed Babaji into the tent and sat down with the feeling that Babaji had brought his seeking to an end.

At that time, Michael had long hair, of which he was rather proud. After a few minutes in the tent, Babaji called Michael to Him and told him to get a mundan, the complete head shave. Knowing that one's guru's orders are to be followed without hesitation, Michael walked out of the tent and had his head shaved. When he went back to the tent, he and other devotees spent the rest of the day and all of the night singing kirtan.

Michael and his girlfriend spent three or four days with Babaji in Allahabad; then Babaji told them to go to Haidakhan. But first they had to go to Benares to get their belongings. Now there were millions of people *leaving* Allahabad and trains and buses were packed. As they walked around, looking for transportation, Michael's head was filled with celestial music and the mantra Om Namah Shivaya. For three days the music and the mantra rang in his head.

They had no luck getting out of Allahabad the first day, so

145

they returned to Srivastava's house and stayed the night. The next day, while they were walking around the city, a stranger walked up to Michael, touched his feet, took him by the hand, and led Michael (whom we now know as Hiraman) and his girlfriend down streets and alleys and finally right into the vacant front seats of a waiting bus. The bus was packed, except for those two seats. They sat down and asked where the bus was going. To Benares, of course!

A Moslem Devotee Visits Babaji

In 1978, Shri Babaji was a guest in Shammi Kapoor's apartment in Bombay, for a yagya (sacred fire ceremonies) of several days. Two or three days after He had come to Bombay, after the evening chandan ceremony, Shri Babaji retired to His room at about six p.m. Almost immediately thereafter, Sheila Devi was called outside by one of the servants and told that someone wanted to talk to her. She found a tall, lean man with a rucksack on his back, looking tired and travel-worn. He had a hooked nose and sharp, 'hungry' eyes. Sheila asked what she could do for him.

The man said he wanted Babaji's darshan immediately. Sheila replied that was impossible; Babaji had just retired and He would not come out or see people until eight o'clock. The man looked so tired that Sheila invited him into the apartment and offered a cold drink. He refused everything: he said he had not eaten for days and he would not eat or drink until he had Baba's darshan.

Sheila asked where he came from and how he knew Babaji was at this place. He said he was a Moslem and that he came from Mecca; he said he had had Shri Babaji's darshan in Mecca. He said that every few years there is a meeting of Moslem leaders in the mountains not far from Mecca - a very secret meeting. He had attended one of those meetings and Babaji was there and he had had Babaji's darshan. He did not know who Babaji was, but he presumed He was from India and he had come to India to find Him. In Delhi, the man had been told that Shri Babaji was in Haidakhan. He had gone to Haidakhan and was told that Babaji was in Bombay (but no one in Haidakhan remembered a man of his description). He said he had walked all this distance.

While talking to Sheila, this man never removed the rucksack from his back. She pressed him to eat something – some fruit – but he refused even a glass of water, saying he had made other arrangements. He said he would wait outside until eight.

When Shri Babaji came out of His room at eight, Sheila Devi told Him that there was someone who had come, but he refused to give his name. Babaji told Sheila to call him immediately; the man was an old devotee. Sheila called the man in and took him to Babaji. Babaji and the Moslem man talked for a good half hour. Sheila, who was standing only a foot or two from them, could see their lips moving, but she could not hear a single word or sound. (Sheila says other people - on rare occasions - have experienced this phenomenon.) Sheila told Shri Babaji that the man had refused food or anything else until he had Babaji's darshan. Babaji - who was usually very insistent that His guests be fed immediately - just smiled and said it did not matter.

For three days this Moslem man came to Shammiji's apartment, morning and evening. He would make a pranam to Babaji -without a word spoken - then go and stand in a corner, without speaking to anyone. He never ate at Shammiji's apartment. Later, Sheila learned from the gardener that the man slept in the street outside the apartment building and took his bath at the garden tap. Sheila tried to get Babaji to say more about His Moslem devotee, but He never responded.

After the man's first appearance at the yagya, Babaji talked frequently about Mecca and the shivalingam there, and He said He had been there many times. During this time, the Illustrated Weekly of India had extensive coverage on Mecca, with pictures and narrative. Babaji showed the pictures to many people and told them all about the places - including the location of the place where the secret meetings are held, outside of Mecca.

To this day, no one in Babaji's circles knows who this man was, where he came from, or where he went.[3]

A German Housewife's Several Experiences of Babaji

Pinti, a German housewife then in her early 40's, met Shri Babaji in November, 1978. She told her story this way:

147

"Since my childhood, I have been acquainted with yoga. My parents were disciples of Paramahansa Yogananda and, my brothers and sisters and I have been following the same path.

"When I was eighteen years old, I went to California, to the center of Self-Realization Fellowship, established by Yoganandaji. For eight years I stayed in his ashram. During this time, I frequently had visions of Yogananda and once of Babaji.

"I especially remember the latter incident. It happened when I passed through a difficult period connected with the internal affairs of the ashram. I was in deep distress then. Needing help, I prayed in my meditation to Paramahansa Yogananda for comprehension and clarity of the situation - and suddenly I had a vision of Babaji. He appeared as a body of light and He raised His hand to bless me. Full of reverence, I mentally bowed down before Him. Afterwards, my difficulties dissolved and disappeared as if they never had existed. Naturally, I questioned myself as to why Babaji had appeared to me and not Yogananda, with whom I had a much closer relationship. After a lot of reflection, I understood that it had been Babaji who had led and guided me over all those years.

"When I saw Babaji's picture on the book 'Babadschi,' printed in Germany in 1978, I experienced the same devotion and reverence I had felt in my vision twenty years earlier. After reading the book, naturally I desired to meet Babaji personally.

"Shortly before I left for India, I had an experience during meditation in which I was lifted into another dimension. The world around me had somehow been effaced and in front of my inner eyes the feet of a young man slowly formed themselves, and the end of a white cloth wrapped around his waist became visible. The vibrations brought about by this event were so strong that I was moved beyond words. Later, when seeing Babaji in His physical form in India, I recognized these feet to be His.

"On the airplane, I again had a vision. I saw Babaji and Yoganandaji, each showing only half of their body - it looked as if they were cut into halves - merged into one person.

"After my arrival in Delhi, I traveled to Vrindaban, where Babaji was staying in a temple... when I saw Him first, I was sitting amongst other devotees in the temple who were chanting Om Namah Shivaya. When Babaji appeared, He sat down on a chair beautifully decorated with yellow flowers, and, looking over the crowd, He noticed me, the foreign newcomer, immediately, in the middle of the people. I watched Him closely, how He blessed His devotees that bowed down before Him and I saw that He distributed prasad among some of them.

"Suddenly, I noticed a duplicate of Babaji, standing next to the actual sitting one. And from this 'duplicate,' which seemed to be of a finer substance than His 'real' physical body, a fine bluish beam emanated. It was directed toward me and seemed to touch my heart. It is simply impossible to describe my emotions during and after this event."

A Swedish Woman is Transported to Haidakhan

Gunnel Minett is a young Swedish woman who met Shri Babaji early in 1980. She was studying psychology at the time. She has written a small book entitled "Babaji: Shri Haidakhan Wale Baba,"[4] from which the following excerpts are taken.

"The very first time I heard about Babaji was a summer night in northern Sweden, 1979. I was sitting with a group of people on a rock by the sea, enjoying the sunset and talking about this remarkable man

149

in India, whom one of the men present had visited. I wasn't paying much attention - my mind was preoccupied with the beauty of our natural surroundings.

"The second time - the first time I paid any attention - was when a collection of writings about Babaji fell into my hands. It was written by Leonard Orr (who has developed Rebirthing, a breathing technique to release physical and psychological tensions in the body and who is a devotee of Shri Babaji) whose ideas I was at that time interested in. So I began to read it. At the beginning of the text, it said that whoever reads this has already made their first contact with Shri Babaji. In many cases, it continued, this would be followed by more vivid and obvious contacts in the form of visions and/or manifestations. I found this a bit frightening, and felt that someone was standing next to me, hovering at my shoulder and watching everything I did - just in the way, as I had been told as a child, that God did...

"From this first reading, I formed an inner impression of a white-bearded, wise, old man who knew and understood everything. I developed a strange curiosity about and longing to meet this person, though I never (at this stage) formed any realistic plan to do this. I knew nothing at all about India and Oriental philosophies held no interest for me whatsoever. India was just another poverty-stricken, underdeveloped country, not worthy of a visit. I was all for the Western way of life and my ambition was to be able to go to America in order to learn more about modern psychotherapy.

"Having finished this compendium about Babaji, nothing further happened for a while - apart from the fact that I couldn't entirely forget the man. Then, a couple of months later, I saw the compendium again. This time it was a professionally produced edition and on the cover was the picture of an exotically beautiful young man. The picture rooted me to the spot. It gradually occurred to me that this was Babaji. I cannot explain the picture's fascination, but I simply couldn't take my eyes off it. In no way did he resemble the old man I had imagined. But this was not all: it was as if the picture itself had the power to attract me.

"When I'd finally torn myself away, I noticed that I was feeling upset. After a while pondering the cause, it came to me: I had decided to go to India and see him. I was upset because of the inconvenience and because of what this would do to my tidy plans for the future...

"Then came the moment when I had to write to Shri Babaji to ask his permission to visit him. I was... more than ever immersed in an inner conflict over whether to go to see him. As writing for permission did not involve making a final decision, I decided that I could at least manage to do that. I got pen and paper out - but what should I write? What do you write to someone who is supposed to be able to see and hear everything, anyway, and is regarded as God in human form? My hand was shaking as I finally managed to get a few words down on the paper. I was afraid of expressing myself in an inappropriate or offensive way: I was not a religious person, and had had no experience as to how to address God.

"Having finished the letter, I went to bed pleased that I had at least been able to write it. I was sleepy and I soon fell asleep. But then I suddenly awoke with the feeling that I was not alone in the room. I thought immediately of Babaji, remembering all the stories about visions people had had, I became very frightened. Not so much at the possibility of Babaji appearing, but at the idea of this happening: If he did appear it would surely mean that I was experiencing an hallucination and that I had probably gone insane. My teeth were chattering and the hair rose on my scalp. I was close to total panic. I pulled the bedcover up to my chin

151

and tried to think of something rational to do. Then, I immediately fell asleep, as if someone had opened a door leading to another world. I realized at once that I was sleeping and had started to dream right away. The dream was about Babaji standing in my bedroom. Now I was calm and could see him clearly without being afraid. He sat down on the side of my bed and looked straight into my eyes, as if he wanted to know exactly what was going on inside me. The fact that it was a dream reassured me, and I remained calm.

"I fell into a deeper sleep, and then was suddenly awake once again. It was still night, or at least very early morning. The light was dim, just enough to make a silhouette of the surrounding landscape. To my left there was a fire burning. I could smell the smoke, and hear the crackling of the burning wood. I could sense, rather than see, that there were people sitting around the fire. On my other side I could hear the sound of running water and see it glimmering some distance away. I had the impression of being on a rock with water below me. I could see a curtain or something, made of some silvery material, so there must have been a house close by.

"'So it wasn't a dream after all,' I said calmly to myself, realizing that things cannot be seen so clearly in dreams. But at the very moment of realization, a surge of fear went through my stomach and I awoke at home in my bed.

"What did it mean? I was totally confused. After some time I succeeded in convincing myself that it was nothing but a dream - sufficiently, at least to get back to sleep. But the dreams came again - vividly realistic, about Babaji and India - throughout the night. The next morning my confusion was total. I was acutely afraid of losing my sanity. I adopted the strategy of dismissing the experience as a bizarre form of intense dreaming - though I knew this was self-deception.

"I never received a written reply from Shri Babaji, but I left for India anyway. I went to Vrindaban, Krishna's hometown, where Babaji was staying at the time...

"Then came the moment - which had grown so important - when I saw Shri Babaji for the first time. I was sitting in his ashram, with a group of Westerners, when, after a long period of waiting, he came out to see us. My inner turmoil on first seeing him can only be described as a psychic earthquake. All I can recall now are the words I repeated over and over to myself: "It's true - He is God." I felt as if I knew and understood everything, without really having any idea what it was that I understood. No more could I explain what his being God meant, since I considered myself an atheist. Yet I felt sure that I was sitting at the feet of God himself in human form.

"I could add that I experienced him as different from everyone else I had ever met. He felt 'whole' to me, as if all the energy radiated from him in a perfect egg-like shape. Ordinary people, I decided, are more formless, adjusting their form to the surroundings. Such ideas had never occurred to me before - it came as a revelation. After the first emotional turmoil, it became clear that he was exactly as I had seen him in my dreams. I had previously seen several pictures of him, but there were also other things which I recognized: Things that cannot be seen in a picture.

"Despite my determination not to speculate as to the meaning of my strange dreams, I suddenly felt the need to receive some sort of sign from him that could confirm my feelings. I tried to discreetly catch his eye. I was far too afraid to simply go up to him and ask for such confirmation. When it finally became necessary to approach him, in order to avoid rudeness, I was too frightened to glance up at him, even once.

"The day after, however, when it was time to go up to him once again, I worked up the courage to look up and take a glance at him. He turned towards me at once and looked straight into my eyes, slowly nodding and with a look of infinite love. Another psychic upheaval shook me. I returned to my seat with tears burning my eyes. Gradually, I realized that I was experiencing the feeling of being fully recognized as a human being for the first time in my life. I was overwhelmed by grief.

"Back at the hotel, I started crying. I cried for hours and could not stop. I was crying about every sad event in my whole life. After this, I experienced other kinds of physical reactions, as if I had been exposed to some great natural force: I could neither eat, sleep nor relax. Finally I developed a fever and had to stay away from the ashram. Not until I left Vrindaban for New Delhi, after a few hours on the train, did I recover a sense of bodily normality...

"The second time I went to see Shri Babaji was a totally different experience...

"[Babaji] was completely different. To begin with, what made the biggest impression this time, was Haidakhan itself, with its endless peace and beauty. It was hard to imagine that such a paradisical place could exist on earth. I felt immediately that I wanted to stay forever, just enjoying being alive and living in peace for the rest of my days.

"As we walked up the 108 steps to the ashram, an Indian man rushed up to us, just before we reached the top, telling us to hurry, since Shri Babaji wanted to see us right away. I felt a bit of the old fear, at seeing him again, but didn't really have time to worry. I just had to drop everything and run after the man. We rushed into a crowded room. In the middle was Babaji. The man who had come to fetch us pushed us gently forward and gave us a sign to greet Shri Babaji, by kneeling, in the Indian way. As we did so Babaji gave us each some candy and told us to make ourselves at home in his ashram. It was all over in less than a minute...

"When, some moments later, we had unpacked and were sitting on the steps in front of our guest house, I was suddenly overcome with shock. It was the place I was looking at - I had just recognized it. It was where I had 'woken up' during my strange dream. I could precisely locate where I had been, even though the fire and the people were not there and it was full daylight. Later though, I was to experience even that, because this place, beside Shri Babaji's room, was where every-one gathered for the fire ceremony, held every morn-ing just before dawn...

"... Still today, I cannot fully explain what made me set out on these eventful journeys nor the real sig-nificance of the things that happened during them. It was as if a part of me, whose existence I had never even suspected before, took over the first time I saw Babaji's picture and started making decisions for me.

"That this happened no longer frightens me. I now trust my sane mind, although I still experience Shri Babaji's presence. I still cannot explain God - only describe him, and Shri Babaji still represents God to me. I have learnt about immense love, through him. I have experienced states of peace and happiness which I had never known before. I have learnt a lot about my-self - to like myself and others more - and about unity with everything.

"For all this I am very grateful. This is all I can say. "Bhole Baba Ki Jai!" (Hail to the Simple Father!)

NOTES

1. See Baba Ram Das' book about Neem Karoli Baba, "Miracle of Love"; E.P. Dutton, 2 Park Avenue, New York, N.Y.10016.
2. Honor (or glory) to the Most Revered Lord Haidakhan Baba!
3. The Sufis (a sect of Islam), also, have a tradition of a 'secret teacher,' named Khidr, who comes and goes in much the same fashion as Shri Babaji.
4. Printed in Stockholm, Sweden, 1986; copyright by Gunnel Minett, available at www.BabajiAshram.org.

"Thine eyes are wet with compassion and full of mercy;
O Lord, let the whole creation be fulfilled.
God's play,
which Thou performest in human form put on,
is wonderful!
Hail, hail, O King of Sages,
Remover of the pain of Thy devotees!"
From the Haidakhan Aarati

CHAPTER VII

SOME LEELAS OF BABAJI

"Leela," or "lila," is the Sanskrit and Hindi word for the activity or 'play' of The Divine in Its various manifestations in physical form in the created universe. It is usually used for the amazing, humanly inexplicable acts of God, but that limitation is not found in the definition of the word; after all, the very appearance of God in a human form in the Creation is, itself, a "leela."

Almost everyone who spent any time with Shri Babaji has some sort of leela experience to relate; there are far too many to try to collect in one place, and not all of them make interesting reading, though they were of significance to the participants. A few of these leela experiences may give some idea of the powers which Shri Babaji exhibited (though He rarely laid claim to them as His miracles) and what it could be like to be in His presence - or be a devotee of His beyond His immediate physical presence.

Shammi Kapoor is Surprised

Shammi Kapoor, the film star, acknowledges his first meeting with Babaji[1] was a rather unusual and powerful experience, but he prided himself on his clear, rational thinking and was not immediately inclined to 'surrender' to Shri Babaji. His wife and children wanted to invite Babaji to come to their home. Shammiji had no objection to this, but the custom was for the whole family to go to where Babaji was staying and tender the invitation as a united group - and this Shammi refused to do. Babaji was to be invited to their apartment on Monday and the family wanted to go on Sunday to offer the invitation. Shammiji had a busy work schedule and Sunday was his only free day and he insisted on his right to have his customary Sunday lunch and beer, followed by a long nap in his air-conditioned bedroom. Shammiji says he told Neela, his wife, "Babaji is welcome to come; He can have my home and my money, but I will not go to invite Him. I am going to have my beer, my lunch, and my nap!" So the family went off to see Babaji and Shammiji had his lunch and beer.

As Shammiji was getting ready for his afternoon nap in his big bed, Neela and the family knelt before Shri Babaji to ask Him to come to their home. Babaji asked Neela, "Where is your husband?" Unwilling to say that he had stayed home to enjoy his beer and nap, and not wanting to lie, Neela stammered that Shammi was not really well and had stayed at home.

At that time, Shammiji stretched out on his bed for his nap - and suddenly Babaji was standing before him at the foot of his bed! Babaji laughed at Shammiji and said, "Oho! So you are sick? You stayed home and had lots of beer and lunch." Babaji jumped to the right of the bed and teased and laughed at Shammiji, then jumped over the big bed to the other side. Back and forth, to the top and bottom of the bed, Babaji jumped and laughed and teased. For two hours, Babaji kept up this 'game' and Shammiji sat in his bed in a sweat, wondering what in God's name to do with this Baba.

When Neela came home from Babaji's afternoon darshan, she went into the bedroom to wake up the sleeping Shammiji; but she found him sitting on his bed, drenched in sweat, and trembling. A very shaken Shammiji told Neela of his experience with Babaji.

When Babaji came to the apartment the next day, Shammiji related his experience to Babaji, who laughed at Shammiji with twinkling eyes.

Footprints

Din Dayal, "Mahantaji" of the Hanuman Temple at Connaught Place in New Delhi, went with Babaji and a group of devotees to visit Madhuban, a village in Mathura District where there is a Babaji ashram which contains what Babaji said is the oldest existing sacred fire pit (dhuni) in the world. After giving darshan there, Babaji directed that those who came with Him from Vrindaban should be fed first. Nevertheless, the Madhuban villagers scrambled to the prepared places and there was no place for Shri Babaji's party to sit.

After a minute or two, a small black cloud appeared in the otherwise clear blue sky and in a few minutes the open-air dining space

160

was drenched with rain. The villagers ran off to the shelter of their homes. When the rain stopped, Babaji jumped off His dais (which was covered by a tent) and laughingly ran hither and yon through the muddy area. Mahantaji ran after Him. After a few minutes, Babaji returned to His dais and sat cross-legged again. Mahantaji followed Babaji and, approaching the dais, Mahantaji stopped to look at his clothing. His dhoti (a pant-like, cotton garment) and his feet were covered with mud. Quickly, Mahantaji turned to Babaji, thinking of the need to clean His feet and perhaps bring Him a clean white lunghi (a wrap-around, skirt-like garment worn by Indian men). To his astonishment, Babaji's lunghi was still sparkling white and the foot exposed to view was absolutely clean. Shri Babaji caught Mahantaji's startled look, smiled, and tucked his foot under the folds of His clean lunghi.

"Motu" Banerjee, then a fifteen-year-old devotee from Allahabad, was walking immediately behind Shri Babaji in a group of devotees, crossing the sandy area of the riverbed at Haidakhan. She became intrigued with the footprints in the sand and walked along idly watching them. Suddenly, she gave the footprints her full attention and realized that Babaji was leaving no footprints as He walked through the sand.

Ram Dass, on the evening of a different day, was walking with a group escorting Babaji across the riverbed. His eyes fell on Babaji's footprints in the sand and Ram Dass began to walk along placing his feet in Baba's footprints. He was concentrating so carefully on this maneuver that he almost ran into Shri Babaji, who had stopped, turned, and was looking at Ram Dass. As Ram Dass watched, Babaji slowly lifted a foot off the sand; Ram Dass stared at the footprint and saw that it shone in the evening light.

Babaji as a Mind Reader

Ram Dass, an American who, as a child, was a concert violinist, had a charming experience of Babaji's ability to read minds. One evening soon after he first arrived at Haidakhan, Ram Dass was standing by Babaji's dais in the kirtan hall after the aarati service. Shri Babaji had Har Govind play the flute, which he did spontaneously and

beautifully. As Har Govind finished playing, Ram Dass found himself wishing he had brought his violin to Haidakhan so he could play
for Babaji. The thought was barely formulated when Babaji turned to
Ram Dass, pantomimed a man playing a violin, winked and smiled at
Ram Dass, and then turned back to the scene before Him.

*   *   *   *   *   *   *

One day when Shri Babaji was passing out the mail that had
been brought by the postman for Him and for the residents of the
ashram, He showed an envelope to Sheila Devi and asked, "Who is
this for?" He held the letter so she could see the handwriting, which
Sheila recognized as her mother's, so she said the letter was for her.

Babaji slowly turned the envelope over in His hand, looking
intently as He turned it; then He handed the letter, unopened, to Sheila
and picked up the next piece of mail. Sheila took the letter and went to
her room to open and read it before her afternoon nap. The letter was
in the Gujrati language, which no one other than Sheila then present in
the ashram could read. She read her letter and had her nap.

Later in the afternoon, when she met Shri Babaji again, His
first item of conversation with her was to tell her - accurately - the
contents of the letter. When she showed surprise, Babaji told Sheila
that He could do this whenever He wanted to. After she returned
to her home in Bombay, Sheila read a book about Shri Aurobindo,
which noted that he, too, had and used this power.

Gaura Devi, the Italian woman, had many experiences of this
power. She handled most of Shri Babaji's correspondence from abroad.
Baba gave her his foreign mail unopened. Gaura would take it to her
room, read it and make a note of a few words on each envelope to
indicate the nature of the request or comment, then take these letters
back to Shri Babaji, read Him her comments on each letter, and ask His
guidance on how to respond. Usually this was done during Babaji's
darshan. Not infrequently, Baba used to tell Gaura that she had missed
some important point in her comments on a letter and told her precisely what the letter said on the point He wanted to answer.

A year or so after the Lals met Shri Babaji, Vimla Lal had a viv-

162

id dream in which Babaji came to her home. In her dream, Vimla was sitting in her living room and Babaji came to the door of the room and asked for a drink of water. Vimla was aware that the custom was to serve Shri Babaji water (or other drinks) in a stainless steel 'glass' that had been washed and cleaned with <u>vibhuti,</u> the ashes from a sacred fire. In her dream, Vimla went to her kitchen and looked for a steel glass, but there was none. She finally picked up a porcelain cup and then wondered how to clean it, there being no vibhuti in her house. She saw a container of powdered cleanser and used that as her closest substitute. Then she filled the cup with tap water and took it to Babaji. Babaji winced with displeasure, but drank the water.

Vimla's dream was so real that she mentioned it to her husband (but to no one else) and they went out and bought a full set of stainless steel tableware, so they would be prepared if Babaji accepted an invitation to visit them in their house.

Some days later, Dr. and Mrs. Lal went to Haidakhan. As they approached Shri Babaji to make their pranams, Babaji 'angrily' asked Dr. Lal, "What kind of woman is this who cannot properly serve a glass of water to her guru?"

There are many devotees who have stories of Babaji's remarks to them about dreams they had of Him. When asked about dreams, Babaji often said that dreams are gifts from God.

Physical Changes

Babaji was able to change His physical form at will. There are a number of people who saw His face change - to that of Jesus Christ, the Hindu gods, and many well-known saints - in the course of a few minutes, as they sat before Him.

During the Christmas festivities in 1983, an Italian devotee took four pictures, in a period of four or five minutes, of Babaji standing, separately, with four different men, ranging in height from five feet eight inches to six feet. In each photograph, Babaji appears to be the same height as the person He stood with.

Some years earlier, a very tall American doctor - six feet six or seven inches tall - came to the ashram. Everyone was amazed at his height. One day Major Bhupindra Sharma and another devotee were looking for Babaji. From the ashram, which is about one hundred feet above the riverbed, they spotted Babaji, in the riverbed, talking to the doctor, looking up into his face. They ran down the steps and over to Babaji and the doctor. When they arrived, Babaji was talking with the doctor and looking straight into his eyes; both of them were the same height.

Many people experienced Babaji's weight changes. Sita Rami and I once brought a bathroom scale from Delhi for use in the ashram clinic. When we returned to the ashram and made our pranams to Babaji, He asked what was in the box and, when we had opened it, He stepped on the scales and registered a weight of seventy-five kilos (about 165 pounds).

Once when Babaji visited the Raja of Bhavnagar, a retired, old devotee known as "Guard Sahib" asked Shri Babaji to visit him in his son's home. When Babaji came to visit him, Guard Sahib met Babaji at the car. There is an Indian custom of carrying an honored guest into one's home, and this old man insisted on carrying Babaji (who at that time weighed about sixty-five kilos) into the house. Babaji got on Guard Sahib's back like a monkey and was carried the thirty or forty feet into the house. Guard Sahib told people Babaji was as light as a child.

Many people had that experience. Sometimes, as I knelt before Him, Babaji playfully got down off His seat on the wall outside His room by stepping on my back. I often thought He had just placed His foot on my back to test my steadiness, and, before I realized it, He was standing beside me.

Babaji Heals a Woman

There are many stories involving unusual, miraculous healings. Bhupindra Sharma, then a captain in the Indian Army, in his late thirties, related this leela of his wife's illness.

"I was born into a family that always believed in religion, pujas, kirtans; lots of saints visited us. I myself always believed in God as an abstract form - until in 1976 my wife fell ill."

164

His wife, Shakuntala, had an operation to remove her gall-bladder. Though the doctors and surgeon involved were among Delhi's best, there were complications and within twenty days, Shakuntala was at death's door.

"My mother and my aunt, great devotees of Babaji, had told us about Him, but I was not convinced. When my wife's sickness got worse, naturally they took recourse to prayer - so much so that Baba invited my mother to come and stay with Him in Haidakhan. She went there for a long time, but my wife's health did not improve at all. "Finally, a second operation had to be performed. It lasted four and a half hours. Her abdomen was filled with pus; my wife had developed peritonitis. Also, my wife had high jaundice; she had a high fever and was losing weight. Antibiotics did not cure her, and soon she was in a stage where not even analgesia could be given because of fear of death.

"While I sat beside her and nursed her and hoped for the best, my mother and her sister, of course, were hammering away at Babaji. One day He said to them, 'You people are after My blood! You ask Me to cure this woman. Have you ever found out if she believes in Me?'

"So we asked her and she replied, 'No, I don't believe in Him; I don't believe in Him at all."

"'What *do* you believe in?'

"She said, 'I have a lot of faith in the faith *you* have in Babaji.'"

Shakuntala had lost half her body weight; she was down to about thirty kilos, a bag of bones. The doctors thought it necessary to operate again, but feared the operation itself would kill her. Finally, a surgeon with great confidence in his skills and in his faith in God said he would operate. In September, the doctors offered to try another operation. Captain Sharma's mother asked Babaji if the operation should be attempted; He said, "Not right now." On Babaji's instructions, the operation was postponed twice and finally it was performed on December 17. It lasted seven hours and forty minutes. After this operation, Shakuntala's liver stopped producing bile.

"Finally, some of my relatives wrote to my mother in Haidakhan and asked her to tell Babaji that if He does not want to cure her, He might as well finish her off - but quickly: we who attend to her can't take any more.

"On receiving this letter, my mother was in tears. Babaji turned up and asked what the matter was. She related the contents of the letter to Him and Babaji replied that she should return to Delhi immediately. My mother did not want to go, so He went on to say, 'What will the world say? Your daughter-in-law is dying and you are staying with your baba!' Mother only replied, 'I am not bothered about the world. What I *am* bothering about is whether You are going to do something.'

"Right then and there, Babaji ordered her to have a mundan [the head shave]. My mother reflected and said, 'Babaji, one year ago someone mentioned that I should have a mundan. You replied I did not need it. Having spent one year with You, have I become filthy and dirty, so that I require a mundan?'

"Babaji just smiled and said, 'Everything you do is not necessarily for yourself.' She understood at once, went down to the river, and Gaura Devi gave her a shave. When she returned, Baba gave her His own cap and exclaimed, 'Why don't you believe? Your daughter-in-law will be all right. Tell the doctor to stop all medicine.'

"Next morning, in Delhi, it happened that the visiting doctor gave orders to stop administering all medicines. And, without medicines, from January fifth onwards, my wife's health started to improve."

When all medicines had been stopped, the family followed Babaji's instructions to place a bottle of plain tap water in their home temple every evening. In the morning, Captain Sharma's aunt, Vimla

Lal, would take the water to the hospital and serve it to Shakunta-la. The water had changed its color and consistency; by morning, it looked like the bile that her body failed to produce.

"Early one morning, I had to leave my wife's room. She was under a strong anesthesia and a nurse was with her. I had just left when Babaji appeared. The nurse got up and asked, 'Who are you?' He replied, 'I am not a bad chap. Move away!' Babaji approached my wife, held out His hand, which was closed to a fist, and moved His arm seven times around my wife's body. When the nurse was about to ask if He were Babaji, He disappeared.

"Subsequently, on the next occasion in Haida-khan, we asked Him if He had been visiting my wife in hospital. He did not deny the fact, but replied, 'Why don't you ask Swamiji; I think he might have gone.' Approximately a year later Babaji admitted in a con-versation that He had visited my wife."[2]

Shakuntala recovered completely a month or so after Babaji's visit to her hospital room.

Babaji Heals a Child

In 1976, Vivek, the only son of Hem Chand Bhatt, the lawyer from Nainital and Haldwani,[3] was six years old and a student in Class Two at St. Joseph's College in Nainital. One day late in November, Vivek developed a fever. Because it was exam time and Mr. Bhatt thought Vivek had a common cold, Vivek was given aspirin and sent off to school. After two or three days, Vivek developed a high tem-perature and could not go to school so the family shifted him to their home in warmer Haldwani. Soon, they took him to the hospital where Vivek's illness was diagnosed as typhoid; he was also found to have worms. Vivek was treated for typhoid and the fever was broken and in a week or so he was well and discharged from the hospital. He was told to return to the hospital after three weeks for a check-up.

On December 24, Bhattji went to Haidakhan, as was his custom by then; he asked his wife to take Vivek to the hospital for his check-up and to remind the doctor of the diagnosis of worms. Vivek was found to be in good health; he was given some tonics and two pills for worming, to be taken on consecutive days.

After Vivek took the second worming pill, blood showed in his stools; then he began to bleed constantly. He was returned to the hospital. Despite their best efforts, the doctors could not stop the bleeding and there was such great pain in his stomach and abdomen that Vivek could hardly sleep for five minutes at a time and got no more than thirty minutes' sleep a day.

That year, Bhattji stayed unusually long in Haidakhan; he stayed until Babaji came to Haldwani on January 9 for a nine-day yagya at Khanna Mataji's farm outside of Haldwani. When He came to Haldwani, Babaji stayed briefly at Amar Singh's house, and it was there that Bhattji's mother found Bhattji and told him of Vivek's critical condition. Bhattji rushed off to the hospital.

The little boy's condition went from bad to worse. Finally, the doctors conferred and then advised Bhattji that it was beyond their power to save Vivek. They advised that if Vivek could be taken to Delhi, there might be a chance to save him, but they had doubts he would survive the trip.

Bhattji arranged for a taxi to go to Delhi, but his wife and mother insisted that they should take Vivek to Babaji first. So they took him to Khanna Mataji's farm. There, Shri Babaji scolded Bhattji for having no faith in Him.

Dr. S.K. Lal, the famous physician from Delhi, was at the yagya. He checked Vivek and concluded that the child's intestines had ruptured. He wrote a lengthy prescription covering more than a dozen medicines, and he told the Bhatts that every utensil used for Vivek's medicines should be totally disinfected before medicines were administered. By this time, a crowd had gathered around Vivek and practically everyone was of the opinion that there was very little need of any further medicines, because death was very near.

Then a villager named Tikaram came and told Shri Babaji, in Bhattji's presence, that he knew of some herbal medicines that might save the child, if that was Shri Babaji's wish. Babaji told Bhattji to give Vivek those medicines now, instead of the medicines Dr. Lal had prescribed. So Bhattji asked Tikaram to bring his medicines. Tikaram went out into a nearby field and returned with some plant roots which he washed in an irrigation ditch; then he made a pulp of the roots and poured the juice into a tumbler. This medicine was given to Vivek and Babaji told Bhattji to take the child home.

During the night, the boy continued to be in such pain that Shri Bhatt thought it would be a blessing for him to die, to end the suffering. No one slept. At 3:30 a.m., Bhattji's mother asked him to go to Babaji again. Bhattji went on a motorbike to the Khanna Farm, told Babaji about the child's painful and critical condition, and asked Baba to come to his house.

Babaji replied that He had not yet had His bath and He would come later. He gave Bhattji one rose petal and told Bhattji to give a drop of its juice to Vivek.

When Bhattji got home it was 4:30 and Vivek was fast asleep - for the first time in more than two weeks. They gave Vivek the drop of rose juice without awakening him. Babaji came to the house at 9:30 and Vivek was still sleeping. Babaji had Vivek carried to Him and He said Vivek would be perfectly all right. The bleeding and the pain had stopped. Babaji told the Bhatts to continue administering Tikaram's root juice. They did this and Vivek was completely recovered in less than a week.

Two weeks later, the family went to Haidakhan. One of the doctors who had treated Vivek in the Haldwani hospital was also there. Bhattji took Vivek to the doctor and the doctor was amazed to see him. The doctor then told Bhattji that, because of the typhoid, Vivek's intestines had become so weak that when they gave him the worming pills, the intestines burst: only faith and a miracle could have saved Vivek's life.

Babaji Cures Shammi Kapoor's Diabetes

As the Biblical book of Job indicates, one's declared faith is often tested, and strong faith may be strongly tested, not only for the sake of the one of faith, but also for the benefit of those who observe the events.

In the spring of 1975, Shri Babaji had a big yagya in the riverbed at Haidakhan to celebrate the opening of what was known as "the Bombay House," the first major residential building in the ashram, with a big hall downstairs and eight individual rooms above. Shammi Kapoor, by then known as 'Mahatmaji' (Great Soul), came from Bombay for this celebration.

Mahatmaji had not been feeling well for some time and before he came to Haidakhan he had had a routine physical checkup. His doctor - among Bombay's very best - had told Shammiji that he had dangerously high blood sugar, and Mahatmaji was put on a very severe diet - no sugar, no liquor, no carbohydrates.

When Mahatmaji sat with Babaji after his arrival at Haidakhan, Babaji asked Mahatmaji about his health. Mahatmaji said he had been told he had diabetes and told Babaji about his diet. Babaji's response was to hand Mahatmaji a kilo box of sweets. Mahatmaji said, "Babaji, this is poison for me!" Babaji told him to eat it - by himself! And at their next meeting, later in the day, Babaji gave Mahatmaji another box of sweets. Mahatmaji was also told to eat the regular ashram food - rice, potatoes, chappatis (bread); a whole plateful of carbohydrates.

After three days on this diet, Mahatmaji was very sick. His temperature was high and he was too sick to leave his room in the new 'Bombay House.' By the second day of bed-sickness, Mahatmaji was much worse and wandered in and out of a coma state. On the third day, Mahatmaji was in a coma all day.

Everyone in the ashram was concerned about Shammiji's condition. Babaji's prescription for Mahatmaji was a spoonful of water in which 'sunf' (a mouth-sweetener consisting mostly of anise) had been boiled, which could be given to Mahatmaji every few hours. Babaji Himself did not go to Shammiji's room, but He sent someone every few hours to ask about his health; and Shammiji's wife, Neela, was also asked to report. Everyone told Babaji that Mahatmaji was getting worse. A sister-in-law was frantic and said Mahatmaji should be taken out to a hospital. Neela said that she and Shammi had complete faith in Shri Babaji's treatment and Shammi would not be moved.

On the evening before the last day of the yagya, Babaji sent word that the next morning Shammiji was to be given a sponge bath and brought to Babaji's room for chandan and the sunrise fire ceremony. When this message was taken to Shammiji, the coma and the fever had been broken, but Mahatmaji was too weak to move by himself. So Amar Singh said that three or four men would come in the morning and help with Mahatmaji's bath.

Soon after 3 a.m., people went to awaken Shammiji and Neela. Shammiji insisted he would have a full bath, not just a sponge bath, before going to Baba's room for chandan. Because he was so weak, Mahatmaji was supported and half-carried out to Khurak Singh's field, placed on a chair, and a bucket of water was poured over him. Then he was dried and clothed and supported on the walk to Shri Babaji's room.

Babaji took Mahatmaji into His small room and asked how he felt. Gently and lovingly, Baba applied the cooling, yellow chandan (sandalwood) paste across Mahatmaji's forehead and had him sit in the room while the others filed in and out of the room as Shri Babaji applied chandan on other foreheads. When everyone had chandan, Babaji moved outside His room for the sunrise hawan (sacred fire) ceremony, and He had Mahatmaji sit beside Him. When the hawan ceremony was finished and the others had left, Baba sat and talked with Mahatmaji for five or ten minutes, then told Mahatmaji that he would participate in the yagya that morning, down in the riverbed. Mahatmaji protested that he could not possibly make it through the yagya: he had no strength left. Babaji said, "I will take you with Me. Now you go and rest."

Throughout the chandan and hawan ceremonies, Shri Babaji had looked often at the skies. No one else seemed to notice the gathering clouds, but as soon as Mahatmaji had gotten into the "Bombay House," rain came. There was a heavy downpour for two hours, which caused a flash flood in the river. Several hundred people had camped in tents in the wide river valley and hundreds of kilos of foods and other things were in the riverbed, in preparation for the huge fire ceremony and the feast to follow. When warning of the flash flood was given, people fled the riverbed for the high ground of the ashram, and the tents and vast quantities of materials were washed away. Very little more than the hawankund (fire pit), which was on the highest ground of the riverbed, was left. (Later in the day, people were sent downstream and almost everything was retrieved, including purses, watches, jewelry. It is said that no one lost a thing.)

The morning aarati was performed, as usual, at the temple, while some people prepared again for the fire ceremony, taking new supplies down from the ashram storerooms. After aarati, Shri Babaji went down for the hawan, and He took Mahatmaji with Him. The rain was over and the sun was shining brightly.

The hawan ceremony lasted two hours. Mahatmaji sat through it all and participated in it. It clouded and rained again during the hawan and everyone got wet, but the fire did not go out. Shri Babaji stared up at the skies again and the sun came out.

After the ceremony, Shri Babaji walked Mahatmaji slowly to the bottom of the '108 Steps' up to the ashram. There Mahatmaji, who normally takes twelve to fifteen minutes to walk up, resting two or three times because of his bulk, told Babaji that he would come up slowly; he suggested that Babaji should go ahead. Babaji replied, "I will take you with Me," and He took Mahatmaji by the hand and in one minute, somehow, they were at the top of the stairs, where the family was waiting and watching. A person in good physical condition can cover these steep stairs in a minute, but it takes considerable effort.

The next day, Mahatmaji and his family left for Bombay. Babaji told Mahatmaji to have a new physical checkup and inform Him of the results. This was done, and the amazed doctors could find no abnormality in Shammi Kapoor's blood sugar. Shammiji returned to his former style of eating and drinking and has had no recurrence of the blood sugar problem.

Babaji Restores a Man to Life

When the Canadian John Stewart, whom we came to know as Khurak Singh, first came to Haidakhan, in 1977, Shri Babaji sent him to live with Prem Baba in the Haidakhan Cave across the river from the ashram buildings. Prem Baba, then a sturdy man of about seventy years, was known, among other things, for the considerable amount of charas (the local form of marijuana) that he smoked; and Khurak Singh tried to keep up with Prem Baba. Khurak - a 23-year-old who had 'tried everything' - could not handle the charas; he was constantly 'spaced out' and he soon got sick and his body could not heal itself. So Babaji made Khurak Singh the ashram 'doctor,' had a grass hut built near "the Cave" and called it a hospital, and Khurak dispensed aspirin to everyone who came to him, no matter what the ailment.

One day, Prem Baba developed a great infection on one of his legs; in a day or two, it swelled up hugely, oozed with pus, and gave Prem Baba great pain. Babaji told Khurak to lance the swelling and clean out the infection. He told Khurak to put Prem Baba up on a table in the 'restaurant' near the cave, so Prem Baba's leg would be about at Khurak's eye level, and use a big box for Prem Baba to sit on. Babaji left the area and Khurak set up his 'operating theater.'

When everything was ready, Prem Baba got up on the table and on the box and a nervous Khurak Singh sterilized his knife and selected a spot to puncture the swelling. When Khurak lanced the sore, Prem Baba's body lurched and he passed out from the pain. The sudden jump pushed the box off the table and Prem Baba fell off the table, head first. A panicky Khurak Singh tried to make Prem Baba comfortable, but got no life-reaction from him. He felt for Prem Baba's pulse and found none. Khurak screamed for help.

A medical doctor who had come from Delhi the previous day was nearby and he came running. More calmly and professionally, he felt for Prem Baba's pulse, and confirmed that there was none. Khurak began to cry and run around hysterically. The Delhi doctor began to massage Prem Baba's heart and told Khurak to shut up and massage Prem Baba's feet.

Hookum Singh, who, by another name, is an internationally-known photographer, was also near the cave-side 'hospital.' Observing the scene, he had the presence of mind to run to find Babaji. He found Babaji on the ashram side of the river, talking to Swami Fakiranandji. Hookum Singh blurted out the story to Babaji. Babaji took the news very calmly and got up and strolled across the riverbed, talking earnestly with Swamiji on the way.

When Babaji and Swammiji reached the 'hospital,' they walked

in and Babaji looked up at the newly-installed straw roof and proceeded to scold Khurak Singh for having used the wrong kind of bark
to make the 'ropes' that held the stick-and-straw roof together; He
paid no attention whatever to the drama around Prem Baba's body.
After a minute or two of this, Hookum Singh pleaded with Babaji that
He do something quickly.

At last, Shri Babaji turned to Khurak Singh and told him to go
to Chandan Singh's teashop and get some ghee (clarified butter) and
rub it onto Prem Baba's head; He said that after about five minutes of
that treatment Prem Baba would be all right. So Khurak raced across
the riverbed to Chandan Singh's teashop and came running back with
some ghee. Babaji had left the area when Khurak returned.

By then, Prem Baba was losing life fluids; a whitish fluid was
running out of his eyes, ears, nose and mouth. Still, Khurak sat down,
put Prem Baba's head in his lap and began to rub ghee into his head.
Just as Babaji had said, after about five minutes, Prem Baba sat up.
He immediately called for a chillum to be prepared and Hurak Singh,
the British shopkeeper at the ashram, managed to press tobacco and
charas into a clay chillum and light it for Prem Baba.

Prem Baba took one deep pull on the chillum and then sat
back and began to curse Khurak Singh. Prem Baba said he had just
been 'liberated' - his soul had been outside his body, looking down at
the mad scene; he felt released, free! Then Babaji came along and, in
response to Khurak Singh's tears and cries, Babaji had ordered Prem
Baba's soul to get back into his body and return it to life. Prem Baba
was so furious that he took a swing at Khurak and hit him and then
fell back, completely exhausted.

For three days, Prem Baba lay in bed and slept, waking only
to drink some milk and then falling back to sleep. On the fourth day,
Prem Baba got up and went back to work.

Babaji Sends a Gift to Oklahoma

Carol Parrish-Harra, an American mystic teacher, lecturer,
and the founder of the spiritual community of Sparrowhawk, near
Tahlequah, Oklahoma, tells this story of a connection with Babaji,

174

whom she met briefly in 1980 during a trip to India.

Carol says the peacock has been a strong symbol for her for many years. As long as thirty years ago, the symbol of a peacock would come to her in her meditations. She has a collection of peacock artifacts of various materials from all over the world.

In 1981, after the 382-acre Sparrowhawk community was formed, a peacock appeared in the back yard of a family that lived just off the community land. People tried in vain to find the owner. Finally, they built an aviary on top of the Sparrowhawk 'mountain' for the peacock.

During this time, a friend of Carol's from Cincinnati, Ohio, had gone to Haidakhan to visit Babaji for a month. On his return from India, the friend called Carol from New York to tell her about his trip. At the end of the conversation, he added, "By the way, Babaji told me to ask you if you received the peacock He sent you."

Divine Water

In October, 1981, Shri Babaji took a group of devotees on a spiritual pilgrimage (yatra) which included a visit to Benares (Kashi in the ancient scriptures; Varanasi on modern maps of India). This is a city on the Ganges where pilgrims come to bathe away their sins, and many come here to die in its holy atmosphere. Kashi is known as Lord Shiva's city.

Babaji's party all bathed in the Ganges and then took a pleasure boat cruise up and down the river. They left the boat at a landing below the famous temple of Kashi Vishwanath Bhagwan. There was a great throng of pilgrims at the temple and it was with considerable difficulty that each person in Shri Babaji's party was able to make a pranam before the shivalingam (the symbol of Lord Shiva's creative power or energy) in the inner temple.

When Vishnu Dutt Mishra entered the inner temple with Shri Babu Ram Gupta, for whom he had been told by Babaji to perform a special puja, he stood before the shivalingam carrying an offering of flowers in both his hands. Shastriji requested water from the two temple priests, which he needed in order to perform the puja correctly. He was told there was no water inside the temple and that people had to bring their own if they wanted to do puja. Assuming the priests had a bucket of water available somewhere, Shastriji asked again, noting that the temple was so crowded that it just was not possible to go out and get water and come again. He was testily told there was no water in the inner temple area. In disbelief, Shastriji asked a third time and was told angrily that there was no water to be had.

With considerable disappointment, Shastriji and Guptaji sat in front of the shivalingam. Reciting the appropriate mantras, Shastriji offered the flowers. When he recited the mantra used when the worshipper offers water, suddenly a stream of water poured down from out of nowhere and continued to fall on the lingam for two or three minutes.

The people crowded in the inner temple and those waiting to get in saw the stream of water and more people pushed into the little room, crying "Water! Water! Divine water!" The people started to fall over Shastriji and Guptaji; Guptaji struggled to his feet and then helped Shastriji up. Two constables were required to escort them out of the inner temple and to restore order.

Seeing this divine materialization of water, the pilgrims in the temple were greatly moved. But most people did not know of the source of this little miracle because Shri Babaji stood outside, in the courtyard, as though He had no connection with this leela.

NOTES

[1] See pages 138, 139.
[2] From notes in the Haidakhan Ashram files, compiled by Gertraud Reichel, a West German devotee, based on recorded statements by devotees of Shri Babaji.
[3] See pages 129-132.

"...it is the task of the guru to help the disciple to grow. How is it done? One has to merge into the Teacher. Only then the little self will go. It is like a voluntary death in the guru's essence. A complete surrender to the Teacher is the first step leading to complete surrender to the Will of God."

"The teaching is given according to the time, to the place and the state of evolution of the [disciple]. A Saint will never give a bad example. He is free; he obeys only the law of the Spirit, not human Law; but he will always conform to the law of the land. He will never go against any religion, for all religions for him are alike: they are only different roads to the one Truth."

"The Chasm of Fire," Irina Tweedy, pages 70 and 74

"All the living beings, animals, flowers, plants and stones have been given a form by God and this body has been given by God to perform a duty in this world. Even my own body has come only to perform a duty and to serve all human and living beings. "But when human beings come into this world, they forget their duty and they fall into the attachment of maya and into the concepts of 'me' and 'mine,' and they forget God."

Babaji, during His evening bath, 2 February 1983

CHAPTER VIII

BABAJI TEACHES: THE CONCEPTS OF GURU AND SANATAN DHARMA

Babaji as Guru

Lord Shiva, who is considered by Shaivites as the unmanifested and manifested God, is believed to manifest "Himself" in innumerable forms, mostly subtle forms invisible to the untrained human eye, but some - occasionally -visible to ordinary humans. Among these many forms are Nataraj, the dancing Shiva who tramples on the ego and also symbolizes the rhythm of the universes, and Shiva as the Supreme Yogi or the Supreme Guru. The traditions of Babaji, as Haidakhan Baba, center on His coming - again and again throughout human history - as a manifestation of Shiva in a human form to teach and guide mankind on the path to universal harmony and to God-realization. There are some people who suggest that Babaji may have developed, as other souls are believed to grow, through countless births and experiences, into union with The Divine (thousands of years ago) and then embraced the duty of returning to human form to teach. Most of Babaji's followers believe that He is a direct manifestation of God/Shiva who, like Christ in the Christian tradition, was One with God at the time of Creation. Many of Babaji's statements seem to support this latter view.

Whatever Shri Babaji's origin, both in the manifestation of the 1970's and 1980's and in the prior manifestation of Haidakhan Baba (1800's to 1922) of whom we have historical records, He exemplified and exhibited the traditional traits of the guru. He is a teacher of the highest spiritual knowledge and wisdom, whose teachings reflect the basic, ancient Truths, but who makes His teachings practical and relevant for the times, and who teaches each person before Him on the basis of his or her own level of attainments, needs, and aspirations, using spiritual powers beyond the grasp of ordinary teachers. Like the traditional guru, Babaji made no apparent effort to attract people to Himself; it took considerable effort to reach His ashram and presence. He was adept at hiding Himself from those who came to Him

179

without faith - perhaps to scoff, to test, or to see what benefits they could get from Him. He often played the game of being just an illiterate boy from the hills, and there are quite a few people who concluded He was nothing more than that.

In 1976, an American woman came to Babaji. She was full of suspicion and doubt about Him. At one point during what lengthened into an eight-month stay, Babaji told her:

"If you come to doubt, I'll give you reason to doubt. If you come suspicious, I'll give you every reason to be suspicious. But if you come seeking love, I'll show you more love than you've ever known."[1]

To those who came and 'surrendered' to Him, He gave everything.

Babaji was constantly teaching. His whole 'mortal' life was a teaching, because He *lived* what he taught. For the first years of His mission, He spoke very little. In some situations, He is said to have spoken only five or six short sentences in a day, sometimes even less. At other times, He might converse easily with a few individuals; but there were few public teachings or talks. Babaji was busy showing people how to live, through His own example.

When the young Italian devotee whom Babaji called Gaura Devi came to the Haidakhan Ashram for the first time, in April, 1972, after Shri Babaji welcomed her, He went back to painting the columns of the temple, which He had been doing when she arrived. When Gaura settled down to live in the ashram, early in 1973, Babaji put her to work sweeping the ashram and working in the kitchen; He spent hours in the kitchen showing her how to prepare and cook the ashram food, and He served the food with His own hands. He showed people how to cut huge logs efficiently into the sizes needed for the kitchen fire and how to move or break up the immense boulders in the riverbed that were used for ashram construction projects. He showed them, by His example, how to combine worship of The Divine with action and work performed as an offering to The Divine.

In a response to Shri Babaji's welcome to him in October, 1983, Sir C.P.N. Singh, the then Governor of the Indian state of Uttar Pradesh noted this about Babaji:

"In His teachings, His work and His daily routine of life, we can see that He not only gives us blessings, but in His daily practical life He exemplifies what He says. *There is no difference between His speech and His action.*"[2]

Babaji insisted that those who stayed in His presence must make spiritual progress. When He decided what problem area a devotee needed to work on, He managed (like a theatrical director) whatever series of lessons or experiences the person needed. The first encounter with the problem area generally would be a subtle one - sometimes so subtle that the person did not comprehend the situation until the experience had passed. If the first encounter failed to put the lesson across, the devotee got a stronger experience of the situation - obvious, hard to ignore; it might cause physical pain or mental anguish. If the devotee failed to master that lesson, a harder, harsher one was in store - just as in life outside the ashram, but on a faster schedule. Some people wept in self-pity, others from frustration at not knowing how to handle their problem; some got furious at Babaji, others exploded on friends. Usually, when the anger or pain subsided, people understood the teaching and the love behind their lessons and adjusted their behavior as a result of their experiences.

Whenever one lesson was learned, there was another to follow. Shri Babaji always pushed to the individual's limits, but, apparently, not beyond what the person was capable of handling. Some seemed to 'fail' in that process, but we always had the feeling that those people had given up too soon, that the teaching was not really beyond their capacity. When a person reached a plateau in growth and needed opportunity to assimilate the lessons, or if they remained stuck in their problem, they generally left the ashram - either of their own, inner desire or at Babaji's insistence. Often, those who left or were sent away returned, with His permission, at a later time for another stint of learning. Babaji constantly tested His disciples and devotees, even re-tested on matters we thought we had worked through.

On very rare occasions, Babaji discussed with people some of the specific gifts He gave in response to consistent desires. More than once, He let people know that what they desired was dangerous for

181

them or for their spiritual growth - it was better left alone. Still, if the desire remained, Babaji (as the "easily-pleased," wish-fulfilling Lord Shiva) gave what was desired - even though the devotee thereby 'flunked' the test. Babaji did not force people into anything - not into belief in Him; not even into 'goodness.' The choices and the responsibilities are ours.

Shri Babaji rarely gave anyone detailed instructions on what to do, how to do it, or why they should do it. He gave people assignments in general terms and threw them into the work. It was *learn through experience;* "sink or swim." Sometimes, in confusion, a devotee came back to Babaji for more detailed instructions. Often, Babaji would give the person two or three conflicting suggestions or instructions in the space of a minute. The duty had been given; it was the doer's responsibility to observe what was required and get effective results in an efficient way with whatever means were available. In a 'school' based on individual experience, it was no help to the devotee if Babaji gave the person the answers.

One's success or failure was usually quite clear in the end. A job well done was rewarded with a smile, a touch of blessing, a gift (prasad) of some sort, or maybe a public comment. Poor execution might stimulate shouts of 'anger' or frustration and disbelief in the extent of our stupidities, or even a blow with Babaji's hand or staff. Babaji expected of His devotees - demanded of them - that they learn quickly from experience and make their own decisions. God has given mankind free will and Babaji implied that it is not His responsibility - or in His power - to make choices for us. In that respect, a person can defeat God's desire, or will, for the individual in any given circumstance - or can reach higher than predicted.

To help people achieve 'liberation,' Shri Babaji played many roles - gentle teacher, harsh instructor, best friend, guru and God. Although He is quoted as having said, "I am no one's guru, but I am the Guru of gurus," He did assume the traditional role of guru with some, and was a Teacher of all who came into His presence. In the age-old tradition of India, Babaji stated a number of times, "without a guru, there is no Knowledge." One goes to the teacher to seek knowledge and part of the training is total surrender to the guru, in the same way

182

that one must totally surrender to God, if one seeks to achieve God-realization. It is this requirement of surrender, and its accompanying trust in the guru, that makes it so vitally important for a would-be disciple and for the guru to be extremely careful in the establishment of a guru-disciple relationship. In the Buddhist and Hindu literature - indeed, in the literature of all religions - there are many stories of great hardships endured by disciples in their processes of learning 'surrender.' The life of the Tibetan Buddhist saint Milarepa is one of the widely known stories[3] of long, hard service to the guru.

A recorded conversation between Shri Babaji and a strong Western devotee illustrates many of the elements of the traditional guru-disciple relationship which Babaji occasionally assumed. The devotee approached Babaji to ask permission to apply for a long-term visa to India while he was back in his home country, where he planned to go and sell all that he had in order to give the money to Babaji on his return to India. This Westerner had been assigned duties as a temple priest at Haidakhan and he was getting special temple training. He had recently been offered yoga initiation by another devotee of Babaji and he asked Babaji if he could accept that offer.

Babaji told the Westerner to take initiation from someone else; then He told the man to go home to his own country. He continued:

"You are being sent back to your country because you have lost your faith. If you were a true devotee, you would have unshakeable faith and a steady mind. What are you doing, believing that a man who himself is not a yogi could initiate you into yoga? This I do not like.

"By giving you temple duties, I accepted you as a devotee. To devotees I give <u>Abhaya Dhan</u> - the blessing of My protection, by which you will always be protected, which should make you fearless. *I* am responsible for you and your liberation! Whatever initiation you need, I will give to you. Why, then, should you doubt or seek elsewhere?"

The Westerner responded that he had been motivated by spiritual greed. Babaji continued:

"What would you not receive from Me? Your faith must be as mighty as Mount Meru. Even the sun and the moon can move from their course, but the faith of a devotee should not be shaken. A true devotee will be ready to shed his life for God and will have faith to his last breath. Never be moved by false doctrines! You are protected in every moment."

Although sometimes His devotees thought Shri Babaji was a hard teacher, as "the easily-pleased Lord Shiva," His touch was comparatively light. However, inbred habits and social conditioning are not easy to change and the situations Babaji created to help people break through their patterns of living were often emotionally painful, and sometimes physically hard. He said:

"The path of God-realization is a most difficult one. Few are those who will walk it. It is as difficult as walking on the edge of a razor. The grace of the guru is everything. No knowledge is possible without the guru."

As the Guru, Shri Babaji said: "I have come to give liberation to all of you. I have come to give the Light."

Some Learning Experiences with Babaji

Shri Babaji is a Master Teacher. When the time is right for Him to help a devotee with a problem, He goes to work on the person with real love - with a concern that the devotee face Truth, see it, and respond to it in a way that promotes his or her spiritual growth. Babaji has the courage to do anything necessary to achieve that, and He acted with total detachment throughout the process - unmoved, not controlled by the person's reactions of fear, anger, tears, repulsion, or anything. He did whatever had to be done to help His devotee. In this work, sometimes Babaji appeared to be ruthless: even that - with its potential damage to His reputation as a God of love - did not alter His course of action.

One day Babaji instructed Ram Dass to construct a bathing ghat[4] at the riverside, in front of the Moksha Dham dhuni in Haidakhan. Ram Dass asked Babaji's permission to use the karma yoga work force. Babaji allowed that, but He told Ram Dass he had only one day to build the ghat. That day Ram Dass directed the work of the crew and he and they worked very hard, moving and placing big rocks to make solid steps to the water. But at the end of the day, the ghat was not finished. That evening, as Ram Dass and others helped Babaji with His bath (a ritual shared at that time by four or five people), Babaji asked if the ghat was finished. Ram Dass had to say, "No, Babaji, it is not. May I have one more day?" Babaji looked sharply at Ram Dass and said, "O.K. You can have one more day - only."

The next day, the crew worked hard again. Ram Dass laughed with the crew, splashed water onto people, talked about Babaji's teachings on karma yoga as they worked, practically dancing with the energy he threw into the work. But, at five o'clock the ghat still was not finished and Ram Dass had to go up to help Babaji with His bath. He left with the thought that the crew might - should - finish the work by sunset.

Not long after Ram Dass got to Babaji's bathroom, Rajendra Kumar Sharma, a photographer who had been with Babaji since 1971, came to join the bath crew. He also had been working on the ghat and Babaji asked Rajendra, "Is the ghat finished?" Ram Dass hoped Rajendra might say that it was almost finished, but Rajendra simply replied, "No, Baba; it is not."

Babaji turned toward Ram Dass and coolly started to berate him in a manner that ground his still-strong ego into dust. Babaji threw words at Ram Dass that both Baba and Ram Dass knew were not true. Although Ram Dass had an earned reputation in the ashram for constant hard work and a willingness to undertake anything Babaji told him to do, Babaji taunted him with, "How can you be a guru of karma yogis if you show no interest in your work?"

Ram Dass knew Babaji was not interested in hearing excuses or defenses, so he stood silently while Baba's comments, in front of Ram Dass' colleagues and friends, grew more and more scathing and contemptuous. The situation became harder and harder for Ram Dass to stand. Tears of frustration welled up in Ram Dass' eyes, but he stifled the impulse to justify himself.

At last, Babaji, still berating Ram Dass, motioned for Ram Dass to prepare the bath water. Because of the chill of the fall evenings, the bucket of unheated tap water was warmed by adding a thermosful of very hot water. The combination of the hot and cold water was just right and there was no way to further adjust the temperature or volume of the water once they had been mixed; there was just enough water in the full bucket for the ritual bath. The water had to be kept absolutely pure to pour over Shri Babaji's body; the bath-helper could not even stick a finger in the water to test the temperature.

When the water was ready, Babaji stepped into the bathroom and Ram Dass squatted and dipped the <u>lota</u> (a wide-bodied, smaller-mouthed metal bowl) into the water for the first pour. Babaji continued His reviling of Ram Dass in such scathing terms that the tears finally overflowed from Ram Dass' eyes. And they fell into the lota of bath water!

Ram Dass realized, with a sense of horror and shock, that his tears had contaminated Babaji's bath water. He also knew that if he threw out the lota of water there would not be enough water left for Babaji's full bath. Poised with the lota in his hand, Ram Dass was paralyzed with indecision. After a few seconds of his numbed inaction, Babaji slapped Ram Dass on the head and said, "Pour the water!" Still Ram Dass hesitated and Baba again told him to pour the water; so Ram Dass began pouring the water on Shri Babaji's feet.

As he poured, Ram Dass' mind was flooded with thoughts of the stories, from many religious traditions, of devotees who washed their Masters' feet with the tears of their love and devotion, and he realized that he, too, was washing his Master's feet with his tears. As he continued to pour, Ram Dass had a strong sense of release and clearing and a feeling that everything was all right. In that moment, Ram Dass looked up at Babaji's face and found it smiling and beaming at him, with light sparkling from His eyes.

This and similar incidents remind readers of Yogananda's autobiography of the story of Mahavatar Babaji and His disciples sitting around a sacred fire one nineteenth century night, when Babaji suddenly picked up from the fire a blazing stick and lightly hit one of His disciples on his bare shoulder, burning him. When Lahiri Mahasaya protested against the seeming cruelty of Babaji's action,

Babaji asked if he would rather have seen him burned to death in accordance with his past karma. Then Babaji placed His healing hand on the burned shoulder and told the disciple that He had freed him from painful death. The karmic law was satisfied through his slight suffering by burning.[5]

*   *   *   *   *   *   *   *

There were all kinds of people who came to Shri Babaji, for all kinds of reasons. Some came to worship One whom they considered to be God; some came out of curiosity; some for wealth, healing, birth of a child, or other specific desires; some came for His teaching, guidance and support on the path to God-realization; and many came from an assortment of reasons.

They came from everywhere and from many cultures, carrying all sorts of karmic baggage. High caste Indians and an occasional "untouchable"; retired people and people who had never yet held a job, not yet started a working career; physically sick people and all kinds of healers; drug addicts, alcoholics and reformed drinkers and drug-abusers; neurotic people and 'crazies' and psychiatrists and psychologists. Babaji took the measure of each one quickly and worked on each at the level where he or she was and at the speed the person was capable of. He treated them all with courtesy, love, patience - often granting the desires of those who asked from motives of love, faith, or devotion to God. To those who came for teaching and spiritual growth, Shri Babaji - the Supreme Guru - gave a rigorous training; one by one, He forced people to face and master the fears and desires that robbed them of courage and blocked out the divine knowledge needed to walk the difficult path to Self-realization.

Shivani (Dr. Shdema Goodman) is an Israeli-born woman, a trained psychologist who had a consulting practice in New Jersey. She made several visits to Babaji, in Haidakhan and elsewhere, during the last five years of His mission. She has written a book about her experiences with Babaji, from which the following story comes.

"On my third visit to Haidakhan, I found myself being severely tested. Babaji, Shastriji and Tuli, a

187

German woman, were walking toward the river and I saw Babaji motion to me with his hand to join them. I went and we continued walking toward the river. The river was quite high with fairly strong currents of rapids. Babaji motioned to Tuli and me to cross the river. Now I knew that it was dangerous to cross the river when it was that high. This was another test to see how much trust I was willing to give to Babaji. I silently bargained with myself, 'I'll try it out and if it is too deep, I won't go across.' I looked at Babaji questioningly and asked, 'Are you sure that it is all right?'

"Tuli took my hand firmly and said, 'Come on, Shivani, let's say Om Namah Shivaya and we will do it.'

"So we started crossing the river together, saying Om Namah Shivaya. Tuli pressed on my hand so hard that my wedding ring started cutting into my finger. I yelled, 'Ouch!' and let go of her hand. The next thing that I knew was that Tuli was swept away by the water. I stood still, wondering what to do next. As I turned around, I saw Babaji screaming at Tuli. 'Get up, Tuli; get up, Tuli!...' I wondered if I should be heroic and try to save her. There was no way that I could do that because I would just be swept away with her. So, I started calling, too, 'Get up, Tuli, get up!...' I looked again at Babaji and I saw that he had a huge rock in his hand. He was aiming it in my direction and screaming at me 'GO!' I instantly turned around and started walking across the river, not daring to look back. With Babaji, you never knew. I thought he might hit me with the rock. I was not going to take any chances.

"I was almost swept away by the strong current. Fear surged through my body and I started repeating Om Namah Shivaya with fuller concentration. When the current eased up, I found myself stable again, and I glanced quickly towards Tuli's side to see what had happened to her. Again, a strong current almost swept me away, and I almost did not make it. My whole body was shaking with fear and I concentrated again on Om Namaha Shivaya and on the stones in the river. (I was barefoot.) I was sure that this time my feet would be cut badly. Any time my mind wandered, even for an instant, my feet would start wobbling. As long as I was repeating the mantra and concentrating fully on every step, I remained fine.

"I finally made it across to the other side and I looked at my feet to see how much damage had been done. All I had were two cuts. I was amazed. My thoughts were allowed back in me and suddenly I remembered the huge rock that Babaji had aimed at me. I fumed with anger and started swearing at him. Pantaji, an American who lived in India, came over to greet me.

"'Do you know what he made me do...who does he think he is...aiming a stone at me... what am I, a dog? ...I am leaving tomorrow. That's it! I have had enough.'

"Pantaji reassured me and said, 'This is probably the best teaching you have ever had and it may be the most powerful teaching you ever will have. You'll see...believe me, I've been around gurus for many years. Don't quit now, trust me.'

"I really did not want to quit but my ego and my pride were hurt, or so I thought. It was probably more a feeling that I *should* feel angry and hurt. How would I explain it to my family and friends at home? Should I allow myself to be subjected to such treatment? Where is the appropriate place to draw the line? Where do trust and surrender end and where does being a schmuck begin?

"What if he hit me? That is where I also drew the line. I was determined not to put up with that, either. What would I do if he hit me? I would probably leave, I decided to myself.

"I crossed the river in a place that was less dangerous to cross, and even that was difficult for me. I almost toppled over a few times.

"When I returned to the Ashram, I met Tuli. She told me that she was not hurt, but when she met Babaji he hit her over and over again. My mind started racing. Here was the next test. No, he would not do that to me, I thought; after all I had not fallen down. I had made it.

"Tuli told me how jealous she had felt when she saw me safe on the other side. I empathized with her. I felt much calmer by now and decided to forget the whole incident. Later, when I saw Babaji, I stopped and went over to greet him. Whammo! I saw stars and realized that he had hit me. He had slapped my left forehead. I looked at him, feeling puzzled and not knowing how to react.

"'I saved your life!' he screamed at me. 'You were drowning.' And he walked away. Reflecting on that incident now, I am filled with loving tears of gratitude. I understand what he meant, although I did not understand at the time. Then, I felt angry and humiliated that he had dared hit me in front of all those people. It hardly even hurt, only for a second, although it felt and sounded like a very hard hit. I was amazed at the fact that it did not hurt!

"I wondered what I should do now. I went to my room and decided to allow whatever happened to happen. I started crying, feeling somewhat childish and a little confused, but not really caring much. For some unknown reason, my inner self was delighted. I guess that I felt relieved that I had passed that test. I was hit and that was that. It was nothing important. Still, I decided to stick to my original plan and leave the Ashram... I realized that I was supposed to be leaving the next day, anyway, because my five day's permission to stay was up. I decided to wait until morning to try and make a final decision.

"I went to Babaji and asked him whether I could stay for five more days.

"'I will hit you every day,' was his response.

"I closed my eyes to see whether I was willing to allow that to happen and replied, 'If it would lead me to enlightenment, okay; otherwise, no.'

"'You can stay,' he said.

"He never hit me again."[6]

*   *   *   *   *   *   *   *

Nan Singh is a young Englishman who stopped to meet Shri Babaji in 1977 and stayed several months, on his way to Australia, where he now lives. Babaji had Nan Singh work with an Indian man about his own age - the early twenties. Nan Singh and his Indian partner soon discovered they did not like each other; the more they worked together, the more they found to dislike in each other. They made clear to Baba their unhappiness in working as a team, but He just continued to send them on jobs together. In the dry weeks before monsoon, He sent them a mile upstream from the ashram to cut small branches with tender leaves for feeding the ashram cows, and the one who climbed the tree *threw* the branches at the other, hoping to hit and hurt. They 'progressed' to shouting and swearing at each other as they worked.

Nan Singh got ready to leave Haidakhan and go on to Australia. A few days before his departure, Baba put Nan Singh and his Indian partner on a particularly messy job. Babaji took them to the edge of the ashram and pointed to a large, stinking, sloppy pile where ashramites had thrown garbage for months - left-over food, fruit peelings, dirty rags. Baba told them to move the pile from here to there - about two hundred feet. With revulsion for both the job and each other, they started work. It was messy work and they had to concentrate fully on it in order to avoid being covered with the filth themselves. By the time they had moved the ashram garbage two hundred feet, they found that, without any thought, intent, or effort on their

191

part, they had moved their own 'garbage'; they ended the job working in harmony, with respect - even love - for each other.

When Nan Singh left the ashram two or three days later, they embraced like brothers. And when Nan Singh returned to Haidakhan for a visit in 1979, his Indian partner was also at the ashram and they greeted each other with joy and love.

Babaji Teaches the Eternal Law, the Sanatan Dharma

When Babaji takes a human form, He does so for a purpose - to teach, to guide mankind toward its highest capacities and its highest adventure. When people asked Him why He comes in human form, Babaji gave various answers, but they all pointed in the same direction. "I have come to give liberation to all of you. I have come to give the Light." "I have come to restore Sanatan Dharma."

His teachings and example were focused on helping sincere seekers of Truth to realize and *experience* that they are truly one with The Divine and that they can, even while in a physical, human body, live in harmony with The Divine and Its Will and with the whole Creation. When a person attains this "God-realization," he or she is liberated from the ties which hold human beings in the tangled web of desires, anxieties, fears, and the alternating ups and downs of joys and sorrows. One attains a recognition that the human mind, molded by the imperfect societies in which we live, shapes our reactions to events; that the knowledge and experience of our divine origin and end allows and stimulates an inner balance and a detachment from the activities occurring around us, which removes desire and fear and allows the human being to operate on a much higher level - in both the physical and spiritual realms - than the average human being now experiences. Life becomes a purposeful, fully conscious, creative adventure, supported by the harmonious vibration of an orderly universe which itself operates within and exemplifies the Sanatan Dharma - the Eternal Law.

The people who attain this level of understanding we call saints, philosophers and creative geniuses. Babaji, like all great Masters, indicated that any individual who is willing to focus on this goal can attain it; and that when enough people attain this level of life - or even accept and strive toward this goal - there will come a New Age and humankind as a whole will evolve to a higher spiritual level. Then people will live in harmony with the laws of nature and with all aspects of the Creation, rather than struggling, individually and with a sense of loneliness, against what is perceived as a cruel, 'inhuman,' inflexible universe.

Babaji often spoke in terms of His coming in order "to restore Sanatan Dharma [the Eternal Path/Way /Religion]." On one occasion, He said:

"The Sanatan Dharma is the universal Law - eternal, without beginning, without end. No one knows when it came into being; no one knows how long it will last...

"The Sanatan Dharma is the king of all religions. At the beginning of Creation it was the only [Way] and at the end of Creation it will be the only [Way]. Sanatan Dharma is like an ocean; other Dharmas [Paths] are like rivers - eventually they all merge into the Sanatan Dharma. They will lose their separate existence."

Babaji spoke of the Sanatan Dharma as the underlying Law of the universe which guides the process of creation, by which the Creation is expanded and maintained, and which impels the growth of all sentient creatures - governing the results of all activities within the created universe. The laws of physics and chemistry are a part of the Sanatan Dharma; so are the laws of karma - "As ye sow, so shall ye reap."

The Vedic and Hindu traditions of the Creation are quite compatible with modern scientific thinking. The "Big Bang" theory and the subsequent expansion and development of this universe fit in with the concept of the creative process beginning with a stirring within the Formless God and the utterance of the sacred syllable "Om" (or "AUM") to set off a vibration that started the movement of Conscious Energy which resulted in the combination of energies into very subtle entities which combined into larger, grosser particles, and on and on until there is a recognizeable universe which continues to grow in accordance with the universal Law - the Sanatan Dharma.[7]

Scientists have difficulty in "proving" what led up to the "Big Bang." The Vedic and Hindu traditions have, for millennia, described the pre-Creation God as formless, without human attributes, without birth or beginning. Perhaps the best "description" of this Divine Being is Conscious Energy. The belief is that Conscious Energy is behind the creation process, that Its own nature compels It to initiate the creation in order to express and experience Itself through an infinite number of forms and energies. Everything that is created - on subtle levels, not visible to the human eye, as well as every visible object and creature - has developed from the primal Divine Energy which was impelled by the Creative Movement and given order through the Laws of Creation. The tradition of the Sanatan Dharma is that the universes are created by, maintained by, and then drawn back into the Divine Conscious Energy in a process lasting tens of billions of human years. Then the Conscious Energy rests quietly (for perhaps as long a period as the Creation process requires), and the Creation starts over again. There is no end to this cycle of creative activity and quiet.

All living creatures, and even insentient forms like rocks, are in a constant pattern of change. Even mountains crumble; trees and plants grow from seeds, produce a ripened plant, then die and decay, providing a base for other life; animals, including humans, are born, mature, and die. Human beings are considered the highest form of life. Babaji said that even the gods - the subtle energy forms - long for a human existence, because it is only in the human form that a soul can grow in wisdom and spiritual understanding. Only human beings have the power to think and to change their ways through experience and rational thought. Human beings are the physical forms which are closest to The Divine - the only form of earthly life which can experience and realize its unity with The Divine.

It is a belief of this tradition that the human soul does not die with the death of the human body which it inhabits. The soul is a subtle "entity" akin to the gods, a very direct expression of The Divine. The soul is the Divine impulse in a human being, the Observer and Experiencer of life, which, like The Divine, is immortal. When the body dies, the soul reaps the 'rewards' of its human activities (karma), both good and bad, re-experiences its Divine origins, and then returns (reincarnates) to another human life. The soul may have gone through millions of human and non-human lives on its progress through the Creation. It is believed that generally a soul which has attained a human state reincarnates in a human form, but there are said to be exceptions to this general rule. The soul is *bound* to return to physical life as long as it is entangled in karma - in the desires of the physical, created universe and in the activities, and their results, which are spurred by desire. Only when the soul recognizes, realizes and *experiences* its harmony and essential unity with The Divine - and the uselessness of any human-level desire - can it escape the nearly ceaseless round of births and deaths. When that time finally comes, in some lifetime, the soul can end the process of desire and karma and be fully reunited with The Divine, its long process and journey ended in reunion.

The Sanatan Dharma is the Law which governs the created universes. When a person lives in harmony with this Law, life is a growing, enriching process; operating within these universal laws, the advanced soul can perform what we call 'miracles' (because we do not understand the Law governing those events) or provide "divine" guidance to people struggling along their paths. When we break the Law by failure to live in harmony with it - either by ignorance of the Law or by intent - we find the universe a very difficult place to live in; life is a painful struggle. Both courses - the way of life which pro- duces 'miracles' and great thoughts and the life of painful struggle - illustrate the laws of karma: what you sow, you must harvest. Much of the 'harvest' is reaped in the lifetime in which it was sown, but it can also shape later lifetimes.

On an occasion when people were sitting with Babaji in the temple garden at Haidakhan, someone did something that was very wrong. Babaji reacted furiously and beat the man. After Babaji had calmed down, Sheila asked Him if she could ask a difficult question. On receiving His permission, she asked, "Baba, You are the Lord of Forgiveness; why did you do this to that man? Why not forgive the man? You shouldn't be so angry."

Babaji replied, "Forgiveness has gone to the Himalayas! I can- not forgive that."

Sheila persisted, "You are the Master of Forgiveness. If You don't forgive us, who will? We make mistakes all the time."

Babaji said, "I also am bound by the Laws." Sheila was surprised and said, "You are the One who *creates* the Laws; how can You be bound by the Law?"

Babaji looked sharply at Sheila and said, "This is to be understood: there is *nobody* above this Law!"

On later occasions, in discussions with other people, Babaji often looked pointedly at Sheila, when He said, "The Law is above everything: even I am not above the Law."

*   *   *   *   *   *   *   *

The Sanatan Dharma is the eternal Law by which all relationships are directed or controlled. It is the basis for the creation and maintenance of the physical universes, the 'lubricant' which allows, encourages, shapes harmonious relationships among all the varying elements of the Creation.

In the human contribution to the creative process of the expansion of our physical world, in the practice of our religion or way of life, mind is the central element. There is no thought, no understanding without the mind. The process of thinking has the power to create - to create a new house, a machine, a useful process, or a new way in which we experience or relate to the world. Two people involved in the same event or in similar events in different locations can have greatly different reactions to the event, depending on their "mind-sets" - on how they relate to life.

The mind is a generator, or at least a transformer, of energy. Thought waves are a measurable form of energy. Some people have the ability to communicate telepathically and to "read minds." The thoughts we have get results, and every thought sends its energies into the universe and has an effect on the universe. The thoughts of the billions of people now on earth have a very real effect on day-to-day events and the trends of what is to come. Babaji made it clear that our thoughts and actions create effects throughout the universe. He said, "At present, not only humanity is in danger, but all sentient

196

and insentient beings of the universe are in danger." Our thoughts and actions have effects far beyond our "own" limited spheres of physical presence.

Aware of the importance of the mind, for millennia the people of India - even before the Aryan invasion (c. 2000 B.C. or earlier) - have taught the need and the techniques to control the mind. By one means or another, each human being must learn to focus, control, and discipline the mind. The scattered, undisciplined mind is incapable of sustained progress toward achievement of any kind. The scientific genius focuses his or her mind on research and clear thinking in the area of specialization; the musical genius focuses on music; the person who would "realize God" must be similarly one-pointed. Babaji said, "Everything comes from the mind and is created by mind. Control of the mind is the main practice."

*　　*　　*　　*　　*　　*　　*　　*

Over and over, in many ways, Babaji taught of the impermanence of created things; everything is constantly undergoing change; the only permanent "reality" is The Divine.

"This world is transitory; the Name of God is the true reality. Everything in this world is destructible, transient, unlasting...

"The thing is that this whole world is transitory: why do you entertain confusion in your minds? You must have only one aim, *one goal - to serve every living thing in the universe.*"

One reason for this "one aim" is the belief that God is the underlying reality of everything - that all of Creation is 'built' with the building blocks of God's energy. As such, God is literally the substance of everything that exists. Those who worship or revere God should worship and respect The Divine in all Its forms. Humankind should serve and protect - live in real harmony with - every element of the created universe, including, of course, all other human beings. When someone asked Babaji, "Where is God?" His reply was, "God is everywhere, in everything, in the water, in the sky...'He' is inside you."

All of the world's religions reflect basic elements of the Sanatan Dharma. Their founders' perceptions of the Sanatan Dharma are

197

what give validity to the religions. The paths that each of the major religions show to their adherents have been tested through time and each has produced saints who have achieved great spiritual heights and powers through following the paths shown by their religion. On the other hand, the human mind - as great an instrument as it is - is limited. We do not understand infinities; our languages cannot express even what people experience of The Divine; and the infinite aspects of The Divine are so vast that no human being can experience all this in one life-time, much less formulate and propagate a Way which completely expresses The Divine or the Sanatan Dharma. Therefore, none of the religions of the world does or can have the full, exclusive revelation of the Sanatan Dharma or of The Divine: a full mental understanding of the ways of The Divine appears to be beyond the capacity of any soul in a human form. Additionally, all of the world's 'established' religions have, over the course of centuries, accumulated tenets of faith, means of expression, and problems of organization that were not faced by the founders of the religions. Some of the decisions taken have opened the religions to new areas of Truth; others seem to limit or burden the clarity of the founders' insights. But, despite limitations and problems, each of the Paths has led adventurous followers to great spiritual heights and insights and accomplishments.

The present political, economic and religious chaos and confusion in our world indicates a need to re-examine the underlying concepts of our world civilizations. In our eagerness to create a "brave new world," we have abandoned and forgotten some of the basic principles of civilization. Babaji said He comes to restore, or remind people of, the Sanatan Dharma. He did not come to establish a new system of doctrine and worship; He urged people to follow whatever religion is in their hearts. The focus of His life and teachings was to cause people to seek the underlying truths or laws of the universe and to learn to put them into practice and experience the peace, harmony and creative adventure of life lived in accordance with the Eternal Way.

NOTES

1 Dio Urmilla Neff, "The Legend of Herakhan Baba," <u>Yoga Journal</u>, Issue No.32, May-June, 1980, page 53.

2 "Teachings of Babaji," page 87; 1988 edition; page 115; 2004 edition; published by the Haidakhan Samaj, P.O. Haidakhan, District Nainital, U.P., India.

3 "The Life of Milarepa," translated by Lobsang P. Lhalungpa; 1977; Shambala Publications, Inc., 300 Massachusetts Avenue, Boston, Massachusetts 02115. See also, W.Y. Evans-Went's "Tibet's Great Yogi Milarepa."

4 A ghat is a series of steps down a river bank into the water of a river, where people can come to bathe, fill water buckets, wash clothes, etc.

5 Yogananda, op. cit., page 349 of the 11th edition, 1987.

6 Goodman, Shdema, "Babaji - Meeting with Truth at Haidakhan Vishwa Mahadham".

7 Itzhak Bentov's book, "Stalking the Wild Pendulum," presents this concept beautifully and clearly in a scientific manner.

"Love is long-suffering and kind. Love is not jealous, it does not brag, does not get puffed up, does not behave indecently, does not look for its own interests, does not become provoked. It does not keep account of the injury. It does not rejoice over unrighteousness, but rejoices with the truth. It bears all things, believes all things, hopes all things, endures all things. Love never fails."
St. Paul: I Corinthians, 13: 4-8

"Once you love God, you love His creation, and then you do not hate anymore."
"The Chasm of Fire," Irina Tweedy; page 143

"To follow and demonstrate the path of Truth, Simplicity and Love is man's supreme duty and the highest Yoga."
Shri Babaji, 30 September 1982

CHAPTER IX

BABAJI TEACHES:
TRUTH, SIMPLICITY, LOVE, AND UNITY

The Central Message - Truth, Simplicity and Love

In 1977, 1979 and 1981, David Berry, a young man in the American motion picture industry, visited Babaji. David took a camera each time and accumulated movie footage of Shri Babaji - in the Ashram, in neighboring villages, on travel. Babaji told David to make a movie or video tape and David asked Baba what title it should have and what message Babaji wanted to give. The last frames of David Berry's video tape[1] show Babaji stating His central message. Babaji looked into the camera and said, "Prem, saralata, satayut," which is "Truth, Simplicity and Love."

This is the same message which Mahendra Baba said was given to him by Lord Shiva, in preparation for Babaji's return to human form to teach again.[2] As Mahendra Baba expounded the teaching, Truth was described as "whatever the mind thinks, the voice should tell, and the organs should do." The expression of Truth requires a total harmony within an individual. Simplicity means the living of a simple, natural life based on detachment from the materialistic world and a resulting clear conscience. It did not mean renouncing material things necessary for a simple, comfortable life or renouncing an active role in life. Love was described as the basis for devotion to God - in all forms.

The living of a life based on "Truth, Simplicity and Love" requires - and further develops - a strong sense of unity and harmony with the entire Creation and its Creator, starting from within one's self. This is the essential Truth which Babaji comes to show and teach and to help people experience. When an individual can think, speak and act in harmony with the Eternal Law, she or he has found and is living in Truth.

Even before His resumption of the direction and activity of the Haidakhan Ashram in 1970, Babaji lived in the area in a full expression of this central Truth. When people started coming to Haidakhan to be with Him, they saw this teaching exemplified not only by Babaji Himself but in the lifestyle of the ashram. It was certainly simple! For several years, there was no recognizable residential dwelling in the ashram; people slept under the stars, or, when it rained, crowded into the village houses and tea houses. They bathed in the river. They ate simple food. But no one felt deprived; they felt blessed, and came again and again to live in this environment. Even today, with stone-and-cement buildings and electricity, the Haidakhan Ashram provides very simple accommodations, still difficult to reach. It is the Presence of Truth, Simplicity and Love which draws rich and poor, saint and sinner, the powerful and the strugglers to this place.

"You can only know Me through Love"

For a God of Love, Shri Babaji *spoke* rather infrequently about love. In comparison to the talks about jap, karma yoga, changing the world, or prophesies, there are few that place a direct focus on love. Yet Love is what stimulates people to spiritual growth and it is a goal of that growth. Love stirs people into purposeful action - karma yoga, and karma yoga is what Babaji said perfects love. Jap helps to purify the mind so love can be mind's controlling impulse. Everything Babaji teaches, everything He does in human form revolves around love, expresses His love and is aimed at leading the devotee to the perfection of love. But, in keeping with His desire for "practical human beings" to populate the earth, He taught people to *do* things which stimulate the growth of love, reflect their love, and perfect it through experience and constant repetition in action until it becomes the only motivation for human activity. Because He sees the Creation as One - all created things as a manifestation of the Divine substance and energy - there is little or no distinction in His teachings between a human being's love for God and love for created forms.

The love which Shri Babaji exemplified was not a romantic, sexual love; it was not 'namby-pamby,' meekly accepting whatever came His way. His love was clear, rational, detached; He could as easily hit a devotee as He could touch in blessing - depending on which was truly more helpful to His devotee at the moment. The giving and receiving relationship between mother and child is closer to the love which Babaji expressed than that of lover and beloved. In India, and elsewhere, The Divine is often worshipped as The Divine *Mother;* and Babaji was seen by many of His devotees as 'Mother.' There is even a 'Mother aarati' (worship service) which was often offered to Babaji. When He completed His ministry, He left behind Him 'Haidakhandeshwari Mata' (the Divine Mother of Haidakhan) as His Shakti (or consort), as the Energy and Love of God, in much the same way as Christ spoke of the Holy Spirit as Comforter and Guide.

His whole 'life' was one of loving service. When Gaura Devi came to the Haidakhan Ashram, Babaji told her, "Babaji means all people service." His entire day was given in loving, supportive service to His devotees - and not just to those physically present in the ashram. He was patient - working at whatever pace was possible - but He was also capable of jumping into any activity that had lost its momentum and energizing it by drastic action. He was constantly giving - material objects, spiritual blessings, needed knowledge. When He spoke about love and service, it was from practical 'human' experience, as well as from the Divine Wisdom in Him.

Like many spiritual teachers, Shri Babaji used the phrases "God is love" or "Love is God." He seemed to indicate that the formless God - Absolute, complete in Itself - is nevertheless energized by Love. Love is the energy of God which creates, maintains and enlivens the Universe with its pulsing vibrations or waves, and which also stimulates the active, caring, purifying relationship between God in Its many divine forms and the individual, embodied souls that are struggling to recall their unity and oneness with God.

He saw love as the bond or the channel of communication between God and human beings. "You can only know Me through love - Divine Love, love for God, without any selfish purpose." Love is also the unifying force among disparate human beings: "Live here with love for each other, like members of one family. Discard jealousy and envy. Because you are all one, live here in peace. If you are in peace, I am in peace; if you have problems, I have problems."

Babaji took on many people's problems for them. Some found peace just by talking to Babaji and leaving their problems with Him.

Sometimes He solved a problem with a gift, a word of advice, or by instructing another devotee to help the person with a problem. There seemed to be no limit to what He would do for those devotees who came to Him with problems.

*　　*　　*　　*　　*　　*　　*　　*

On one occasion, Babaji said, "I don't want you to *talk* about Truth, Simplicity and Love; I want you to *live* it." Rather than Himself talking about love, He more often talked about how it could be expressed, and frequently He used terms other than "love." One evening in October 1983, during His last visit to the ashram farm near the village of Manda in southern Gujarat State, Shri Babaji spoke of love in terms of "humanism."

"I wish everyone in this country, as well as in all the world, all the best. Nowadays humanism has been completely killed; human beings have become like animals. I want to bring back humanism into the soul of every person. Because of the lack of human spirit, every individual is in tension and fear. I want to relieve everyone from this state.

"Ages ago, sages formed the following mantra:
'Sarve Bhavantu Sukhina
Sarve Santu Niraamayaa
Sarve Bhadraani Pashyantu
Maa Kashahid Dhukhbhag Bhavet.'
(May all be happy;
May all be free from disease;
May all realize what is good;
May none be subject to misery.)

"But in all these Ages, under the guise of bringing peace and happiness, only wars took place - like those in the <u>Ramayana</u> and the <u>Mahabharata</u>. These wars only left millions of women and children in grief.

"Now I want to bring happiness to every living being by transforming the hearts of all individuals.

204

Only by this process can the dream of the sages who formed the mantra come true. For this purpose, the only path is Karma Yoga. Only Karma Yoga can bring satisfaction and good fruits of action. With this, happiness will automatically come into the hearts of the people. Hence, all of you should work hard and follow the path of Karma Yoga."

Often He spoke of love as 'dharma' - a person's duty or moral responsibility to God and humanity. "All of you are soldiers of Haidakhan. Do your duty with faith and devotion. You must remove hatred and jealousy from your hearts to be of real service. All of you must climb the mountain of victory."

Jealousy - which was a prevalent trait among those who vied for Shri Babaji's attention and the sharing of His power or authority - was a frequent target of Baba in His speeches. Jealousy and love are incompatibles.

"You must work to elevate humanity and eradicate pride, jealousy and hatred. Today humanity is in great danger and there exists no security of person or wealth. This problem is not that of one nation, but of the whole universe.

"Unite in love to elevate yourselves! Each one of you must vow today to sacrifice everything to obtain oneness among yourselves. Be rid of attachments in your heart and be ready, for the sake of righteousness, to jump into the flames and water of life. Be prepared to burn your very bones, if necessary, to secure the public good and righteousness."

Shri Babaji played almost any 'game,' 'wore any mask,' did almost anything to project His love in ways which helped His devotees to progress along the spiritual path. What His mind thought necessary, His mouth spoke, and His body immediately accomplished. His detachment allowed Him to do whatever was appropriate in any situation. He could laughingly, lovingly, joyously reward someone for a seemingly insignificant achievement, if that would help the person take another little step along the Path. For some, a smile or a touch of blessing was the only encouragement needed - or appropriate. Others might go 'unrewarded' day after day and then, having passed a greater test, be given special attention, teachings on a deeper level, because they had shown themselves ready to respond to it.

He could just as easily - and from the same well-spring of detached love - mete out appropriate punishment. When someone got lazy in his or her spiritual progress or got 'stuck' on some attachment or fear, Shri Babaji could, for all outward appearances, totally ignore the person; He might scowl and shout 'angrily'; He could smack somebody hard with His open hand; and, occasionally, He took the staff He often carried and administered a sound thrashing. (When Babaji hit, whether with hand or staff, He always knew exactly where and how to hit: although He could use the staff with strength, He never broke a bone or inflicted more than a short-lived pain.) Most people who spoke about these punishments said they were literally helped to move through the internal crisis that prompted the 'punishment' and that, afterwards, they saw it as an act of love.

Some people saw the love immediately. I remember a young German school teacher who giggled through her public scolding as Babaji threw her out of the ashram for disobeying the rules. Though His face was a mask of anger, and though He gave her a whack on the back that resounded through the kirtan hall, she saw only love and laughter in His eyes and felt no fear or pain.

"What I want for you all is Unity"

Shri Babaji spoke often about unity. Learning to do karma yoga in unity with others was an essential part of His teaching and of the experience He gave to those who came to the ashram. Working cooperatively, harmoniously, effectively with others was a training in the practical expression of love.

Babaji often spoke of all things in Creation as ONE: the whole Creation is the manifestation of God, not just an infinite number of manifestations of God. When we study a beehive, one way of looking at it is as an integrated whole, with each bee playing its role in the life of the hive. When we look at our bodies, we see fingers, toes, hands, feet, legs, arms, and are aware of individual organs which we cannot see; but we identify ourselves as whole human beings. Yet, when we look at humankind, we see only a mass of individuals: it is very difficult for a person to see himself or herself as 'only' a part of Creation. Society teaches us to focus on individual interests and achievements; Shri Babaji urged us to live and work for the common good - developing all our individual talents to the fullest, but consciously using them to benefit all of a Creation which works best when it is in harmony.

"Everyone should forget nationality; we are one here. This is a universal family. Have no idea of separation of identity; discard feelings of separateness. Serve all people with mind, body, wealth, brain.

"The progress of Vishwa Mahadham [the greatest place in the universe - Babaji's name for the Haidakhan area] is the progress of the world. When you work and learn here, you help the world. Make Vishwa Mahadham perfect. Work as a unit; there is no caste or creed here; there are no differences."

"I have come to help you realize unity beyond division. I am not talking about the kind of unity they talk about in party politics; I am talking about a unity never before achieved, a unity we will obtain by way of mutual understanding; no bombs, guns or force. You must all seek that unity.

"I will build a water hole where the lion and the goat may come together to drink. What I want for you all is unity and an awareness that we are all the same."

Babaji often noted that human beings get so focused on their misconceived concept of individuality, so impressed with their own, individual physical forms and mental conceptions, that they lose the concept of their real divinity and their oneness with the whole Creation. The 'unbodied soul' sees and understands the unity of the Creation, but when the soul enters a physical body it becomes enraptured by that form to the point where the soul identifies itself with the *form*, rather than recognizing itself as divine and the body as a *tool* of the soul, as a means of service or a means of expression of the essence

207

of the soul. It is this confusion of the mind and soul that keeps humankind tied to its lower nature and to the cycle of births and deaths. When the individual entity experiences its essential divinity and the unity of the divine Creation, then it recognizes all beings as a part of itself and can discard attitudes of separation, competitiveness, fear and hostility, leaving love and compassion as the essential motivating spirits.

"...we must annihilate the feelings of 'I-ness' and 'my-ness' from our minds. You must march forward like a soldier, dutifully and bravely. The thing which brings man down is attachment to his own kith and kin. When you all belong to this whole universe, where is the place for 'I' and 'mine?' We must unite as one universal family and march forward in unity. By this means only will the world be benefited. This is not the concern of one individual, but that of the whole universe. Every person must cultivate the qualities of 'humanity.' This is the only way to success.

"...Humanity will not be elevated by lecturing and talking, but we must awaken the spirit of humanism in all of humankind. Everyone must remove the differences between themselves and others and work in the world in unity; otherwise the disorder which is spreading in the world will go on increasing and there will be no cure for it.

"There is only one way for humankind to be saved and that is by changing the hearts of all people. Shri Mahaprabhuji will give His full spiritual power to this, but every man and woman will also have to make their best efforts toward this end. As long as there is no change of heart, humanity is in great danger."

With Shri Babaji's strong energy to direct it, the Haidakhan Ashram hummed with purposeful action; useful projects were accomplished, people learned to work with each other without much thought of nationality or creed or color; and as they worked they learned about themselves and grew spiritually. Many of the people who came remarked about the sense of peace, unity, and purposeful activity in the ashram. Government officers of many levels visited Haidakhan frequently and some of them understood the importance and beauty of what Shri Babaji was doing. One of these was the then Kumaon Commissioner, Shri A.K. Das, the senior state government officer of the three districts that comprise the Kumaon area in the foothills of the Indian Himalayas. Speaking to a large gathering one evening after aarati, he said:

> "We are all very much impressed to see that people from thousands of miles away have sent their offerings of thousands of rupees and have themselves come here to sit, without distinction of caste, color, or creed, at His lotus feet. We have never seen such gatherings anywhere else."[3]

Babaji preached unity in many ways, over and over.

> "Think of the Earth as a Mother. This is one Earth. Don't be divided by thinking of yourselves as belonging to different countries. We belong to one earth. Proceed with this in mind. Look to the future with a vision of good deeds for the whole world, not just one country."

> "Everyone must take a vow...that we are all one and that we must all live in unity. Everyone must remove differences, distinctions from their hearts. There must be more stress on unity. We must put an end to all kinds of differences of opinion and other differences, too. We must step forward, keeping in mind the problems that the coming great crisis will bring.

> "There is great power in union. If there is unity and love among you, then only can you lead a peaceful and happy life."

An Experience of Working in Unity

Major Bhupindra ("Bhoopie") Sharma told the story of an early karma yoga project in Haidakhan - the construction of the major stone wall by the Haidakhan Cave. This wall is about fifteen feet high and, rounding a corner, has a lineal measurement of twenty-five or thirty feet.

At the start of a nine-day celebration of the Divine Mother in Haidakhan, Babaji called Bhoopie to Him and said it would be Bhoopie's duty to organize and supervise the construction of the wall, which had to be finished by the ninth day. Babaji gave Bhoopie a work crew of three or four middle-aged and old men and four or five women. The base of the wall had to have the largest stones and by the end of the day the whole crew managed to push, shove, roll, and lever four or five major rocks into place.

The next day three or four more people joined Bhoopie's crew and the team worked all day, except for a break at noon. When Babaji came to the work site late in the afternoon, not even one full base row of big stones had been completed. Babaji remarked acidly that the work would never be finished at that rate.

With more people arriving for the celebration, the third day saw more people on Bhoopie's work crew, but there were still not enough people and they were working at less than maximum output. At noon, Bhoopie went to the area below the room where Babaji ate. Bhoopie was told no one could interrupt Babaji's meal or talk to Him after it; this was no time to try to see Him. Major Sharma stood on his rights and insisted on talking to Babaji when He left the room. While people were standing and arguing noisily about this, Shri Babaji came out of the room and asked Bhoopie what he wanted. Bhoopie said the work was going too slowly; he needed more men and he suggested they work from dawn to dusk - even through aarati. Babaji granted the time and indicated He would send more people. That afternoon, with a few more men and women working harder and longer, the first and second row of major stones were completed; but with one-third of the time gone, less than twenty per cent of the work was done.

Each day more people came and joined the work crew. At the end of the period, Major Sharma had a Central Government cabinet minister and an Indian Army general working under his direction, and a total of fifty or sixty people. With the spur of Babaji's presence in frequent visits, the wall leapt upwards and it was, through the combined efforts of old and young, men and women, rich and poor, completed well and on time.

The experience provided lessons on many levels for many people. They learned to work as a unit and they learned they could do far more physical work than they thought they could. Some of them learned a lesson that Shri Babaji has taught to many throughout the world: when you learn what your duty (dharma) is, do not be daunted by its size and your responsibility; just start working with what you have and, if your work is good, others will come to help you.

The Teaching of "Humanity"

On Christmas Day, 1983, with about one hundred and fifty foreigners and almost as many Indian devotees in Haidakhan to celebrate Christmas, Commissioner A.K. Das spoke again about the sense of unity, despite diversity, which he found in the ashram.

"The message of Christ was to love everyone, to have no hatred or jealousy toward anyone. Babaji teaches the same...

"...I have a tremendous faith in Babaji, particularly because we have His message of humanity here. So many foreign friends have come from all over the world. There is much difference between the ways of life and the religious beliefs, but there is something unique here - that is why people come from all over the world to sit here. This great gathering of humanity teaches us that though we come from all over the world, we are all from the same spring of humanity. We should love each other; we should gain experience of each other's views and exchange views of our faiths.

"On this auspicious day, let us all pray to Christ - and to Baba - for blessing and for the mental courage to perform our destined jobs honestly, properly, and with dedication."[4]

Shri Babaji emphasized the need for courageous hard working individuals, working in real unity, performing humane service to all, as a necessity for universal peace.

211

"Our main aim is that there be universal peace. How can we obtain this peace? We can achieve this by eliminating all inhumanity among us. There must be only one 'caste' and one 'creed' - humanity. Become human!

"The only religion is humanity. There must be tolerance and forgiveness. It is our duty to set an example for this. Everyone must be 'human.' Everyone must be courageous, facing the difficulties of life with bravery. Save yourselves and others from the lawlessness of the world. Cowardly people are like dead people. I want to create a world of brave people who face life as it comes. We want to save the victims of atrocities and bring them out of their trouble. We want to bring peace not only to one country, but to the whole world; our aim is universal peace.

"All of you must take a vow to go from house to house, from place to place, and help the needy. You have to root out the inaction which is destroying man. Inaction and idleness are the chief obstacles to man's progress. If you learn right action, you can do *anything!* Action is mahayoga - the highest yoga. You should progress through action. Man is meant for action."

*   *   *   *   *   *   *   *

On September 23, 1983, a black American couple from Milwaukee, Wisconsin, was re-married according to Vedic rites before Shri Babaji. In the darshan following their marriage, Babaji spoke again about 'humanity,' unity and hard work.

"...now we focus not only on the matter of this marriage, but of the whole world. The world now is in a state of turmoil. It is suffering from three kinds of pain - physical, mental, spiritual - and there is only one way of being cured from these. We have to root out inhumanity and replace it with humanity. I have told you before that I do not want differences of caste,

212

creed, color, or race. When there is only one Humanity, how can there be different creeds and castes? This is quite unreal.

"I think it was like this: some shrewd people invented all the differences in order to divide people, to be able to rule over them. So they created castes, their aim being to divide and rule. Differences were created for selfish motives. There are people in this world who, when they see someone else's house is burning, are happy. There are people who want to live in comfort at the expense of the labor of others. There is only one God, who created *all* people in His image. This is why we have to re-establish 'humanity.'

"What I want to instill in humankind is courage. I want to have a creation of courageous people. Only courageous people can survive such critical times...

"I want a creation where there is no dependency of any kind. Everyone should be able to stand on his or her own feet. The problems of all countries can be solved when everyone becomes hard-working. As long as there is laziness in the world, people cannot attain happiness. Materialism is rising like a great storm and we have to face it."

A month later, Sir C.P.N. Singh, the Governor of Uttar Pradesh, as he responded to Babaji's welcome to him, noted the unity that Shri Babaji taught:

"...in this place, as a result of the appearance of Shankar Swayambhu [the Self-created Lord Shiva], the essential thing is that there are no differences here. Hindus, Moslems, Germans, Italians, rich and poor - all come to the holy feet of Bhagwan.

"... The degenerated human race starts its purification automatically from His lotus feet to effortlessly spread throughout the world. For that purpose only, this forgotten, neglected land is now getting new life.

"The work we are all engaged in here is for the

213

purpose of making Man a true human being. At present, men have become like animals!"[5]

To foster this unity among those ready to work together for "universal service" and to spread His teachings of 'humanity,' Shri Babaji encouraged people to organize.

"The message that is given here must be spread like electricity throughout the world. Do it quickly!

"We must create many institutions; we must spread the Message by making committees."

Babaji Himself stimulated the creation of ashram trusts and committees to print material, and He authorized and enlivened the Haidakhandi Samaj, an Indian-registered society (Samaj means 'society' in Hindi) with affiliated organizations now in Europe, North America, Africa, and Australia. In addressing the annual meeting of the Samaj in April, 1983, Shri Babaji had Vishnu Dutt Shastriji speak these words for Him:

"The main purpose of the Samaj is service to humanity. Service to humanity is the best service to God. Our motto is 'work is worship.' It is our duty, as those working within the Samaj, to show the path to those who are in need of help, inspiring them to overcome lethargy which is the cause for inaction in the world, inspiring them to work. Therefore, I want first to root out lethargy in you. In this Yuga, the only way to obtain siddhis - to become really strong - is Karma, action...

"Whenever true progress was made in the world, it was due to hard-working individuals of a particular Age. Today it is our task to go everywhere, from house to house, spreading righteousness, guiding everyone on the path of karma, giving them practical instructions - *being ourselves examples*. By karma alone can we be come prosperous. We have to work to our last breath."

To provide leadership for the Haidakhan Samaj, Babaji named Shri Trilok Singh of Haldwani as the Samaj chairman, from the inauguration of the Samaj in 1979. Babaji had given Trilok Singh the name of Muniraj (King of the Sages) and specifically made him the guru of many of the foreigners who came to Babaji. Over a period of several years, Babaji told His followers that Munirajji is a present incarnation of Lord Dattatreya, a great teacher of the Sanatan Dharma who is said to embody all three of the Hindu trinity of gods - Brahma, Vishnu and Maheshwara (or Shiva). Babaji said of Munirajji that "his work begins when I leave."

Service as the Highest Activity

Shri Babaji considered service to others as the highest activity, greater than the rituals of worship - and the absence of a sense of service as a great impairment to life. He exhorted people to serve others always. Such work is a useful contribution to society and is the best and highest means of attaining personal spiritual growth and perfection, as well. There is no service which is needed by others which is beneath the dignity of a true server.

"The world demands hard work and constructive action, so you must apply yourselves fully to your work. Do not fall back, but go on. Each step you take will benefit the whole world.

"Fulfilling your duty is the highest accomplishment - higher than other sadhana, penance, and the rest...

"To engage in work is the duty of everyone, whether rich or poor, high or low, old or young, man or woman. You should not hesitate to do the lowest kind of service, if it is needed. If a man of high position is prepared to perform any service - even the lowest service - he sets an example for others.

"By working hard, a man can achieve peace within himself and in the world around him. If everyone works diligently and with love, there will be peace throughout the world."

*   *   *   *   *   *   *   *

The status of a "sweeper" in India - one who sweeps the streets

215

and sidewalks or cleans latrines and toilets - is one of the lowest in the economic and social hierarchy. Although 'untouchability' is forbidden now in India by legislation, discrimination is widely practiced still, in some regions of India, against sweepers and other 'untouchables,' and this remains a problem which Government and society still work at.

Neem Karoli Baba was a great saint of the Kumaon area who left his body in 1973.[6] He knew 'Old Haidakhan Baba' and often spoke of Him. While He was wandering as a boy in the Kumaon Hills in the 1960's, Babaji had spent some months in Neem Karoli's ashram, sweeping the ashram and serving others: performing "even the lowest service" was completely consistent with Shri Babaji's teachings.

Neem Karoli Baba, in a fashion observed by many saints, apparently told different people different things about the "new" Babaji in the early 1970's. It appears that he told most people that this new Haidakhan Baba was an imposter. (No teacher who has established a guru-disciple relationship with someone will encourage the disciple to "shop around" for another teacher or guru.) But I have a recollection that some devotee of Haidakhan Baba told me that he came to Babaji because Neem Karoli Baba told him that He was the manifestation of Lord Shiva Himself and that He would not stay long in that form. "Go and serve Him."

Babaji constantly urged on people the need to perform service in unity; but there is no need to wait for others to get the work started for you: do your own duty; set the example.

"There should be humanity in you. People of all countries should unite with each other as brothers.

All of you must be happy and healthy and appreciate the joys of life...

"...spread the light of righteousness to the hearts of others. Let the seed of human love and 'humanity' which is in you flower and be fruitful. Organized powers are always stronger than individual ones....

"Remove hatred and jealousy from the heart. The same thing has been written repeatedly in the Bible and spoken through Christ. Where there is jealousy and hatred, this is no religion. If there had been 'humanity' in people, there would have been no necessity for making atom bombs; years ago people would have left fighting instruments."

"I am Against the Non-Violence that makes a Human Being a Coward. Fight for Truth!"

In this Age (Kali Yuga), with people in general so unthinking of and inhuman to each other, Shri Babaji was not in favor of turning the other cheek to the aggressor or exploiter of other human beings. He was not averse to using His hand or His stick on someone who did not respond to reason or the gentle word, and He had no use for the coward or one who accepted ill treatment and later 'bleated' about being mistreated.

"The theory of non-violence has spoiled the mind and courage of people today. I am for fighting - fighting against evil and crime everywhere, which should no longer be tolerated!

"I want to weed out the prevailing non-violence in this world. It is a cause of apathy and idleness. *This* non-violence has cooled the blood of men so that it has become like cold water. This attitude of non-violence produces a lack of discrimination between good and evil. Everyone should lead a life of bravery and courage. A man without courage is like a dead man. Life without courage is no life.

"At present, many atrocities are being committed in the world. No one has had the courage to stand up against these atrocities, but everyone should be brave and resist them. Everyone must be of firm determination and stick to what he believes to be true. Be constant in your actions, and dutiful."

Learning to oppose and resist inhumanity and atrocities may also be a learning and growing process for those who serve and stand up for righteousness. It takes discrimination to know what to oppose, when to resist, and what means to use - what is appropriate for different situations. It requires some experience of God's support in difficult situations to build up one's courage. The knowledge of when and how best to resist does not come without testing; fear is not conquered by one successful act of bravery or courage. Shri Babaji once prompted Vishnu Dutt Shastriji, sentence by sentence, to say the following:

> "Non-violence is now contaminating the world. Non-violence of itself should be removed from the world. Culprits *must* be punished; for security we must employ strength. Babaji wants *some* violent people, so that others may grow in wisdom and discrimination and learn to make decisions."

Although many saints and sages have taught and employed non-violence as a way of life, in this century the most famous practitioners of non-violence have been Mahatma Gandhi and Martin Luther King, Jr. Their non-violence was an active, disciplined, powerful weapon which, through the courage of many people, was successfully used to win a revolution for the independence of India and to break centuries-old patterns of racial discrimination, domination and exploitation of black people in the United States of America. The Philippine revolution against Ferdinand Marcos gained strength from and built on their experience, risking lives, unarmed, against armed governmental might. There was nothing 'weak-kneed' or 'lily-livered' about their non-violence; it took great courage to stand up against the armed might of the British Empire, the American 'establishment' and Marcos' army. Hundreds died in the exercise of their non-violent efforts to change their corners of the world. Their examples not only changed their own countries but inspired and set the stage for the astounding, basically peaceful revolution in Eastern Europe in 1989.

For the past two or three decades, "non-violence" has often been an excuse for avoidance of responsibility, for averting our gaze from the atrocities that jump out of television screens and newspapers every day, for walking to the other side of the street when some stranger is assaulted, robbed or abused. Governments practice genocide, large corporations have crushed those whose interests conflict with theirs, terrorists involve non-participants in their 'war games,' organized crime enforces its authority through violence and fear. There is violence and inhumane action on every level, from within ourselves to the level of international affairs, and - in the name of non-violence, but often from simple indifference or fear - we make little effective response. There certainly is no sense of the oneness of all of Creation that is at the base of Shri Babaji's teaching; the exercise of a truly unselfish human response to these situations is so rare that it makes news headlines.

"I want to make the people who have come here true citizens. I don't want *this* non-violence. The people preach non-violence, and they make water out of their blood. I want to wake up the sense of true humanity. With great difficulty you get this human body. I want brave and courageous people. A man must have great courage..."

"I want a creation of brave, fearless and courageous people. I want people with a strong revolutionary spirit who are willing to fight for the Truth. I want to root out the present spirit of non-violence from the world; this emphasis on non-violence has brought an increase in atrocities and injustice in the world. I do not want a world in which the rights of human beings are trampled, as the world is today. This practice of non-violence has led people into ignorance, instead of leading them to knowledge. Due to this kind of non-violence, man has been deprived of his rights and he is afraid of his own shadow. I want a creation of powerful people throughout the world."

Shri Babaji was not in favor of mindless or excessive violence, either. "It is My desire that there be harmony in the universe. My plan is one of love - one where the lion and the goat can drink from the same pond." For those who are truly non-violent in thought and deed, He commented, "The concept of violence should be understood like this: those who are non-violent should have no part in violence." This is the ideal way.

But for those who do not have the courage and strength to be and remain truly non-violent, He said, "I am against the non-violence that makes a human being a coward. Fight for truth! To face life, you must have great courage every day."

"You should seek Harmony in everything you do."

Teaching and living the concept that the entire universe is one great, integrated manifestation of the Divine Energy, Shri Babaji knew that the entire Creation should - that the laws of the universe *require* it to - operate in harmony. To the extent that any element of the Creation is out of harmony with its perfect, prescribed course of action, the whole universe is affected by that deviation. Thoughts, actions, and movements in nature vibrate far beyond their locality of origin and have effects like the widening ripples stirred by a stone dropped into a still pond of water.[7] Of course, the acts of an individual person have minor effect on the universe as a whole, but the cumulative effects of billions of thoughts and actions every minute in our world alone have a *very* substantial effect on events and patterns.

Human beings are becoming increasingly aware of how our thoughtless, selfish actions are polluting the atmosphere, the air we breathe, the water we drink and use to raise crops and animals, and the earth on which we live. Unless we quickly develop a respect and protection for "Mother Earth" and "Father Sky," human beings will poison themselves out of existence. There are serious questions about the ability of humans to survive on this planet if we fail to take effective corrective actions against the widespread pollution of our planet.

The pollution of human minds is equally or more dangerous: if we fail to learn to discipline our minds against envy, jealousy, hatred, and lack of respect for all beings, if we fail to develop a sense of love and compassion for and of unity with all beings, we may blow ourselves off the face of the earth sooner than the elements can bring an end to *homo sapiens.* Our human attitudes, thoughts, speech and actions have a very significant effect on the quality - even the possibility - of life in this universe. Lives lived in the "Truth, Simplicity and Love" taught by Shri Babaji contribute to the healing and harmony of this world and universe.

Shri Babaji urged all people to become inwardly peaceful, balanced and harmonious with every level of existence - from the earth on which we live, through our families, through our villages and cities, countries, and the whole world and the universe beyond us. Only then can we know real peace and security, either individually or collectively. To the extent we give expression to *disharmony* - to the fears, jealousies, greed, lusts, and hatreds that ego and attachment breed - we can see, from our own experience of ourselves and the world around us, the harmful, disruptive, unsettling results. If people can, through self-examination, self-knowledge, and enlightened self-interest, rise above these "enemies of yoga," they live and vibrate in harmony with the entire universe. And that universe supports them.

Babaji worked consistently, through His example and speech, to restore humanity's lost focus on its relationship and unity with The Divine throughout the universe - and of the unity of all created beings with each other. On one occasion, He stated:

> "If you are at peace, I am in peace. If you are troubled, I am troubled. If you have problems, I have problems.
>
> "There will always be hills and mountains to overcome on the way to God. Do not be disturbed by the mountain falling down; it is the duty of the mountain to fall down. And it is the duty of the soldier to remove the mountain. "You should seek harmony in everything you do. *I am harmony.* Thank you for your love."

NOTES

[1] "Have Guru Darshan"; video by David Berry, music by Turkantam. Available from www.babaji.net or www.babajiashram.org.

[2] See page 62-63.

[3] "Teachings of Babaji," 1988 edition, page 88; 2004 edition, page 116.

[4] Ibid, page 99; 2004 edition, page 129

[5] "Teachings of Babaji," 1988 edition, page 85; 2004 edition, page 112.

[6] See "Miracle of Love," by Baba Ram Das, E.P. Dutton, New York, N.Y.10016, for a wonderful book about Neem Karoli Baba.

[7] Refer to Note 3 on page xv.

"Remember the name of your Lord and dedicate yourself to Him utterly. He is the Lord of the East and the West: there is no God but Him. Accept Him for your Protector."
The Koran, "The Mantled One"

"Set thy heart upon thy work, but never on its reward. Work not for a reward, but never cease to do thy work. Do thy work in the peace of yoga and, free from selfish desires, be not moved in success or failure. Yoga is evenness of mind - a peace that is ever the same.
"Work done for a reward is much lower than work done in the Yoga of wisdom. Seek salvation in the wisdom of reason.
How poor those who work for a reward!"
Bhagavad-Gita, Chapter 2, verses 47-49
(Translation by Juan Mascaro, Penguin Classics)

"This is the nature of the excellent people that they cannot bear others' misery. They consider others' misery their own and try to eradicate it."
<u>Siva Purana</u>, Vol. III, pages 1350 and 1351.

CHAPTER X

BABAJI AS TEACHER:
JAP AND KARMA YOGA

The Practice of Japa

Shri Babaji's first formal public teaching was given at the top of the Kumaon Mount Kailash, just across the river from the temple and ashram that 'Old Haidakhan Baba' had built. In November, 1970, Babaji invited people from the valley villages and from Haldwani and Nainital to come back to Mount Kailash, and several hundred people made the difficult trek. The message they heard from Him was to constantly repeat the mantra "Om Namah Shivaya," which translates to "I bow to Shiva" or "I surrender to, or take refuge in, Shiva [the Divinity within us]." It is a statement of surrender to God; a vow to put God first and foremost, constantly, in one's life; a commitment to walk a Path toward God-realization.

This ancient mantra is so closely connected with Lord Shiva that it is counted as one of His names. Shri Babaji used it as His signature. The mantra is sung to many different tunes, as <u>kirtan</u>; or it can be repeated, silently or aloud, while passing mala beads through one's fingers - like a Catholic rosary or a Muslim's prayer beads; or one can keep the mantra dancing through the mind while doing a routine activity, like cutting wood, driving, doing dishes, or pulling weeds from the garden. Because of its use as one of Lord Shiva's names, it fits into the category of <u>nama jap</u> (or <u>nama japa</u>), which means "repetition of a name."

The purpose of <u>nama japa</u> is to help focus the mind on The Divine. Frequent repetition of the mantra focuses one's mind more and more on The Divine and other, unnecessary, distracting thoughts are crowded out. So a mantra helps focus the mind in two ways - toward The Divine and away from the "trash" that often accumulates in our minds and clutters up our mental computer discs. Who cares what witty response you might have made to the put-down at last night's party, and how long do you remember the dreams you spin as you go to work? How many hours a day are our minds half-focused on idle "mind-chatter"?

Lord Krishna, in the Bhagavad-Gita, told Arjuna, "...you must remember me at all times and do your duty. If your mind and heart are set on me constantly, you will come to Me. Never doubt this."[1] Isaiah commented on the power of this focus on The Divine in these words: "Thou wilt keep him in perfect peace, whose mind is stayed on thee, because he trusteth in thee."[2]

Babaji taught the practice of jap, or nama jap, to all who came to Him throughout His ministry. When Gaura Devi came to live in the ashram, she asked Babaji for a sadhana (spiritual practice). His response was that Gaura would constantly repeat Om Namah Shivaya, mentally or aloud, eat one meal a day, and drink no tea. He set up a schedule of manual labor for her (sweeping the ashram and cleaning kitchen pots and pans) which allowed her to keep her mind on the mantra while she worked. Gaura says that she kept the mantra going in her mind from twelve to twenty hours a day for most of her first four years with Shri Babaji. Then He taught her a different practice.

Nama japa was a frequent subject of Babaji's conversation or public talks throughout His ministry; it was one of His basic teachings. Its value lies in its use in the devotee's efforts to "turn around," to initiate a basic change in one's life patterns. Our minds normally are scattered all over the landscape, literally. Whatever we see, whatever comes to mind, captures our mental attention for some brief or longer time. In a real sense, we human beings are the *prisoners* of our minds, instead of their masters.

Nama japa is a tool to help the individual tame and eventually master his or her mind. It is a major step toward disciplining the mind. It sounds easy, but, for many people, it is not. In Babaji's presence, it was fairly easy to sit for an hour or so singing or saying Om Namah Shivaya; but when He was gone, almost every time I sat down to do jap, my mind flew off to thoughts of work or family or 'whatever' before the fifth bead passed through my fingers. Babaji, who in the nineteenth century taught many people Kriya yoga with a strong emphasis on meditation, said that almost no one now can meditate like the ancient sages and rishis, so, in this manifestation, He taught people this simpler form of concentration - the repetition of a Name of God. But even nama japa is difficult for most Western minds, at first.

Nama japa has another value besides helping to turn off unwanted, valueless thoughts. The Haidakhan aarati, in a statement which reflects the traditional thought of the Sanatan Dharma, states that "by drinking the nectar of God's Name, one attains God's holy eternal abode." This refers to nama japa, wherein the devotee "drinks the nectar" by the repetition of a Name of God. It is believed that the soul which is focused on God goes to "God's abode."

There is an even more immediate and practical result of nama japa. By focusing on a specific form or aspect of The Divine, one gradually takes on the attributes of that form. For instance, when a person wants to be physically strong and greatly devoted to God, he or she may focus on Hanuman, who is celebrated for his super-human strength and his constant devotion to Lord Ram and to His consort, Sita. The person who seeks wealth may become a devotee of Lakshmi, the goddess of wealth, beauty and harmony. By repeating the mantra Om Namah Shivaya and focusing on Shri Babaji, one tends to become more and more like Him - to take on His attributes, to walk the Path to God-realization. This is as normal and natural as a person's taking on the characteristics of her or his ideal person, or idol; we tend to become like that which we admire. And we *may* reach something like a Babaji state even before our souls "leave the body."

So nama japa not only turns our minds away from idle, useless thoughts, but turns us in the direction of The Divine. Getting into the practice of repeating a Name of God - whatever Name you feel is appropriate for you - is a BIG step toward changing your focus and patterns in life. This is why Babaji urged His followers to make nama japa a constant practice. He said of it:

> "The Lord's Name is like divine nectar; repeat it all the time." "In this Dark Age [Kali Yuga], the mind of man is weak and restless from the day of birth. Because of this, no one is able to do the real practice of meditation any more; but everyone can pray and repeat and chant the name of the Lord, using whichever divine name his religion teaches." "Chant the name of the Lord always. By chanting the mantra, its vibrations spread all around you. You will then 'meditate' for

225

yourself and others."

Babaji Himself spent a great deal of time with a mantra or in deep meditation. For the first several years, in Haidakhan, He lived in an open hut. People slept around this hut and whenever anyone woke up in the night they always saw Babaji sitting in meditation.

Sheila Devi spent many months every year at the Haidakhan Ashram and spent many hours serving Babaji or sitting in His presence. She said He constantly stressed nama japa in His conversations with her and others; He told her it is the only thing which can take a person "across the ocean of life"; it is very powerful. He told many that it does not matter much what mantra is used - use any appropriate name of God. If a mantra is used constantly, until it keeps going subconsciously, that is better yet; then the mantra may continue to be lively in the mind always. If a person goes to sleep with the mantra in mind and wakes up with it, that person has attained a very high level of yoga. He said that constant use of a mantra eventually makes the devotee one with the form of God whose name is used.

Although one can achieve a state in which the mantra is repeated subconsciously, almost unconsciously, it should also - particularly in the early stages of nama japa - be repeated with concentration on the words, the vibrations, and the meaning of the mantra. Devotees used to sit for hours in Shri Babaji's presence either silently repeating a mantra or (more often) singing Om Namah Shivaya to different tunes. This is kirtan.

Dr. V.P. Tiwari (Mahant Baba) tells of a time in the Vrindaban ashram when a large group of devotees was sitting before Shri Babaji chanting Om Namah Shivaya. After many minutes of this kirtan, Babaji suddenly stopped the singing and told everyone to go and have their tea.

Dr. Tiwari was aware of Babaji's prohibition of tea in the Haidakhan Ashram (at that time: later, He lifted the ban and even gave tea parties) and was puzzled by Baba's action. Seeing the confusion on Dr. Tiwari's face as the people left to go and get their tea and biscuits, Babaji said, "How do you think they can concentrate on the mantra when they are all wishing they had their morning tea?"

In the 1980's, Babaji asked Vishnu Dutt Shastriji to add a ninth chapter to his scriptural book, <u>Shri Sadashiv Charitamrit,</u> to relate the activities and teaching of Babaji in His most recent manifestation. The following verses are quoted from a draft translation of Chapter Nine to give an idea of Shri Babaji's concept of <u>nama japa</u>. Shastriji cited Babaji as saying:

> "The only way to happily control the mind is to worship the Lord and remember His Name at every moment. The power of the Lord's Name is unfathomable. Keeping it always in mind, the traveler on the Path overcomes every obstacle.

> "When the Name of the Lord, as His supreme power, enters the heart, happiness begins to pervade it. By remembering His Name, the Lord Himself comes to reside within the heart, and the devotee immediately reaps the fruit of all his endeavors.

> "The little self of man then begins to merge with the Divine Self, and the Lord, most merciful, gives fearlessness to it. The constant remembrance of the Lord transforms the individual self into the Self Supreme...the self, by constantly remembering God, becomes like Him."[3]

In one of His talks in November, 1982, Shri Babaji said:

> "Of greatest importance is that the repetition of God's Name increases daily. In this way your heart and mind will be purified; only then will you find God in yourself.

> "The mind can be purified only by jap. This is the only medicine for the disease of the mind. While your mind and heart are impure, how can God live in your heart? The water to clean your heart is the Name of God. So teach everyone to repeat the Name of God - everywhere."

Shri Babaji told Gaura Devi, "Repetition of the Name is the most powerful process of purification for the mind - to rid our minds of all unnecessary thoughts; because meditation is, finally, a process of purification. Repetition of a mantra is the first step of every meditation."

The repetition of God's Names is an essential part of Shri Babaji's teachings, but only rarely did He instruct someone to stop other activities and only 'do jap' - or meditate. He said:

"I do not want idle people. Jap does not take the place of karma [work]. Jap and work go together. You must be active in God's work, like King Janaka who ruled his kingdom always with his mantra in his mind. Arjuna fought the Mahabharata battle, constantly remembering God's Name. I do not want jap to be a pretext for idleness. *Do jap with your work* and be liberated. I do not want God's Name to be like stagnant, muddy water, but like sparkling, running water. Work and be Light! Repeat God's Name. With a concentrated mind, always repeat God's Name."

The Teaching of Karma Yoga - Service in Harmony with The Divine

Jap may have been Shri Babaji's first public message, but Karma Yoga was the teaching He stressed most often and most forcibly. Karma yoga is work (activity) performed in harmony with the Creator and with all the Creation, without selfish motive or aim. It is the activity one performs as the expression of one's duty (dharma) in the world. Each person has his or her own duty: policing, teaching, mothering, writing, farming, constructing, healing, governing - whatever. If the duty is performed with the aim of helping the Creation function harmoniously as a contribution to the welfare of the family and community, in harmony with the perceived Divine Will, rather than for purely selfish, ego-inspired reasons, the activity is probably definable as karma yoga. Activities motivated by hatred, jealousy, greed, lust, revenge, and the like cannot pass muster as karma yoga.

Babaji's daily activity throughout His ministry was a constant example of karma yoga; the schedule of the day at the Haidakhan Ashram emphasized Karma Yoga; and His speeches hammered away at karma yoga so frequently that just before the New Year, 1984, He said: "Shri Mahaprabhuji says, 'I am always telling you about working hard. My head has become very hot from the constant repetition

228

of this same thing.'"

As Lord Krishna taught in the <u>Bhagavad-Gita</u> so also Babaji taught that human life is given for the opportunity for spiritual advancement of the soul, and spiritual growth is achieved through activity more effectively than through renunciation; complete renunciation of action is a physical impossibility.

> "You have come into the world to work. You must always be eager to work. The one who is idle is like a dead man. You have come to this world to live, not to die."

> "...this Earth is a field of Karma. Everyone must be active, working. The great people who lived in the past thrived by doing Karma Yoga; now, also, people who thrive are those who are working diligently. Only through Karma Yoga can you make progress...

> "Until you breathe your last breath, you should not abandon Karma Yoga. Inaction is like death: that is why you must go on working, advancing, and making progress."

> "I want very much that everybody be brave, active, and hard-working. Never lose courage! Because you have taken this birth, you must seek achievement. And to be successful, you must work hard. The world requires fortitude. Become courageous and lead others to courage."

Shri Babaji described Karma Yoga as *the most important act of religion..* The forms of religious worship are of secondary importance to the devotee's work. The phrase Work is worship' was frequently on His lips.

> "Go on working while repeating God's Name. You cannot conceive the high value of karma performed while repeating God's Name.

> "Man's mind is very fast, faster than the wind. By doing work while repeating God's Name, your mind becomes cleansed of thoughts and useless, negative thoughts cannot enter it. To uplift man

- for the progress of the whole of Humanity - karma is a great sadhana."

"I say all of this in the service of humanity. To work, think good thoughts, and dedicate your life to Humanity is the best thing. The only necessity of this Age is karma yoga through service. Everybody must spread this message."

"In every Age, people have reached salvation through different types of action and sadhana; but in this Age one can reach liberation only through hard work. I want real, practical human beings, and only he is a true human being who lives in accordance with this Age. We need not consider religion or caste, but look only to hard work. The troubles that beset this Age can be resolved through Karma Yoga. You should become pioneers of this Age and search for Truth. You have to become adventurous and awaken Truth within you. This is real Yoga."

For more than two millennia, India has known several forms of yoga. Babaji stated that Karma Yoga has special significance during these times, for this Age.

"I have told you before that there are many kinds of yogas, but Karma Yoga is of supreme importance. Karma Yoga must come first; then other types of yoga can be added."

"Karma Yoga is the highest religious practice of this time and it will liberate you. The scriptures declare that at the end of each Yuga only Karma Yoga will help you."

"Only through karma yoga is it possible to change the Era. All other forms of yoga are unable to achieve this. Whenever there is a change of Era, karma yoga expresses itself in scientific progress and other developments as the fruit of human activity."

Not only did Shri Babaji see work - karma yoga - as a blessing, but its absence in one's life is more than just missing an opportunity to progress. Idleness is harmful, a danger to the individual soul and to society. "Lethargy must have no place in your lives. Lethargy is the weakest trait in man. The day mankind becomes hard-working, the world will lack nothing. Man *must* live and improve through work. Work is the highest form of worship: you can evolve in all ways by doing work."

Although Babaji appreciated modern technology and expressed great respect for the dedicated scientists and engineers who produced these wonders, He was concerned about the effects on humankind in general of our application of these things.

"Science has made great progress in this world. Where we used to engage a thousand men to work, now a bulldozer does the work in seconds. But that makes a thousand people useless and unemployed. While unemployment is increasing in this world, people have lost their peace of mind. The reason for this is because man has ceased to work. Due to this inaction, all kinds of pains and sicknesses are increasing in the world.

"I want you to take the energy of the machines into yourselves and work like machines! In one respect, if you correctly observe, you see that science is weakening human beings. How can you test your own talents and faculties, if you do not use them? For example, take a soldier; how can he show his strength and valor, if he is only using a machine?

"We must follow a path which will strengthen us, so we must not be dependent on machines. How can that be done? It can only be done when you are hard-working and active. Everyone must advance by the practice of Karma Yoga. This is the eternal, unshakeable way. Everything - all knowledge, all science - came through karma, hard work."

"Anyone who is an active and hard-working Karma Yogi has no problems in this world. To give up Karma and become lazy or idle is the greatest problem and unhappiness - and also danger - that you can face in your life."

"Since the time of Lord Rama and Lord Krishna, many scriptures have come into being. They all describe the significance of Karma Yoga and teach its greatness. Christ was a Karma Yogi and the Prophet Mohammed followed the path of Karma Yoga. All the Great Ones who have come advanced through Karma Yoga Only Karma Yoga is able to transform the world. Inaction is the cause of pain and all troubles....

"In the name of Lord Rama, Karma Yoga gives immediate results."

Karma Yoga for Spiritual Growth

Shri Babaji emphasized karma yoga as work that is service; and in doing service for others - in performing work that is in harmony with the proper functioning of the Universe as a whole - the individual also attains spiritual growth.

"This work [the karma yoga project of that time was digging out a steep hillside at the base of the Kumaon Mount Kailash, to make a garden area the size of a football field] is not only for this purpose. This work will go with you wherever you go; even after you leave the body and go to the other world, this work will go with you; you will be benefitted by it. *Whatever kind of garden you will make here,* and whatever seeds you will sow here, *you will get there, also.*

"This is spiritual work, not material. This is neither My work nor yours; this is the work of the whole universe. Do you understand?

"It is good that you spend as much time as you can in this work; this will be good for you in the future.

232

The more time and the more energy you use there, the more beneficial it will be for you. Your health will also improve by this; your digestion will be all right and you will sleep well, also. Your mind will be purified...

"See the ant. How small is the ant, yet how big a load she carries. You should not become dejected or disheartened. If we want, we can blow the whole of this mountain - if we all want to; if we have the will. Don't lose your heart; when you lose courage, this is death. Don't lose courage. You can move the mountain!

"Yoga is to be courageous. To get dejected or to lose courage is not yoga."

"Do your duty! Do not be idle. This is an Age of Action! Perform your karma yoga. Show the world ideal actions. Service to humanity is service to and worship of God."

"Babaji likes human beings. Humanitarian work should be done by all of us. A person who follows this and who always keeps humanitarian rules in mind will be loved by everyone and shall survive all this [coming] destruction and shall remain happy. One should try to bring these humanitarian ideas to everyone who does not have them.

"What does one mean by humanitarian rules and humanity? Babaji says one should not have any hatred toward anyone; one should try not to let down other people; one should try to help others; one should try to love all."

One day Babaji called Ila, a devotee from Bombay, to come and sit with Him. He sat on a wall on the porch outside His rooms, where He could look over a small stream and the rear part of the ashram. Ila sat at His feet. The "International Guest House" was then under construction and a mixed crew of paid village laborers and karma yoga devotees was working on the site. There were many foreigners - especially Italians and Germans - and a few Indian devotees in the ashram. Babaji mentioned His karma yoga to Ila.

"I am doing all this karma yoga; but what is the need for Me to do karma yoga? Do you ever see Me sitting idly? One should always be doing something. I do not like <u>akarmanyata</u> [the lack of action, or idleness].

"Look at the foreigners. How hard they are working! I feel like handing over everything to them and going away. I am giving Chilianaula to the military. The Indians don't believe in working; they just do talking. They should take an example from the foreigners."

Babaji sometimes exaggerated to make His point but there were and are many followers - both Indian and foreign - who would rather talk than work. The foreigners came mostly from countries with a strong work ethic and those who resisted karma yoga were sent on their way. But in every possible way - by example or instruction, reward or punishment - Shri Babaji urged His devotees to "talk less, work more."

"I have told you many times before that you must all keep your duty before you always. We must all have one purpose before us - to sacrifice ourselves for the sake of humanity. We must live for humanity and die for humanity. We must all offer our lives for the welfare and security of society. This must be our main aim, our bhajan [hymn]. This is our bhajan, our kirtan; this is our repetition of the Name. We should always proceed with this in mind."

"Karma is an inevitable law of cause and effect by which all living beings reap the fruits of their actions and thoughts. Jesus stated the law of karma in the words, 'As ye sow, so shall ye reap.' The law of karma is above all things. Karma starts when movement starts in the mind. To stop karma, we must bring the mind to that state of silence and voidness beyond which God can be known... Otherwise, as long as a man breathes, he is creating karma. No one can remain without action, even for a minute. Therefore, *learn how to dedicate your every action to the Lord."*

In April 1973, when Gaura Devi took up residence in the Hai-dakhan Ashram, Shri Babaji told her, "Now you will serve Lord Shiva for twelve years; after twelve years you will start to realize something spiritual." Karma yoga is no casual dedication to service; it is a way of life. Although, as Babaji said, its practice does bring instant and visible results, in most instances it takes a person more than a brief practice before karma yoga can supplant the society-taught, inbred patterns of thinking and working for personal gain and personal ends. Karma yoga requires a strong focus on The Divine and constant, consistent practice; it takes time to establish one's self in karma yoga. When the karma yogi has tamed the ego, then new vistas of spiritual growth open up. The traditional period of training for the person who wishes to become a yogi is twelve years.

> "Everyone who comes here should be prepared to do *any* kind of work. In this Age, work purifies you and is the best spiritual practice."

> "You must intensify your courage and enthusi-asm. I want all work to be done punctually - on time. Whatever work you do, do it with a sense of duty. I do not need *more* work to be done, but I want work done with concentration, efficiently and expeditious-ly. Everyone must do his or her work here as his or her own work. I want everybody to be very active and hardworking. Activity - hard work - is the only way to infuse new life into your country."

"Advance with Courage!"

Babaji emphasized the need for courage in the practice of karma yoga and pointed out that courageous action develops and strengthens the worker's personal courage.

> "You should do your work with courage. Kar-ma Yoga is what will make you like lions; it will make you strong in this life.

> "Don't disappoint Babaji. Don't be afraid of death, nor of the storm of water and fire. This life itself

235

is water and fire. Don't try to stop it but rather become like lions!" In whatever condition or position you find yourself, *always go forward.* Go ahead! Go ahead! Advance with courage!"

It is human nature to seek stability and security. People seek these goals through family, through material wealth, through strong houses; they seek governments to foster these ends on a wide scale. Shri Babaji, looking at Creation on a long-term view, saw everything in a state of change. The plant or tree grows from its seed, matures, bears fruit, dies and decays. Buildings decay and crumble. Great fortunes and empires are made and lost or dissipated over time. Man grows, waxes strong, ages, and dies. Even the mightiest mountains crumble into hills. In His view, all of Creation is 'transitory' ; it comes into being, it is maintained over billions of years - always changing - and it is dissolved; to come again, after a time. Though not in any way depreciating man's striving for peaceful order, simple comfort and stability, Shri Babaji said that real stability comes through karma yoga.

"The world is transitory. You will find stability only on the path of karma yoga. Only action can take a person to God and give liberation. The law of karma is so deep that no words are great enough to describe it. The day karma stops on this earth will be the day of its dissolution [pralaya].

"Brave ones, all of you, continue to work! Through karma alone will you be able to change the world. It is the only way.

"Today the world is playing with fire. We have to be ready to face fire, water and great storms and not be shaken. We have to go beyond the hope of life and the fear of death. Whatever happens, we must go ahead; then only can we benefit the world. We have to bring the path of karma into the light. Now the world is in deep darkness. The Revolution [Mahakranti] spreading in this world can be controlled only by karma."

Shri Babaji seemed to teach, through the experiences He led us to, that real stability or security is an inner attainment; all that is exterior, material, is subject to change and loss. His concept of stability seems to be the balance that Shri Krishna - and countless others - taught: by rising above desires, that is, not being controlled or 'driven' by them, being unswerved by pleasure or pain, though experiencing them in normal life, by being like a detached observer or witness to the events in our lives, it is possible to attain an unshakeable balance. Where there is balance, Truth can operate freely: "mind, speech, and action are in unity." Where anger, hatred, greed, lust, confusion, or fear upset our balance, Truth flees and we lack the inner harmony (stability) which allows clear, strong, purposeful, 'right' action. The constant practice of karma yoga develops and strengthens this stability, so that its possessor is not shaken by the storms of life that whirl around him or her.

In the summer of 1983, Babaji sent me into the ashram office, where I had often worked before, and gradually, as other 'office staff' left the ashram, He put me in charge of the office. My working career had been office work and I basically enjoy it; soon I was keeping the office open more hours than before and I was swamped with work and more people came to help in the office.

Babaji used to visit the office three or four times a week and they were usually moments of delight and blessing. But on several occasions, He came in and pounced 'angrily' on some facet of work not done to His satisfaction. Because He was normally the embodiment of Love in action and because we loved Him so much, his apparent anger was devastating to those on whom it was turned. On the first occasion, one's reaction was almost always panic and guilt. But to anyone who observed Him, it became clear that Babaji's 'anger' was only a mask, a method of teaching, of shocking a person out of established, comfortable reactions to a situation. He could shout 'angrily' at someone - even hit a person - and in a fraction of a second look at the next person with such a look of love that it melted the heart: He was not motivated or ruled by anger.

It did not take long for most people to learn this about Babaji, so the panic born of fear was diluted or dissolved, sooner or later. During an early experience of Babaji's 'wrath,' my reaction was one of inner, unexpressed anger toward Babaji and self-justification: why do You jump on me like this when You know I am working as hard and as well as I can? Over and over, Shri Babaji criticized my management of the office until I learned to react with reasonable calmness and simply agree to clear up the matter He threw at me - and to proceed expeditiously to do it.

My last lesson from Babaji on this point came the week before Christmas 1983. Baba had given to Lok Nath and me major responsibilities to organize the ashram for the big Christmas celebration. One thing He had specifically reminded us to do was to station people at the bottom of the '108 steps' to welcome new arrivals to the ashram, register the foreigners on the police registration forms, and assign rooms where each would stay. We had made certain this was done and was operating well.

On the 17th of December, at 6 p.m., when total darkness had fallen, the 'greeters' at the bottom of the stairs decided no one else would come that night and they left their post. Fifteen minutes later Amar Singh's truck came up the valley road and unloaded a party of eighteen Italian devotees. They walked up the stairs and found Babaji sitting on a bench at the top landing. They made their pranams and Filippo asked Babaji where they all should go. Babaji shouted for Lok Nath and Radhe Shyam. Someone ran to the office and told us to hurry to Babaji: He was angry.

Lok Nath is younger and faster than I, so when I reached the landing, Babaji was already berating Lok Nath in harsh terms that made one's toes curl with embarrassment. Om Shanti's translations could not take the sting out of Babaji's comments. When I arrived, Babaji turned it on me. The translation of His comments to me was on the order of "Can't you manage anything? Even when I tell you what to do, there was no one to meet these people! Where do they go? Why don't you take care of these things?"

After a second or so of sheer panic, my mind screamed at me, "This is a test! Don't panic!" And then, as the stinging words kept coming from Baba and the translator, I recalled that we had set up the system, that it had worked unusually well so far, and that we had better make sure that tomorrow night after six someone from the greeting group would sit in the teashop where the trucks stop.

As I was concentrating my mind on the problem, suddenly Babaji had a warm, approving smile on His face and He started a chant of "Budhe Radhe Shyam, Bhudhe Radhe Shyam." "Bhudhe" generally means "old" and seasoned, but I am told it can also mean "one who is learning." He had read my thoughts and was congratulating me on reaching a new level of balance - stability under fire! He was blessing me for standing without fear or without anger toward my guru in the face of His 'anger.' It is that quality - at a still higher level after longer practice - that enables the karma yogi to react calmly, dispassionately, quickly and intelligently in the face of disaster. It is the long, constant practice of karma yoga that develops the courage, fearlessness and steadfastness that are needed in this era of change and destruction.

Karma Yoga as a Practical Way of Life

Shri Babaji often told us He wanted *practical* people and He pointed out how practical karma yoga is.

"Any material desire you may have can be fulfilled by karma yoga... Karma yoga is Supreme Yoga. Lord Rama and Lord Krishna taught this, too. Not only did they teach it, they also practiced it and were successful in it...

"Karma Yoga is the only type of yoga that gives immediate results. Whatever you do in the morning, you can see the results in the evening, standing before you like a picture. The seeds sown in the morning sprout by the evening. The farmer harvests the results of his karma yoga after six months.

"Everyone does karma naturally; no one can remain without it. We must perform those actions which will benefit others - and not only other people, but the whole of Creation.

"It is of no use to give birth to millions of sheep. One hard-working human being is enough to save the world. We must all become hard-working and teach

239

coming generations as well. All other forms of yoga come second only to karma yoga, because the whole world is maintained by karma. So practice karma yoga and progress. People in the world nowadays have become very cowardly. That is why we have to be courageous, adventurous."

"If you are engaged in doing good deeds and go on doing good acts, you will have good sleep, good appetite, and bad thoughts will not cross your mind. In *inaction*, your minds will always be engaged in thinking critically of each other. Karma - activity - is the only thing which can drive out all evils."

In the late nineteenth century, Mahavatar Babaji focused His teaching mostly on <u>Kriya yoga</u>. In November 1983, Babaji had this to say about Kriya yoga and the karma yoga that He emphasized in this manifestation.

"The fact is that your daily routine work from morning till night is the real Kriya Yoga. The union of that work which is started in the morning and finished in the evening is real Kriya Yoga. There is nothing like Kriya Yoga. There is nothing in this world that is not Kriya Yoga. Perfection in work is the real Kriya Yoga.

"Every action in this world, including eating and drinking, is Kriya Yoga. The digestive process in your body is Kriya. The process of uniting any two or more things is Kriya Yoga...

"Only that is Kriya which brings peace and happiness and all kinds of benefits to people. To do good actions is Kriya Yoga. Worship is also Kriya Yoga; worship of any deity is Kriya Yoga.

"You must all do service to humanity. *That* is Kriya Yoga. The times now demand this of you in this world."

Karma yoga can embrace all kinds of arts and sciences, all the skills that humans have developed. Babaji did not seek mindless, plodding 'servers'; life is given for growth through experience; we are expected to use it and to develop talents to the fullest. Babaji often sent young people back to their homes to develop their skills and live useful "practical" lives, so they could benefit "the whole of Creation" at their highest possible level of attainment. He expected everyone to learn and grow.

Babaji tried consistently to make people alert and aware of what was going on around them. During the last years of His ministry, He often had a group of men (mostly Western devotees) who walked with Him on the "ceremonial" walks in the ashram, such as when Babaji walked from His room through the temple garden to the kirtan hall to give darshan after the evening aarati. On these occasions, the young men would walk before and behind Babaji shouting "Hoshyar! Savadhan! Shri Shri Mahaprabhuji pedar rahe hai!" (Be alert! Be on your guard! The Revered Great Lord is walking here!)

This custom may have arisen from a desire of His followers to give The Lord His due, while He walked among men, many of whom did not recognize Him as The Lord; but Babaji never lost His sense of humor - even of the ridiculous - and He was always alert to opportunities for teaching His devotees. One evening, at dusk, as He was walking through the temple garden on His way to give darshan, with six or eight strong young men shouting to "Be alert! Be on your guard!," and to make way for The Lord, Babaji suddenly jumped off the sidewalk on which they were all walking and leaped into the garden. He lifted the stout staff which He often carried and started slamming it into a plant about four feet from the sidewalk. The surprised men followed Babaji into the garden to see what was happening, and when Baba turned away to the temple they saw a battered, highly poisonous lizard lying dead in a corner of the garden. Babaji seemed to be making a point: shouting for other people to be alert and to pay attention is not enough. *KEEP YOUR OWN EYES OPEN! OBSERVE WHAT IS GOING ON AROUND YOU ALWAYS!*

Changing Nature Through Karma Yoga

Karma Yoga and jap, used together, are powerful tools for change. Babaji put all who came to see Him on this Path to help them

241

change their patterns of life and re-establish their focus on The Divine. With these "tools," He wrought changes both in Nature and in human nature.

In 1981, Babaji started karma yogis working on developing a garden out of a portion of the riverbed which was a little higher than the rest of the riverbed and in a corner of a bend. Sometimes, in a weak monsoon, this area was not badly flooded; most of the year it was dry. Babaji set people moving big stones out of this perhaps-four-acre area and piling them up on the edge of the plot. Big stones were dug up and rolled into place by strong men; smaller stones and pebbles were picked up and put into baskets and carried to the pile on the edge by women, children and old men. As they worked, they repeated their mantras.

After this work had gone on for some time, the piles of stones on the edge of the lot began to look like a wall, or a levee against the monsoon floods. The work looked pretty impressive when Sita Rami and I left for Nepal in July, in search of long-term visas to India. When we returned to Haidakhan after the monsoon, we found people working on the wall and moving stones again; the monsoon floods had wiped out big sections of the wall, flooded the area, and supplied a new "crop" of stones and pebbles.

In 1982, the wall - broader and higher than before, with bigger boulders at its base - held against the monsoon floods. Gaurhari, the young priest at the nine temples, brought the ashram oxen over to the plot and ploughed, and crops of grain were planted in the winter and spring.

During the spring and summer of 1983, karma yogis planted flower gardens and trees at the foot of the steps from the ashram down to the river, and Babaji Himself carefully supervised the construction of big concrete blocks upstream of the garden to push the river's flow away from the new garden. He also supervised the construction of a new dhuni over a sacred fire pit.

All this work, over a three-year period - the moving of stones, the building of the wall, ploughing and planting, the construction of the new dhuni - was performed by hundreds of karma yogis, repeating millions of mantras as they worked.

In August, 1983, the newly-built Moksha Dham[4] Dhuni was inaugurated by Shri Babaji in the midst of the newly landscaped and planted "Company Garden." Babaji spoke about the accomplishments of this work.

> "In the name of Lord Rama, the sages of this Age have shown great self-sacrifice in order to build this place. In the name of Lord Rama, just as 'Pramodavan' was the beautiful garden of Lord Rama in Ayodhya, so this is the beautiful garden of Lord Shiva. Its name is 'Nandan Van.' This divine manifestation, this garden, is not of an ordinary type; it has come into being through the sweat and blood of all devotees. That is why it is so beautiful....

> "I have told you that I will bring heaven down to earth and today you all are eyewitnesses to this fact. In the name of Lord Rama, I have told Har Govind many times that I shall make Switzerland and Sweden here. In the name of Lord Rama, now you can see the verdure all around. That the place is what you can see today is due to those who have done penance here.

> "In the name of Lord Rama, what is here today is the outcome of your hard labor and sadhana - of your winning the challenge Nature posed to you. You have conquered Nature and have created this beautiful garden."

> **"When Karma Yoga is such a high thing, why don't you all adopt this as your practice?"**

NOTES

1   Bhagavad-Gita, Chapter 8, verse 7. Annie Besant's translation.
2   Isaiah 26:3.
3   "Shri Sadashiv Charitamrit" by Vishnu Dutt Mishra; Chapter 9, verses 468-470.
4   Moksha Dham means Place of Liberation.

"We destroyed many generations before you
when they did wrong and denied the veritable signs
which their apostles had given them.
Thus shall the guilty be rewarded.
Then we made you their successors in the land,
so that We might see how you would conduct yourselves."
The Koran

"When you see a 'gourd of ashes' in the sky,
you will know that the Great Purification is at hand."
Ancient Hopi prophesy

"Shri Mahaprabhuji has this wish that we all must
work for the welfare of the whole universe.
Whatever we do - we will to do - must be based on the universal good.
I tell you that you must all spend your time and energy
working for the good of the entire universe.
Only by doing this will you be benefitted."
Shri Babaji, 17 December 1983

CHAPTER XI

BABAJI PROPHESIES

Statements about "Revolution" and Destruction

Shri Babaji teaches that the Creation is "One" - that all things are created from the same Energy and Substance - and that all should work in harmony with the laws of Creation. The inert and the insentient forms and the non-human living creatures of the earth, left to their own devices, seem to operate pretty closely in accordance with the Laws of Nature; but humankind, with active, independent minds and free will, has more difficulty in submitting to any authority which it perceives as being 'outside' or beyond itself. Babaji had something to say to the world about what may happen if human beings fail to heed the Sanatan Dharma, or the Laws of Nature.

Our thoughts and actions inevitably have results; we reap what we sow; and what the world in general has been sowing in past decades is producing a great harvest of bad fruit. Babaji spoke of the need for a "Revolution" (He used the Hindi word "Mahakranti," which means "great upheaval" or "great revolution") in the world to change humanity's course from destruction.

Throughout His ministry, but especially in the last half of it, Babaji made prophesies about wars, natural disasters and upheavals. During the 1980's, and in many of His speeches He made additional comments on these prophesies. Some of His statements appear to have been intended to be understood literally and others figuratively. Some of the events He prophesied occurred as Babaji foretold them; many have not yet happened; and many may never occur, or may not occur "on schedule." The past is written into the universe and can be seen or recalled by saints and seers; but the future of human events, subject as they are to the free will of human beings, cannot be accurately foretold, in detail, even by The Divine. Babaji constantly urged us to be alert and work hard to change the course of human and natural events. His whole ministry was focused on showing people how to focus on The Divine and to live in harmony with The Divine and all of Its Creation, thus breaking the patterns of disharmony that lead to disastrous results.

Although Babaji did not spell it out for us, in retrospect, it seems clear that He spoke about *two* "Revolutions," for both of which He used the word <u>Mahakranti</u>. It seems to me that Babaji predicted, and considered probable and perhaps necessary, physical, violent upheaval in the material world, as the certain result of the increasingly heavy load of 'bad' karma that the world is carrying and that human beings are piling onto themselves and the earth at increasing speed. The other revolution - which He came to initiate, guide and support - is a spiritual revolution.

Babaji said of these two revolutions:

"Terrible calamities and wars are approaching in the world. After much destruction, a new Age of Goodness will come. I Myself have come to prepare the world for a new kingdom."

Certainly by the time of His first trip from Haidakhan to Vrindaban, early in 1971, Shri Babaji must have told people about the coming destruction, because the handbill issued prior to His April visit to Bandikui warned of the coming destruction and great loss of lives![1]

The next printed statement of Babaji's prophesies that I have found comes through Dr. V.V.S. Rao's report of an incident that took place on March 15, 1976, in the home of Shri Jain during a visit Babaji made to Jaipur. On the morning of that day two decorated seats were prepared in a room in Mr. Jain's house where Shri Babaji was to give darshan. Babaji came in at 9 a.m. and sat. Then Mr. Jain was garlanded with flowers, at Babaji's direction, and seated on the other <u>asan</u>. Babaji went into meditation and apparently put Mr. Jain into a trance; Mr. Jain started to speak slowly.

Mr. Jain uttered Babaji's prediction in some detail. He said that the unrighteousness and evil and violence then prevalent would increase and that all "living beings" will go through bad times; the world situation would continue to deteriorate. By 1979 a very bad period would start and for the next ten years there would be large-scale destruction, until by 1989 only about one quarter of the present world population would remain.

During this period of destruction, everyone should worship

246

God in accordance with his or her religion. In those families where God is regularly worshipped and His Names are chanted, there will be no great problems; in other families there will be cruel destruction. Mr. Jain said that some time after 1989, when the world population has been severely reduced, a <u>Satyayuga</u> (Age of Truth) will begin.

At 9:25, Mr. Jain ended his pronouncement; Babaji opened His eyes and aarati was performed to Him - and to Mr. Jain. Mr. Jain was completely exhausted by this brief experience![2]

In July 1979, Babaji made two statements concerning the prophesies for the 1980's. Someone wrote a summary of His statements. On July 26, Shri Babaji stated:

>"The change of the present, which is full of turmoil, will be brought about by bloody revolution. Peace will return only after the revolution reaches its zenith.

>"In the aftermath of the revolution - which will be total; no country, big or small, will be spared - some countries will be totally erased, leaving no sign of their existence. In some, three to five per cent of the population will be spared and will survive.

>"The destruction will be brought about by earthquakes, floods, accidents, collisions, and wars. The destructive elements, which were kept in check by Shri Babaji, have been released to do their worst. Those who pray to their chosen Divinity will not be affected."

Two days later, Shri Babaji made the following additional comments about The Revolution:

>"People today are full of misery and unhappiness. Misery and unhappiness are not confined to the poor, but rich people are affected, too. All are suffering from difficulties, misery, and unhappiness.

>"The leaders of all countries are busy safeguarding their positions and have totally ignored their people's needs and interests. These leaders are misguiding the public. There is complete insecurity; there is no safety of person or property. New leaders are being trained and prepared to take over from the corrupt

247

leaders. The new leaders will restore justice and proper order and bring peace.

"At present, demonic influences have engulfed men. Men will fight and devour men and they will destroy each other. First, destruction will take place, then a lull, and then peace will prevail. Some countries will be completely destroyed.

"Prayer will be the only safeguard and savior against destruction. Forget past and future; abolish all other thoughts; but pray with total concentration of mind and soul and have full faith in God. Chant Om Namah Shivaya and you can defy death. No evil influence will ever come near you if you pray with purity of heart and mind and with all faith and concentration."[3]

After these three prophetic statements in 1976 and 1979, most of Shri Babaji's subsequent statements on <u>Mahakranti</u> were amplifications of or comments on the coming "Revolution."

"The problem is one which affects the whole universe. It is not the problem of one caste or creed, but of all living beings of this Creation. It is the problem of the 8,400,000 species of sentient beings. In the name of Lord Rama, it is not only the problem of all sentient beings, but also of all insentient beings. The task now before Me is to make the goat and the lion drink from the same water source."

Why It Must Come

Babaji spoke a few times on the need for the destruction - the reasons why destruction must come.

"I want to create brave people in this world. I want to remove violence from the world. I will remove idleness. There are certain elements that are destroying the Creation, but they will be destroyed."

"Courage is necessary. I want to root out idleness and create a world of brave, intelligent beings."

Babaji's devotees used to question among themselves whether He spoke literally or figuratively about the Mahakranti. Would there really be such terrible destruction, or was Babaji just threatening mankind, as a father might threaten his children with dire punishments if they misbehave? If He really did see widespread destruction in the near future, could one take precise dates literally? After all, those who see past, present and future in a single glance may have a different concept of time; and some of Babaji's other predicted events had not occurred "on schedule."

There certainly were indications that Babaji's predictions, if not necessarily their timings, were to be taken literally.

> "Be strong in the time of great revolution, which is coming. No one can stop the 'fire' coming in the world now. The bells of great destruction are already ringing."

> "The fact is, a great 'fire' of sins and sorrows is burning throughout the world. Everyone living walks and works through this 'fire.' People have become disheartened; Death is dancing before everyone's eyes; everyone has this experience.

> "At present, not only humanity is in danger, but all sentient and insentient beings of the universe are in danger. I have not only to consider human beings but I have to save the entire Creation. How is this possible? (A long pause.) It is quite *impossible.* The calamities which are coming to this world are unavoidable. Only he who has strong determination to do good acts and who is strongly devoted to God can survive this destruction."

Our scientists are now foremost among those who warn of life-threatening human damage to the Earth and its atmosphere. In addition to predicting massive earthquakes as the continental plates shift and a possible shift in the earth's axis, they have shown us, with mounting heaps of data, that we are polluting the air we breathe, the water we drink, and the earth in which we grow our food. We are destroying the forms of life which have, until this time, been able to purify our atmosphere - the great tropical rain forests and life forms in our fresh and ocean water and in the soil. Our acts of ravaging the earth for the immediate satisfaction of our fleeting and mounting desires and covering the earth with the polluted wastes of our lifestyles have readily predictable and serious consequences for human existence. If we do not make some revolutionary changes in our patterns of living, humanity may largely poison itself off the face of the earth. And, of course, there is always the possibility that - without a revolution in the way nations and peoples deal with each other - humankind may simply blow itself off the face of the earth.

The issue of <u>Newsweek</u> for January 22, 1990, contained a series of statements and comments relating to human destruction of a balanced world ecology. One of the comments read:

> "Today there are 5 billion of us, twice as many as in 1950; by 2040 we will number 10 billion. Within a decade, 23 cities will have more than 10 million people apiece. This burgeoning population is the single greatest threat to the health of the planet: the need for food and fuel causes deforestation and the spread of deserts, overcrowding pollutes air and water, megacities breed disease..."

If human beings fail to curb their destructive patterns of living, it would seem that Nature must take drastic steps to curb the upsetting element of humankind within its realm. Humankind is not any more exempt from inclusion on the lists of endangered or failed species in the history of Earth than the dinosaurs.

For those who believe that science and engineering can develop ultimate weapons to protect their countries from destruction by war, Babaji had these comments:

> "Countries which believe that they can save themselves through the newly invented weapons can forget this thought, for they will not be able to do so. Everyone knows of the present-day [1983] events taking place in Iran: no one had ever heard of the name of Khomeini before, and suddenly he captured everything he wanted."

"The flames of revolution are presently spreading in the world. There is no power which can stop the fire and reduce the heat. Super powers like Russia and America will not be able to face the 'fire'; even with their new weapons. Nothing that they have invented will be of any use. Everything can be destroyed."

There is no apparent escape from humankind's responsibility to learn to live in harmony with each other, with other forms of life on this earth, and with the Divine Order of the Creation. Individuals, groups, governments, and international organizations have finally begun to see and deal with the necessity of living and working in harmony with Nature. We need to be alert to the ways in which human thought and action influence and affect other elements of the Creation.

How can We Mitigate the Damage?

In September 1981, someone asked Shri Babaji how His devotees could help other people during this period of upheaval and change. Babaji replied that His devotees should spread the word of His presence and teachings; it was their foremost duty to tell the world of His message. People who were forewarned and alert might develop the courage, bravery, faith, detachment, love and respect for The Divine and Its Creation, and the willingness to help and serve others that are the requirements either for avoidance of the vast destruction of the "Revolution" or for survival and growth after it.

Babaji said that saints appear in the world according to the needs of the time, as the world situation demands, and, at the present time, there are many "God-men" throughout the world because of the great need for them.

On the evening of January 8, 1984, Shri Babaji prompted Amar Singh, line by line, in a speech which outlined how Babaji will 'direct' the Great Revolution.

"This is how Babaji will accomplish His work. In every place He will put one of His devotees and fill him with His Energy and, through him - making him an instrument of God's will - He will benefit the whole

251

area. Like this, the world will be saved.

"He puts His representatives everywhere and through them He works out His plan without Himself going anywhere.

"At the time of the battle of the Mahabharata, between the families of two brothers - the Kauravas and the Pandavas - it appeared to be a fight between cousins; but it was really a fight between Righteousness and Unrighteousness (Dharma and Adharma). At that time, God took the form of Lord Krishna and saved the world. He became the charioteer of Arjuna. He was seen as one who only handled Arjuna's chariot, but, in reality, He was directing all the fighting and inspiring all the warriors [on both sides]. Like that, Shri Mahaprabhuji is putting His energies into and through His disciples, sitting in the hearts of His chosen disciples, guiding them for the benefit of the whole world.

"Now we can compare these disciples with Arjuna. Actually, Baba is doing everything, making the disciples His instruments for the welfare of the whole world."

If human beings are so foolish and blind as to allow a widespread, violent Mahakranti to occur, in a "world turned upside down," where "nothing will remain the same," obviously survivors will need special talents and skills for continued life, growth, and the establishment of a higher society and culture.

"Only those will survive who have adventure in their hearts, those who are wed to the Truth. You should all go forward with courage and adventure. This is why you should proceed with your duty always foremost in your mind. To do karma is the true path and in that only is there happiness and peace."

"Wherever you live, be prepared to face the Revolution. Whatever occupation you might have, take part in the Revolution. Only that person can take part who is prepared to face death, who is prepared to die at any moment. Only the man who is daring and has courage, who is prepared to die for the sake of righteousness, is fit to face the Revolution."

"This is not the time for sleep. Awake family, friends, and country! Awake! Every man and woman in this world must *live*, be alert, not lazy like death. Work as much as possible and never be lethargic. All of you must become powerful and energetic and make others like that."

The Spiritual Revolution

All the time, interspersed in the talks and comments about the great physical upheavals in the physical, material world, there were hints and comments about the spiritual revolution which Shri Babaji came to foster and guide.

On one occasion, Babaji prompted Vishnu Dutt Shastriji to make the following remarks:

"Up to this time, many incarnations of the Lord have brought war and violence to bring peace to the world. He is now preparing your hearts for the coming revolution so you can face it peacefully. He has faith in no particular army; each human being is part of His 'army' and He will face atomic bombs and cannons with the power of the Word of God. On the one hand, certain countries are busy creating weapons and armaments; and on the other hand, Babaji is nullifying these by having people loudly repeat the Word of God, bringing spiritual change.

"In the eyes of God, no one is big or small. In every heart, the consciousness there is His Reflection. In a short time, He is going to destroy the bad elements and then change the Revolution into peace."[4]

Again, Shastriji, prompted by Shri Babaji, offered these comments on Babaji's mission:

"Babaji has come to change the world - not by

fighting or with weapons and armaments. He transforms by changing the hearts of people through a simple method - repetition of God's Holy Name. The vibrations of the Name will change the world. There will be universal understanding - one nation, one family. This is Babaji's intent and it will soon come about.

"Great armaments have been made which can destroy humanity and most of the earth. But there is a greater protection sitting before us and He has given a means of protection more powerful than the atomic bomb. Those who want to kill will be destroyed. *You* must concentrate on the Name of God and the instructions that Babaji has given you. Repeat 'Om Namah Shivaya' and you will receive Babaji's blessings."[5]

Shri Babaji emphasized the need for revolutionary spiritual change in order to create a world in which peace - within the individual and throughout society - can flourish. The alternative to this peace is violence, or 'fire.'

"In the world today 'fire' is bursting out on one side, while nectar flows on the other. You must decide if you choose 'fire' or nectar. While flames of the fire are spreading, it is up to us to save ourselves and others. We must be alert.

"At this moment, people are jumping into the fire because of their ignorance. We must save these people, and we can do so only if we have great courage. We should give this courage to others, as nothing can be accomplished without it. Courage is the most important thing. Shri Mahaprabhuji has told you many times to wake up. Wake up yourselves and others! Control your mind and have firm determination.

"All must be prepared for this Revolution... Whether young or old, private or public, those working or not - *all* must take part. It is devotion, love, and yoga for you to save the world and join in [this] Revolution. For those who are true devotees of Babaji, the flames of this fire will become cool. Face the fire and it will turn to ice! This requires control of mind and a firm determination.

"Everyone must consider himself a soldier and be active. Everyone will have to face the fire."

"With people going their own ways and conflicting with each other, it seems that a time of great crisis is very near. The world needs change from its roots upwards. Oh, My children! Youth of the world! Be brave and courageous and be prepared to face life as it comes, because as long as there is no fundamental 'root change' in the world there can be no improvement.

"You have to be strong and capable of facing these coming difficult times. O, youth! Remove all differences from your minds and unite like one great chain. We have to do good, not bad, for the whole world. You have to gather your courage, leave behind the fear of death to face life with hope and courage. Forget profit and loss; do not be concerned for praise or abuse; march on! You will have to walk through the blazing fire; only then can this world be saved."

"There is only one way for mankind to be saved and that is by changing the hearts of all people. Shri Mahaprabhuji will give His full spiritual power to this, but every man and woman will also have to make their best efforts toward this end. As long as there is no change of heart, humanity is in great danger."

Although Shri Babaji made it clear that these changes must take place in each individual, that the decisions and struggles - and the Revolution itself - are inner actions in each person's heart and mind, the reflection and 'proof' of these individual changes are seen in the individual's interactions and relationships with all the rest of Creation - and particularly in our relationships with "Mother Earth" and with other human beings. Babaji often exhorted His devotees to work in unity and harmony with others, on a grand scale.

"Awake! Arise! *Everybody* must make a firm resolve. Men and women from all over the world must take part. In other Ages, only men took part in revolutions and wars, but now women are coming forward, so it is necessary for them, too, to take part in this Revolution. Everybody must make contacts on all sides of the world and unite together."

"You must all step together and form a great international organization - bigger than anything organized in the history of the world. I do not want you all to be ruined or destroyed. A great revolution is going to take place, such as has never before occurred in the world. The hearts of people who read or hear of this Revolution will melt. This is an era of great destruction; no other time can be compared to this. The Revolution will last not for minutes but only for some seconds. The countries which have invented these destructive weapons will themselves be destroyed; they should not think they are secure. Only he who has surrendered completely at the feet of God is secure..."

Some Comments about After the Revolution

In the spring of 1982, I went to Shri Babaji and asked Him for guidance and understanding in using the prophesies. He told me to talk to Vishnu Dutt Shastriji about them. For the most part, Shastriji's statements, which he checked against a notebook on the subject that he kept, corroborated the quotations above. He emphasized that he (Shastriji) expected the period of upheaval to last through 1988,[6] after which the "lull" of which Baba spoke would begin, to be followed by a spreading peace.

I asked Shastriji about predictions of what may come after the "Revolution." He said that, with the purging of the treacherous, untruthful, insatiably desirous and violent elements of mankind, the 'remnant' would be those who had achieved a higher spiritual level through the challenges and testing of the Mahakranti. These people will be living in a world society where loving, truthful thoughts and actions will not be overwhelmed by the vibrations and actions stimulated by greed, fear, hate, lust, and the other desires and attachments of lower human nature. In these circumstances, spiritual growth will be easier and more and more people will rise to the level which until now has only occasionally been attained by spiritually advanced people: powers to heal, read minds, change forms, be in more than one body in different locations, to materialize objects, to know anything; and a host of other 'powers.' People will still be human beings with freedom of will to make 'poor' choices and decisions as well as 'good' choices, but the culture and society in which they live will tend to support spiritual growth and uplift people, instead of nurturing the baser human natures.

Somewhere about 1990 (Babaji gave no date), after the wars have ceased, Shastriji said that Babaji stated an <u>avatar</u> will appear - or be recognized - at that time. This avatar will be a many-faceted person with knowledge of all areas of life, a very high spiritual being, who will be an earthly ruler. In the tradition of the ancient scriptures and mythology, the avatar would rule over the entire earth as one nation, restoring peace, harmony, righteousness, justice, and joy to all people on a level beyond our present imagination. Like King Janaka, he would rule with his mind focused on God and his duty. Business and industry would be organized on a cooperative basis; people will be free - and encouraged - to develop to their fullest spiritual, intellectual, and creative capacities.

I was told that Shri Babaji would also return (His departure in the 1980's was anticipated) in a human form at some unstated but near date and be a spiritual adviser to the world. Shri Babaji did not say a great deal about the Age of Truth (Satyayuga) which is to follow the Great Upheaval; His focus was on His teaching mission; but He did tell Mahendra Maharaj, Shastriji, and others that He will be present in a physical form to inaugurate the Golden Age.

Shri Babaji made only one specific, public reference to the future period in His printed talks. In August 1983, He made this comment:

"Nature and the elements are now in our favor.
Whenever you will *face* a challenge, you will win it.
Now the sounds of victory can already be heard.

257

"The kingdom that will come now will be a religious kingdom. There will be high morals. At every crossroads, bells will be hung, and if anyone is in trouble, he may go and ring them, and he will receive justice.

"I will root out all fear from the world. I will give the boon of fearlessness to all. I will stop the use of weapons. The disarmament campaign will be greatly strengthened. World leaders are now only *talking* about this, but I will *show* you disarmament in practice... In the Name of the Lord, advance!"

The Revolution as a Purifier - a Force for Change and Growth

Shri Babaji often spoke of His desire to create a world of practical human beings - intelligent, rational, spiritually developed people not limited or enslaved by their lower natures. His concept of the "Revolution" and the changes it will bring about are 'practical' and rational.

Although the Mahakranti did not take place in the 1980's, as Babaji predicted, it does not take a seer or an intellectual giant to see where present human desires for material gain and wealth and national policies based on them are leading. Armaments are not manufactured to rust through disuse and even within the major military alliances and in the non-aligned 'Third World' the forces of competition and disunity could explode into <u>Mahakranti</u> at any time. For decades the political and economic world has been sowing the seeds of competition, dominance, jealousy, hatred and disharmony and polluting and destroying the world around us. Our societies create higher aspirations for *material* things and the satisfaction of all human desires; our economies thrive only by stimulating new, unfulfilled desires among people. There is no possibility of fulfilling all desires because the material desires spawn more desires in an endless progression. There has been little evidence of corporate, governmental, or even much individual concern for "Mother Earth" and the delicate balance of Nature until very recently. The relentless search for 'more and better' leads inevitably to greed, jealousy, competition, hatred, aggression, and to pollution and destruction of the Earth and its atmosphere.

When this happens on a world-wide scale, Mahakranti follows. Sooner or later, the majority of people - who number among themselves those who are harmed, exploited, oppressed, persecuted, and the helpless, non-combatant victims of both economic and military wars - will call a halt to the system which creates and sustains such widespread damage, injustice and unrighteousness; or the forces of disunity and aggression put into motion by the exploiters and oppressors will get out of hand. This has already happened in Eastern Europe and elsewhere. One way or another, Shri Babaji - as the Lord of Change, or Destruction - saw that the present system will - must! - crumble and make way for needed changes.

If the change comes violently, as Shri Babaji predicted, it will require the survivors of destruction to develop the qualities which Babaji has emphasized are necessary for spiritual growth. The material objects on which the present society is based and focused would be largely destroyed; how can people be 'attached' to objects they no longer possess or can acquire? The production of food and restoration to any widespread degree of water supplies, transportation and communication, commerce and industry will require unity and cooperation to a degree not known before. If people do not learn to live courageously and work together in Truth, Simplicity and Love, they may simply not survive.

The Mahakranti has all the elements of Shri Babaji's system of teaching. God has given mankind many, many teachings and examples of how to live happily and harmoniously on this earth. When we fail to heed the lessons and learn from the experiences The Divine gives to us, it puts us into a heavier 'learning situation'; and if we refuse to move then, we feel the staff on us. The Mahakranti may be seen as God's wielding of His staff in a world which pays little heed to the lessons He sends, or as the inexorable operation of the Law of Karma on a world-wide basis.

In August 1983, Shri Babaji, talking with an American reporter, said:

"My message will reach into the depths of the sea and into the heights of the sky. All modern weapons, atom bombs, and arms are ineffective against Mahaprabhuji's message and power. The Message that came from a cave in the Himalayas has now come out into the world at large."

A month later, He spoke again about 'broadcasting' His Message.

"The fact is Our radio communication is weak. The sound is very feeble. The 'radio' has to be beamed to many places and the transmission is difficult; 'radios' are not receiving up to their full capacity because today the news has to be broadcast throughout the whole universe. This broadcast is being transmitted to every single being in this Creation - to each one of the 8,400,000 existing species. Due to the fact that the sound waves have to reach every distant corner of the universe, reception is somewhat weak.

"Not only is Man in danger, but every one of the 8,400,000 species, as well, and the sound of the 'radio' has to reach every single one of them.

"This is where the radio's transmission ends today.

"Sabka kalian ho! May all beings be liberated!"

In His tenderness and love for mankind, Babaji - who seems to have predicted the physical Mahakranti from a knowledge that it is the result and harvest of humanity's present heavy load of 'bad' karma - gave a final hint that even now this fate can be averted or abated. In His last speech to His devotees in Haidakhan, on February 4, 1984, Shri Babaji made this comment:

"All the great sages, saints, yogis and sanyasis that the world has seen and all the Messengers of God have achieved all that they did through hard work and karma yoga. Through Karma Yoga they changed Nature itself. Therefore, you must never be disappointed in life and you must remember that what even God cannot achieve, *you* can achieve through hard work. **Karma yoga is a thing which can even change the course laid down by God."**

"The Messenger of Revolution has come!"

NOTES

1   See page 98-99.
2   "Baba Ji:" by Dr. V. V.S. Rao, pages 67 and 68; or by K.L. Jand, pages 114 and 115.
3   For a similar, but more detailed picture of a 1990's Mahakranti scenario see the chapter entitled "Tomorrow - A Changed World" in Mary Summer Rain's book, "Spirit Song: The Visionary Wisdom of No-Eyes."
4   "Teachings of Babaji," 1983 edition, page 20; 2004 edition, page 31.
5   Ibid., pages 30-31; 2004 edition, page 41.
6   A young Italian devotee given the name Ram Lota told me that one day in 1982, when he and Gaura Devi were sitting with Baba-ji, Babaji told them that the Mahakranti would begin the next time India and Pakistan went to war.

"I have set before you life and death,
blessing and curse; therefore, choose life,
that you and your descendants may live."
Deuteronomy: 30:19.

"Go in through the narrow gate;
because broad and spacious is the road leading off into destruction,
and many are the ones going through it;
whereas narrow is the gate and cramped the road leading off into life,
and few are the ones finding it."
Jesus: Matthew 7: 13 and 14.

"Can he who follows the guidance of his Lord be compared to him who is led
by his appetites and whose foul deeds seem fair to him?"
The Koran

CHAPTER XII

BABAJI SHOWS A PATH TO
GOD-REALIZATION

Babaji's Mission

According to Mahendra Maharaj, writing more than a decade before Shri Babaji's return to the Haidakhan Ashram in 1970, Babaji explained His mission in this manifestation in the following terms:

"...I have decided to go into the human world - go to each person and remove his ties of sorrow. I have to teach them how to stay detached even [while] completely attached to day-to-day life."

"The basic work would be to change the hearts; only then would all living beings obtain happiness. Hence my most important work would be to change the hearts and minds of men."[1]

Babaji's actions and His oral teachings during His thirteen-year mission give validity to this forecast. His example and His teachings on jap, karma yoga, worship and self-discipline were aids in developing love in the human heart and a sense of harmony and unity in serving all living beings. These are means of changing and elevating the basic character of humanity. The changes in human hearts and minds come about in the individual through slow, steady growth which overturns the embedded patterns of thought and action. By constant, long practice, a person can develop a spirit, or character, that spontaneously responds to events in a manner which is in harmony with Divine Will and with all of Creation. Babaji offered a number of self-disciplines to encourage and develop this spirit.

"Now everyone feels insecure. I want to raise the character of man so high that people as different as the lion and the goat can live together without jealousy or hatred - only in love.

"Kindle the Light in yourself, then kindle It in others - one by one. Just as when the lamp burns it consumes oil, so this Light will consume idleness, laziness and greed.

"Your duty is to spread My message and bring
people to the level of humanity, rather than their animal level....

"Like spreading a light by lighting one candle
from another all around a room, so we should spread
love from heart to heart."[2]

Vishnu Dutt Shastriji commented one day, "Two traits which
Shri Babaji dislikes in people are acting like sheep, one blindly running after the other, and deceitfulness or cunning." Both traits are
opposites of the Truth which Babaji and Mahendra Baba taught and
exemplified. And, through Shastriji, Shri Babaji gave the advice of
two ancient mantras which offer an antidote to these ruinous traits.
"He who has control over himself will succeed in life." This is the
method by which one can live a fulfilling life and find the way to
God-realization. And where to find it? "Awake! Arise! Go to the wise
and learn from them."

"Nothing Can Be Achieved Without Discipline"

Babaji placed great emphasis on self-control and discipline.

"You must have perfect control over your self
and a firm determination. You must not be shaken
from your determination, even at the time of total dissolution of the world. One who is firm in his determination can change the whole world."

"Nothing can be achieved without discipline.
You should have the strong discipline of a soldier. Be a
soldier of God, and act with courage and discipline."

Discipline and courage are essential to this process because
the Path is very difficult to follow. There are far more enticements in
modern life to leave the Path than there are to follow it. Babaji commented on the strength required for this journey in these terms:

"...you must resolve in your hearts to be industri-
ous and courageous. Those who are strong like iron are
fit to flourish. To become strong does not mean to become

264

harsh and heartless; to become strong means to grow beyond pleasure and pain, beyond heat and cold."

The strength Babaji sought to instill was the strength of character lauded in all the ancient scriptures - a willingness to face Truth,
an inner discipline, strength of will which is not shaken by offers or
threats of pleasure or pain, not deflected or 'ruled' by desires or fears.
To practice or to build this strength, Babaji advised devotees, "Learn
not to make projects and fantasies about your future. Forget your past
and old habits. Learn how to concentrate your mind on the Divine
only - here and now."

Although Shri Babaji has an earned reputation for helping
people attain their material desires, what He *taught*, by example, by
His speech, through the routine of ashram life, and by His interactions with people, was discipline and 'purification,' or the strengthening of the individuals' bodies, hearts and minds. The body was
disciplined and strengthened by early rising, learning to endure cold
winter morning baths in the river and the heat of working in the summer sun, controlling hunger and thirst, controlling desires and rising above physical pleasure and pain. The mind was given practice
in self-control through prayer, singing, jap (either silent or chanting
together), meditation; and through mind-shaking experiences whenever a devotee got 'stuck' in fears, desires, or complacency. The heart
was purified through worship, service to others, devotion to and love
for God in many forms, but especially for the living manifestation of
God whom we could relate to as Babaji.

Too Many Desires

These teachings are in harmony with the ancient Indian scriptures, but Babaji, focused on modern man's situation, suggested a
slight change in the devotee's practice from what the ancient scriptures taught.

"In this Age it is not possible to renounce the
world. The only practice of renunciation now is to offer
all work and actions to God. If you want God, be ready
to devote *everything* to God."

Babaji gave this teaching to people in different ways. Shdema Goodman, the Israeli-born American psychologist whom we in the ashram knew as Shivani, reported this experience with Babaji.

"It was...during my second visit to Babaji that I suddenly felt that I was crazy to be there, so far away from home, away from my husband, my son, my work, my style of life, etc. I was out in the jungle with snakes and with worms in my stool. I had insects biting me all night long. It was hot. I wondered, am I a masochist or what? What did I need all of this for? So I decided to ask Babaji specifically what it was that he could teach me. I thought to myself that if he could teach me tele-portation, then it would be worth my while to endure the suffering.

"I gathered courage, for it had been recom-mended to me to never ask him for anything. I had been told that he knows exactly what I need and that he would supply me with the appropriate teachings at the right time. Still, I asked him, 'What can you teach me and can I learn teleportation?'

"He answered, 'I can teach you how to be si-lent and how to obey my orders. You talk too much. I don't like people who talk too much... You can leave tomorrow.'

"So, I had to leave the next day. A part of me was happy and a part was sad. I packed my luggage and was ready to leave. As I sat on the steps waiting for my horse, after I had said goodbye to everyone, I closed my eyes and started to question myself, 'Where did I go wrong?' In my mind, I posed my question to Babaji and asked him again, 'Where did I go wrong? What did I do? All I asked was whether you could teach me teleportation.'

"What I heard in my mind was, 'You have too many desires.' Aha! So that's what it was, I thought. Okay, I was willing to let go of all my desires. I tuned inward to make sure that I meant it and I saw a few desires here and there that I did not think I could let go. I started repeating silently in my mind that I was now truly willing to give up all my desires. To make sure that I really meant it, I repeated it again with my name. 'I, Shdema, Shivani, am now willing (I relaxed into the willing part, letting go of all tension or holding on anywhere inside my body) to give up all of my desires.' I felt that I was sincere. I opened my eyes and saw Babaji standing right next to me. He told me, 'You can stay.' I smiled and took my luggage back to my room."[3]

"Don't Waste Anything"

Babaji did not like idle speech any more than idleness of any other kind. "Talk less, work more" was one of His mottos. Another time He said, "Speak as little as possible. Don't waste your time. Be concentrated all of the time on the Lord's Name."

He was against waste of any kind. "Concentrate energy, conserve it. Don't waste anything; use it only when needed."

Babaji pushed hard to get electricity brought up the valley and into Haidakhan village and the ashram. When it came, in 1983, He had lights installed in many open places where there were stairs or changes in levels in the ashram walkways and in other public areas. Lights in these places were kept on all through the night for safety reasons. After the dawn hawan ceremony outside His room, Babaji often sat alone on the porch outside His bathroom, where He could see much of the ashram, and as the morning light became brighter He would shout across the ashram to tell passers-by to turn off the lights. He did not like to see water taps left running, and He shouted at people who took too much food on their plates and threw it away. Waste of any kind was abhorrent to Shri Babaji.

Another waste Babaji spoke against was the use of drugs. "Drugs are harmful and useless for any spiritual practice." One evening He spoke specifically to the Italian devotees present, but the message was for all.

267

"Don't use intoxicating drugs, but learn from Gaura Devi's devotion and purity. Why do you travel so far from your home, only to lose yourself in drugs? It is strictly forbidden to use drugs and you must leave if you do so, *because there is no progress; you remain the same.*"

People learn through physical and emotional pain and sorrow as much as they learn through pleasure and success; we learn most when we are confronted by obstacles and challenges. When nerves and emotions and brains are dulled by drugs or alcohol it is difficult to face problems and easy to avoid them; there is little or no discipline in the user. Time and life are wasted. After one exhortation against drugs and drug-users, Babaji concluded:

"Everyone here is a soldier of Haidakhan. Be dutiful for the sake of duty. Be prepared to make sacrifices. Do not fear the floods and flames of life. Be alert and prepared to face changes. The time has come! Do you understand? Be alert!"

Despite His strong teachings against the use of drugs, and despite the fact that the ashram rules, printed at Babaji's instructions, forbade the purchase, sale, possession or use of <u>charas</u>, the common local form of marijuana, Babaji Himself used to buy it from the valley dwellers and give it, by the kilo, half kilo, or piece, to devotees who wanted it. After all, He is Lord Shiva, who grants the wishes of His devotees; and, as the Sadguru [True Guru], He has the responsibility of making people aware of their problems and shortcomings and helping them through the confrontations with Truth. Rather understandably, there was confusion as to what Babaji really meant.

During one of Shri Babaji's trips away from Haidakhan, in a moment of comparative quiet, He called into His room two foreign devotees whom He knew used charas. Through an interpreter, Babaji talked to them as a father to his sons. He told the young men that many temptations would come in their lives and that a man becomes a real man when he can recognize the temptations and avoid them. He asked if they used charas, and they acknowledged that 'sometimes' they did. Babaji told them this is a very bad thing and that they

268

should not indulge in it. He said He expected them to give it up. They responded, "Yes, yes."

In the afternoon, the two young men were sitting outside of Babaji's room talking about the morning's conversation. They asked the interpreter to clarify what had been said. It was repeated to them and they responded that this was one of Babaji's leelas: He *speaks* against charas, but He *gives* it to us.

After the evening aarati and darshan, Babaji talked to the young men again. He told them that He did not like anyone to take any kind of intoxicants or drugs. "I don't like addicts. Even if I give it to you, you should not use it." The interpreter told Babaji that they were confused by the fact that He gave them, and others, these things. Babaji's response was, "It is a test. Even if I give it, they should not use it."

The next day, Babaji gave them a half kilo of charas and said, "Smoke it." And they took the charas and smoked it.

Another wasteful act that pained Babaji was suicide, the intentional taking of one's own life because the person does not want to face a current situation. Among the basic beliefs of the Sanatan Dharma is the concept that lifetimes in human form are not easily attained and that they are granted for the purpose of the growth of the soul. The beginning and the end of human lifetimes are in the hands of The Divine. For an individual to bring a God-given life to a premature end is to defy God and waste the full learning opportunities of life. This is not to say that a person should not risk or even give his or her life to help or to save another person. Babaji often told us to "go beyond the fear of death and the hope of life." But to consciously put an end to one's life out of fear or lack of courage is abhorrent to The Divine.

Changing Hearts through Experiences

Babaji exposed people to the experiences they needed in order to work through problems and develop inner discipline. He would throw angry people together, let them explode in fury at each other; and if they failed to learn to control their tempers at that level, He let them taste His anger - and their anger directed at Him. To those with

269

over-strong or uncontrolled desires for drugs, alcohol, sex, money, whatever, He could either allow them to indulge themselves to the point of stimulating their own desire to control the urge or He could put them into situations where they were unable to gratify their desires and had to learn to control them.

As the Divine Psychologist, Shri Babaji charged into His devotees' failings and weaknesses and threw them in their faces until they could not fail to recognize them. He worked hard and constantly at exposing people to themselves so that they could pull away from their false, limited, unnecessary identifications of themselves. He had told Mahendra Maharaj that He would come to remove mankind's "ties of sorrow," which are the attachments and desires which cause our worries, our pains and sufferings. This He did by helping people rise above the desires and fears which constrain them and keep them from realizing the freedom, peace and happiness that humankind is meant to attain and enjoy.

Babaji did this at no small cost to Himself. His constant activity in serving His devotees was a physical strain on His human body. He literally absorbed much of the heavy karmas of His devotees; He acted, on behalf of His devotees, in ways which brought criticism to Himself, and He rarely bothered to defend His actions or His reputation. He kept His equanimity in situations which would infuriate or disgust most people. For His devotees, in a world in which the general moral and spiritual level of people has sunk low, He descended into the whirlpool of human emotions and activities in order to mirror people to themselves. There are some devotees who feel that this 'descent' cost Shri Babaji some of His 'siddhi' powers; some who think it hastened the end of His 'life'. Whatever the cost to Him was, Babaji did not spare Himself in His service to others, as He did not spare those who sincerely sought His guidance and training on the Path to God-realization.

"This," He said, "more than others, is an Age of great destruction. Man has become enslaved by his lower nature. I do not belong to any particular religion, but respect all religions. I seek the elevation of all mankind. The higher self in people must be developed

270

and enthrallment with the lower nature destroyed. It will be destroyed in countries all around the world by changing the hearts of mankind. Do you understand?

"Now that you understand, you must live in Truth, Simplicity and Love, and take this message into the world."

On Sex and Marriage

Because attachment to sex and its pleasures is so strong in humankind, so difficult to control, it played a large part in Shri Babaji's teachings -not so much in speech as in the experiences to which He guided His devotees, who, like any other cross section of people, were frequently involved in sexual thoughts, desires and activities on one level or another. One of the few statements He made concerning sex was.

"In this Kali Yuga (Dark Age), almost no one has the strength to remain celibate. Although this is the best condition, marriage is better than undisciplined relations. Union between a man and woman with love can bring peace and help in spiritual practice."

Vishnu Dutt Shastriji, speaking for Shri Babaji prior to a wedding at Haidakhan, said, "Marriage is of great importance in one's life. This relationship may last for centuries. In marriage, two souls coming from different places unite through an inner inspiration."[4] Marriage is an opportunity to develop the unity, harmony, and sense of duty and service which are essential elements of the humanitarianism which Babaji taught. A couple can work through their sexual desires, have and raise children, and live together as caring, sharing friends, helping each other to grow in creativity and spirituality, outgrowing the lower human nature. But marriage is also an 'opportunity' to fall deeply into sexuality and attachment, and this may be a reason for Babaji's (and St. Paul's} indication that celibacy is better for the devoted seeker of God than marriage. However, at least from Babaji's initiation of Shri Lahiri Mahasaya into kriya yoga in 1861, on through this last manifestation, He has concentrated His teachings on 'householders' - married people with family and business responsibilities.

271

Lahiri Mahasaya, the father of several children, became a great saint with many 'siddhis' (spiritual powers)[5]; but within his marriage, after his initiation, he learned to practice celibacy.

Babaji, completely in harmony with the ancient teachings and traditions, encouraged people to marry, have children, provide for them, and, in this process, to learn detachment from sexual desire, as one element in learning to control and rise above *all* desires, which is a prerequisite for the highest experiences of The Divine. There is a tradition within the Sanatan Dharma that the saint or enlightened person who has followed the path of the householder and has experienced and mastered all the desires of normal life on his or her pathway to God-realization has achieved more than the 'renunciate' who has mastered his attachments to the desires and pleasures of life in a cave in the Himalayas, far away from the 'material world.' The ancient rishis (master teachers} often had more than one wife and many children. Both ways have led people to enlightenment - and both paths are very difficult to tread, requiring a strong inner discipline.

Gaura Devi once asked Shri Babaji about tantric teachings and practices regarding sex, which, at least in theory, use sex to teach detachment from sexual pleasures. She says His response was that these sexual practices are just lower temptations along the path; that *attachment* to sex, by whatever name, is a major hurdle on the path to enlightenment. It is more than a little difficult to maintain one's focus on The Divine while engaging in sexual activities or fantasies. However, when people were not ready for celibacy, when they were still caught up in sexual desires, Babaji guided them into situations where they could satisfy that desire. Although He did not - so far as I can find - enunciate this practice, He appeared to urge (in some cases, require) people to attain their major desires fully before they sought to 'detach' themselves from desires. There are few, indeed, who can learn to rise above a desire without experience of its satisfaction.

Once someone asked Babaji, "How can I put together my love for my girlfriend and my love for God?" Babaji's reply was, "You can concentrate first on the love for the girlfriend and, when you are satisfied, then come to God."

The ancient Indian scriptures are not 'sexist;' they describe

272

Absolute God as being without form and without sex; and, among the 'physical' manifestations which they describe, the female forms are as powerful and important as the male forms. In fact, as noted before, the female aspect of God (and the gods) is the active, creative Force of God, without which the 'male' aspect is inert and useless. The Divine Mother is worshipped in many forms, in many scriptures and cultures. The human women in the scriptural tales were in no way lesser creatures than the men.

Women coming to the ashram from the West of the 'liberated' woman were often shaken by what they saw as the position of women in the Uttar Pradesh countryside. To many Western women, the ashram requirement that women wear a saree (a really beautiful garment when properly worn) and, particularly, the age-old requirement that during menstruation women must stay away from the kitchen, the temples, and from holy men (including Shri Babaji) seemed to be an unnecessary and demeaning discrimination against women. Some Western women, not knowing the sensible underlying cultural reasons for these requirements (like giving the hard-working women three or four days of rest in a month) initially considered the ashram a 'sexist,' male-dominated community.

One young American woman once asked Shri Babaji, "What is the difference between man and woman?" Babaji replied, "There is NO difference!" He explained that both men and women have male and female 'energies' in them; only the form is different; there is no generic difference that makes one superior or inferior to the other. They are, after all, in His view, created from the same substance' and energy of God; each 'houses' a soul which is one with God; each has its duty which is essential to society, civilization and the continuance of life itself.

Although Babaji could read people's minds, He did not manipulate minds. He would lead people into situations, but it was up to the disciple to learn the lessons from the experiences. Although the rule of the ashram was celibacy, Babaji steered many people into the sexual experiences they desired (or needed), apparently with the hope that they would learn that the experience and pleasure of sex is fleeting, impermanent, and not worth being 'attached to,' 'ruled by,' or addicted to. Almost all people who were involved in some sort of sexual <u>leela</u> and discussed it with others came to the conclusion that Shri Babaji was teaching them to rise above sexual desire (not necessarily to renounce sex for procreation or as a means of giving expression to love within a marriage relationship), so they might be freed from this strong attachment to the lower human nature that impedes progress on the path to God-realization.

One young man who was not yet ready for celibacy was sent by Babaji on a business trip to Bangkok. When he returned from Thailand, he found Babaji in Vrindaban for a celebration. After the celebration was over, Babaji told the young man to return to Haidakhan with Him. The young man, hesitantly and sheepishly, told Babaji that he needed to go to Delhi and get some medical treatment because he had contracted a 'social disease' while in Bangkok. Babaji laughed and said, "I *like* your problems! Do not go to Delhi, but come with Me to Haidakhan; you will be all right." With some concern, the young man went with Babaji's party straight back to Haidakhan and, within a few days, the symptoms disappeared. He had been thrown into an experience he desired; it had caused a foreseeable problem; and he had learned something from his experience. Step by step, he went on learning and growing through his experiences.

Babaji continued to nudge and push people as they progressed along the Path. The 'yogis' (renunciates who seek God-realization in 'this' lifetime) from abroad found it very difficult to rise above sexuality. Some yogis (as well as other devotees) were married at Babaji's direction and were surprised to experience pressures in their marriages as Babaji continued to teach them renunciation and detachment. Marriage is fine for the 'householder,' but yogis, by tradition, are those who renounce *all* attachments and desires.

In one case of a marriage of a yogi and yogini, a month or so after Babaji married the couple, He spoke to them privately, scolded them gently, and told them to stop living together. He told them, "When I come to this world, I always come to give divine nectar, but people always choose poison." When the baffled groom protested that Babaji had married them Himself, Baba replied, "Yes! But that was My *test!*"

274

On an earlier occasion, Babaji had said, "If you want God, be ready to devote *everything* to God;" and for the yogin or yogini that is the standard. The person who seeks unity with God must leave behind personal, physical, ego-born desires and devote everything to God, serving God by serving all God's creatures. Desires for wealth, sex, success, material objects - even desire for enlightenment - break one's focus on God; *any* desire forms a blockage between the devotee and God.

During a spiritual discussion, someone asked Vishnu Dutt Shastriji a question about renunciation. "I heard that Lord Shiva is a God who is easily pleased, but also considered a very hard one. What do you think about that?"

Shastriji replied:

"Lord Shiva is truly the one who is easily pleased with His devotees, but on the other hand, He requires that people who want to become His *disciples* give up everything, as He has given up everything. This is necessary because we must become like the Guru we have chosen as our own.

"To give up everything is not so easy, because it doesn't mean giving up material things only. It actually means giving up the ego and the sense of 'I' in whatever action we perform."[6]

One day, on the porch outside His room, Babaji sang a hill song to Gaura Devi, the words of which translate to: "I gave you the highest Path - the Path of Yoga. Don't look back; don't look around. Don't look to what man and woman do together; that is the path which leads to hell."

Shri Babaji was very concerned with today's heavy focus on sex as a 'recreation,' as a goal in itself, as an overpowering desire and distraction to society. In the last weeks of His ministry, Babaji commented, in the quiet of His quarters, that the Western world, especially, had to learn to control sexual desires, impulses, and activity. To Gaura Devi, in this same period, He remarked bitterly, in pithy Hill dialect, referring to human beings in general, "They are *all* fornicators! They don't know how to do anything but that!"

Ashram Life as a Stimulus to Change and Growth

The schedule and style of life at the Haidakhan Ashram were established and maintained by Babaji to help people break old patterns of living, establish a new focus on The Divine, and to establish new patterns of living which foster the self-discipline and spiritual growth of the person who seeks God-realization, or a life lived fully in harmony and unity with The Divine. This kind of life, on a permanent basis, is not for everyone; in fact, Babaji (like Krishna in the <u>Bhagavad Gita</u>) suggested that perhaps one person in a million might seek this kind of life. But the lifestyle and the rules of the Ashram offer some guidelines or suggestions for people who, as householders, would like to break their current patterns and bring their lives into greater harmony with the divine order of the Creation. An ashram can be a good place of 'retreat' for the person who wants to experience this pattern of life, as a help in breaking old patterns of daily life.

The first rule of the day at the Ashram was to arise early and take a bath in the river and dress in clean clothes before aarati, which was performed at dawn. If you had a personal program of meditation or yoga asanas in your schedule, that, too, should be done before aarati; Babaji said the best time for meditation was the hours between 2 and 4 a.m. Early rising combated the laziness or lethargy so abhorrent to Babaji, and the 'bath facilities' and the simple clothing worn at the ashram promoted the simplicity that Babaji urged His followers to observe in their lives. After aarati, a few minutes were allowed for a quick, simple breakfast or snack from the village teahouses for those who felt a morning meal was necessary. Everyone then went to perform karma yoga - either to a previously-assigned regular duty, such as preparing the ashram's noon meal or working in the office - or to the major work project of the day. This might be digging out the hillside to form the garden of the nine temples, preparing the "Company Garden" at the foot of the "108 Steps," constructing a new building, creating stone-and-log bridges across the streams that run through the wide riverbed in the dry seasons, or whatever Babaji made the main task of the day. The work was some useful contribution to the activities or facilities of the ashram, which was to be performed while one kept the preferred mantra running through his or her mind.

We broke our work before noon to wash and gather together for a communal meal of vegetarian foods which first had been offered to The Divine at the temple. Food was put on a plate (either a plate of leaves sewn together or of stainless steel) by ashram servers from buckets of food and no one ate until all were served. You could have as much food as you cared to eat, but you were expected to eat all that was put on your plate; Babaji detested waste of food. When your meal was finished, leaf plates were thrown where the cattle could eat them; metal plates were cleaned by the users and returned immediately. After the meal, there was a rest period which, in the heat of the summer, might extend until 2:30 or 3 o'clock, when work began again. Most people used this rest time to take their afternoon baths - a requirement before the evening aarati - and wash their clothes and dry them on the rocks in the hot sun.

The afternoon work generally went on until shortly before sunset, when time was given to wash up before the evening aarati, which started at about sundown. On rare occasions, like cement pours, activity continued until 10:30 or 11 at night. The aarati itself took about an hour. Near the end of the service, Babaji came to the kirtan hall to give darshan. Usually for an hour, or sometimes two hours, Babaji sat with us, directing the singing of kirtan and bhajans, sometimes giving a little talk, giving valley residents or visitors an opportunity to perform their songs and dances, letting others give little talks, sharing gifts of food with everyone, and occasionally Babaji had private talks with people as the group sang songs. It was an informal, usually lively and happy time, spent in the presence of Divinity. It was also a busy time, on inner levels; many people, sitting in Babaji's presence, had powerful inner spiritual experiences. When Babaji got up from His asan and left the kirtan hall, a few people went to the door outside His quarters to wish Him a good night and to be blessed, and all went to their rooms for the night - or to sit outside their rooms to watch the stars (and sometimes the divine lights[7] on Mount Kailash) and talk quietly before bed.

The schedule and discipline of daily life in the ashram promoted the qualities which Babaji asked His followers to observe for their spiritual growth. The performance of karma yoga while repeating a mantra was the leading activity of the day; our work was not personally centered or for personal enrichment, but performed for the well-being of the community. Jap and the many hours spent in Babaji's presence kept the mind focused on The Divine. The rules of the ashram prescribed cleanliness of person and belongings (our rooms were to be cleaned daily, and Babaji often popped in to visit and inspect), a simple lifestyle, and celibacy (while resident in the ashram) to keep mind and body focused away from the 'lower nature' and on The Divine. The lives lived in this atmosphere and on this schedule were changed and the Ashram had a power and vibration of its own. One morning at Babaji's darshan, He said of this situation:

> "You have come here for spiritual growth. Try to make spiritual progress. Spend your time here doing bhajans, meditation, kirtan and service.
>
> "The peaceful vibration of Haidakhan must be preserved. Do not disturb the peaceful vibrations of the ashram by wrong actions. Mahaprabhuji is very strict about this. Those who disturb the peace of the ashram must leave.
>
> "Those who come to Haidakhan must cooperate in maintaining the harmony of the ashram. They must participate in the aarati and in all the activities."

Babaji supervised and supported the construction of several ashrams in India and encouraged foreign devotees to return to their countries and create ashrams. In January 1984, Babaji said, "In the near future, all of you will establish ashrams and centers throughout the world and do Karma Yoga there and create the same vibrations wherever you go." He told us: "As there are islands in the sea, you should make ashrams in the ocean of the material world." And He told us, "In this ashram and in the ashrams abroad, discipline is the primary thing. Life abroad should be led the same as it is in Haidakhan."

Ashrams are built as places to live for both those who want to focus totally on God-realization, living a monk-like life of service, and for those who want to experience that atmosphere for shorter or longer periods of time to refocus their thoughts and lives, to find balance, inner peace and the courage to live actively in the 'normal,' 'real' world, while still retaining a focus on The Divine. Ashrams have served this dual purpose in India for thousands of years - as schools to teach the young, centers of 'retreat' for active 'householders,' and a place to focus entirely on spiritual development for householders who have raised their children and established them in marriage and business.

Detachment and Renunciation

In one way or another, Shri Babaji consistently taught people to be unattached to material things, to the objects of human desires. That does not mean that one does not acquire or own material things but simply that one is not compelled by desire to acquire or retain objects - or experiences; one is not ruled by temporary pleasures or pains. All objects are 'transient' and all experiences are fleeting; they cannot be held, made secure against change or loss. To be attached to these things, 'ruled' by desire for them, limits human freedom, makes people competitive, greedy, fearful or jealous of others, constantly on guard to 'protect my own' or acquire more. In Shri Babaji's philosophy, true freedom begins to be achievable when a person rises above attachment to and desire for sense objects: then a person is not 'unbalanced' by pleasure or pain, 'gain' or 'loss'; there is nothing to seek and nothing to defend. In this condition, a person can freely serve others and find contentment, happiness, and salvation in this human life. He or she may also find wealth and 'power' or great talents through dedicated service emanating from a peaceful, balanced inner center.

Not everyone is ready or able to seek or attain this condition in life; in fact, our current societies are built on the opposites of these teachings. But merely to acknowledge detachment of this nature as an eventual goal of life loosens the hold which our desires have on our lives, allows a more balanced, detached concept of living. Unless a person is panting for "Enlightenment now!," it is not harmful to experience pleasure and pain, to satisfy desires, provided one can do so without becoming 'addicted' to them - 'attached' to and ruled by the desires.

One evening Shri Babaji said:

"You may know about Shirdi Maulana. He

lived during the Muslim rule in India. He is now making the rounds everywhere, going here and there to help humanity. Now he is here, speaking through Shri Mahaprabhuji.

"He says that 'I' and 'my' have put a veil over the hearts of people. People have become self-centered and selfish. How can there be peace when the mind is full of ego and selfishness? Who is big enough in this world now to sacrifice himself for universal service and love? People have degenerated to the point that they are prepared to kill or harm others for their own selfish works or motives.

"All of you must try to destroy the corrupted law and establish true Law in the world."

On another evening, Babaji's statement was, "Everyone must consider his country as heaven and remove 'I' and 'my' from his mind. Put all your effort into service of country and humanity." He was constantly trying to lift people's goals and attention from the pursuit of *personal* pleasures and gain to a focus on selfless service to others. The unbalanced craving for and focus on personal satisfaction and gain necessarily fosters competitiveness, greed, jealousy and anger and strengthens ego and attachment to the material world - all of which are described in the scriptures (as a result of the experiences of the sages) as "the chief enemies of yoga" (union). When a person is able to see beyond himself or herself and focus attention on serving others, the activities and thoughts of that person weaken the negative traits and strengthen the traits of love, service, inner peace, harmony and unity with the entire universe. These are the traits which assist the soul in its search for Self-realization.

"There is no place for fear: people must work fearlessly in the world. Maharshi Markandeya has said that we must be fearless. When a man is fearless, no man can stand against him in battle - either a battle in material life or in spiritual life; he is victorious in all the battles of life.

"Now Babaji is suggesting another point -that

we must annihilate the feelings of 'I-ness' and 'my-ness' from our minds. You must march forward like a soldier, dutifully and bravely. The thing which brings man down is attachment to his own kith and kin. When you all belong to this whole universe, where is the place for 'I' and 'mine'? We must unite as one universal family and march forward in unity. By this means only will the world be benefitted. This is not a concern of one individual but that of the whole universe. The only true man is one who practices 'humanism.' Every man must cultivate the qualities of humanity: this is the only way to success in life."

*   *   *   *   *   *   *   *

Gaura Devi states that Shri Babaji frequently told her that renunciation is 'the only thing' for the person who wants to walk the spiritual path; that success on the spiritual path depends on the strength which comes from renunciation. He encouraged His devotees (those who were especially interested in spiritual growth and progress) to renounce every attachment to material life, even while actively living and functioning within the material world. He told Gaura, "The body will die one day and will be burned to ashes; how can you be so attached to it?"

In 1983, Shri Babaji was putting me through many detachment experiences. (Not only me; many people got these lessons as they progressed along the spiritual path and as He prepared us for His physical departure.) I was very confused in my efforts to assimilate 'detachment' with my concepts of duty - to wife, family, friends, the ashram, to society as a whole, and to 'the universe.'

At this time, Sita Rami (Margaret) became certain that Babaji, through experiences He gave her in the ashram and through inner guidance, was telling her to leave the Haidakhan Ashram and serve the Divine Mother elsewhere. After considerable confusion, she left the ashram, flew to the United States, in a brief, unsuccessful effort to raise money for a project she wanted to support, and then returned to

Haidakhan. Babaji greeted Sita Rami with an angry-sounding "Hopeless lady!" but when she made her pranam, He garlanded her with flowers and she saw a loving welcome in His eyes.

But in June she again felt pressure from Babaji to leave the Haidakhan Ashram, and she left again, early one morning, without asking Babaji's permission. This time, she felt less certain that she had done the right thing; she was reluctant to leave India and she was afraid to return to Haidakhan because of her uncertainty and fear of Babaji's displeasure. Sita Rami and I kept the Indian postal service busy with our efforts to support and encourage each other, but whenever I asked Babaji's permission to leave the ashram to see Sita Rami, He made it clear that my departure would be without His permission and, on one occasion, He said that if I left I could go anywhere I liked, except to return to Haidakhan. I, who, along with Sita Rami and others, had been initiated as a yogi in Babaji's tradition in November, 1982, considered myself well launched on that path. Now Babaji was giving us a severe test of our sincerity: which commitment was stronger? We were both very uncomfortable with Babaji's testing; this wasn't quite what we had in mind when we asked His permission to stay when we returned to Haidakhan at New Year's, 1981, or when we eagerly accepted His invitation for initiation in 1982.

One evening in August, after much thought, I went to Babaji during darshan and asked Him three questions concerning 'detachment.' What is the definition of detachment? What is it for, or to what does it lead? And, when you don't have it, how do you 'practice' it? Babaji, who had been coughing violently, told me to ask tomorrow, so I went back to my seat.

Later, Vishnu Dutt Shastriji came out of Swamiji's room and went to touch Shri Babaji's feet. When Shastriji stood up by Babaji's side, Babaji called me back. I came forward and made my pranam and Babaji told me to ask my questions of Shastriji.

The questions were repeated and Shastriji replied that detachment is knowing that the world is illusion. This did not mean much to me and I felt further confused and disappointed. At that point, Shri Babaji leaned forward and entered into the conversation, saying there were many kinds of detachments (vairagyas). For instance, the men who invented the atom bomb were 'detached'; they focused all their attention on one problem, forgetting everything else. The main theme, He said, is to focus your attention completely, to concentrate on your goal, whatever it is, forgetting all other things. This is renunciation; it leads to God-realization.

Shri Babaji added that being one-pointed is 'vairagya.' He told me that I was 'liberated,' that I was 'most detached.' I felt neither liberated nor detached, but I touched Babaji's feet and headed to my seat. Babaji - aware that I did not realize He had answered my questions fully - called me back. He re-emphasized that whatever decision a person makes, whatever goal he sets, he should go after it with great faith and firm determination, focused on it entirely. Babaji said that just by shaving one's head, or putting on orange garb, one does not become 'detached.' One must have firm faith, strong will, and complete concentration. I again touched Shri Babaji's feet, thinking the conversation was over.

However, Shastriji told me to stand up and he began to speak again. He said that Shukadeva had asked the same three questions of his father, Vyasa.[8] Vyasa had told Shukadeva to go to King Janaka and ask these questions of him. When the questions were put to him, King Janaka instructed Shukadeva to circumambulate the city of Mithila, carrying a full bowl of milk. Shukadeva was to be accompanied by two guards with bared swords and if he spilled even one drop of milk they were under orders to cut off his head.

Shukadeva was then sent on his walk, holding the very full bowl of milk. Hours later, he came back into the presence of King Janaka, who asked him what he had seen of the city. Shukadeva replied that he had not seen a thing of the city because he had focused entirely on not spilling the milk, the sword of death hanging in his mind. King Janaka then explained that this was how he had to concentrate on his goal - with complete concentration. This was 'detachment' from all the things in life.

I thanked Shastriji and, again, with gratitude, touched Shri Babaji's feet. At this, Babaji turned from another conversation and asked, "What was your third question?" It was, "How does one practice detachment when he doesn't have it?"

Shastriji answered, "Dhire, dhire (slowly, slowly)," and I laughed. Shri Babaji leaned forward and pointed His finger at me and clarified: "With total concentration and great faith and determination! Focus on your goal and everything else fades from view. Then you have detachment."

At last I had a pretty clear mental conception of the 'renunciation' and 'detachment' which Shri Babaji was constantly urging on us. But mental conceptions were only early stages in Babaji's method of teaching; the *experiences* which lead to - or prod one to - the attainment of pure detachment have continued without end.

"I Want the Welfare of the Whole Universe"

The spiritual concepts which Shri Babaji expounded to His devotees dealt mainly with living actively in the created universe without being a 'prisoner' of it. Although He honored the forms of worship and sometimes encouraged some foreigners to learn the traditional Hindu methods of worship, His emphasis was clearly on developing the inner spiritual life of the devotee of God so that person could become 'detached,' 'pure,' 'one with God,' and live in the material world, giving expression to 'unity with God' through loving, selfless service to all living beings that he or she could 'touch.' Shri Babaji called this 'humanitarianism.'

One can practice humanitarianism as one makes progress on the path toward God-realization; this is what Babaji urged all people to do. Even if a person is not ready to 'give everything' to attain God-realization in this lifetime, a humanitarian outlook on life, together with a conscious control over one's desires for worldly pleasures, is very practical for everyone. The whole created universe is God's manifestation and when a person is in harmony with the rest of Creation there is peace, harmony, and happiness within and around that person.

Babaji commented:

"All great saints and spiritual leaders who have appeared in the world have come to establish world peace and unity for humanity <u>as a whole</u>. Jealousy and hatred are the two causes by which humanity is ruined.

284

In your lives, these two vices should have no place."

Vishnu Dutt Shastriji continued this theme with the statement,
"When the Supreme manifests and comes on to
the stage of life, the ships of all world religions come
to sail the seas. Books written thousands of years ago
make it clear that God comes for the benefit of devotees of different religious paths and, by doing so, He
unites the different paths, making them one."[9]

On New Year's Day, 1984, Shri Babaji concluded His New
Year greetings to devotees with the introduction of a new slogan.
"JAI VISHWA!"[10] There is an Indian slogan,
'Jai Hind!' It means 'Victory [or honor] to India!' But I
want the welfare of the whole universe, so I am starting a new slogan - JAI VISHWA!' [Victory, or honor, to
the universe!]"

We honor the Universe by respecting it and consciously seeking to live in harmony with it and its Creator. **"You should seek harmony in everything you do."**

NOTES

1   "Baba Ji," by Dr. V. V.S. Rao, page 15; translating from Mahendra
Maharaj's "Divya Kathamrit."

2   "Teachings of Babaji," 1988 edition, page 34; 2004 edition, page 38.

3   "Babaji - Meeting With Truth" by Shdema Shivani Goodman,
page 44-45.

4   "Teachings of Babaji," 1988 edition, page 23; 2004 edition, page 40.

5   Read Autobiography of a Yogi by Paramahansa Yogananda.

6   Quoted from "The Eternal Way," May 1989, page 5.

7   People occasionally saw unexplainable lights moving on Mount Kailash - too quick for human movement, or on the unclimbable slopes
of Mount Kailash. Babaji said they were light-forms of the gods.

8   Vyasa is the sage who wrote the Ramayana, the Mahabharata, the
Srimad Bhagavatam, and other early, great scriptural books.

9   "Teachings of Babaji," 1988 edition, page 50; 2004 edition, page 70.

10 Vish'-wa means universe.

"Not everyone saying to me, 'Lord, Lord,'
will enter into the kingdom of the heavens,
but the one doing the will of my Father who is in the heavens will."
Jesus Matthew 7:2

"He created life and death that He might put you to the proof and find out
which of you acquitted himself best. He is the Mighty,
the Forgiving One."
The Koran 67:2

"The true, eternal religion, full of generosity,
Tells of knowledge combined with holy work."
From the Haidakhan Aarati

"Those who will meditate and do penance here and sing the praises of Lord
Shiva will attain liberation. Those who will hear of the
importance of Haidakhan Vishwa Mahadham and
describe it to others will also attain liberation."
Shri Babaji

CHAPTER XIII

BABAJI TEACHES ABOUT RELIGION AND THE SIGNIFICANCE OF HAIDAKHAN

Some Basic Concepts of Religion

A devotee from New Delhi who met Shri Babaji in the early 1970's says his first conversation with Babaji went like this:

He asked Babaji, "What is the Truth?"

Babaji answered, "The voice of your <u>atma</u> (soul, self or conscience)."

"What religion should one follow?"

"Humanitarianism: that is the real <u>dharma</u> (religion, duty)."

That was the simplest way of stating Shri Babaji's message on religion. If all created things are manifested from the 'substance' and Energy of the Absolute, the Formless Soul, then all things are truly One, and all the parts of that One Whole should live and function in harmony with each other. For a human being, religion - the expressions of one's belief in the Absolute and Its Creation - to a large extent, must be expressed in 'humanitarian' thought, speech and action. Shri Babaji briefly summarized 'humanitarianism' in these terms: 'The Creation is vast and there are many doctrines. Adhere to one principle - that of Truth, Simplicity and Love. *Live* in Truth, Simplicity and Love and practice Karma Yoga."

In many different ways, Babaji taught of the impermanence of created things. Movement, activity, change constitute a basic law of the universe. Human unhappiness, sorrow, anger and hatred stem from attachment to things, to people, to situations, to constant efforts to stabilize, control, retain things to which we are 'attached.' In a universe in which everything is transient, constantly undergoing change, human beings are always trying 'to swim upstream,' trying to hold on to things which, in accordance with the laws of Nature, are flowing past them.

Babaji often spoke an ancient saying: "Pinda kacha, shabda sacha." "The body is perishable; the Word is eternal."

He elaborated on this theme frequently.

287

"The fact is...everything in this world is...transient. It has no 'reality.' True reality is to proceed on the Path of Truth, to keep the company of saintly people, and to render service to men."

"Leaving behind the fear of death and the hope of life, you must advance. You should not be afraid of fire and water. When the need arises, we will have to jump into the ocean; when the time comes, we must be prepared to jump into the fire. That is why all of you must be as firm as Mount Meru."[1]

But just because the body is "perishable" was no reason to treat it with disdain. Babaji noted many times that it is difficult for a soul to get a human body and all people should use that opportunity to make progress on the spiritual path. It is necessary to do our best to keep the body clean and in good health.

"You must all advance by taking good care of your health. Only by taking good care of your health can you gain success. The fact is that if your health is not good, how can you do your service? Taking care of your health is as important as any of the other duties of your life. It is your duty towards your body. If your body does not work, how will you function and advance?"

"Shri Mahaprabhuji wants to impress on us all that cleanliness is a very high thing. Cleanliness is next to godliness. Shri Mahaprabhuji says that God only resides in cleanliness. If there is impurity inside you, how can God reside in your heart? So practicing cleanliness is one of the most important acts in your life to realize God...."

"Those who live in Haidakhan - and the fakirs of Haidakhan, especially - must be very clean. They must have a daily bath, clean their clothes, and everywhere they must observe neatness and tidiness. Things must be kept in order. Cleanliness is the first step in reaching God."

A basic tenet of the Sanatan Dharma is that the individual soul

288

is a part of the Supreme Soul (the Formless God) manifested in this created universe. The individual soul (jivatma) has been embodied in physical forms through many lifetimes and, identifying itself with those physical forms, has forgotten its true identity and reality as being One with -a true part of - the Supreme Soul. The soul is the real force in the human body; it is the Experiencer, that spark of The Divine which goes out from the Formless Soul to experience Itself in innumerable ways. The human form is like a set of clothes with which the soul is covered, which the soul sheds at 'death,' and with which the soul is reclothed when it takes on another human form. The soul is immortal; the body is mortal. The individual soul retains general knowledge from its experiences from life to life; its cumulative experience through its past lives in physical forms is what shapes the human being's reactions to experiences in the current life. With every experience of life there is an opportunity to progress toward the higher nature of humanity or toward humanity's lower nature; the choices are ours and they are heavily influenced - but not inevitably determined - by the soul's accumulated experience and wisdom. This concept of reincarnation was assumed to be understood by all who came to Haidakhan. It was not a concept which Shri Babaji discussed in any detail, but He often made references to it.

"The rhythm is that those who are born must die and those who die must be born."

"You are all rishis of ancient times, residents of this divine place. You all do not know yourselves. You do not know your own greatness - like Hanuman [in the story of the Ramayana] who did not know his own greatness; he had to be reminded of it."

The human life lived in the delusions of the permanence and 'reality' of the physical universe and 'attached' to material objects and the desires, pleasures and sorrows of the senses is the cause of the almost-never-ending cycle of births and deaths. Attachment to material things brings the soul back to the material life and its 'school of hard knocks.' Only when a person rises above the desires of the physical body and becomes detached from the physical objects of the universe can he or she constantly experience The Divine in the universe. When a person attains control over the mind and senses, then he or she becomes open to experiences of The Divine which can lead to the soul's true unity with The Divine - the experience of the individual soul as one with the Supreme Soul. It is not enough to know this truth intellectually; the attainment of that unity must be experienced over and over, strengthened through constant practice over many lifetimes, until it becomes the underlying Truth of one's life.

Babaji had Vishnu Dutt Shastriji recite a Vedic mantra, on more than one occasion, which translates to:

"Only he who for many lifetimes practices severe sadhana can attain to the highest abode of God [that is, liberation from the cycle of births and deaths through 'reunion' with God]."

The sadhana that Shri Babaji taught included, but was by no means dominated by, religious worship. He considered the forms of worship a valuable means of preparation of the heart for the journey on the path to Self-Realization, but not ends in themselves. When I first went to Haidakhan and was struggling to learn to sing the nearly hour-long aarati service, I asked why we sang it morning and evening. Sita Rami, who had already asked that question, said that Babaji had told someone that the aarati was performed for the benefit of the devotee: "I have no need for the worship; the benefit is what the worshipper receives." And if the worshipper does not carry the spirit of worship and service out of the temple and through her or his whole working day, the worshipper has failed to get the full benefit. "Work is worship."

A devotee tells of being seated near Shri Babaji one day when another devotee came to the ashram from a distant place. The new arrival made his pranam to Babaji and proceeded to tell Babaji in detail how he did his worship at home and asked Babaji what further to do and what not to do. He made a big verbal display of what he was doing and how devoted he was.

Finally, Babaji, with a frown on His face, interrupted the flow of words with, "What is it that you are saying? Make your *heart* your temple!"

Shri Babaji made it clear that He, as a manifestation of The Divine, does not need to be worshipped; The Divine is complete in Itself. Formalized religion - the ritual of worship, the belief systems, the deities which people experience and the facts and myths surrounding them - is a vital help and guide for human beings, but God's existence and activity within Creation are not dependent on humankind's worship or belief. Finite human minds can neither fully comprehend nor express the Infinite. All religions contain much Truth and each presents a viable and tested system for reaching toward and experiencing The Divine. There have been great saints and Masters in all of the great religions, but no religion has *all* the Truth of The Divine, because The Divine is found and experienced through an infinite number of ways by the many who seek. Because of the limitations of human languages and the variety of spiritual experiences, the forms of worship and the scriptures of any religion can guide the seeker only to a certain point on the Path: the last steps to the experience of unity with The Divine are uncharted, and are mapped out between the seeker and The Divine in each case.

Babaji lived in a Hindu ashram. The basic pattern of the ashram was in the ancient Hindu tradition, but He did not press Hindu forms of worship on people of other faiths. If a person asked to be taught Hindu rituals or beliefs, Babaji usually sent them to someone else for teaching, though He occasionally gave a specific response to questioners. Of Himself, He said: "I have come to guide humanity to a higher path. I do not belong to any particular religion, but I respect all religions. I seek the elevation of all mankind."

He did not like religious proselytization, no matter who was trying to convert whom. "Follow the religion that is in your heart." What Babaji emphasized was the Sanatan Dharma - not as a religion, but as a way of life. When life is lived in harmony with The Divine and all of Its Creation, the form and tenets of the religion which guides the person to that harmony is a matter for individual choice and use.

The religious wars in the Near East and Northern Ireland are ghastly examples of what happens when people get so fixed on their own cultish forms and tenets of religion that they cannot see the validity and Truth in other belief systems. Babaji commented that where there is hatred, there is no religion. These battles have little to do with spirituality or religion, but are struggles for power and domination over other people. The defense of one's right to exercise one's religious beliefs is one thing; attempting to force others to conform to one's own beliefs is despicable.

One form of worship in which Babaji actively participated throughout His ministry was the fire ceremony - the hawan or yagnya. One devotee says she heard Babaji say, "If you want to worship God, worship the fire."

As a pre-Christmas hawan was getting under way in Haidakhan in 1983, Shri Babaji stopped the ceremony to allow another foreign devotee to sit for the ceremony and then He spoke a few words about the meaning of the hawan:

> "Hawan it is that brings rain, which brings grain. The origin of Creation stems from the hawan. [In another talk, He had stated that original humans performed hawan ceremonies and 'extended' creation - through procreation and through development of implements, agriculture, society, culture, etc.] The hawan is the real form of the gods: whatever we offer to the hawan goes directly to the gods who are being invoked.
>
> "By doing hawan, people gain happiness and all the pleasures of life; they all have good thoughts and love - for each other. By the smoke from the hawan, the harmful germs in the atmosphere are destroyed and the good bacteria, useful to life, grow in it. This increases the plenty and prosperity of the world."

The hawan ceremony also provides a drama for human beings to symbolize their role in maintaining, expanding and perpetuating the Creation. As The Divine gives of Itself to manifest the Creation, the participants offer, with thanksgiving, back to The Divine, some small portion of the Earth's bounty to them. The fire, worshipped since very ancient times as a form of The Divine, transforms the offerings and takes their essences to the deities invoked by the recited mantras. In this way, participants in the ceremony have a sense of being a part of the cycle of Creation.

One of the names given to the early Vedic peoples was "the People of the Sacrifice." They tried to take the spirit of sacrifice from the fire ceremony into and through the activity of their whole day: the 'sacrifice' did not come to an end when they left the ceremonial area. It was apparently this spirit of sacrifice in daily living that led Babaji to say that He came to restore the yagya ceremony in modern society and religious practice.

Whatever form of worship one uses in the process of preparing the individual soul for finding the Absolute, Formless God, the experience of saints and sages, past and present, has been that one goes through the *Form* to the Formless. It is much easier for a person to focus on a form of God than to launch a search for the Formless, Attributeless God. Through worship of and devotion and service to a Form of God (a statue, a painting or photograph, or guru), the individual prepares for the experience of the Formless God - "beyond name and form." When the devotee understands and experiences something of the Formless One, the forms of worship lose much of their meaning in the life of the devotee: when one experiences God within and beyond his or her human frame, worship of a Form and the forms of worship lose some of their charm. Traditionally, the yogin or yogini does not participate in ceremonial worship, unless he or she does so as an example for others in the course of service to mankind. Although Babaji sat as a murti (statue or idol) when aarati was offered to Him, He did not (but once or twice to the Divine Mother) *perform* the aarati ceremony. However, apparently because He wanted to encourage worship through the hawan, Babaji Himself performed hawan just about every day of His ministry, and sometimes twice or three times in a day.

The Divine Takes Human Forms to Help Humanity

Completely in harmony with the teaching of the scriptures, Vishnu Dutt Shastriji made these comments about God's many appearances in human form and the unity of religions:

"Since the creation of the earth, God has always come to see and protect His garden of the universe. So He appears from time to time to weed out the tares and guide the devotees and all good people in the proper line."[2]

293

"Whenever the world faces grave problems, the Lord takes human incarnation and comes to fulfill the needs and desires of human kind. However, when the Lord comes in human form, few recognize Him. It was thus with Ram and Krishna, Christ and Mohammed. Only those to whom the Lord wishes to reveal Himself realize that He is in fact more than just a normal human. He will put suspicion in our minds and hearts and it is our duty to pray to Him for the wisdom to know Him.

"Without Babaji's blessing, one will only see His play at the human level, like that of Krishna with the gopis [the cowherds who tended cattle with Him in His youth].[3]

"Whenever God is incarnated in human form, we see that the question of caste and creed does not arise. This is the real acknowledgement of God: whenever He comes, He unites all religions of the world into one religion."[4]

On Christmas Eve, 1981, Shri Babaji had Shastriji give His message to those who came to Haidakhan for the celebration.

"The message to all of you is that the most important thing in the world is humanitarianism, or humanism. For this, we should sacrifice all our self-comfort. Do not think of yourself or your comfort, but think of others. This is the great humanitarian principle.

"In any town there is always a central place; all the roads in the town or from out of town lead to that central place. Similarly, all religions lead to one point, and that is God Himself; and, therefore, following any religion, you will ultimately reach God."[5]

There was really little new in the religious ideas which Shri Babaji spoke; probably every concept He taught can be found stated clearly in the ancient scriptures of more than one religion. But He spoke the ancient, eternal truths to people of this Age, in language they can understand, focused on problems of this day.

Shastriji's words again help to make the point:

"His principle is service to humanity without expectation of reward He teaches us to share with all equally, whatever we possess. Whatever is a part of the Lord's creation belongs to no particular person, but rather to all.

"He is not preaching any new religion. He has come to preach the religion which occurred at the time of Creation, and that is the <u>Sanatan Dharma</u> - the Eternal Religion. He has come to preach the Sanatan Dharma only."[6]

Babaji as a Manifestation of The Divine

To His devotees, Shri Babaji is a Form of the Formless God - a physical, human manifestation of the Absolute God. The ancient scriptures and religious commentaries of India describe the process of Creation as a progressive descent from the subtle, formless Supreme Soul through various limitless, changeable, occasionally visible forms of God, through the grosser, limited form of man, to animals and other sentient creatures, and to the still grosser, nearly inert forms of rock, earth, etc. The grosser the form, the more limited is its awareness of the Universal Consciousness, and the greater are its limitations. Human beings - at the mid-point of this process - are capable of breaking through this 'ignorance,' but only through great effort, detachment, and Divine Grace. In the Shaivite tradition, the first 'form' which the formless God made for 'Himself' was Ishwara. From Ishwara came the more identifiable forms of Sambasadashiv, the Divine Mother (Amba) and the Eternal Shiva. All these names, and more, were attributed to Shri Babaji by Mahendra Baba when he composed the Haidakhan worship service. Babaji was sometimes addressed by these names; and occasionally, when people asked who He was, He would use one of these names.

Sometimes He played 'Babaji' or 'Bhole Baba' (the Simple Father) as a simple, jolly, roly-poly friend to all. Sometimes He was worshipped as Haidakhandeshwari Ma (the feminine aspect - the Energy or Shakti - of the Lord of Haidakhan); there were many people whose predominant experience of Him was as The Divine Mother. At other times, He was Bhagwan Haidakhan (the Lord of Haidakhan). He sometimes acknowledged Himself to be 'Mahavatar Babaji.' One of the songs that was sung before Him chanted one hundred and eight names of Lord Shiva. All these names referred to different aspects of the One, Supreme God.

But perhaps the most relevant and consistently apt descriptions of the manifestation of Shri Babaji that we knew were the two following statements which Babaji made about Himself.

"I am Bhole Baba. I am nobody and nothing. I am only like a mirror in which you can see yourself.

"I am like a fire. Don't keep too far away or you will not get the warmth. But don't get too near or you may burn yourself. Learn the right distance.

"My name is Maha Prabhuji [the Great Lord]."

In His talks and in His conversation, Babaji often referred to Himself as 'Mahaprabhuji.' And He lived a 'life' consistent with that concept.

Educated, experienced, skeptical, practical people experienced Him strongly and clearly as a manifestation of God. The Governor of Uttar Pradesh, Sir C.P.N. Singh, who, in his eighty-odd years had spent a good deal of time with powerful Indian saints and avatars, said of Shri Babaji:

"There is no doubt about His incarnation, which is most significantly for the purpose of entering into the deep consciousness of Man - to awaken Man. This could not have been accomplished without this incarnation. This incarnation happens only when the people do not accomplish those righteous acts which Absolute Truth requires of them...

"For this purpose only, He had to come, to manifest the Ideal. He has to take a human form to guide and show the Ideal, not by talking, but by *living* it."[7]

Babaji had this to say about 'Mahaprabhuji':

"Sitting here at Haidakhan, Mahaprabhuji has

296

control over every particle of the Creation by the power of His mere wish; by His every thought Mahaprabhuji has control over the elements, the spiritual world - to say nothing of the world of men. He is the Creator, Sustainer and Destroyer of the world. Not a single blade of grass can grow but that He wills it. He has incarnated in a human body for the welfare of mankind. His sole desire is to make it possible for the whole world to be liberated. He shall do His utmost to achieve liberation of the whole world."

In some previous manifestations, there are indications that Shri Babaji showed a large number of 'miracles' involving His physical form. 'Old Haidakhan Baba,' for instance, sat for hours within blazing fires; there were a few people who saw Him die and who cremated His body - and then found Him teaching people in another town. Shri Babaji's miracles in this manifestation were not of that spectacular nature. Mahendra Maharaj wrote, years before Babaji's appearance in Haidakhan, that Babaji would come to show human beings how to live - how to remain detached in the midst of day-to-day human life. In this manifestation, He lived very much as a 'normal human being' in order to show people what they can accomplish by aligning themselves with The Divine. Most of the miracles He performed can be attained by a strongly focused and devoted human being.

On a few occasions, Babaji emphasized the human qualities of His body (not His <u>Atman</u>, or Soul). One day in the winter of 1976, Shri Babaji told Sheila (who then 'played doctor' in the ashram) to get her medicines; He had a fever. She laughed; she thought He was joking. Baba put His hand out and told her to take His pulse. She laughingly refused, still thinking He was joking: "Who am I to take Your pulse? You are God!" Babaji replied, "This is a human body. It has to work through its karma." He insisted on taking proper pills and later in the day His aches and pains were gone and His pulse returned to normal. Over the years, Sheila treated Him three or four times for colds and fevers. Other devotees also were called for treatment and medicines.

Babaji often behaved as a mirror. If children came to Him happy and ready for fun, He would spend time playing with them on His lap, as He sat for darshan; if they came crying or whining, He would mimic their cries and tears until they got tired of it and either began to play with Him or became quiet or fell asleep in His arms. He would laugh and joke with devotees who sought that; He would talk seriously and soberly with those who were thoughtful - or pedantic; He sometimes shouted at the angry ones and could turn in an instant to mirror the love and devotion of the person who followed.

On one occasion He took a large group of devotees on a hike to a Shiva temple on "the back side" of Mount Kailash. After a meal, Shri Babaji sat on a seat and gave darshan to all. During the hour He sat there, He called a number of foreign devotees to sit at His feet and have a picture taken, with Him, on a Polaroid camera. Each of us sat with our backs to Baba, facing the camera. Later, as the photographs were passed around, people noticed that Babaji's face reflected the face of the devotee who sat before Him; if the devotee smiled, Babaji's face bore a large smile; if the devotee's face was stern, or pensive, so was Baba's. His 'mirror game' often caused confusion among devotees who tried to analyze Babaji and comprehend Him in terms of consistent patterns.

In January 1983, Shri Babaji made this statement to Gaura Devi one day as they sat quietly in His quarters:

"I am nothing. Bhole Baba is nothing. Only the Will [Adesh - God's Will] is.

"In the whole world - the whole universe - only The Will is, and only The Will will work from now on. No Baba; no Baba; only The Will.

"I never cry, because nothing of this world touches Me anymore. Whoever comes or goes, is born or dies with no attachment whatever, is in Me.

"But who asks, anyway, about My pain?"[8]

Haidakhan as a Very Special Place

Twice in the past two centuries, Shri Babaji has appeared near the little village of Haidakhan and has made it His 'headquarters' for enough time to earn Him - as one of His many names - the name of

'Haidakhan Baba.' During the course of the years of this most recent manifestation, Babaji made many references to 'Haidakhan Vishwa Mahadham' - Haidakhan, the Greatest Place in the Universe. This was not idle talk for Him: He considered it the most sacred place on earth, and He treated it with the respect due to such a Place.

He spoke of the 'Kurmanchal Kailash,' across the river from the main ashram buildings, as the original Mount Kailash. (There is a great mountain in Tibet known as Mount Kailash. It is sacred to Lord Shiva and has been a goal of pilgrimages for thousands of years.) Babaji said that when the mountains first rose from the seas, before the land creation was 'completed,' the Kumaon Kailash was the earthly seat of Lord Shiva. Shiva, with the lesser gods as courtiers, did <u>tapas</u> (spiritual and physical austerities) here for thousands of years for the benefit of mankind. It is this penance which has given the area its special, holy quality.

Babaji noted, "You must not think that the Creation was always like what you see now. There have been many total transformations." When civilization crept through the forests to this area, Lord Shiva and His divine 'court' moved to the Tibetan Mount Kailash. Babaji said He had returned to Haidakhan and the Kumaon Hills to give new life to this old, holy Place. Haidakhan Vishwa Mahadham was again the home of the gods.

"Always," He said, "all heavenly beings - the gods and goddesses - are present here. They come and go. They bathe in the Gautam Ganga. Many divinities reside here permanently, not wishing to leave this Place."

"You are all blessed to be present in this great pilgrim center, at the Court of the actual Kailash Mahadham. Here, only those can live and are living who are very fortunate in this world. How can unlucky people live here? To those who have impurity in them, not even their shadow can come near this place, because this is a sacred, divine center. Here only heavenly beings can reside."

People saw and heard the <u>devas</u> (gods). Many people have seen - sat and watched with others - during the night 'jyotis' (generally, bluish-white lights totally unexplainable as 'natural' phenomena) playing on Mount Kailash and in the Gautam Ganga riverbed. Rarely, they came close to the watching people - tenuous, floating, light-forms. They were quite frequent visitors before 1978, and were less frequently seen when the population of the ashram increased; but their appearances have been reported even since Babaji left Haidakhan.

Prem Lal, a sophisticated, well-educated woman devotee from Delhi, tells of awakening one May night in 1975 in Haidakhan to the sounds of; Om Namah Shivaya' being sung by a chorus of deep, male voices. She could not believe her ears and, to make certain she was awake, she got up and walked to the door of the room and was surrounded by the sound. It came from the trees, the stream, the river, everywhere. She covered her ears and shut out the sound, but when she listened again, the sound was still clear -'Om Namah Shivaya.' She tried to convince herself that it was her imagination; she went back to bed, covered her ears again, then listened. The sound still came. The next morning, as she recalled the experience, Prem remembered that Babaji had recently told a group of people that, if you listen, you can hear saints and rishis chanting 'Om Namah Shivaya.'

Babaji said of Haidakhan that:

"Those who have a darshan of this place have all their wishes fulfilled." "Those who live here for some time automatically get many kinds of yogic powers." "One who lives here for some time becomes a real yogi." "If we call this Place a heaven on earth, it will not be an exaggeration."

Shri Babaji was very careful about who He allowed to come to His holy place. Many people wrote to ask if they could come to Haidakhan: usually the answer was yes, but occasionally He denied the request. Frequently, people came to the ashram without previous correspondence: usually they were welcomed, but occasionally Babaji would meet a group of new arrivals in the riverbed and sharply tell them to turn around and leave - before they ever had a chance to speak a word. He did not explain individual cases, but occasionally Babaji made statements which may explain the basis for His selection process.

"When a man's bad karmas are coming to an end, then he is naturally drawn to a sacred place and the company of good people."

"Only he can come here in whose life a turning-point has come, when the spiritual energy is rising. Only he can come here whose sins have been destroyed. Lord Rama says that only he can come here who has done great penance in his previous lives."

Babaji had Shastriji say that "those coming from the West have been saints in their former lives and were born in technologically advanced cultures to fulfill karmic desires, but are drawn to Shri Babaji when that karma is about to be satisfied."[9]

In August 1983, Shri Babaji said:

"A new world is being created here. The new Creation is beginning here. What you see here are already the beginnings of the new world. Here in Haidakhan the old world has been destroyed. I am teaching you this: THE NEW WORLD BEGINS FROM HERE! I want you to be happy and in peace."

Although Shri Babaji was clearly the 'Director' at the Haidakhan Ashram, He did not treat it as His own. He often told us, as He walked through the ashram like an inspector, that this ashram belonged to all of us. Mostly, we chuckled as people scurried to carry out the orders of Bhagwan Haidakhan. But Babaji meant what He said: one day, as the last building was being readied for occupancy, He left us, and left the ashram in the hands of His devotees. He had told us:

"This ashram belongs to you. Learn the rules and follow the discipline while you are here. Then, wherever you go, teach others the same discipline. Become powerful and help others to do the same. Be very attentive and alert and prepare to face life in the times that will come."

"Haidakhan Vishwa Mahadham is not the property of one person; it is the property of all mankind. Progress made at Haidakhan Vishwa Mahadham benefits the universe. You are fortunate to be in Haida-

301

khan, because even the gods long to be here."

"At Haidakhan, no one is restricted to only one kind of devotion or learning. All have a right to their form of devotion to God."

"There are many holy places that are limited to a particular religion. There have been and are many temples, churches and religious centers; but this is the only *universal* pilgrim center. That is what gives this Place its great significance."

In addition to the celebration of the major Hindu religious festivals, there were several occasions when the Sikh community among Shri Babaji's devotees organized 48-hour, continuous readings of the Guru Granth Sahib the holy scriptures of the Sikhs. (Christmas was another major celebration at Haidakhan.) After one recitation of the Guru Granth Sahib Shastriji noted:

"When such studies are undertaken in sacred places, it charges them with divine energy and, like the flow of the waters of the Ganges, benefits the whole world. Whenever recitations of such sacred scriptures take place, the vibrations go throughout the three worlds - earth, atmosphere, and the heavens."[10]

The Moksha Dham Dhuni, Liberation Sanctuary

During His stay in Haidakhan, Shri Babaji built nine small temples to Hindu deities on 'the Cave side' of the ashram. He spoke to several people of plans for three more temples - a Sikh temple, a Christian temple, and a Moslem shrine. They were needed to give a clearer universal character to Vishwa Mahadham. But Babaji left before these temples got under way; He left them for His devotees to complete.

The last shrine which Shri Babaji built at Haidakhan was the Moksha Dham 'dhuni' in the Company Garden, at the bottom of the '108 steps.' The garden itself had been reclaimed from the wide river-bed over a three-year period of karma yoga activity. In the third year, Shri Babaji had built a dhuni - sacred fire pit - with His own hands and then supervised and helped in the construction of a temporary structure around and over the dhuni. During the monsoon of 1983, He built a 'permanent' structure of stone and cement around the first structure and then removed the temporary building and dedicated the Moksha Dham Dhuni on August 17, 1983, with a great, roaring hawan fire.

The evening before the dedication, after the aarati service, Shri Babaji spoke about the dhuni.

> "The dhuni down below has living consciousness. In the Name of Lord Rama, in it is always the presence of Divine Light...
>
> "The dhuni is one of the wonders of the world!
>
> "You may see many types of dhunis, such as Parsi dhunis, but nowhere else will you find an eight-sided dhuni. The eight sides symbolize the eight arms of Jagadamba, the Universal Mother. In the name of Lord Rama, as long as there is Creation, the dhuni will be there with living consciousness. A boon has been given to this dhuni - that whosoever comes to have its darshan, whosoever meditates and does puja there will be relieved of all ailments, whether physical, mental or spiritual."

Another name that Shri Babaji gave this dhuni is "Maha Shakti Dhuni." "Maha" means "great" and "shakti" has many meanings and connotations which are appropriate for this dhuni. A literal translation is "Energy" or "power." The dhuni is a strong source of God's Energy. "Shakti" is also the Sanskrit word used to identify the female aspects of God or the gods. As noted earlier, in the Hindu pantheon, every major god has a female aspect which is the "Energy," the creative, moving aspect of the god. God (or the lesser god) represents and presents the pure quality; the "Shakti" is that Quality in action in the Creation. So the "Maha Shakti Dhuni" represents and symbolizes Babaji's moving Force in Creation; and the "Shakti" of God is always worshipped as the Divine Mother (Jagadamba) - the loving, caring, creative, nurturing, supportive, protective, tender character of God.

Shri Babaji often told people that when He left, He would leave Haidakhandeshwari Ma behind Him to give His devotees guidance, comfort, support and energy to do His work. She is worshipped in this dhuni (Her aarati is sung morning and evening) and the eight-sided dhuni is cared for as Her living form. Her presence is strongly felt by many who worship or meditate there, and Her form has been seen more than once.

Once, when the ashram was 'emptied' for a celebration in honor of the Divine Mother at another place, Ram Dass focused his worship on Her. One evening, while he was doing the Mother aarati, he experienced a pure white Light - tall, like a human form, but without any distinguishing features other than eight outstretched arms - rising out of the dhuni fire, which, after some seconds, embraced him in an eight-armed hug that left him in a state of bliss. The experience of the Divine Mother is there, in the dhuni, for those who seek it with faith and determination and devotion.

As the structure around the dhuni was nearing completion, Babaji commented:

"The door and windows of the dhuni building which houses the new holy seat have been left open. This means that the sanctuary is open to all, whoever they are, from whichever place they come. It is of vital importance to everyone who comes here and wants to be benefitted spiritually to have the darshan of the dhuni.

"This dhuni is not new, although it has recently been newly housed. It is a most ancient dhuni. Mahaprabhuji not only made this dhuni with His own hands, He Himself supervised and directed every detail of the work."

"...Mahaprabhuji has given a boon to this place - that whosoever drinks the holy water of Ram-Dhara [the spring below the dhuni] and whoever comes to have darshan of the dhuni, takes vibhuti [sacred ash from the fire], and performs any spiritual practice here, will have the guarantee of being liberated. This is what Mahaprabhuji tells you. That is why it is called "Moksha Dham" - liberation sanctuary. It is a manifestation of Lord Rama and a center of pilgrimage. It is the entrance door to the Lord."

Haidakhan, the center of the universe, according to Shri Babaji, is very special for a number of reasons. Babaji says it has been a holy seat for perhaps millions of years - a focus of Divine Energy in this world, a place where a physical form of Lord Shiva did spiritual practices for ages for the benefit of humankind, helping in the development of human forms from the lowest, early stages to the present stage of humanity. The presence of the Energy and form of Lord Shiva attracted the subtle and other forms of divine beings and ancient rishis and sages to this area. And still, in our period, Babaji had the constant sense of the presence of other divine beings in Haidakhan. He said they bathed in the river, danced on the mountainside and in the riverbed; they sometimes spoke through Him. And there are many people - Indian and Western - who experienced some of these forms in many ways that were very real to them.

It was special, too, in the sense that Haidakhan was a spiritual center which welcomed people from all spiritual paths. Babaji made no effort to convert people to any religion, but He tried to enliven all people's sense of The Divine and of the divine harmony of the universe. Whatever their religious, spiritual or philosophical background, Babaji did everything possible to help people experience the unity of the Creation and the sense of beauty, harmony, bliss and power that can come from lives based on Truth, Simplicity and Love for all created things.

Perhaps the chief significance of Haidakhan under Babaji's guidance was as a model for the New Age, or the New World which He sought to encourage and shape. The Revolution that He came to guide and inspire was taking shape in the tiny, remote hill village and ashram of Haidakhan as the "storm of water and fire" gathered strength outside the valley. Babaji showed those who came to the Ashram how to live active, useful, creative lives, in harmony with the earth, with other human beings, and even to send vibrations of harmonious energy out into the universe beyond earth's atmosphere. "A NEW WORLD IS BEING CREATED HERE.... THE NEW WORLD BEGINS FROM HERE!"

For thirteen and a half years, Babaji gave His whole Energy to showing people a higher, more peaceful, creative, loving way of life, and He made Haidakhan a model of that way of life. In the last few years, and more urgently in the last months of His ministry, Babaji urged His followers to go to their home countries and create ashrams based on the model He had shown them at Haidakhan. Babaji seemed to have made this ancient, holy place into an Eden for the New World.

NOTES

[1] Mount Meru (Sanskrit) is also known as Mount Kailash (Hindi) and as Mount Tisi to Buddhists. It is regarded by Buddhists and Hindus as the center, or firm base, of the Earth.

[2] "Teachings of Babaji," 1988 edition, page 41; 2004 edition, page 24.

[3] Ibid., page 8; 2004 edition, page 20.

[4] Ibid., pages 12 and 13; 2004 edition, page 25.

[5] Ibid., page 11; 2004 edition, page 23.

[6] Ibid., page 19; 2004 edition, page 32.

[7] Ibid., pages 87 and 88; 2004 edition, page 114 and 115.

[8] From Gaura Devi's unpublished notes. (Now published in her new book, "Fire of Transformation," see page 375.)

[9] "Teachings of Babaji," 1988 edition, page 79; 2004 edition, page 105.

[10] Ibid., page 51; 2004 edition, page 71.

"When I refuse attachment to those devoted to me, my reason is,
to make their devotion more intense. I disappeared so that your hearts should
be so absorbed in me that you would
be unable to think of anything else."
Lord Krishna to the gopis.
Translated from the Harivamsa (an appendix to the Mahabharata),
in Joseph Campbell's "The Masks of God: Oriental Mythology,"
pp. 348 and 349; Penguin Books.

Milarepa, preparing to die from poisoning by a jealous lama, said to
his disciples: *"There is no reality in my sickness. There is no reality in my*
death. I have manifested here the appearance of sickness. At Chuwar, I am
going to manifest the appearance of death."
From "The Life of Milarepa"
translated by Lobsang P. Lhalungpa, page 169.

308

CHAPTER XIV

MAHASAMADHI

Some Hints of Departure

The leela - the 'play' - of Shri Babaji's manifestation had a surprise ending. I think almost everyone - out of love and longing for and dependence on Babaji's physical presence - confidently accepted Shastriji's statement that he expected Babaji would stay with us until some time in 1988; and, furthermore, most people seemed to assume that, like 'Old Haidakhan Baba,' He would 'dematerialize' into a ball of Light when He left. There was even a story that Babaji had said that when He 'dematerialized' He would take eleven devotees with Him.

The Babaji that we knew played on thousands of His devotees the trick that 'Old Haidakhan Baba' had played on the young man who wanted to see the scar on Babaji's head that came from the battle at Kurukshetra: He gave us plenty of opportunities to know what was coming, but almost no one understood or was prepared for his mahasamadhi.[1]

After He left, many statements by Babaji, by saints, and experiences people remembered took on meaning and made it seem clear that His departure occurred according to a long- established plan, which He had teasingly revealed to us and covered up with His maya.

In 1972, Shri Nantin Baba, when he stated that Haidakhan Babaji was a manifestation of Lord Shiva, said also that He had come for a very specific purpose and that He would "disappear" after "some years" but reappear again.

In February 1973, Shri Gangotri Baba had confirmed Nantin Baba's statement and added that Shri Babaji would probably disappear in the next seven or eight years, unless a very great devotee would come, for whose sake He might extend His stay for a few years.

Not until Babaji had left did we learn that He had told Master Ram Singh of Okhaldunga, in 1970, that He would leave in 1984. Ram Singh, who had been visiting the ashram in Haidakhan once every three to six months for some years, began coming for Shri Babaji's darshan weekly in 1984.

Gaura Devi met Babaji in February 1972. When she came to live in the Haidakhan Ashram in 1973, Babaji told her she would serve Him for twelve years. She wondered if He would send her away: she had no thought that it was He who would leave.

One day in 1980, when Shri Babaji took a group of devotees on a pilgrimage, Hem Chand Bhatt was alone with Baba in His room. While they were chatting, Babaji told Bhattji that He would be leaving Haidakhan in 1984. Mr. Bhatt had no thought other than that Babaji might do as 'Old Haidakhan Baba' had done frequently and go off into the Himalayas for some time. He casually asked Baba when He would return, and Babaji replied that He would come back only if a devotee like Mahendra Maharaj would come and draw Him back.

An Illness in 1983

On June 8, 1983, Babaji became very ill with what appeared to be a summer cold which developed into serious congestion. He looked miserable and obviously felt that way in His body. One morning, darshan was quite late and when it was granted, people found Shri Babaji propped up in a chair, wrapped in a blanket, sitting in the doorway of the dressing room outside His bath-room. He was in such pain that He could barely sit and people just quickly made their pranams, touched His feet, and left their offerings of prasad beside Him, instead of requiring Him to move to receive their gifts. People sat outside His room and sang kirtan softly, and some wept to see His pain. At one point during this illness, Ram Dass found Babaji beating His head against a wall to distract His mind from the pain of the illness.

At that time, plans were being made for Babaji to go to the ashram in Chilianaula to give His darshan to the Governor of Uttar Pradesh and to dedicate the ceremonial gate of the ashram. When Governor Singh learned of Babaji's illness, he sent his own doctor from Nainital (the summer capital) to treat Babaji. A young German intern who was staying in the ashram had diagnosed Baba's illness as extreme congestion and had given Babaji a course of antibiotics. The Governor's doctor confirmed that diagnosis and the prescription, but cut the dosage in half saying Indians were not used to the heavy doses of antibiotics that Westerners needed. The doctor told Shri Babaji to rest for five or six days and forget the trip to Chilianaula, which was scheduled to start the next day. Baba agreed to rest and the Governor's doctor started his trip back to Nainital.

The doctor could hardly have gotten down the '108 steps' before Shri Babaji sent someone to the office to telephone to Haldwani and make certain that Amar Singh's truck would come early the next morning to take Babaji and His party to Haldwani, on the first leg of the trip to Chilianaula.

Also on June 8, two carloads of devotees were on their ways home from visits to Haidakhan. In one was Shri 'Nandi Baba' - Sib Narayan Nandi of Calcutta - and members of his family. East of Benares, near a bridge, the brakes on the car failed and the car went off the road and fell twenty feet into a ravine, rolling over three times. As the incident began, the people in the car started shouting Baba's name and they heard a voice saying, "Don't be afraid!" (Daro math!) The car was smashed and people were hurt, but not badly.

The other car, headed to Delhi, hit a rough spot in the road and flipped over. Everyone in the car was thrown out, except for Shri Manherlal K. Vora of Bombay, then in his 70's, who was found upside down in the overturned car, suffering from sprained muscles in his back. The only other injury was a very minor cut on Arun Vora's ring finger.

When news of these two incidents reached Haidakhan a few days later, Shri Babaji said He had taken on the karma of these two carloads of people; they were saved from death or serious injury, but someone has to reap the harvest of those karmas, He said. As their Guru, He had taken their karmas onto Himself. On receiving news of the accidents, Babaji took His first food in three days and made rapid progress toward recovery. He went to Chilianaula on schedule and spent three days there, sparing Himself only a little, and by the time He returned to Haidakhan on the 16th, there was no sign of illness.

More Hints

For a year or so before that illness, Shri Babaji had often commented to people that He was tired of this body and wanted to leave it. In His little talks, He noted "My work here is half done," then three-quarters done. His body became heavier; He walked up the '108 steps' slowly and sometimes leaned heavily on people; sometimes He had trouble breathing as He walked up stairs.

In the late spring of 1983, when Maria Elena Martinez and her daughters, Debbie and Laura Herring, were visiting Shri Babaji in Haidakhan, Maria Elena was told that Babaji had said that He was tired of His body and would leave it soon, but that He would stay about another six months "out of love for His devotees."

During the monsoon of 1983, Babaji, when He invited some-one to come to His side and speak to the people gathered for darshan, began to use the Hindi word "rona" - weep - instead of the word for "speak" to the people.

In August, before the Gautam Ganga became swollen by the monsoon rains, Shri Babaji was taking His evening bath in the river, after dismissing the work crews that labored on a new concrete river control block. On one occasion, when only Ram Dass was assisting Him with His bath, Babaji told Ram Dass, "After six months I will go into samadhi." And, then, a few moments later, He said, "I will be in samadhi for six months." A puzzled Ram Dass mentioned this to me and I remember we calculated that six months would make a certain day in February 1984. I told Ram Dass that Shastriji - at Babaji's in-struction - had told me about the prophesies and that Shastriji was sure Baba would stay with us until 1988. I could not make any sense of Babaji's statement: it remained in my mind for perhaps a month and then I forgot it entirely. Ram Dass later told me that he had con-cluded that Shri Babaji, who was obviously ailing, had decided to go sit at the top of Mount Siddeshwar in samadhi for six months and restore His health.

During the monsoon, in late August, a party came from Italy with a proposed layout for the 1984 Babaji calendar. They brought ten or twelve color photographs of Babaji and two or three black-and-white photos and asked for Baba's guidance and approval before the calendar was sent to the printer. We were accustomed to lovely color photographs of Babaji, but this time He told the Italians to print the whole calendar in black and white - even the color photographs were to be printed without color; and the March photograph was a photograph of the Haidakhan ashram, instead of Babaji. We thought it a very dull calendar - until February made it very appropriate for a year of mourning.

In February 1983, Shri Babaji had instructed Yogendra Madhavlal, the chairman of the board of trustees of His ashram in Vapi, in Gujarat State, to construct a temple on the 'Manda Farm,' outside of Vapi, and have metal murtis of Mahakali, Kalbhairav, and Shri Ganesh ready to install during Baba's visit to Vapi during the fall Navratri celebration (in honor of the Divine Mother) in October. Monsoon is not a good season for construction - the whole area becomes a sea of mud. Letters flew back and forth between Bombay and Haidakhan, asking whether and assuring that the building would be completed on time. Not only the temple, but also guest quarters were under construction. Babaji pushed the Vapi trustees hard and it was completed, with finishing touches made to the temple and housing, in unseasonably late rains, after Babaji's arrival at the Farm. Babaji was very pleased to have this done: it was His last visit to Vapi.

Late in November, Shri Babaji and a sizeable party of people from the Haidakhan Ashram went for a yagya (fire ceremonies, scripture readings, and darshan) at the Jadar, Gujarat, home of then-deceased 'Pujari Baba,' Prahalad M. Vyas. Babaji usually rode one of the ashram horses the four or five kilometers to the 'dam site.' On the morning of departure for this trip, the horses were not ready and, after waiting for some minutes, Babaji started walking - accompanied by those who were going with Him and by many of us who were staying behind. After a while, as He walked, Shri Babaji started singing and teaching a new song to us all, by singing it to Ram Dass and making him repeat it. Its words were "Sita Ram, Sita Ram bol pyaare; Radhe Shyam, Radhe Shyam, bol pyaare." It translates to something like "Sing the beloved name of Sita Ram" [Lord Ram and His wife, Sita] and "Sing the beloved name of Radhe Shyam" [Lord Krishna and His most devoted female follower]. When Ram Dass was able to sing the song to Babaji, Baba sent those of us who would stay in Haidakhan back up the river to the ashram and He mounted His now-saddled horse and rode on down the valley.

313

Babaji taught this song also to His ganas (attendants of Lord Shiva) on the Jadar trip and in December, January, and into February, this song was sung often. Frequently, Babaji would start this song when I went to make my pranam to Him and many people thought Babaji was playing with me and Sita Ramiji, who was then in the United States. It was not until after Babaji's mahasamadhi that we foreigners learned that the name of Ram is sung as mourners carry a body to be cremated.

During this winter period, Babaji also said several times, in public, "My body is here but I am going abroad." A number of people got thrilled by the thought of traveling with Babaji through Europe and North America.

When the evenings turned chilly in the fall, Babaji started having His evening bath in His bathroom, near the little room He stayed in, slept in. A regular group of attendants - plus occasional visitors - were with Him for an hour or more every afternoon, before and during His bath. Sometimes these people meditated in Babaji's presence, sometimes He talked with them; but more and more frequently Babaji had them turn on a radio or play a tape of devotional songs - and He went off into deep meditation.

Although a few advance copies of Vishnu Dutt Shastriji's scriptural book about Babaji, Shrisadashiv Charitamrit, with the new ninth chapter about 'our' Shri Babaji's manifestation, had been put together for the Guru Purnima (the Full Moon of the Guru) celebration in July 1983, it was December before the printing and binding was complete. When the finished copies of the book were available in Haidakhan, Babaji urged everyone to buy it - even those who could not read Hindi. Babaji 'autographed' many copies for devotees with His signature - 'Om Namah Shivaya' in Hindi characters. At that time, seeing the 'leela' of His life in print, one or two devotees wondered if the 'leela' was coming to an end.

Also during December, 1983, the marble murti of 'Old Haidakhan Baba,' which Babaji had installed in the little ashram temple that 'Old Haidakhan Baba' had built, developed a 'tear' below the left eye. For several months - two months before mahasamadhi and for some months after - the tear was visible; but it is there no longer.

314

Shri Babaji had an almost constant cough through this winter of 1983-84 and there were stories of frequent black vomiting in His toilet. His body was obviously unwell, but His spirit was still strong; He maintained His own disciplined schedule. Man Singh, who served Babaji daily for about ten years, awakened Him at 3:30 or 4 a.m. and gave Babaji His bath; then Babaji gave chandan to His devotees in His little room, followed by the hawan ceremony in the dhuni on the terrace outside His room. Until the last three or four days, Babaji maintained His schedule, no matter how He felt. During the Christmas festival of 1983, few people had any serious concern about Babaji's health, other than noting how stubbornly His cold hung onto Him. Throughout the fall and winter; many new people came to meet Babaji and were overwhelmed by His beauty and by the force of His presence.

Perhaps Babaji gave us another hint on Christmas Eve, 1983. After a traditional Christmas play for the people in the ashram and for the people of the valley, followed by a long darshan with people giving gifts to Babaji and He giving out those gifts to those who came for darshan, Babaji made this comment before He left the crowded tent-hall:

"Now there is only half an hour before twelve o'clock. Don't get up and disturb the rhythm of this holy time.

"There is a proverb in Hindi which has the hero of the drama telling the heroine, 'Most of the play is over; little is left, and this little is about to finish. Please do not disturb the rhythm of the music for this short remaining time.'

"So please stay seated and go on singing kirtans and bhajans until twelve o'clock. Whatever kirtans, bhajans and prayers you offer today, Christ will hear. Sing kirtan; sing' Alleluia!"'

Babaji Describes His Burial Ceremonies

January 8, 1984, was my 56th birthday and I requested and received permission to perform the aarati service to Shri Babaji during evening darshan. Several foreign and Indian friends and I offered incense, ceremonially bathed His feet, applied chandan and kum kum to His toes and placed flowers on each foot, put a sandalwood mala and a 'sacred thread' and a flower garland around His neck, a cotton shawl over His head; offered Him fruits, nuts, sweets, and then performed aarati to Him with a ghee lamp. It is a beautiful experience to worship the Lord in that way. Sometimes Shri Babaji sat as still as a stone murti when aarati was offered to Him. In Haidakhan, He frequently participated more actively in the aarati - helping the fumbling worshipper to untangle the snarled sacred thread, maybe tucking one foot under Him so that only one foot needed to be washed and given chandan; and sometimes, with twinkling eyes and a broad smile, He would reach for an article out of its 'proper' order - perhaps to test our 'confusion quotient,' or maybe to indicate to us that the carefully memorized order and form of worship is less important than the love, devotion, and purity in the heart of the worshipper.

After the aarati, while the food items which had been offered to Babaji were being passed to all the people in the kirtan hall, Shri Babaji called Amar Singh to Him and had Amar Singh give a speech, which Babaji prompted, often line by line. He made some complimentary comments about me, then prompted the speech reported above[2] on how Babaji would carry out His work around the world through His devotees.

On the following evening, Babaji, who, on the 8th, had joked about being able to make me nine years old, said He could just as easily make me 159 years old. This speech was not officially recorded and it was not fully translated into English at that time; I have pieced things together from three or four people's recollections.

Babaji went on to say, laughingly, that Radhe Shyam would die in Haidakhan. He said my body would be burned - then He stopped and said, "No; Radhe Shyam is a Christian; he will be buried here." He went on to say that my body would be laid out on a bed of ice for three days, to allow people to have a last darshan; and that then my body would be buried, covered with perfumed oils, malas, flowers, incense, dried fruits and nuts, and covered with salt and dirt. And over the grave a samadhi temple would be built with a murti of 'Old

316

Radhe Shyam.' He told Nagini, an American woman who had painted many beautiful images of the gods and goddesses in the Haidakhan ashram, to make sketches of me and of an appropriate temple.

At the time, I thought Shri Babaji had rather overdone it. Five weeks later, it turned out that He had only used my name to describe what would happen to His body. Everything was done to His body that He had said would be done to mine. And the decisions on what to do were all made by people who were not in the kirtan hall at Haidakhan on that January 9th evening.

Babaji's Last Trip from Haidakhan

Late in January, Shri Babaji made His last trip outside of Haidakhan. In response to Governor Singh's pleas, Babaji stayed for three days in the Governor's Palace at Lucknow, with a party of His attendants. He enjoyed walking in the gardens and sat often in a square, twelve-pillared shelter in the' garden. He commented several times to Dr. Rao that He liked this style of building very much. In February, that building became the basis of the design for the samadhi temple that was built over Shri Babaji's grave.

Babaji went from Lucknow to Allahabad. For many months, the Banerjee family had been constructing a temple to Kali Ma - a form of the Divine Mother to whom the family had been offering daily puja for 108 years - and rooms for Shri Babaji and His attendants, plus a kitchen to serve guests who came for His darshan. When Babaji had reached Lucknow, the building in Allahabad was still not finished and He said He would not go to Allahabad. Construction work was re-doubled and the family pleaded with Babaji to go to their home and inaugurate the temple and 'give life' to the murti. Babaji finally agreed to go and of course the construction work was completed just in time.

I am told that Vishnu Dutt Shastriji was nervous about Babaji's inauguration of these Kali temples in Manda and Allahabad. Kali represents Time, Space, Death - the limitations in the created universe, the 'last' aspects before Creation is absorbed back into the Formlessness of God. Shastriji was said to think it was not 'good' for Babaji to be putting so much emphasis on this aspect of God; but Babaji said it

317

was all right and went ahead with the inauguration of these two Kali temples in the last four months of His ministry.

On the day of the 'life-giving' ceremony at the Allahabad temple, when the doors of the temple were opened, the devotees saw Shri Babaji sitting on the asan on which the murti was to be installed. Babaji had a cotton shawl over His head and He looked very feminine. Prem Lal, who has always seen Shri Babaji as "Ma," the Divine Mother, burst into tears and sobbed loudly at the sight of Him sitting there, partly because He looked so very tired and worn and partly because He had a distant, 'far away' look which gave her the feeling He might be going. Babaji snapped back to alertness and pushed Prem roughly away; He rarely encouraged tears near Him.

During the 'life-giving' ceremony, Babaji stroked the murti lovingly and whispered the mantra in Kali Ma's ear that gave the murti shakti (energy, 'life'). When the ceremony was concluded, Babaji got up without a word and walked quickly to a waiting car.

Prem Lal walked more slowly but she walked through the house instead of around it and when she reached the front porch, Shri Babaji was seated in the car, ready to go. He turned toward Prem and now His skin was glowing with Light; she says she had never seen Him so radiant. He beamed love at Prem - poured love on her. As the car started, Babaji called to Prem, "Be happy! Be happy!" That was Prem's last view of Babaji until she came to Haidakhan to bury Him.

On the way back to Haidakhan, Shri Babaji acceded to the request of Shri Saubhagya Chandra and Shri Himatlal Parikh that He stop at their family home in Kanpur, a major manufacturing center in the southwest part of Uttar Pradesh. At the Parikh home and at stops along the way back to Haldwani, Babaji told people to be sure to have a gun in their homes because "now the Mahakranti is coming."

When He returned to Haidakhan, Babaji told Swami Fakiranand, "I performed the ceremony [at Allahabad] because at a later date it would not have been possible."

Some Final Preparations

On the fourth of February, Anton and Marlise Waelti, a Swiss

318

couple whom Babaji called Jamansingh and Janki, arrived in Haidakhan. On the next morning at darshan they presented to Baba twenty copies each of sixteen photographs they had taken of Him on previous visits. I was behind them in the darshan line and Babaji had me sort out one copy of each photograph. He handed this bundle of photographs to Gaura Devi and told her to put them in an album and give them to Governor Singh "when he comes." Then Baba sent Gayatridevi (Stacey McCullough) to the office and told her to bring back one copy of every photograph of Him in the office and add it to the album for the Governor. Gaura wondered why Babaji would tell her to give the album to the Governor when He was there to make the gift. Gaura put all the photographs in Babaji's dressing room and forgot all about them. When Baba went for His afternoon bath, He found the photographs and scolded Gaura for not taking them to her room, as He had instructed her. He told her again that she must give them to the Governor.

Soon after His return to Haidakhan, Shri Babaji had sent a letter to Makhan Singh Baba, the priest who maintains the temple at Babaji's ashram in the village of Madhuban, in the Mathura District of Uttar Pradesh. The dhuni at this place, which was unearthed, along with ancient utensils of worship, in the time of Mahendra Baba, is said by Babaji to be tens of thousands of years old - the oldest existing site of fire worship ceremonies in the world. Babaji told Makhan Singh Baba to come quickly to Haidakhan and he arrived on February 9. Makhan Singh says that soon after his arrival at Haidakhan, Babaji told him that He was going to leave His body on the morning of the 14th, but said Makhan Singh should speak to no one of this.

At about the same time, Babaji was talking one day with Guiseppe D'Allessio, an Italian man to whom Babaji had given the names of Kali and Shanni Maharaj, and made the 'King of the Italians' (of whom there were many in the ashram). Babaji told Kali: "Son, now the moment has come to keep the spine erect; for now is the time to go ahead. For your own good, for the good of the whole world, for the good of all, it is necessary to keep the spine straight. For the time has come!"

On the tenth of February, 1984, morning darshan was very late. I went to work rather than wait in line outside Baba's closed door. Darshan started at about 10 a.m. and people found Baba sitting in a chair on His porch, bundled in sweaters and shawls and a woolen blanket. Word soon got around that Babaji was quite sick. When I went to make my pranam at about 10:30, I was surprised by the heaviness, puffiness of His face and the weary look. I inanely asked Baba how He felt. With a broad smile on His face and His hand on His heart, Babaji replied, in Hindi, "My health is eaten up." As Gaura translated that for me, I thought Baba was exaggerating things a bit. I did not know how to respond to a remark like that, given with such a smile, so I smiled back at Him and went back to my work in the office.

Other people also asked Babaji how He felt. To several He answered, with His hand on the left side of His chest, "There are a thousand knives in My heart," and then, moving His hand to the center of His chest, to the heart <u>chakra</u>, He said, "and there are a million knives in this heart." According to the tradition of the <u>Sanatan Dharma</u>, a true guru literally takes on himself the karmas of the disciples whom he accepts: in His thirteen years of public ministry, Shri Babaji had taken on a tremendous karmic load.

Later in the morning, Babaji walked slowly through the upper area of the ashram and sat and rested wearily. In the afternoon, He came up the steps from His quarters and sat on the benches at the top of the '108 steps.' He did not again go down to the river or across to the Cave and the nine temples at the foot of Mount Kailash.

That evening, Babaji came to darshan after aarati and seemed to be improving. He was more subdued than usual, but He spoke with people, laughed, sang a bit. During the evening, Babaji called me to His side. I had arranged for an appointment in New Delhi on February 18 with Shri N. D. Tiwari, then Minister for Industries, a man who came from the Kumaon area and had had Babaji's darshan. Babaji had Gaura Devi translate and He told me, "When you come back from Delhi on the 19th, you stay at Amar Singh's house overnight, and go to Munirajji's son's wedding on the 20th in My place." Neither Gaura nor I understood why Babaji would think of not attending such an important function in Munirajji's house; Babaji made special trips out of Haidakhan for major functions in Shri Trilok Singh's family; and He did not seem so sick that He would not be fully recovered in eight days. But, like many others, neither of us asked why.

On the morning of February 11, Babaji was up at the usual hour of 4 a.m. to give chandan in His room. On this morning He had given only eight men permission to come for this ceremony. After He gave them chandan, He sent them all down to the Moksha Dham dhuni for the morning aarati service. He told them that now the dhuni was the <u>Mahashakti</u> Dhuni (the dhuni of the Great, Divine Energy or Force); now it represented not only the Universal Mother (the eight-armed Jagadamba) but Shiva and Shakti in union.

At morning darshan - not quite so late this day as on the tenth - Babaji announced that Chairman Andropov of the Soviet Union had died, and He asked for a minute of silence in Andropov's memory. Someone gave Babaji a picture book of the destruction caused by the atomic bomb at Hiroshima, and another person offered Baba some oranges wrapped in a map of the world. Babaji spent many minutes looking at the book and the map thoughtfully and somewhat sadly.

It was probably on this morning that Babaji made His last walk through the ashram. With two or three Indian members of the ashram, Babaji walked to the house of old Baij Singh Sammal, whose house adjoins the ashram. Shri Baij Singh was then 83 or 84. As a young man, he had known 'Old Haidakhan Baba' and as an old man he had revered this 'Babaji.' Baba used to stop frequently at Baij Singh's house and have a glass of chai and a chat. Babaji had encouraged Baij Singh's sons to open a tea shop and had helped Prem Singh, the oldest son, marry off the first few of his seven daughters.

On this day, Shri Babaji greeted Baij Singh with, "How are you, old man?" Baij Singh said he was not feeling very well. Babaji turned to Baij Singh's sons and said, "He is an old man. He should be well cared for by all of you." And with a smile, He added, "If you don't want to take care of him nicely, you should beat him to death, so he does not suffer from your neglect." Then Babaji turned back to Baij Singh and said, "You are sick? Maybe you die. And when you die, I may not be here [Babaji had told Bombay devotees He would go to Bombay early in March], so let Me weep for you now." Babaji made the face and sounds of mourning for Baij Singh and then took His leave of his old neighbor.

Babaji spent most of the day in His quarters - in and out of His room, on and off His bed, on His porch. In the afternoon, He called His 'ganas' (Lord Shiva's attendants) - Gaura Devi, Har Govind, Kali, Ram Dass, Khurak Singh, Lok Nath, and Raghuvir - to sit with Him for the usual afternoon bath time; but He did not take a full bath, only washed His hands and face. Babaji spoke with them somewhat and there was also much silence. He went to evening darshan again that night, giving all present His blessings and talking charmingly with people; but He was obviously weary and He left a bit earlier than usual.

On the morning of February 12 there was no chandan ceremony. Khurak went to Babaji's room at about 5 a.m. and sat with Him in silence. Other 'ganas' joined them and they sat with Baba until morning darshan, which started an hour later than usual and lasted only thirty minutes. The twelfth was Gayatridevi's birthday and she wanted very much to do aarati to Babaji that day. She asked if she could perform the aarati that evening in the kirtan hall. After a brief pause, Babaji said she could.

Treatments for the Illness

After the morning darshan, a doctor and an Indian Army colonel came from Haldwani to visit Babaji. Babaji let the doctor check His condition and while this was being done Baba talked with the colonel, who said he had wanted for a long time to have just half an hour of talk with Shri Babaji. Babaji talked with him about spiritual matters while the doctor plied his trade on Baba's body. During the conversation, Babaji told the colonel, "Now destruction will come in the world, because people are always thinking of 'me' and 'mine'; everybody wants to be BIG; nobody wants to sit on the floor."

After the brief check-up, the doctor told several of us whom he met in the ashram that Babaji had pneumonitis; he had given proper medication to Baba, and He would be all right in two or three days.

322

"Don't worry!"

People who were attending Babaji said He chuckled when they begged Him to take the prescribed medicines, for pneumonia and bronchitis; but He swallowed the pills. He complained that He could not breathe, could not fill His lungs.

That afternoon, Babaji's attendants stayed with Him. Sometimes Babaji moaned and grimaced with pain; at other times He talked with the ganas - even sang to them. He had Khurak hold a Shri Yantra (a spiritual, symbolic design, in this case produced on brass) against His heart while He sang the love songs of Meera, a great devotee of Lord Krishna. Meera was a queen of the 16th century who abandoned palace and family in her worship of Krishna; her songs of devotion are still widely sung in India. He had Gaura Devi translate the songs for the group.

Perhaps it was this afternoon that, as He washed His hands in the bathroom, while Ram Dass was wondering silently why Babaji was suffering all this pain, Babaji stopped moaning, straightened His back, put His face close to Ram Dass', and gave Ram Dass a big 'stage wink.' Then He bent over again, moaned, and walked into the dressing area where the other attendants waited. It was difficult to know how seriously to take Babaji's illness.

A number of people asked each other this day - and later - if Babaji might "leave His body"; but, thinking of Shastriji's 1988 'departure date,' or remembering the sudden recovery from the illness of the previous June, people waited for the news that would signal the start of Babaji's recovery. And while we waited for the recovery, Shri Babaji told Gaura Devi, "My heart is broken, wounded by thousands of knives. My body has thousands of wounds and nobody is there to heal Me. Why, oh, why? The moon, sun and stars are all within Me and I carry the whole burden of the universe."

That evening Shri Babaji did not come to the kirtan hall for darshan. When it became clear He would not be coming, a pair of Babaji's sandals was placed on His asan and Gayatridevi and others performed aarati to His sandals. Worshipping the guru's or God's sandals has been a tradition at least since the days of Lord Ram, when Ram's younger brother ruled the kingdom in Ram's name through the symbol of Ram's sandals, while Ram, Sita, and Ram's brother Lakshman lived in exile for fourteen years.

As the aarati was ending, Babaji sent word that He wanted some of the ganas (attendants) and they quickly went to His bedside. Again they held metal Shri Yantras against Babaji's body to ease the pain which caused Baba to twist and turn on the bed.

When Ram Dass used the Shri Yantra, he 'massaged' Baba's body with it. Babaji rolled over onto His stomach and, after Ram Dass had run the Shri Yantra over His back and legs once, Baba pointed to the small of His back and told Ram Dass to hold the Shri Yantra there. Ram Dass stood next to Baba's bed, bent over, holding the Shri Yantra in position lightly with both hands, and silently repeated a healing mantra. Babaji's restless movements stopped and His breathing slowed down. Because Ram Dass was holding the Shri Yantra to Babaji's body, he fell into the rhythm of Baba's breathing; as Baba's breathing became slower and deeper, Ram Dass' breathing became synchronized with His. They breathed together in this way for perhaps two minutes.

With his eyes closed and the mantra filling his mind, Ram Dass sensed inner feelings; he felt light and then felt a lifting, rushing sensation. His inner gaze shifted from looking toward Babaji's body to looking up and he 'saw' black space. Out of that 'black space' very minute particles of light appeared, like a mist of light in a black night. They started at the edges of Ram Dass' vision, then suddenly congealed in the center. The rushing, lifting sensation increased and then a veritable movie of yantras (religious designs) came flying out of 'space' toward him, one form after another. He recalls seven different forms, but thinks there were nine. One stayed in his 'sight' long enough for him to remember it very clearly and then it 'exploded,' as if a mirror had been smashed with a hammer.

Ram Dass had the sensation of shooting up into that black space and then, in the blackness, he 'saw' a very pure white light, with edges of soft white light. At that moment, Ram Dass had the thought, "This is liberation!", and then, "This is how the soul leaves the body." At that point, Ram Dass opened his eyes and found himself still holding the Shri Yantra on Babaji's back. Babaji was still teaching, still giving, even as He lay sick in His bed.

The Final Darshan

On the morning of the 13th there was no chandan ceremony, no hawan ceremony, and no morning darshan; people were asked to go to work quietly and let Babaji rest. His attendants sat quietly with Him, ready to be of service.

When someone came to clean Babaji's little room, He decided to sit in the 'Sheesh Mahal,' the room where He often received guests - a room with mirrors on two sides. It is about twelve or fifteen meters from His room to the Sheesh Mahal; He leaned heavily on Kali and Har Govind, walking very slowly, His face grey with pain. As Babaji sat in the Sheesh Mahal, He again picked up the book on Hiroshima and, as He turned the pages, He said softly, "Too many diseases I have eaten; now I have to eat My own disease."

Just before noon, Babaji got off His bed and stood outside His room. He visibly gathered His strength and told the people with Him that He was going to the kirtan hall to give darshan and they should tell everyone to come. They protested that He should conserve His strength, not go up the stairs and exert Himself; but He insisted and put His arm across Makhan Singh Baba's shoulders and struggled up the steps to the first landing, then up more steps to the level of the temple garden.

By chance, I happened to be walking through the garden when Baba came up the steps, so I followed Him and the ganas into the kirtan hall. It was His custom always to stop at the temple and look in at the murti of 'Old Haidakhan Baba' before He went to His asan in the kirtan hall; however, this day He did not stop, but went straight to His asan and sat heavily and a bit slowly, but managed to tuck His legs into a half-lotus position.

As people filed to make pranam, He had a word or gesture of blessing for each. As I made my pranam, He started the chanting of "Bhudhe Radhe Shyam, Bhudhe Radhe Shyam." For a few minutes, some of us thought Babaji might have turned the corner and started to recover. After about ten minutes, when those present had all made pranams and were seated, quietly singing 'Om Namah Shivaya,' Babaji had Gaura Devi pile up pillows to His right and then He leaned heavily on them and breathed with difficulty, moaning softly with each breath. It was heart-rending to see His suffering.

After two or three minutes, Babaji asked, "Where is Colonel Sharma?" "Bhoopie" had been a major in the Indian Army but had been retired as a colonel. Just before his retirement, Bhoopie began 'playing' with morphine and in retirement he had quickly become a morphine addict. For four years he had lived the miserable life of an addict - losing his retirement business, living in the streets of Delhi - until Swiss friends and his aunt brought him to Haidakhan late in October, 1983. Babaji had cut Bhoopie off morphine 'cold turkey,' which came close to killing Bhoopie, but he survived and slowly regained strength and weight. Bhoopie, who had been a star athlete with Indian Army teams, a runner-up for Mr. India, and the man who had helped move huge boulders to make the wall under the nine temples at Haidakhan, could only sit and toss pebbles from one pile to another in his first days of karma yoga. By Christmas, Bhoopie had redeemed himself in Baba's eyes and those of his friends in the ashram and he was involved in work projects all over the ashram. In February, he was running the ashram clinic, on the far end of the ashram, and word of Baba's darshan had not reached him and the Western nurse. All these months, Baba had purposely addressed Bhoopie as "Major Sharma," to let Bhoopie know he had not made colonel in Baba's 'army.' But on this day, Baba sent someone to the clinic to bring "Colonel Sharma" for darshan.

When Bhoopie and the nurse had made their pranams, Baba signaled Bhoopie to come to His side. In addition to his several other duties, Bhoopie had been keeping track of the karma yoga projects at the ashram, and Babaji asked Bhoopie if the stone work for a big new river control block on the Kailash side of the river had been completed. Bhoopie had to answer that it was not yet done and Baba flared briefly. "Do I bloody well have to *die* before you finish it?" Bhoopie answered that it was a big project and people were working well but it would still take two or three more days to complete. Quietly, but with emphasis and concern, Babaji told Bhoopie, "The work *must* go on!"

At this point, Om Shanti, who usually translated for Babaji and spent much time serving Him, pleaded with Babaji to go back to His room and rest. He got up slowly and walked out of the kirtan hall, leaning on Makhan Singh Baba's shoulder, again without stopping at the murti. Bhoopie and Amar Singh, following Babaji, commented to each other that the murti looked lifeless and they wondered aloud if Babaji might be leaving.

During the afternoon, several times Shri Babaji got up from His bed and walked out of His room to the ganas (attendants) who waited on the terrace. He put the men in a circle and He stood in the middle; He had them put their arms out so they touched Him. Some of the ganas felt that, for a change, Babaji was drawing energy from His ganas, instead of pouring His energy into them.

By evening, Babaji was in such discomfort that a message was sent up to the temple that the evening aarati should be performed without the usual eight or ten minutes of loud bell- ringing and conch-blowing that accompanies the offering of light. Babaji needed the chance to rest. The aarati and the worshippers were subdued that night. People were greatly concerned by the discomfort and pain that Baba suffered, but still there were very few who thought He would let this body die at that time.

That evening, Babaji called Swami Fakiranand to His side and said to him, "I have shown the Path; quickly call the Governor." Swamiji says he asked, "So You are going to leave us?" Babaji made no reply.

Shri Trilok Singh - Munirajji - had come in the afternoon and that night he and Ramesh Bhatt and Gaurhari, the young temple priest, waited on Babaji. Late in the evening, Babaji was in such pain that Amar Singh took his truck down the awful road through the riverbed and went to Haldwani. He got a doctor out of his bed and brought him back to Haidakhan at about midnight. The doctor examined Bab-aji and said His problem was not congestion but a heart problem. The doctor administered the most effective drug he had with him - a shot of morphine, to cover Baba's pain and help Him rest. He assured Baba and His attendants that if Baba would just rest very quietly for two or three days, He would recover. He spent another hour or so

327

with Baba and then Amar Singh took the doctor back to Haldwani. Babaji, still having trouble with His breathing, asked to have oxygen sent in to Him; there was none in the ashram.

Saint Valentine's Day

On the morning of February 14, Babaji lay silent, rarely moving, on His bed. Once or twice He asked to be raised up and He vomited a black substance; phlegm in His throat added to His difficulty in breathing.

At about 7 a.m., just as the first bells of aarati were lightly, tentatively rung, Om Shanti came again to the temple and told people not to ring the bells. Babaji had not slept during the night, she said, and He needed complete rest, so there should be no noise in the temple garden. She said Babaji was all right, but He needed complete rest. So we performed another very quiet aarati service, had our breakfasts, and turned to the morning work.

At about 9:15, there were six people in the room with Shri Babaji. Khurak Singh, who was sitting in the kirtan hall, purposely avoiding what he feared was an already-overcrowded room, felt a strong pull to Baba's room and he ran down to it.

Some time between 9:15 and 9:25, Shri Babaji whispered, "Get Me up; sit Me up," and Ramesh Bhatt and Gaurhari, standing at the head of Babaji's bed, lifted Baba to a sitting position. Babaji gave a half cough, gasped for air, blew the air out of His lungs and settled back into Ramesh's and Gaurhari's arms. They laid Him back onto His bed and tears fell from Ramesh's eyes. Gaurhari asked Ramesh why he was crying and Ramesh answered, "Baba has gone!"

With a sense of ironic humor to the last, operating through great physical pain in His human body, Shri Babaji, who came into the world to change the hearts of all mankind, abandoned His physical body because of a heart problem on Saint Valentine's Day - the day this Christian saint is honored by people sending messages of love to those whom they love. Babaji, having completed His mission, gave the last 'possession' He had, in order to send His Message of love throughout the world.

NOTES

[1] Mahasamadhi is the conscious departure of a saint's soul from the body.

[2] See page 263.

"Holy Shiva is residing in your heart;
Find Him there; leave ignorance and disappointment behind."
From the Haidakhan aarati

"OM This is perfect, that is perfect;
From perfection, perfection comes;
Take away perfection from perfection, perfection remains.
OM Peace, peace, peace."
From the Haidakhan aarati

"Then [God] realized, I indeed, I am this creation for I have poured it forth
from myself. In that way he became this creation. Verily, he who knows this
becomes in this creation a creator.
From the Upanishads[1]

330

CHAPTER XV

AFTERWARDS

Mahasamadhi as an Element of Babaji's Teachings

Years before Shri Babaji made His appearance in Haidakhan, He had appeared to Mahendra Maharaj and told him about His coming and what the purpose of His coming would be. These predictions were published by Mahendra Baba in the 1950's. Babaji came - in a form described by Mahendra Maharaj and at the time foretold by him; He *lived* His message; He gave devotees experiences of what He was teaching; He spoke about it in the last years of His mission; His message was published; and He left.

There were people who thought Babaji was crazy; others who thought Him a clever boy from the Nepali hills who rode a hoary tradition to a comfortable living by fooling a lot of people. A few thought of Him as an advanced 'siddha' - a boy who had attained some 'siddhis' and used them to impress and to teach people - and maybe got a little lost in the process. But there was a patient tenacity, a consistency, strong power, clarity and purpose that are reflected in His message to humanity throughout His whole public ministry of thirteen and a half years. There are many people whose transformed and uplifted lives of service bear testimony to the wisdom and power of His life and teachings. He exemplified His teachings of selfless service to others in harmony with The Divine and the whole Creation. He showed how to be unattached to things, people, fears or desires while yet living actively and lovingly in the world; and throughout His 'life' He quietly displayed knowledge and power beyond that enjoyed by mortals. He showed Himself to those who were open to and ready for the experience; most of the time He 'covered' His divinity through His powers of 'maya' - illusion - as all 'the Great Ones' have done, and must do if they want to change and uplift people rather than just gain a large following through display of miraculous powers.

While He was in the form we knew as 'Babaji,' all His devotees ran to Him with all their problems and fears and hopes. With great patience, He led His devotees from one learning crisis to another, step by step, along the Path to Self-knowledge. And what a slow, tedious, tendentious, fumbling, bumbling lot we were! As Baba commented to a devotee standing beside Him, "Vishnu gets the cream devotees; look at what comes to Me!" Slowly, through an infinite variety of methods, tailored to each person's changing needs, Babaji taught His message to those who stayed with Him. In thirteen years He planted a lot of seeds but there was precious little to 'harvest' at the time He left. Big decisions and small decisions in our lives were all brought to Baba's feet and He was asked to tell us what to do.

But Babaji came to teach mankind how to *live*, not to make people dependent - on Him or anyone else. He told Mahendra Maharaj, "I have to teach [human beings] how to stay detached even [while] completely [involved in] day-to-day life." For thirteen years He taught what we needed to know, but His method of teaching was for people to assimilate the lessons in their lives and grow strong through their own personal experience and practice. He made several comments which indicate that He wanted people to learn how to act and live without dependence on His physical form.

"I have told you that I want active and hard-working people. I do not want to live in a world of inaction."

"You will have to do something practical, something useful. Babaji says you must work hard and put things into practice. First, be inspired yourselves; then inspire others with this message of karma."

"Everyone must use his own common sense; he should do his duty without waiting to be told what to do. To do your duty is the greatest worship, the greatest service, the greatest devotion and penance."

"It is not necessary for all of you to come running here again and again. You must all be busy in doing your own work, and by doing that you will be cooperating in the universal work. You must all be prepared to contribute to the universal good. Go, and remain in your own place! I do not like people roaming about like dogs. If you go anywhere, go for a purpose. If you do anything, do it for a good purpose. Use that time which you would waste in coming and going to and from here to do good to some human being - to *any* living being!"

Shri Babaji's <u>mahasamadhi</u> - the conscious, planned departure of the Soul from His physical body - was another method, and effort, in His teaching. Without His Form to run to, without a 'human' voice which our human ears can hear, Babaji's devotees are forced to focus on His teachings and to seek Him 'inside' - in the heart, where the <u>Sanatan Dharma</u> has always told humanity to seek God. His method of teaching was as 'practical' as everything He did during His mission: if a person listened to what Baba said or observed what He did, he or she could gain considerable knowledge about life and its purpose; but only through implementing the teachings - putting them into practice in one's daily life - could the devotee gain the full benefits of what Babaji came to give. His physical body, to which we all ran, was as much a product of His Maya, the Illusion of 'Creation,' as any other created form in the universe. On several occasions, He is said to have touched Himself and said, "This body is only dirt (earth)." He often told us, "The body is perishable; the Word is eternal." He left His body to make His devotees focus their lives on Truth, and to make it possible for people who could not accept the idea of a living Master to approach His teachings without that block.

His departure emphasized another important aspect of His teachings, also. Although He foretold political and social upheaval on a universal scale, and urged people to take active roles in "the Revolution," He did not seek political power for Himself - as some people feared and others hoped he would. Shri Babaji's message was a spiritual one - a practical message for people of this Age, but deeply spiritual, an encouragement for the best and highest aspirations of the individual soul residing in each human body.

The tradition of the <u>Sanatan Dharma</u> is that the guru leads his or her disciples to God; one finds the Formless, Absolute God through the many Forms of God. Shri Babaji played His role as Guru and as God, and when those roles had been completed - when the Form stood in the way of the Formless - He ended that 'play.'

But the 'leela' of His life was not simply 'play-acting'; Babaji *lived* in the human form that He assumed. He experienced, and rose above, hunger, thirst, anger, pleasure, pain, sickness, apparent failures or defeats, adulation - the whole gamut of human woes and joys - in order to show humankind how to live. His painful 'death,' stoically and fearlessly accepted by Babaji, was also a teaching for humankind. Even Babaji paid a price for taking on a 'human' life. He willingly and lovingly accepted and paid the price, but His body, too, was not "above the Law" and, like Ram, Krishna, Buddha, Christ, Mohammed, and others, Shri Babaji had to work through the karma of His human body.

Signs of Babaji's Departure

In Brussels, Belgium, on the morning of February 11, 1984, when Nicole DeClerck got up, she told her husband and children: "I met Babaji in my sleep. I felt Him very forcefully, and He told me clearly, in English, 'I need to be alone now; I shall go back; I shall leave this world.'" On the 14th, Nicole spent Valentine's Day with her husband and during the day she became very sick. She told her husband, "I want just one thing now - that is to be with Babaji." She had never said anything like that before. She became so sick during the day that she told her husband she thought she was going to die. Nicole slept through the night and when she awoke on the morning of the 15th, she was informed that Babaji had left His body on Valentine's Day.

On the 12th of February, 1984, in Ahmedabad, Gujarat, just before he woke up, Shri Balbir Singh Sethi had a vivid dream of Shri Babaji. Balbir Singh, whom Babaji's devotees know simply as "Sardarji," is a Sikh industrialist who was a generous host for two of Babaji's trips to Bombay and the organizer and donor for two or more of the ceremonial readings of the Guru Granth Sahib, the Sikh scriptures, at Haidakhan. In his dream, Shri Babaji told "Sardarji" to organize a reading of the Guru Granth Sahib. The command was so urgent and his recollection of it so vivid, that when he awoke, "Sardarji" started making arrangements in Ahmedabad for the priests to read and for feasts during the three days of the reading. Without any foreknowledge of what was happening in Haidakhan, the reading of the Guru

<u>Granth Sahib</u> started a few minutes after 9:30 a.m. on February 14 and it was completed just after 11:30 a.m. on February 16 - about the time when Shri Babaji's body was lowered into its grave.

On the 14th, in the city of Gwalior, the day before the news of Babaji's mahasamadhi reached the city, a three-and-a-half-year-old boy who has clear remembrances of his last life as a 19th century Tibetan saint, told his aunt and others in his family, "God has disappeared from His temple. The Sun has gone; there is darkness, only darkness."

The Scene at Haidakhan

Haidakhan was the scene of quiet confusion on the 14th of February. There was no general announcement of Babaji's mahasamadhi made in the ashram and many people had gone for karma yoga, so ashram residents were still hearing the news as late as noon.

At 9:35 a.m., Nagini called up to the office that Babaji wanted to see me, so I closed the office and hurried to Baba's room, wondering what He might want me for. As I reached the patio outside Babaji's room, I found Ramesh Bhatt standing alone outside and I asked him, "Sick as He is, do you really think Baba wants to see me?" Ramesh's eyes overflowed with tears and without a word he led me into the room, to Baba's bed. Despite the fact that there were seven or eight quietly sobbing people in the little room, I found my way to Baba's feet and made my pranam and looked to His face to receive His instructions. Only then, as Ramesh lifted the blanket to reveal Baba's pained, lifeless face, did I realize Babaji had 'left His body.' Stunned, I looked around for a place to sit and meditate, but before I could find a spot, Swami Fakiranand led me from the room and told me I must go to Lucknow, to tell Governor Singh to come. As usual, the Haidakhan telephone was out of order, and notice had to be given somehow.

By 10:30, having packed a few things and having gotten my orders amended to allow me to inform the Governor by a 'lightning' telephone call from Haldwani, instead of by an overnight train trip to Lucknow, I was on my way down the river valley - ten minutes behind two Indian devotees who were going to Delhi to advise Dr. Rao, the General Secretary of the Haidakhandi Samaj, and to tell him to bring Vishnu Dutt Shastriji from his home, 110 miles south of Delhi. When the three of us arrived in Haldwani, at Munirajji's shop we found people shouting into the telephone to Delhi, spreading the news of Babaji's departure. The Haidakhan telephone had started to work again and Bhoopie had achieved the nearly impossible by reaching not only Haldwani but also Lucknow and Delhi on the weak and reluctant ashram phone.

I returned to the ashram late in the afternoon, in Munirajji's truck, bringing a load of ice and of sad and weeping family members. The ashram was still in a state of shock, confusion, uncertainty - some people in a state of joyous ecstasy, feeling filled with Babaji's spirit and energy; others in tears, realizing the enormity of their loss. Many people half expected Babaji to 'wake up' from a deep meditation, laugh at us all, and walk into the kirtan hall to give darshan that evening. I learned that late in the afternoon, Chandramani, who had found Babaji in the Haidakhan Cave in 1970, had come for Baba's darshan and brought with him a young shaman (spiritual healer and 'sorcerer') who had given Babaji's body the aura-cleansing jhara, applied vibhuti to His forehead, and confidently announced that Baba's pulse would start again within three hours. Since Babaji had performed miracles for others, and knowing the traditions of 'Old Haidakhan Baba' 'dying' and being cremated and yet maintaining a physical body, it was easy to fall into this hopeful frame of mind. But after evening aarati there was still no pulse and even the most hopeful of us began to realize that our thirteen-year darshan was ended.

The next morning, Baba's body was bathed (again) and placed outside His room on a bed covered with ice, then blankets, under the pipal tree where He had often sat and talked with disciples. (See the photo on page 308.) People poured into the ashram - Valley people, people from Haldwani and Nainital; the government officers came to be on hand to greet, protect, and serve the Governor when he arrived by helicopter. Soon Babaji's body was almost smothered by costly silks and woolen blankets and shawls, and by garlands of rudraksha beads, of flowers, and of rupees. His hands and feet were rubbed with scented oils as people streamed in to pay their respects and have a last darshan. The pained expression on Babaji's face was gone and for some time there was a peaceful smile on His face.

At about 1:30 in the afternoon, the Governor's helicopter flew in and, at the same time, Amar Singh's truck, with Shastriji, Dr. Rao, and dozens of devotees, from Delhi and as far away as Bombay, came up the river road. They all met at Babaji's gate at about 2 p.m. and went for darshan under the pipal tree.

During the morning there had been questions floating through the ashram about what to do with Shri Babaji's body. Some thought the body should be cremated; others said it should be buried. There seemed to be a tradition for any solution suggested and another tradition opposed to any solution offered. The morning's decision was to "wait for Shastriji," but it was Governor C.P.N. Singh who made the decision. After having Babaji's darshan under the pipal tree, the Governor went up to the kirtan hall and sat with Dr. Rao and discussed plans for a 'samadhi temple' to be erected over Shri Babaji's grave; and from that point on there was no further talk of cremation.

Vishnu Dutt Shastriji and "Bihar Shastriji" delved into their astrology charts and determined that 7 a.m. on the 16th would be an appropriate time for the burial service; but by evening of the 15th there were doubts expressed that the ceremonies would be at 7:00. The next morning we were told the ceremony might begin at 11:00. We then learned that, on the fifteenth, a political organization in Haldwani which had opposed Shri Babaji and tried to tarnish His reputation during His ministry, had filed a written complaint with the police that Babaji had "died by foul play" and that hundreds of thousands of rupees had been carried down the valley in the confusion after His death. Apparently, on the night of the 14th, when Shri Nantin Baba had been informed of Shri Babaji's leaving, Nantin Baba had told someone that Babaji had been poisoned by foreign devotees. Whether Nantin Baba meant this literally, figuratively, or even seriously has never been determined[2]; there is a strong "saintly" tradition for a saint to confuse people who come for factual information and, true to the tradition, Nantin Baba told different people different things.

Whether the complaint was filed to increase the confusion in the ashram and Samaj (the Haldwani police chief said he turned away a group that came from Haldwani to "take over the ashram"), or to embarrass the Governor in a state noted for its turbulent politics, or for other reasons, it created the need for governmental investigation and a political solution before the burial ceremonies could start. State medical officers and police made an investigation, interviewing many people around the ashram who tended Babaji or observed Him in His last days. They may have wished they could have performed an autopsy, but by mid-morning there were more than a thousand upset devotees in the ashram (including one who arrived from Europe) and even an attempt to perform an autopsy would have caused a riot. Having investigated the situation as thoroughly as possible under the circumstances, the State authorities accepted petitions from Babaji's devotees from India and abroad, requesting that the burial be allowed to proceed.

At 11:30 a.m. the ceremonies got under way. Babaji's terrace was still crowded with people who did not want to leave His side. His body was still piled high with shawls, malas, and flower garlands. Now there was a sardonic smile on His face, as if He were inwardly chuckling about the awkward situations - learning opportunities - He had created by His sudden departure.

At one time Babaji had remarked to Gaura Devi, "People criticize Me because I am wearing beautiful clothes; but this is what they give to Me. I came 'naked'[3] and I will go naked." The many cloths and malas were removed from Baba's body and the body was stripped to Baba's lunghoti and lifted to the shoulders of a mixed group of pall bearers, composed of long-time Indian devotees and newer foreign attendants. They had to push and shove their way through the crowd of people reluctant to see Baba's body going - as had always been the case when Shri Babaji left a place.

A deep and wide grave had been dug in the temple garden, adjacent to the kirtan hall, and Saddhu Singh Baba (Dr. V. V.S. Rao) had made a bed of blankets and sheets for Babaji's body to lie on, facing holy Mount Kailash. Sadhu Singh Baba and Gaurhari (the young temple priest) stood in the grave to receive the body and others jumped into the grave to ease Baba onto His bed. One of them was the fully-uniformed Circle Officer (Chief of Police) from Haldwani, Shri M. K. Tyagi, who had come often to the ashram with officials as an escort officer and, as a trained observer, had seen and appreciated what Babaji sought to accomplish through the ashram and His teachings. Governor Singh and Vishnu Dutt Shastriji and Munirajji performed the pujas, with many helping hands. At the appropriate time, Shri Babaji's body was covered again with fresh silk, cotton, and woolen cloths and scarves, rudraksha malas, garlands of flowers and of various denominations of rupee notes; many bottles of perfumed oils were sprinkled, kilos of incense and rice were packed around the body, and then more kilos of dried fruits and nuts. When the body was covered in this way, five hundred kilos of salt were put in the grave as the next layer, and then the grave was filled and mounded with earth. All was done as described in the kirtan hall by Shri Babaji on January 9, 1984.

There are several "usually reliable witnesses" who swear that the murti of "Old Haidakhan Baba" in the temple wept from both eyes during the ceremony.

Later, as people recalled the event, it was interesting to see how many people were involved in the activities they had long performed for Shri Babaji. Governor Singh, Vishnu Dutt Shastriji and Munirajji (Shri Trilok Singh) were performing the rites and giving a degree of order and leadership in a very critical, chaotic and sensitive time. Sadhu Singh Baba was serving Babaji in the grave, making certain the ritual was correctly and reverently done at that level. Ramesh Bhatt, Gaurhari, Navin Joshi and the ganas, all of whom had attended Babaji with love and devotion during His life, were in the grave performing their last loving service to His body. Bhoopie, who had served others as service to Babaji, was called to the ashram clinic as the ceremonies started and missed half of the ceremonies and saw the rest from a distance. As Baba's body was brought up the stairs to the grave, I was called to the office on some now-forgotten errand that 'had' to be done immediately, and I, too, saw most of the ceremonies from a distance. Ram Dass, to whom Baba had assigned duties in the Company Bagh (the garden by the river), did not come up for the burial but stood in the riverbed lifting and throwing the biggest stones he could handle onto the river wall: and he swears he heard Babaji's happy laughter as he worked. As the Canadian Khurak Singh, in the grave, covered Baba's face with fruits and nuts, he realized how constantly Babaji was treated like a <u>murti</u> (a religious statue). He was bathed ceremonially, clothed, decked with malas and flower garlands, perfumed oils were rubbed on His hands and feet, aarati offered to Him, foods and gifts were offered to Him; throughout His human life, Babaji was both a real human being and a true symbol and manifestation of God.

As Khurak Singh climbed out of the grave, he was overcome with the sadness and pain of seeing for the last time Shri Babaji's form which he had served for so many years - and especially closely for the months just preceding His departure. Khurak went to his room and wept and howled. Suddenly his alarm watch started to 'beep,' and it would not turn off. For an hour it continued its 'beep, beep, beep.' Then the hours started changing at each second. Even in his tears, Khurak got the message: "Sound the alarm! Time is running out!"

An Official Audit

In the middle of the afternoon on the 16th, after the Governor and many people had left the ashram, the State officers who had known Babaji and had had His darshan often, came to the ashram to initiate an audit of the valuables in the ashram, to help protect the ashram and Samaj against the accusations of theft and pilferage. A committee of State officers and Samaj and ashram officers, named by the Governor, went through the ashram, identified places where valuables might be found, and made certain all those doors were locked carefully and then gave the keys to the District Magistrate. The State officers then went to Haldwani for the night.

On the morning of the 17th, the Kumaon Commissioner, Shri A.K. Das, the District Magistrate, the Sub-District Magistrate from Haldwani, the Circle Officer from Haldwani, and others came to participate in the 'treasure hunt' and 'audit.' For about seven hours - sometimes laughing, sometimes tearful, as memories of Baba came flooding in - a dozen or more of us went from room to room, looking through cupboards, boxes, purses, all sorts of containers, identifying intrinsically valuable items to be placed in a safety deposit box, pulling currency notes and small change from purses and pockets and from the rooms of Gaura Devi and Man Singh, who served Babaji daily and to whom Babaji had entrusted the money given to Him - the money which had not yet been sent off to one of His other ashrams, or was kept on hand for the financial emergencies of the ashram or Samaj, or forgotten. When a bank teller counted the money in the Haldwani Treasury on the 18th, he counted 194,000 rupees and about $16,000 worth of foreign currencies.

The 18th was also the day I was supposed to have gone to Delhi to meet Minister Tiwari, and it was the day of the marriage of the first of Munirajji's two oldest sons. After the money was deposited in the Samaj's bank account, I attended that marriage and then went back to Haidakhan. For the next two days there were unseasonable, torrential rains at Haidakhan. (Babaji always brought rain soon after big meetings at Haidakhan to clean out the Valley.) The Gautam Ganga became so swollen that we could not walk out through the river route and the path across the hills was also washed out, so I could not attend Munirajji's second son's wedding on the 20th, in Babaji's place, as He had directed me to do ten days earlier.

One of Amar Singh's trucks was also stranded at Haidakhan. He had taken it in to Haidakhan on the 18th "to have Baba's darshan." Amar Singh's other truck had been filled with 100 liters of diesel fuel on the 13th of February, when Amar Singh brought Munirajji and others to Haidakhan. In the days that followed, Amar Singh and his truck had gone back and forth many times. On the 17th, when he realized he needed to refill the tank, he measured the fuel and found 100 liters still in the tank. So on the 18th, Amar Singh had driven his other truck to Haidakhan "for darshan."

Experiences of Babaji at Haidakhan

According to Hindu custom, the twelfth day after death a 'shradh' ceremony is offered for the soul - to seek the release of the soul from its accumulated karmas that tie it to the cycle of births and deaths. This ceremony is usually performed by the sons of the deceased. We really did not think Shri Babaji needed 'liberation' from rebirth and death, but the ceremony was held for the sake of tradition.

341

About fifty or sixty people struggled (Munirajji's mother got swept off her feet by the rushing, chest-high water at one crossing point) up the still-swollen Gautam Ganga on the 25th to attend the ceremonies along with those still living in the ashram.

Bhoopie (Colonel Sharma), who considered Shri Babaji as his father, had been concerned about the shradh ceremony all day on the 24th. He had been trying to convince himself that his 'father' had not died, so why should he take part in the shradh ceremony? But Bhoopie did not feel any certainty about his answers, so as he went to sleep that night he appealed, "Please, Baba, clarify."

At about 3:45 a.m., Bhoopie had a dream that was crystal clear to him. Shri Babaji walked into Bhoopie's room and Bhoopie jumped out of his bed and made a pranam to Babaji. Babaji sat on the very corner of the bed and Bhoopie, rather embarrassed, apologized that he did not have a proper asan prepared for Babaji, but would Baba consider making Himself more comfortable on the bed? Babaji smiled and said, "But, my son, there is no space on the bed." When Bhoopie looked carefully at the bed, he saw his own body lying there, asleep.

Before Bhoopie could even register his surprise at seeing his body in bed while some awake, alert aspect of himself was standing before Shri Babaji, Babaji started firing questions at Bhoopie: "How's the work? Why does it take so much time? How's Jamwant? How's Khimanand? Jaimal?" Bhoopie stammered out some brief answers, but before he could ask *his* questions, Babaji moved out - "like a tornado."

With Babaji's departure, the dream ended and Bhoopie woke up. As he struggled to fix the line between his dream and waking states, Bhoopie realized that the door to his room, which he always locked before going to bed, was standing wide open.

After that experience, Bhoopie considered he had the answer to his plea for clarity: his Father certainly was not dead and he had no need to participate in the shradh ceremony. And Babaji had given Bhoopie another clarification, too; He had given Bhoopie an experience of his active, vital self standing before Babaji while his physical body lay inert on the bed. Whether that was a conscious or subconscious experience, it gave Bhoopie a clear concept of the separation of body and soul, which helped him greatly as a six-month bout with cancer separated his soul from that body.

Bhoopie was also the one who found the ashram dogs having Baba's darshan at night. Babaji had always cared for the ashram dogs; sometimes He would hold them in His lap during darshan, and He made sure they were bathed regularly - often getting into the river to bathe them Himself.

Bhoopie was a light sleeper and he heard the dogs barking and running here and there in the ashram. He got out of bed at about 2 a.m. one night and followed the dogs, curious to see what excited them. They led Bhoopie through the temple garden, down the '108 steps' and into the riverbed. There the dogs' barking got higher pitched and more excited. Bhoopie sat on a bench outside one of the teahouses and, as he watched, the three dogs wagged their tails, whined happily, and moved their heads around as "Someone" was clearly petting them. After a minute or so of this experience, the dogs barked happily and ran off.

The next morning, Bhoopie told of this experience as he had his morning tea in Hira's teashop. A young German woman protested that he should not spread such stories - they were unnecessary, divisive, and could not be 'proved.' So Bhoopie said no more that day. But that night he and the dogs had the same experience.

On the third night, there was all-night kirtan (singing) held in the Moksha Dham dhuni. Bhoopie and the German woman were among those who participated in the singing. At about 2 a.m., they walked to a riverbed teahouse, woke up Chandan Singh, and asked for tea. As they sipped the tea, the ashram dogs came dashing across the riverbed chasing a cat, which they caught and killed a few yards in front of the tea-drinkers. Bhoopie retrieved the dead cat, dug a hole in the sand, and buried the cat under a big stone.

As he sat down, the dogs began their happy yelping again, and danced up to "Someone" who petted them. They went through the routine of wagging their tails and putting their heads up to be petted; but this night the head of Janki Prasad - the lord of the ashram dogs - was bathed in an aura of blue light.

When the 'display' was over and the dogs had bounded away, Bhoopie turned to the German woman to ask, "Did you see? Do you

343

believe?" But he did not have to ask: her jaw hung down, her eyes bulged, and she was shaking with fear and excitement.[4]

It seemed to Gaura Devi that everyone was having experiences of Shri Babaji but her. She was upset that, after twelve years of close attendance on Him, Babaji had 'abandoned' her. One morning, feeling a bit angry about this situation, Gaura went into Babaji's room and left four bananas, as an offering. She said to Babaji, "If You are still around here, as others say, eat the bananas to show me." She went out and locked the door and went off to do some work elsewhere.

At that time, there was only one key to the padlock on the door to Babaji's room, and Gaura had it all day. Man Singh, who also tended to Baba's room, did not ask for it that day. In the evening, Gaura went to Baba's room to do aarati there; by that time, she had forgotten about the four bananas. When she unlocked the door and walked in, she saw the bananas lying there - but there were only three.

And Experiences Elsewhere

Devotees' experiences of Shri Babaji did not cease with His mahasamadhi; in fact, His leaving His physical body acted like a release from human limitations and bondage. People all over the world continue to have strong experiences of Shri Babaji. He continues to appear to people, in dreams, visions, and, apparently, to some, in physical form. Many of His followers feel led by Him into growth experiences they need, and people continue to feel His divine, sometimes miraculous, support in their daily lives. I am continually amazed by the numbers of people who have never been to India but who have had some vivid experience of Babaji which stimulated their search for more knowledge of Him and strongly affected their lives.

David Davis and Lorain Fox had visited Babaji in Haidakhan in 1979. Babaji had advised them that when they considered getting involved in a major work commitment to first learn the rules and the "price" of the interaction with any group they might plan to work with. When they returned to the U.S.A., they began to involve themselves in work with Native Americans. Lorraine is a Blackfoot-Cree Indian.

344

On February 14, 1984, David and Lorraine Fox were anguishing over a matter arising from their work with Native Americans. They decided to go to the Great Sand Dunes National Monument, not far from their home in Crestone, Colorado, to walk in the dunes, get quiet, and review their lessons from Babaji, to see how they might be applied to the problem that worried them.

As they walked in the dunes and quietly talked about Babaji, suddenly David 'saw,' out of the back of his head, a streak of intense pink color - a flash of light with a long tail, "like a meteor" - which came from behind them, sizzled between the two of them, and buried itself in the dune they were climbing, leaving no trace of itself. It startled David with its clarity. Lorain did not see it but felt the presence of its energy. They remarked that Babaji had just "done something" but they did not know what.

When they returned to their home that evening, with an answer to their Indian problem, they found a message on their telephone message recorder. Babaji had left His body.

Late in June, 1984, members of the American-organized Haidakhan Samaj met to consider the future of the group and to elect officers for the coming year. The number of people in the American Samaj was very small in comparison with the number of Americans who had visited Babaji in Haidakhan and there was no clarity on how (or even whether) to try to make the American Samaj an effective channel for spreading Shri Babaji's message.

In the morning, before the Samaj meeting, members performed a <u>yagya</u>, a fire ceremony. As the fire flared, a large ember popped out of the fire, flew past one woman's ear, and landed under Morgan Bates' knee. After a few moments, the heat caused Morgan to look and she found the ember had burned two holes in the dhoti she was wearing, which had been given to her when Shri Babaji initiated her as a yogini. One hole had a definite heart shape and the other was shaped like an open mouth.

As Morgan participated in the yagya, she got the feeling that Babaji was sending a message for all; that He lives in the heart of the fire and in the hearts of all people, and that we are always to speak with love from that place where He resides within us.

345

The experience inspired her and others at the meeting to speak truth lovingly. Deborah Wood (Ramloti) was made president of the American Samaj and decisions made at that meeting launched a drowsing Samaj onto an active, useful course which is spreading Shri Babaji's message - as He told His devotees to do.

Babaji's Return is Expected

Shri Babaji's devotees literally expect Him to return in a human body. There are many views on *when* He will return, but few doubt that He will come again soon. There are also a number of predictions and 'clues' which indicate a return in the 'near' future.

Shri Nantin Baba, in 1972, when he identified Shri Babaji as the manifestation of Lord Shiva, also said He would leave after a few years and return again as a young boy.

In 1980, when Babaji told Hem Chand Bhatt He would leave in 1984, He also said He would return, if someone like Mahendra Maharaj called Him back.

To both Mahendra Maharaj and Shri Vishnu Dutt Shastriji, Babaji spoke of coming "to rule the world," or to be the spiritual Guide of the Golden Age. He mentioned this as well to His ganas. This is something that has not yet taken place yet and people expect Babaji to fulfill this statement in the period after "the Great Revolution."

Babaji told many people, "When I return, I will call you by your name," referring to the names He had given to people. He gave several people objects to hold for Him, as 'Old Haidakhan Baba' gave His rudraksha mala to Gangotri Baba, which could be an indication to those devotees of His identity when He returns.

His Departure was an Essential Part of Babaji's Mission

In the view of many of His devotees, Shri Babaji *had* to leave in order to allow His teachings to take root and to give His disciples and devotees a chance to integrate the teachings into their lives. His "revolution" is an inner revolution which even He cannot bring about at the level of the individual soul; choices and commitments must be freely made by each human being. God can lead devotees to the experiences they need, 'He' can stimulate them to aspire to higher things, but free will makes the choices ours. He had to allow time for repeated experiences of life in the Light of His teachings. This is also the time of great testing - the Mahakranti. It is an opportunity for growth, and individuals do not grow by blindly following someone else's orders; we must learn to find answers in that divine calmness and stillness that lies within ourselves.

In one speech, Shri Babaji said, "Now you see a sweet form of God, but in the future you will see a fierce form of God." During the Mahakranti, God plays the role of Nataraj, the Divine Dancer whose fierce dancing brings destruction (or change and purification) in its wake. As Babaji said, destruction and change are necessary parts of creation; the Golden Age comes only after the Revolution. Shri Babaji said He would leave the Divine Mother - the Spirit of Love and Divine Energy which operates on the inner levels of humankind - as the Protector during the Great Revolution.

Gayatridevi, a young American woman, expressed the power and significance of Shri Babaji's mahasamadhi in a poem.

"My Lord, why do they cry? It's ever so simple and true.
Can't they know that what we see is an illusion
And what we feel, attachment to illusion?
You are more alive than ever now,
In this heart of mine which is flooded with peace.
And through grace I have awakened within
To the wonder of Love's everlasting Oneness.
Thank you for coming and going; for it is in
                    your seeming absence
That I have come to know my Self."

NOTES

[1]   Read by Joseph Campbell. See "The Power of Myth," page 45.
[2]   Shri Nantin Baba has also left his body.
[3]   Shri Babaji came to Haidakhan wearing only a lunghoti.
[4]   From a letter from Col. B.K. Sharma to JoAnn Hongslo, 3/11/84.

"The old Lakota was wise. He knew that man's heart, away from nature, becomes hard; he knew that lack of respect for growing, living things soon led to lack of respect for humans too."
Luther Standing Bear, a Lakota (Sioux) Indian
Quoted from "In the Spirit of Crazy Horse," by Peter Matthiessen.

"If we only knew deeply, absolutely, that our smallest act, our smallest thought, has such far-reaching effects; setting forces in motion; reaching out to the galaxy; how carefully we would act and speak and think. How precious life would become in its integral wholeness. "It is wonderful and frightening. The responsibility is terrifying and fascinating in its depth and completeness, containing as it does the perplexing insecurity of being unique and the profound consolation of forming part of the Eternal Undivided Whole. And we all have the right to, and can achieve, the real-ization of this wonderful meaning of life; one is quite simply part of it all; a single vision of wholeness."
From "The Chasm of Fire," Irina Tweedy

CHAPTER XVI
A CHALLENGE TO ADVENTURE

"The Messenger of Revolution has come!" The Revolution Babaji espoused is one which brings joy, the highest fulfillment in life, balance and peace to all who participate in it. It is a message for transformation of humankind to a higher level of evolution, as individuals and as societies, and of our Earth to an Eden in which every element of the Creation nurtures and supports the others.

Babaji came to show and to teach human beings how to live in a very troubled time of great changes and potential growth. You do not have to read His prophesies and warnings as divine threats of dire punishment for an evil, sinful world; just read the newspapers and magazines that abound with warnings from scientists, political observers, philosophers and daily-wage-earners that our societies and even the basic supports of all kinds of life on this earth are threatened with irreversible damage that could destroy life as we know it.

In little over a century, human beings have put into jeopardy the world eco-system which has developed over billions of years and human civilizations which have been progressing for tens of thousands of years. We have created weapons which are too terrible for sane persons to consider using and we are now trying desperately to "back-pedal" and develop means of controlling and prohibiting their use. We have put into motion methods of production and distribution of food and manufactured articles and have stimulated lifestyles that ravage the earth for our supposed benefit, at the cost of literally poisoning the air we breathe, the water we drink, and the earth in which we grow our food.

Our present ways of living are suicidal for human beings and all forms of life on this earth! Unless we human beings make conscious, drastic changes in our ways of living, the results of our abuses of Nature and human life will impose changes upon us which could bring an end to the human experiment on this planet.

Shri Babaji teaches that The Divine and Its Creation are **One**. The Creation is one great Manifestation of The Divine. It is designed to grow and develop under a system and self-discipline in harmony

349

and unity with a Divine Purpose or Plan. According to the traditions of the Sanatan Dharma, which Babaji teaches, that Purpose is to allow the Divine Conscious Energy to experience Itself in an infinite variety of ways through a nearly infinite variety of "vehicles" or means.

Human beings have developed a higher degree of intelligence and manual skills than other created beings and, with free will, have the ability and power to work in harmony with the Divine Order and Purpose or to oppose it, either by design or through ignorance. Babaji showed that when we disregard the harmony and balance of the created universe, we cause chaos and disintegration in our own lives, in our societies, and, indeed, that our disruptive forces have effects throughout our world and into the universe beyond earth's atmosphere. We can see these results on all levels of life, if we observe what goes on around us.

Although human beings are brainier than dinosaurs, that does not make us impervious to extinction through our own stupidity and failure to take necessary actions. In His life and teachings, Babaji showed that self-disciplined, pure, enlightened, focused and hard-working human beings can counterbalance the forces of disruption and self-destruction and even yet guide human society into an elevated Age of Truth, in harmony and unity with The Divine and the Divine Plan for Creation.

Babaji was constantly reminding His devotees to "BE AWARE! BE ALERT!" He forcefully broke into people's set ways of looking at themselves and the world. The ashram experience is deliberately different from normal, daily lifestyles and routines, partly in order to get us out of our established patterns and put us into a different mold, temporarily, so we can look with fresh eyes on how we live and how we interact with and affect the world around us.

Look around you. Observe what we are doing to this Earth of ours. In the 1850's, the United States Government pressured Chief Seathl (Seattle) and his tribe of Native Americans to sell their Puget Sound traditional hunting and living territory to the Government - two million acres and a way of life for $150,000. Part of the proposal was that the United States Government would create a "reservation" for the tribe and support the tribe on this land. Chief Seattle responded in a speech which scathingly depicted the urban society of the United States in the 1850's and frighteningly foreshadowed the still worse picture of this country in our time - and that which is happening all around the world today. His response is one of the most powerful statements of concern for the environment that has ever been made.[1]

"The Great Chief sends word that he wishes to buy our land. The Great Chief also sends words of friendship and good will. This is kind of him, since we know he has little need of our friendship in return. But we will consider your offer, for we know that if we do not sell, the white man may come with guns and take our land.[2]

"How can you buy or sell the sky, the warmth of the land? The idea is strange to us. If we do not own the freshness of the air and the sparkle of the water, how can you buy them?

"The white man's dead forget the country of their birth when they go to walk among the stars. Our dead never forget this beautiful earth, for it is the mother of the red man. We are part of the earth and it is part of us. The perfumed flowers are our sisters; the deer, the horse, the great eagle - these are our brothers. The rocky crests, the juices in the meadows, the body heat of the pony, and man - all belong to the same family.

"So, when the Great Chief in Washington sends word that he wishes to buy our land, he asks much of us. The Great Chief sends word he will reserve us a place so that we can live comfortably to ourselves. He will be our father and we will be his children. So we will consider your offer to buy our land. But it will not be easy, for this land is sacred to us. I here and now make this the first condition - that we will not be denied the privilege, without molestation, of visiting at will the graves of our ancestors, friends and children.

"This shining water that moves in the streams and rivers is not just water, but the blood of our ancestors. If we sell you land, you must remember that it is sacred, and you must teach your children that it is sacred and that each ghostly reflection in the clear water of the lakes tells of events and memories in the life of my people. The water's murmur is the voice of my father's father.

"The rivers are our brothers; they quench our thirst. The rivers carry our canoes and feed our children. If we sell you our land, you must remember and teach your children that the rivers are our brothers - and yours; and you must henceforth give the rivers the kindness you would give any brother.

"The red man has ever fled the approach of the white man as the changing mist on the mountains flees before the blazing sun. But the ashes of our fathers are sacred. Their graves are holy ground, and so these hills, these trees, this portion of the earth is sacred to us.

"We know that the white man does not understand our ways. One portion of land is the same to him as the next, for he is a stranger who comes in the night and takes from the land whatever he needs. The earth is not his brother, but his enemy; and when he has conquered it, he moves on.

"He leaves his fathers' graves behind, and he does not care. He kidnaps the earth from his children, and he does not care. His father's grave and his children's birthright are forgotten. He treats his mother, the earth, and his brother, the sky, as things to be bought, plundered, sold like sheep or bright beads. His appetite will devour the earth and leave behind only a desert. I do not know. Our ways are different from your ways. The sight of your cities pains the eyes of the red man. But perhaps it is because the red man is a savage and does not understand.

"There is no quiet place in the white man's cities; no place to hear the unfurling of leaves in spring, or the rustle of an insect's wings.

"But perhaps it is because I am a savage and do not understand.

"The clatter only seems to insult the ears. And what is there to life if a man cannot hear the lonely cry of the whippoorwill or the arguments of the frogs around a pond at night? I am a red man and do not understand.

"The Indian prefers the soft sound of the wind darting over the face of a pond, and the smell of the wind itself, cleaned by a midday rain, or scented with the pinyon pine.

"The air is precious to the red man, for all things share the same breath; the beast, the tree, the man - they all share the same breath. The white man does not seem to notice the air he breathes. Like a man dying for many days, he is numb to the stench.

"But if we sell you our land, you must remember that the air is precious to us, that the air shares its spirit with all the life it supports. The wind that gave our grandfather his first breath also receives his last sigh.

"And if we sell you our land, you must keep it apart and sacred, as a place where even the white man can go to taste the wind that is sweetened by the meadow's flowers.

"So we will consider your offer to buy our land. If we decide to accept, I will make another condition: The white man must treat the beasts of this land as his brothers. I am a savage and do not understand any other way. I have seen a thousand rotting buffaloes on the prairie, left by the white man who shot them from a passing train. I am a savage and I do not understand how the smoking iron horse can be more important than the buffalo that we kill only to stay alive.

"What is man without the beasts? If all the beasts were gone, man would die from a great loneliness of spirit. For whatever happens to the beasts, soon happens to man. All things are connected.

"You must teach your children that the ground beneath their feet is the ashes of your grandfathers. So that they will respect the land, tell your children that the earth is rich with the lives of our kin. Teach your children what we have taught our children, that the earth is our mother. Whatever befalls the earth befalls the sons of the earth. If men spit upon the ground, they spit upon themselves.

"This we know: The earth does not belong to man; man belongs to the earth. This we know.

"All things are connected, like the blood which unites one family. All things are connected. Whatever befalls the earth befalls the sons of the earth. Man did not weave the web of life; he is merely a strand in it. Whatever he does to the web, he does to himself.

"But we will consider your offer to go to the reservation you have for my people. We will live apart, and in peace. It matters little where we spend the remnant of our days; they are not many. Our children have seen their fathers humbled in defeat. Our warriors have felt shame, and after defeat they turn their days in idleness and strong drink. A few more hours, a few more winters, and none of the children of the great tribes that once lived on this broad land or that roam now in small bands in the woods will be left to weep over the graves of a people once as powerful and hopeful as yours.

"But why should I mourn the passing of my people? Tribes are made of individuals and are no better than they. Men come and go, like the waves of the sea. It is the order of Nature. Even the white man, whose God walked and talked with him as friend to friend, cannot be exempt from the common destiny. We may be brothers, after all. We shall see.

"One thing we know, which the white man may one day discover - our God is the same God. You may think now that you own Him, as you wish to own our land; but you cannot. He is the God of man, and His compassion is equal for the red man and the white. This earth is precious to Him, and to harm the earth is to heap contempt on its Creator.

"The whites, too, shall pass; perhaps sooner than all other tribes. Contaminate your bed, and you will one night suffocate in your own waste.

"But in your perishing, you will shine brightly fired by the strength of the God who brought you to this land and for some special purpose gave you dominion over this land and over the red man. That destiny is a mystery to us, for we do not understand when the buffalo are all slaughtered, the wild horses are tamed, the secret corners of the forest heavy with scent of many men, and the view of the ripe hills blotted by talking wires.

"Where is the thicket? Gone. Where is the eagle? Gone. The end of living and the beginning of survival.

"So we will consider your offer to buy our land. If we agree, it will be to secure the reservation you have promised. There, perhaps, we may live out our brief days as we wish. When the last Red Man shall have perished from the earth, and his memory among the white men shall have become a myth, these shores will swarm with the invisible dead of my tribe. They love this earth as the newborn loves its mother's heartbeat.

"The white man will never be alone. Let him be just and deal kindly with my people for the dead are not powerless. "'Dead' did I say? There is no death. Only a change of worlds!

"So if we sell you our land, love it as we have loved it. Care for it as we have cared for it. Hold in your mind the memory of the land as it is when you take it.

"And with all your strength, with all your mind, with all your heart, preserve it for your children, and love it...as God loves us. One thing we know. Our God is the same God. This earth is precious to Him."

In the last one hundred fifty years, our "civilized" societies have not learned from the experience of native peoples all around the world to respect the Earth. We are even now destroying these people and their cultures on every continent. In our insatiable rush for more and better "things" in our lives, our Western cultures are exhausting natural resources and are creating wastes, fetid garbage and nuclear leavings so quickly that we cannot get rid of them. They come back to haunt us - and literally to poison us. We have trade wars over the right to sell all these "things" to countries that may not even want or need them. I believe it is true that the two largest categories of expenditures in the United States today are, first, the military defense of this way of life and, second, the healing of the mental and physical ailments that arise from our over-eating, malnutrition and excessive indulgences, such as smoking, drinking, and the abuse of sex and drugs, and the tensions and stresses that arise from this style of life. If we add the costs of policing, punishing, supporting and rehabilitating those people who cannot cope in our society, these social ills and problems probably cost much more than our military establishment. And if that is not sufficiently ironic or insane, consider that the rest of the world is madly scrambling, exhausting resources and destroying cultures, to duplicate this way of life! We are like lemmings rushing over a cliff to destruction.

Babaji showed us a simpler way of life, more in harmony with the rest of Creation, respectful of all forms of life - including those forms which we rarely consider to have life, like rocks, plants and water. He showed us that we should keep our personal needs simple and few; take only what we need; take it in a manner that does not destroy the eco-system; and do not waste anything.

People brought or mailed many gifts to Babaji; there was a good deal of packaging. Babaji carefully and patiently untied each string or ribbon, opened each package carefully, in order to save the paper, and He gave the string and paper to Raghuvir or Kharku or whoever was running the ashram shop at the time. Every possible item brought to Babaji was used and used again; recycled.

As Lord Shiva, the God of Change, Babaji did not hesitate to change the landscape and improve the facilities of the Haidakhan Ashram for human use. The lovely little temple in the ashram was built in the nineteenth century and He added several buildings in the 1970's and 1980's. When He dedicated the Company Bagh (garden) and the Moksha Dham Dhuni (a place of worship) in the summer of 1983, Babaji congratulated those who worked in the garden, which was created out of river "wasteland." "You have conquered Nature and have created this beautiful garden." He taught us, by His example, to use the resources of the earth to create what is needed to maintain human life and simple comfort, but to take what is needed *with respect and care,* not ravaging the earth or leaving it desolate and lifeless in our wake.

Western societies - and the United States of America, above all - are terribly wasteful. We waste electricity and other forms of power; we waste water. We have a whole industry of "throw-away" items. We waste vanishing resources of petroleum and use great quantities of energy to make plastic items for one-time use; but they may take longer than the period of written human history to disintegrate! We create mountains of waste out of things - like paper, metal, glass, even human wastes - which can be recycled and put to beneficial use more cheaply and with less use of energy than making new items from raw materials.

The Rocky Mountain Institute of Snowmass, Colorado, an organization devoted to the conservation of energy and water and other resources, estimated, in the 1980's, that the huge United States national debt could be paid off in ten or twelve years with the potential savings in expenditures for energy alone, if individuals and organizations shifted to the use of light-bulbs that use one-third to one-half of the wattage of the normal, wasteful bulb, heated with solar heat, and used other means of conserving energy and thus avoided the necessity for construction of costly new nuclear or other fueled

356

power plants. The reduction of demand for increasingly scarce resources would also reduce international tensions. In many fields, the technical means for careful and efficient use of our limited resources are now available to us, but we are so stuck in our patterns that we do not take even the relatively easy means of protecting our natural, basic life-support systems! If we do not begin now to use the many available methods of recycling and conservation in our homes and work places, we will soon, as Chief Seattle said, "suffocate in [our] own waste." Or we may find ourselves totally without many of the items we take for granted today.

Babaji taught us to learn to see and treat all created things as containing the substance and Energy of The Divine, using them with respect, living in harmony with Nature. If we live this way, there will be far less destruction and pollution of the Earth and a greatly reduced level of stress for all sentient beings.

Babaji emphasized the great need to restore respect for human beings and the societies which nurture them. Human beings are the creatures closest to The Divine; it is apparently only from the human form that the soul can make its transition to reunion with The Divine. Although the process of purification and spiritual growth is accomplished on an individual basis - different for each person because our experiences and our levels of growth are widely varied - the societies which we create and maintain have a great influence on the training, growth and welfare of those who are born into them.

Today, in most countries of the world, three, sometimes four, generations of a family still live together in one home. This was basically true in the West until the last sixty years. Now, in the name of progress, we in the West have facilitated the break-up of the family through Social Security, through road systems that provide great mobility, through our methods of hiring, and through our once-cheap housing. These policies facilitate moving people allover the country - or the world - in order to follow job opportunities. There are benefits to this mobility, but it certainly has contributed to our rootlessness.

Partly as the result of the weakening of family ties, the 1960's and 1970's saw the breakdown of once-accepted social standards and mores, the introduction of "social" use of drugs and of casual and commercial sex. Now we find ourselves without the traditional moral standards and role models which our more experienced and often wiser elders once supplied; we have worshipped youth and denigrated the wisdom and experience of age. We have opened the way for individual and social license that exceeds the limits of freedom or common sense, and we are reaping a harvest of illnesses, strains and tensions, drug abuse and AIDS (as if gonorrhea and syphilis weren't reason enough for caution), the commercialization of sex, and gang warfare in our cities that makes the Mafia seem civilized. We tolerate cruelties and injustices against individuals and nations which many times in the past have stirred us to take up arms. And although we have accomplished most of this ourselves in the past sixty years, we are upset and saddened when the children take up and amplify our little secret faults and our established ways that threaten life on this planet.

Babaji reminded us of the old scriptural advice: "The good is one thing; the pleasant is another. The wise prefer the good to the pleasant; the foolish, driven by fleshly desires, prefer the pleasant to the good."

In this age, when we rush headlong in pursuit of "the pleasant," oblivious to the damage we are doing to ourselves, our societies and the world around us, we need to recall and study the benefits and the less frenetic joys of "the good." Inner balance and self-discipline, developed through awareness of and reflection on the experiences that come to us through life, provide a basis for making sensible choices among "the good" and "the pleasant" circumstances or challenges which arise. The person who is "spaced out" on drugs, "bombed out" on liquor, or mesmerized by the pursuit of fleeting pleasures, is unable to make balanced, aware choices, unable to make progress in life, unable to enjoy the fullness of life, and unable to know and develop herself or himself to the fullest capacity.

Babaji urged people to "go to the wise and learn." Although not everyone attains wisdom with the passage of time, it is still probable that grandparents are a better source of advice about the challenges and opportunities of life than are the latest popular young singer, actor, actress or athlete. There is a difference between celebrity and wisdom. We should be able to enjoy and respect both - and to distinguish between them as we should make distinctions between "the good" and "the pleasant." Our role models need to be selected with greater care. Our models for the societies we seek to develop and live in, or to provide for our children, are also deserving of more thought and careful selection. If we do not start exercising thoughtful care about the world around us, we will not have much to leave for our children and grandchildren. As Chief Seattle observed, "He kidnaps the earth from his children, and he does not care."

We call our times "modern times." Probably the Greeks of Alexander's day, the Romans under the Caesars, the Norman kings and Peter the Great - and certainly the Victorians in England - referred to their eras as "modern times," as they lived through them. Babaji calls this "The Dark Age," the Kali Yuga. His view of the world is that we are in a time when humankind chases after material things and fleeting sensual pleasures, forgetting the divine origin and aspect of the human race and of its earthly surroundings; a time when the darkness of Ignorance prevails. It all depends on your focus - on the basis from which one views and considers life.

At a time when people are seeking more "things," searching for greater excitement, thrills and pleasures, we are also overpopulating the earth. More people wanting more things leads to ecological disaster. We cut down or burn almost one hundred thousand acres of forests every week, plough up marginal land for farming, pave over and inhabit fertile lands, pollute the once-sparkling streams and rivers, and belch smoke and cancer-causing fumes into the air. While we chase after "the better life," we are destroying the very means of maintaining life itself. The purifying filters of Nature - the earth, air and water - are so clogged with the trash and poisons of our modern societies that they cannot cope. On every side, Nature is regurgitating our human garbage.

Naturally - foreseeably - this gives rise to some tensions within ourselves and our societies. Our economies are fueled by a great outpouring of manufactured "things," most of which have to be advertised heavily in order to convince people to buy them. When we buy and consume them (or throw them away) in sufficient quantity to support the manufacturers, we are berated for not saving enough money to create new industries and more "things." When we cannot sell enough of our "things" in our home markets, we get into disputes with other countries because they do not buy enough of our "things" to keep our economies running at full speed.

In this process, many people get trampled or pushed to one side, out of the way of the stampeding herd. Hundreds of millions of people on this earth are without work or means of earning a decent living. Both they and those who are scrambling along on "the fast lane" are generally - at least subconsciously - on the alert for difficulty or attack from the "outside." As Chief Seattle put it, people see the earth as an enemy. Many people see other people basically as competitors; they find life "hard."

Not all people are burdened with these views of life. Many find the earth a wonderful place to live, to work, to experiment and grow. It depends on one's outlook. Our minds, our thoughts have great power; they shape our outlook on life, our successes in life, and our relationships with others.

If we can acknowledge - or even accept as a working hypothesis - that the Creation is One, that all created things are interconnected and have a common origin and destiny, then it is possible to learn to live and work and grow strong and wise, in harmony with The Divine and the Divine Plan. If we have respect for all created things and treat all human beings and all living things with love and respect, being aware and careful of their capacities to hurt or help in our activities, we are spared the need to live in fear or tension. We can face the world without drugs or violence; we can face our partners in life without hostility or overt defensive tactics. If, as Babaji recommends, we become more interested in serving others than in attaining things for ourselves, we can attain a detachment that dilutes or erases the causes of sorrow and suffering in our lives. If we realize that we do not need a mansion or three cars in the garage, we are relieved of the tensions of attaining those goals and of the jealousy directed at those who may have them. We might experience an inner peace, a more constant joy, and release our latent resources of creativity.

Think of how we live. We eat "junk food" that we know is not healthy for us. We buy useless and unnecessary things, store them in our houses, unused, for months and years, and trash them and other things onto "Mother Earth." By being more thoughtful and careful, we might help lift some of these burdens from Mother Earth, and, in doing so, save our money, live more simply and easily, and save the earth from having to process billions of tons of indigestible trash.

Living simply and carefully does not mean living dully or in impoverishment. On the contrary, simple, quiet living provides more time for deep enjoyment of life and for developing and expressing individual creativity. There was a time when urban dwellers had great respect for the farmers who produced our food and who lived close to Nature and had respect and awe of Nature. Now we have taught - even pressured - farmers to become the greatest users of chemicals and polluters of land and water and to treat the earth as another commodity to exploit and try to subvert to their own wills. The simple life, lived in harmony and unity with The Divine and Its whole Creation, has a balance and meaning that is lacking in our modern day scramble for pleasures and profits. And it has never foreclosed people from attaining a comfortable living, or even riches and power. The life lived in harmony and unity with The Divine produces or provides what is necessary to accomplish one's goals in life.

Although Babaji lived in a Hindu ashram and society, He did not emphasize religion or religiosity. He stated that He was above religions and urged those who came to Him to "follow the religion that is in your heart." "Every religion is equally good and leads to the same divine goal." Over and over, He said that "humanitarianism is the only religion." He made no attempt to export India's religion to the rest of the world: what He espoused and expounded is a way of life - a way of life that exalts and improves the condition and quality of human beings and human life, and helps all Creation live in ever-closer harmony and unity with The Divine from which all forms of life and energy spring.

In the ashram at Haidakhan, Babaji gave us a vision and example of what this life can be. He said, "The new world begins from here!" and that, I think, is the major significance of Haidakhan. He told those who came to Him, "Learn the rules and follow the discipline while you are here. Then, wherever you go, teach others the same discipline." It was the discipline of living life in harmony with other beings and with all of Nature; of being alert to and aware of the lessons, challenges and opportunities that arise for us in daily life; of learning to serve others as a direct expression of devotion to and worship of The Divine - the highest form of worship. As we learned in His Presence to love Him more and more deeply, Babaji guided us to the knowledge that if one is devoted to The Divine a person comes to love all created things. Therefore, one treats all human beings, the Earth, the beasts, birds, flowers, water - all - with the love and respect which we have for The Divine.

This is a rational goal which brings happiness to individuals, both "inside" and around us. One can seek this goal, this way of life, on a purely secular basis, but it helps a great deal to have a belief in The Divine as the basis and support of one's efforts.

It is difficult to practice this way of life in a very secular world, geared to profit and loss statements and the search for new thrills and pleasures. That is why visits to ashrams, monasteries, and similar places of "retreat" can be helpful in developing a new focus on life and getting some experience in living in accordance with new patterns. One can attain a growing degree of detachment from the hectic life and its lures, a significant reduction of fear and distrust, an openness to - even eagerness for - the learning experiences and opportunities of life. And, with these, comes a growing balance and stability which leaves one standing tall and straight even through the buffetting of life's storms. This way of life lessens or removes one's dependence on others for happiness or "success" and allows the expression of love without attachment or "strings."

There was, and still is, much common sense in the manner in which the old culture of India divided the stages of human life. The first twenty or twenty-five years were spent as the celibate student (brahmachari), growing up and learning the skills to earn and to live by, within the shelter of the family and the culture of the community. In ancient days, children often were sent to live and study for many years with learned gurus and sages, who taught all areas of education within a spiritual and religious family framework - in ashrams.

The next stage in life was that of the householder - or the warrior, ruler, or priest. This was the time for marriage, the bearing and raising of children, the pleasures, the strivings, the adventures and joys of practicing the skills, arts and fundamental principles learned as a student. In dealing with other people and cultures, in making their businesses prosper, and in teaching their children by word and example, the householders deepened their experience of human life and of The Divine.

When their children were married and established in business or profession, the parents were ready to enter a third stage of life, in which they focused on their relationships with The Divine, detaching themselves from the focus on building families or businesses or wealth or fame. Often this meant going to live in an ashram or other spiritual community where they could concentrate on spiritual matters and on service to others.

There was a fourth stage, too, for those who attained the spiritual courage, strength and insight to support it. These people renounced even the attachment to and support of the community to which they had "retired." They went into the world as wanderers to share with others the knowledge and experience they had gained in a life-time, living briefly (the tradition is that the sadhu stays no longer than three days in any place) on the charity of those with whom they shared their wisdom, work and love.

Babaji urged us all to help others; to exercise and develop our humanity through unselfish service to others. "To work, think good thoughts, and dedicate your life to Humanity is the best thing." This is Karma Yoga. Through service, while we experience the joys and "highs" of helping others, we are also helping ourselves greatly - both spiritually and practically. Karma Yoga, Babaji said, is the most efficacious way to enlightenment and unity with the Divine in this Age.

Babaji often noted that there is strength in unity. None of us, however rich or talented, is able to cope with all the problems of our neighborhoods or of the world. There are many groups - in towns, in cities, on national and international levels -which work effectively to assist people in practical ways. These organizations are overwhelmed by the effects of poverty, drugs, or the ravages of wars, droughts, or storms. They need both caring workers and money. There are many people, of all ages, who are getting involved in local groups to combat drugs, poverty, and ignorance. The retired people are likely to have many of the skills, the wisdom, patience and time to be of real help to those who are struggling.

And in helping others, they help themselves. As Babaji noted, when a person performs karma yoga (service), he or she eats well, digests well, sleeps well; we feel energized, useful, happy. These effects all help with the maintenance of good health, a ready memory, and interest in life. And if one has - through the experiences of life and through conscious effort - attained a degree of detachment, one can perform this karma yoga constantly, with real dedication and devotion, but without stress, without anger, without getting ulcers.

The work is there to do; there will always be more to do than an individual or group can accomplish. Just go at it as lovingly, efficiently and effectively as you can. Set the example. Others will come to help you and one day those who are being helped will be helpers.

Even people who are crippled or ill can help to heal themselves and the world. Many spiritual teachers, and now even scientists, tell us that our thoughts, as well as our actions, have effects far, far beyond our little personal spheres in life. The Tibetan Buddhist saint Milarepa meditated, prayed and lived for "all sentient beings." He and many other saints and teachers have transformed the areas around them by the power of their spiritual vibrations and by the examples of divine living which they provide. In 1977, Itzhak Bentov wrote of and documented something of the power of group meditation in his marvelous book, "Stalking the Wild Pendulum." Maharishi Mahesh Yogi, the teacher of Transcendental Meditation, and Swami Rama of the Himalayan Institute have been working with groups of meditators and doing research on the powers for good which can come with a mere one per cent of a population meditating for the common good. Those who do not have the physical strength to work to help others can gather (or even sit separately, but in conjunction with others) to meditate, pray, repeat a healing mantra, or just think good, healing, harmonious thoughts for the whole universe. People - young and old - willing to help and work can organize neighborhood assistance groups, meet to send out healing vibrations through the universe, and to plan work in the neighborhood for the day or week.

There are many ways to help in the healing of this confused, challenged, and upset world. But nothing will be accomplished by endless discussion or by neglect or withdrawing from unpleasantness. Babaji's instruction was "Talk less, work more." Only caring action - service to others - can cleanse and improve this world. If we realize and experience the unity of the created universe, then our brother's or sister's, or our neighbor's problems, or the problems of people on the other side of the earth are ours, also, to be concerned with and to move to help with. Then we will say, along with Babaji, "If you are at peace, I am in peace. If you are troubled, I am troubled. If you have problems, I have problems."

The goal of living in harmony and unity with The Divine and all of the Creation is not achieved overnight. It takes years of new experiences and new, improved reactions to break old habits and establish new ways of life. One may not fully attain the goal in this lifetime. But the mere setting of the goal and an earnest striving toward it, will change one's values, choices, policies, decisions on what to desire or acquire for yourself, what to eat, what to put your thought and energy into. With more and more people making choices and decisions and acting on these bases, our cities, our countries, our world - the whole Creation - will be affected by our changes.

It is late, but perhaps not yet too late to make some vital, basic changes in our individual and social attitudes and relationships with each other, with our Earth, and with The Divine. Babaji taught rational, humanitarian values and goals - inextricably linked to The Divine, but not entangled in religious disputes or "religiosity" - which can cure the ills and sorrows of our times and lift humankind to higher levels.

We have all experienced physical and emotional hurts, discomforts, or diseases. Although the human body can function if some part or parts of it are out of order - or even missing - we know that the whole body can feel miserable because of one area which hurts, from a cut, a bruise, a burn, from over-eating, from over-exertion, or from a diagnosable disease. The body may even die because of one part which malfunctions. Certainly, the human body is not able to function at its highest level or its fullest capacity, when one or more of its parts fail to work in perfect harmony with the rest.

It is the same with the Creation, with the entire created universe. As a whole, the Creation is so vast that it can accommodate much pain and disharmony. But so long as any element of the whole does not, or is not allowed to, operate in harmony with its purpose and with the rest of the Creation, the whole of Creation is less than the Perfection from which it came and which it can be.

Human beings - as vibrating, creative, intelligent elements of the Creation, as conscious protectors and extenders of the Creation - have much to do with the balance, peace, joy, harmony and unity of the Creation. Our every thought and action sends impulses throughout the universe and helps shape what occurs in it. If we want to change, improve, perfect what goes on around us, we need to heal and perfect ourselves, and project good thoughts and good works into the world around us. As Babaji said, "You must all be busy in doing your own work (dharma) and by doing that you will be cooperating in the universal work. You must all be prepared to contribute to the universal good."

The healing of our battered Earth and its disordered societies must be humanity's highest priority in the next decades. Failure to take positive, thoughtful corrective measures will leave our children in an earthly hell where ten billion people may be scrambling for meaning and a decent standard of living in a depleted and poisoned Earth. If we look at this challenge of our time from a balanced, peaceful concerned and loving viewpoint, living in this Age can be a great adventure, where human beings, as real co-creators with The Divine, can shape -and *improve* - our destiny.

Babaji returned, in 1970, to His little ashram in Haidakhan, in the foothills of the Indian Himalayas, to teach - to show - human beings how to live in harmony with each other, with the rest of Creation, and with its Creator. He transformed the tiny village of Haidakhan into a new Eden, where the New World, in an Age of Truth, could take on form and a new birth. He gave to us all the impulse and the means to bring about the dawn of a golden Age of Enlightenment.

366

NOTES

[1] In 1988 someone handed me a mimeographed sheet with Chief Seattle's speech on it. I had heard and seen bits and pieces of it for years. In February 1989, I found the story of the speech in Eva Greenslit Anderson's book, "Chief Seattle," along with a few quoted lines. In March, 1989, I went to the Bancroft Library at Stanford University to search for an accurate, authentic version of the speech. I found four different versions, one from the nineteenth century, published years after the event, by Dr. Henry A. Smith, who had translated the speech into English as Chief Seattle gave it. There were also three twentieth century versions. All four versions contain many identical sentences, but no two are alike. Puzzled, and uncertain which version to use - because some statements in some versions seem contradictory to the basic themes of the speech - I was grateful to find, at the end of Dr. Smith's published version, these final words: "The above is but a fragment of Chief Seattle's speech, and lacks all the charm lent by the grace and earnestness of the sable old orator and the occasion." So the version of Chief Seattle's speech which I have given here is my own compilation, using quoted material which best illustrates and supports the points which Babaji taught.

[2] The federal government had already allotted to white settlers some of the land in Chief Seattle's domain.

GLOSSARY OF TERMS

Most of the words in this glossary come from Sanskrit or Hindi. They are transliterated into English. The attempts to come up with an English spelling that produces pronunciations that are close to the Sanskrit or Hindi pronunciations (Hindi has 52 letters in its alphabet and many sounds different from English) often result in varied spellings of the same word. The spellings of some words in the text vary depending on the spelling used in quoted or referenced material.

A major example of this is the spelling of the name of the village where Shri Babaji's principal ashram is located. The two major spellings - Hairakhan and Haidakhan - result from a Hindi consonant which sounds something between 'd' and 'r'. Most Westerners who came to Haidakhan used the pronunciation Hairakhan, or Herakhan. When Shri Babaji learned that it was being spelled Herakhan in English-language correspondence, He insisted that we change the spelling to Haidakhan.

Another frequent cause of confusion is the English addition of the letter 'a' to many words ending in a consonant, such as Rama for Ram and japa for jap. In spoken Hindi, a short 'a' sound is often added to a word ending in a consonant to help it flow into the next word, but the Hindi letter for 'a' is not used in the Hindi spelling of the word. 'A' is always pronounced as in 'ah.'

AARATI, or arati (ar'-ti) - A worship service in which light (usually a lamp burning ghee) is offered to an image of God.

ASAN (a'-san) - In this book, asan refers to a seat, usually one prepared for a holy person. Asan also refers to yoga positions.

ASHRAM (ash'-ram) - Now used most often to mean a spiritual teaching community, or a place of 'retreat.' The Sanskrit meaning also denotes a period or stage in the traditional concept of a person's life: the student period, the householder period, the ashram or spiritual-growing period, and the life of the sanyasin, or wandering renunciate.

AVATAR (a'-va-tar) - A manifestation of The Divine in human form; a great spiritual teacher.

BABA or BABAJI (ba'-ba or ba'-ba-jee) - Father; generally used

368

for a holy man. The 'ji' is an added term of respect or reverence.

BHAGWAN (bag-wan') - God; the Lord.

BHAJAN (ba'-jan) - A song of praise to the Lord.

BRAHMACHARI (bra-ma-cha'-ree) - A person in the first period of a Hindu's life; a celibate who studies the scriptures and other traditional knowledge.

BRAHMAN (bra'-mon) - A name for the Formless Divine.

CHAKRA (chock'-ra) - One of the psychic or energy centers of a human being. Generally refers to one of the seven major power centers, rising up the spine, from base to the crown of the head. See also page 128, Note 12.

CHANDAN (chan'-dan) - Used in this book as a ground sandalwood paste used by many Hindu sects to 'paint' their foreheads with sacred symbols.

DARSHAN (dar'-shan) - Either a vision of a deity or a saint's sharing of his or her presence with disciples.

DEV or DEVA (masc.), DEVI (fem.) (dave or day'vee) - A deity; a form of God. Devi is often used for the consort of Lord Shiva; also used as the shakti or (feminine) energy form of a male deity.

DHARMA (dar'-muh) - The eternal Truth by which the creation operates; the Truth or the sacred Law; a righteous way of living.

DHOTI (doe'-tea) - A long, wide strip of cloth wound around the lower half of the body, which makes a pant-like garment for men.

DHUNI (do'-nee) - A sacred fire; it is usually kept burning continually in a ritually-constructed pit, and is usually tended by a saint or other dedicated person.

FAKIR -(fa-keer') - a Hindu ascetic.

GANA (ga'-na) - A heavenly 'soldier' or attendant of Lord Shiva.

GANGA (gaang'-ga) - A river. With a capital 'G', it is Ganga, the goddess of rivers. Ganga is also the Sanskrit and Hindi word for the Ganges River.

GHEE (gee, with a hard 'g') - Clarified butter; used for making offerings to the gods; also used in cooking.

369

GURU (goo'-roo) - A spiritual teacher and guide who undertakes to lead his or her disciples to God-realization.

HANUMAN (Ha'-noo-maan) - A very popular Hindu deity with the form of a monkey; said to be a manifestation of Shiva, who helped Lord Ram in His struggle to regain His wife Sita after Her capture by a demon. (See the Ramayana epic.) Hanuman is known and loved as a symbol of strength and of devotion to Lord Ram.

HAWAN (Ha'-wan) - Also called Yagya. The sacred fire ceremony in which worshippers offer back to The Divine portions of the five elements which sustain Creation. A symbolic drama of sacrificial living.

HINDI (hin'-dee) - One of the major languages of India, which stems from Sanskrit.

HINDU (hin'-do) - The Greeks, under Alexander the Great, gave this name to the people who lived east of the Indus River. The name has stuck to the Indians who follow the Vedic and later spiritual traditions. Many "Hindus" prefer to be called followers of the Sanatan Dharma, but that is a pretty big mouthful when one word is available.

ISHWARA (eesh-wa'-ra) - The first, most subtle, 'form' of the Formless Divine, according to Hindu belief.

JAI! (jay) - Honor or glory, as in Jai Vishwa! - Honor to the Universe!

JAP or JAPA (jop) - Repetition of God's name(s) or of a mantra over an extended period of time. Often performed while using a mala or rosary.

JHARA (jar'-a) - A method of healing through cleansing the aura by 'sweeping' with a 'broom' of peacock feathers or other material (such as a leafy branch). The jhara practitioner repeats a special healing mantra while he or she 'sweeps.'

-JI (gee) - A suffix added to a deity's name or a person's name to express the speaker's love, respect or reverence for the deity or person addressed.

JYOTI (jyo'-tea) - Illimination or light; especially an unexplainable, holy light.

KAILASH (Kai'-laash) - A mountain held sacred by followers

of Lord Shiva, because He is said to have spent millennia in meditation and doing penance on it for the sake of humanity. Shri Babaji said the original Mount Kailash is the mount in the Kumaon district opposite the Haidakhan Ashram. There is a major mountain in Tibet by this name, which has been an object of pilgrimage for several millennia.

KALI YUG or YUGA (kali, rhymes with collie) - The Dark (kali) Age (yug); also translated as the Iron Age or Age of Strife. It is one of four Eras or Ages in the Hindu tradition, each Yug becoming more gross than the previous one. After the Kali Yug, the cycle starts over with a Satyayug - the Age of Truth.

KARMA (car'-muh) - The Law of Causation; action or work; the fruit (either 'good' or 'bad') of one's action. Jesus stated the Law of Karma as "As ye sow, so shall ye reap."

KHUMBA MELA (khoom'-ba may'-la) - A mela is a fair or gathering. The khumba melas are spiritual gatherings held in four Indian cities (scheduled so the four melas are held three years apart, once in each city every twelve years). Seekers and devotees come for several days to spend time with saints and other spiritual leaders and teachers.

KIRTAN (kir'-tan) - Religious songs which repeat the names of deities.

KRISHNA (kreesh'-na) - A divine manifestation of Lord Vishnu; the central figure of the Mahabharata epic. Lord Krishna's conversation with His disciple Arjuna, before the great Mahabharata battle, is recorded in the Bhagavad-Gita.

KUMAON (koo'-ma-own') - A large district in the northwestern part of the Indian state of Uttar Pradesh, which includes the three magisterial districts of Almora, Nainital and Pithoragarh. It is an area of foothills and mountains of the Himalaya range.

KUNDALINI (koon-da-lee'-nee) - The cosmic energy lying within each individual. It is pictured as a snake, coiled at the base of the spine. As the process of enlightenment, or Self-realization, proceeds, the kundalini (divine energy) rises higher in the individual.

KURTA (koor'-ta) - a simple Indian long shirt.

LAHIRI MAHASAYA (La-hee'-ree Ma-ha-sai'-ya) - The ac-

371

countant whom Mahavatar Babaji initiated in 1861. He became a great teacher of kriya yoga and a saint.

LAKULIN or LAKULISH (la-koo-leen') - A great teaching saint.

LEELA or LILA - The 'play' or 'sport' or activity of God in human form. Often, lila is used synonymously with miracle.

LINGAM (ling'-gam) - A phallic symbol of Shaivite worship, symbolizing the creative energy of God.

LOTUS - The lotus flower is used as a symbol of purity growing out of the muck of materialism and ignorance. The lotus grows in still waters; its roots are in the mud, its leaves float on the surface of the water, and the beautiful blossom rises above all in purity.

LUNGHI (1oong'-gi -with a hard 'g') - a wide, long strip of cotton cloth used to wrap around a man's waist and legs, like a skirt; a sarong.

MAHA - Great.

MAHAPRABHUJI (Ma'-ha-pra-boo'-jee) - The Great (maha) Lord (prabhu).

MAHARAJ (ma'-ha'-radge') - Literally, great king. Also used as a title of respect, especially for a holy man.

MAHASAMADHI (ma-ha-sa-ma'-dee) - The consciously-willed departure of the soul from a saint's body.

MAHAVATAR (ma-ha'-va-tar) - A great avatar, or manifestation of The Divine in human form.

MALA (ma'-la) - A Hindu rosary, often containing 108 beads.

MANTRA (man'-tra) - A sacred word or set of words which, through repetition and reflection, helps a person quiet the mind and attain perfection or God-realization.

MAYA (my'-uh) - Illusion; the illusive power of The Divine.

MOUNT KAILASH - See KAILASH.

MUNDAN (mun'-dan) - The shaving of all hair on the head for a religious purpose.

MURTI - (moor'-tee) - A religious statue or idol.

OM NAMAHA SHIVAI or OM NAMAH SHIVAYA - A Shaivite mantra which can be translated as "I take refuge in God (Shiva)" or "I surrender to Shiva (God)".

PARAMATMA (par-am-at'-muh) - the Divine Soul (atma).

PRABHU (pra'-boo) - God.

PRANAM (pra-nam') - A form of greeting in which one bows the head and touches joined hands to the forehead. A "full pranam" to a holy person may be made by lying flat on the ground with joined hands touching the feet of the holy person.

PRASAD (pra-sad') - Usually food which has been consecrated by being offered to an idol or to a living saint. The food is distributed among the worshippers at the place and sometimes sent to absent devotees or other persons as a blessing.

PUJA (poo'-ja) - Hindu worship ritual.

PUJARI (poo-ja'-ree) - One who performs puja; a priest.

RAJAH (ra'-ja) - (Formerly) an independent Hindu king, a sovereign ruler.

RAM or RAMA - The first of the human-formed manifestations of Lord Vishnu. The chief protagonist of The Ramayana.

RISHI (ree'-shee) - An ancient sage or seer; especially those who initiated the early scriptures and religious concepts.

SADASHIV or SADASHIVA (sa-da'-sheev) - The first (sometimes) 'visible form ' of God in the Shaivite cosmology.

SADHU sometimes SADDHU (sod'-dhoo) - A renunciate; usually a wanderer.

SADGURU (sod'-goo-roo) - One's true [sat] guru, or supreme teacher.

SADHANA (sod'-a-na) - Spiritual practice or discipline, such as fasting, meditating, performing karma yoga.

SAMBASADASHIV (sam'-ba-sa-da'-sheev) - Sadashiva with 'His' Shakti, or female energy, Amba.

SANATAN DHARMA (sa'-na'-tan dar'-muh) - The Eternal (sanatan) Way or Law of the Universe (or Religion).

SANYASI or SANYASIN (san-ya '-see) - One who has renounced social ties for a life of spiritual meditation and activity; often a wanderer.

SATSANG (sot'-saang) - An exchange or discussion of spiritual truths.

SELF-REALIZATION - The knowledge and experience of the

individual soul as one, in union with the Universal Soul, or Self.

SHAIVITE (shave'-ite) - a person who worships Lord Shiva.

SHAKTI (shock'-tee) - Energy; often used as the feminine, creative Energy of a deity, which is assumed to have a balanced male-female energy.

SHIVA (shee'-va) - In the Hindu trinity of gods - Brahma, Vishnu and Maheshwara, or Shiva - Shiva is the one who brings about destruction (change) and purification in the Creation. In the Shaivite tradition (those who worship Lord Shiva as the supreme form of God) Shiva is Absolute God, the Creator of all, as well as the Destroyer.

SHRI (shree) - a term of reverence and respect. In ordinary oral or written correspondence, it is used like "Mister" in English.

SIDDHI (sid '-dhee) - An extraordinary power gained through religious practices and austerities.

SITA (see'-ta) - The wife and consort of Lord Ram; still held in India as the ideal of womanhood.

TAPAS (ta'-pas) - Austerities; self-denial; religious disciplines.

VIBHUTI (vi-boo'-tee) - In this book, Vibhuti is used as the ashes from the sacred fire (yagya or hawan), which have healing powers. Vibhuti is also a word for a special human manifestation of God, sent to perform a specific duty.

YAGYA or YAGNYA - See HAWAN.

YOGA - Literally, it means 'union.' It is used for union with The Divine; or for a course of study or a discipline leading toward union with The Divine.

YOGANANDA, Paramahansa - The Indian yogi who was sent by Mahavatar Babaji and Shri Yukteswar to America to teach kriya yoga. He is the author of "Autobiography of a Yogi," which first spread the name of Babaji in the West.

YOGI (yo'-gi; with a hard 'g') - A follower or practitioner of Yoga; or, more usually, one who has, through practice of yoga, attained 'supernatural' powers.

YOGINI (yo-gee'-nee, with a hard 'g') is the feminine form.

YUKTESWAR - Paramahansa Yogananda's guru; a disciple of Lahiri Mahasaya.

BIBLIOGRAPHY
AND
RECOMMENDED FURTHER READING

Abbott, Justin E. - THE LIFE OF TUKARAM, Motilal Banarsidass, Delhi, India.

Anzar, Naosherwan - THE ANCIENT ONE, A DISCIPLE'S MEMOIRS OF MEHER BABA; Beloved Books, Englishtown, New Jersey, U.S.A.

Bentov, Itzhak - STALKING THE WILD PENDULUM, Destiny Books, One Park Street, Rochester, VT 05767; 1977; Destiny Books edition, 1988.

Berry, David - HAVE GURU DARSHAN: HAIRAKHAN BABAJI; video by D. Berry, music by Turkantam; available from Jai Vishwa Distribution, www.babaji.net or www.BabajiAshram.org.

BHAGAVAD GITA - Translation by Juan Mascaro; Penguin Classics,1962.

BHAGAVAD GITA (The Song of God) - Translation by Swami Prabhavananda and Christopher Isherwood; a Mentor Book; 1944.

Bharatiya Vidya Bhawan - THE AGE OF IMPERIAL UNITY; Vol. II of The History and Culture of the Indian People, Bombay; 1954.

Campbell, Joseph, with Bill Moyers - THE POWER OF MYTH; Doubleday, New York, London, Toronto, Sydney, Auckland; 1988.

Carter, Jimmy and Rosalynn - EVERYTHING TO GAIN, Making the Most of the Rest of Your Life; Fawcett Gold Medal, New York, 1987.

Gaura Devi - FIRE OF TRANSFORMATION, Nymet Press, England, 2003. Available at Maha Lakshmi Shop, www.BabajiAshram.org.

Goodman, Shdema Shivani - BABAJI, MEETING WITH TRUTH, third printing, 1997. Available at www.BabajiAshram.org.

Gupta, Shakti M. - LEGENDS AROUND SHIVA; Somaiya Publications Pvt. Ltd., Bombay; 1979.

Haengdi, M. U. - NITYANANDA, THE DIVINE PRESENCE; Rudra Press, Cambridge, Massachusetts.

Isherwood, Christopher - RAMAKRISHNA AND HIS DISCIPLES; Vedanta Press, Hollywood, California.

Jand, K. L. - BABA JI; self-published in Ludhiana, India.

Javna, John - 50 SIMPLE THINGS YOU CAN DO TO SAVE THE EARTH; Earthworks Group, Box 25, 1400 Shattuck Ave., Berkeley, CA 94709.

Joshi, Hem Chand - HAIDAKHANDI LEELAS; published in 1970's, in Hindi.

Mahadevan, T.M.P. - RAMANA MAHARSHI, THE SAGE OF ARUNACALA; Mandala Books, Unwin Paperbacks, London.

Mahendra Baba - ANUPAM KRIPA; 1957; in Hindi.

Mahendra Baba - BLESSINGS AND PRECEPTS; translated by Prof. D.C. Das; published in 1963 by Shri Bankelal Pathak, Samba Sadashiv Kunj, Gopinath Bazar, Brahmakund, Vrindaban, U.P., India.

SHRI MAHENDRA MAHARAJ SMRITI GRANTH - Compiled by his disciples; published by Shri Mahendra Maharaj Smriti-Granth Samati; Samba Sadashiv Kunj, Brahmakund, Gopinath Bazar, Vrindaban, U.P., India; 1983; in Hindi.

Matthiessen, Peter - IN THE SPIRIT OF CRAZY HORSE; Viking Press.

THE MEANING OF THE GLORIOUS KORAN; translated by Mohammed Marmaduke Pickthall; a Mentor Book.

Minett, Gunnel - BABAJI: SHRI HAIDAKHAN WALE BABA; Stockholm, Sweden, 1986; available at www.BabajiAshram.org

Mishra, Vishnu Datt - SHRISADASHIV CHARITAMRIT; in Hindi; printed in 1959; enlarged and reprinted in 1983.

Muktananda, Swami - THE PLAY OF CONSCIOUSNESS; Harper & Row, New York, N.Y.

Murphet, Howard - SAI BABA AVATAR; Birthday Publishing Co., San Diego, California.

Rain, Mary Summer - SPIRIT SONG: The Visionary Wisdom of No-Eyes; Whitford Press, 1469 Morstein Road, West Chester, Pennsylvania 19380; 1985.

Ram Dass (Richard Alpert) - MIRACLE OF LOVE, STORIES ABOUT NEEM KAROLI BABA; E.P. Dutton, N.Y.; 1979.

Rao, Dr. V. V.S. - BABA JI; New Delhi, India. Out of print.

Reichel, Gertraud - BABAJI THE UNFATHOMABLE; G. Reichel Verlag, Reifenberg, West Germany; 1988, available from Maha Lakshmi Shop, www.BabajiAshram.org.

The RIG VEDA - Translated by Wendy Doniger O'Flaherty; Penguin Classics; 1981.

Satprem - SHRI AUROBINDO; Institute for Evolutionary Research, 200 Park Avenue, Suite 303 East, New York, N.Y. 10166.

Sivananda, Swami - LORD SHIVA AND HIS WORSHIP; The Divine Life Society, P.O. Shivanandanagar, Dist. Tehri- garhwal, U.P., India; 3rd edition, 1978.

SHANKARA'S CREST-JEWEL OF DISCRIMINATION - Translated by Swami Prabhavananda and Christopher Isherwood; Vedanta Press, Hollywoood, CA; 3d. ed., 1978.

SIVA PURANA - Ancient Indian Tradition & Mythology Series; published by Motilal Banarsidass, Bungalow Road, Delhi 110007; 1978.

Szekely, Edmond Bordeaux - CREATIVE WORK, Karma Yoga; 1973; International Biogenic Society, I.B.S. Internacional, Apartado 372, Cartago, Costa Rica, Central America.

TEACHINGS OF BABAJI - Haidakhandi Samaj, Haidakhan Vishwa Mahadham, P.O. Haidakhan, Dist. Nainital, U.A., India; 4th Edition, 2004; 3rd edition, 1988 and first edition published in two Volumes in 1983 and 1984. Available at www.BabajiAshram.org.

THE UPANISHADS, BREATH OF THE ETERNAL - Edited and translated by Swami Prabhavananda and Frederick Manchester; a Mentor Book; 1948.

Tweedy, Irina - THE CHASM OF FIRE; Element Books, Longmead Shaftesbury, Dorset SP7 8PL England; 1979. See also the complete unabridged edition of Ms. Tweedy's diary of her time with her Teacher, DAUGHTER OF FIRE, Blue Dolphin Publishing, Inc., P.O. Box 1908, Nevada City, CA 95959; 1986.

Wosien, Maria-Gabriele - BABADSCHI; published in German in Germany, 1978. An English translation, MESSAGE FROM THE HIMALAYAS is now available from Maha Lakshmi Shop, www.BabajiAshram.org.

Yogananda, Paramahansa - AUTOBIOGRAPHY OF A YOGI; Self-Realization Fellowship of Los Angeles, CA 90065, U.S.A.; 1946.

Yukteswar - THE HOLY SCIENCE; published by the Self-Realization Fellowship of Los Angeles; and in India by the Yogoda Satsang Society, Ranchi, Bihar.

INDEX

Datta (district of Gujarat State) - 49, 50

Dayal, Din - 139, 160

Dhan Singh of Haidakhan - 82, 83, 87, 88, 92

Dhanyan (Ashram in Almora District of U.P.) - 16, 25, 44, 131

Divya Kathamrit (a book by Mahendra Baba) - 60, 90, 92, 285

Dronagiri Mountain - 19, 120, 121, 122, 123

Drugs - 267, 268, 269, 270, 354, 357, 363, 364

Durga, Goddess - 47, 50

Eternal Way, the - See Sanatan Dharma.

Fakiranand - See Swami Fakiranand.

Gangotri Baba - 27, 42, 43, 45, 116, 117, 309, 346

Gaura Devi - 134, 140, 141, 162, 166, 180, 202, 224, 227, 235, 261, 268,
    272, 274, 281, 298, 306, 310, 319, 320, 322, 323, 326, 338, 341, 344

Gaurhari (the temple priest) - 242, 327, 382, 338, 339

Gautam Ganga - 8, 10, 28, 69, 114, 299, 300, 312, 341, 342

Gold, Margaret - See Sita Rami.

Goodman, Shdema (Shivani) - 187, 199, 266, 285, 375

"Guard Sahib" - 164

Haidakhan Vishwa Mahadham - 69, 86, 199, 286, 299, 301, 375

Haidakhan Wale Baba - See Babaji.

Haidakhandeshwari Ma (The Divine Mother of Haidakhan) - 203,
    295, 303

Haidakhan Samaj (of India) - 199, 214, 345

Haldwani (city in Nainital District of Uttar Pradesh State) - 7, 28,
    34, 43, 58, 67, 71, 72, 75, 76, 80, 81, 88, 93, 101, 102, 103, 104, 108,
    110, 112, 113, 114, 115, 123, 129, 131, 136, 167, 168, 169, 214, 223,
    311, 318, 322, 326, 328, 335, 336, 337, 338, 340, 341

Hanuman, Lord - 9, 16, 67, 80, 86, 139, 160, 225, 289, 370

Har Govind (Swiss psychologist) - 161, 162, 243, 322, 324

Hawan (or yagya) - 29, 44, 97, 126, 171, 172, 267, 292, 293, 303, 315,
    325, 370, 374

Humanitarianism - 271, 284, 287, 294, 361

Inamdar, Ambalal - 96, 67, 117-119,

Jagadamba (Universal Mother) - 25, 68, 303, 321

Jain, Shri - 59, 141, 246, 247

Jaman Singh and Babaji's property - 114

Jap, or japa - 49, 69, 70, 85, 223-227, 368, 370

Jaukshu Lama - 26, 27

Jesus Christ - 25, 163

379

Marston, J.D. - See Ram Dass.

Martinez, Maria Elena - 312

McCulloch, Stacey (Gayatridevi) - 319, 322-3, 347

Milarepa - 25, 183, 199, 308, 364

Mishra, Giridhari Lal - 30, 39, 45, 59, 63, 71

Mishra, Vishnu Dutt - See Vishnu Dutt Shastri.

Mittal, Laxmi Narayan - 60

Mohammed - xiv, 232, 294, 334, 376

Moksha Dham Dhuni - 184, 302-3, 321, 343, 356

Moti Bhagwan - 14

Moti Singh - 30, 45

Mount Kailash - See Kailash.

Munindra Baba, or Munindra Maharaj, or Shri Munindra - 29, 31, 56

Munirajji (Shri Trilok Singh) - v, 80, 102, 214, 215, 320-1, 327, 336, 339, 341-2, 359

Nagini - 317, 335

Nainital (city and district in Uttar Pradesh State) - 28, 31, 88, 103, 106-7, 110, 114, 120, 129, 131, 167, 199 223, 310, 311, 336, 371, 377, 385

Nandi, Sib Narayan (a.k.a. Nandi Baba) - 124-5, 311

Nan Singh - 191-2

Nantin Baba (a saint) - 75-80, 103, 114-116, 309, 337, 346, 367

Navratri - 25, 84, 87, 88, 313

Neem Karoli Baba (a saint) - xiv, 132, 1333, 156

Okhaldunga (village in Nainital Dist., U.P.) - 75-6, 83, 85-6, 93, 137, 309

'Old Haidakhan Baba' - v, 12, 28, 39, 45, 56-60, 65-6, 71, 75, 79-83, 86-7, 89, 95, 96, 102, 112, 114, 116, 123 135, 142, 216, 223, 297, 309, 310, 314, 321, 325, 336, 339, 346

Om Shanti Devi - v, 106, 238, 327-8

Opplinger, Mary (Tara Devi) - 134, 141

Orr, Leonard - 11, 150

Pant, Dinesh - 83, 88, 89, 93

Pant, Padma Datt - 104, 111

Parrish-Harra, Carol - 174

Pathak, Bankelal - 73, 93, 95, 376

Pinti - 147

Prem Baba - 172-4

Radha (Krishna's "Shakti") - 15, 72
Radhe Shyam, meaning of - 15
Raghuvir - 322, 356
Rajgarh (town in Rajasthan State) - 64-7, 71, 93, 98
Ram Dass (J.D. Marston) - vi, 161-2, 184-6, 304, 310-3, 322-4, 339
Ram, Lord - 9, 15, 23, 25, 47, 66, 68, 225, 232, 239, 243, 248, 301, 303-4, 313, 323, 370, 374
Ramloti (Deborah Wood) - ii, vi-vii, 346
Ram Singh - See Sammal.
Ranikhet (town in Uttar Pradesh) - 19, 20, 29, 120
Rao, Dr. V. V.S. - 45, 126, 261, 285, 317, 338, 335, 337
Reichel, Gertraud - vi, 176
Reynolds, Michael (Hiraman) - 142-6
Rocky Mountain Institute of Snowmass, Colorado -. 356
Sadashiv or Samba Sadashiv - 25, 30, 40, 53, 70-1, 295, 33, 385
"Sadguru Stuti Kusmanjali" (a book by Vishnu Dutt Mishra)- 65
Sammal, Baij Singh - 321
Sammal, Ram Singh - vi, 75-80, 85-89, 309
Sanatan Dharma (the Eternal Law) - iv, xi, 19, 192-8, 215, 225, 245, 269, 272, 288, 291, 295, 320, 333, 350, 370, 373
Seattle (Seathl), Chief - 350, 357, 359-60, 367
Sethi, Shri Balbir Singh - vi, 334
Sex and Marriage - 271
Shankara (788-820 A.D.) - 19, 25
Sharma, Col. Bhupindra (Bhoopie) - 164, 209-10, 326-7, 336, 339, 342-3
Sharma, Rajendra Kumar - vi, 185
Sharma, Ramesh Chandra - 90
Shastriji - See Vishnu Dutt Shastri.
Sheetlakhet Ashram - 29, 39, 51, 54
Sheila Devi Singh - v, 138, 146-7, 162, 195-6, 226, 297
Shivani - See Goodman, Shdema.
Shiromani Pathak - 29, 39-42, 51, 54-5
Shiva, or Lord Shiva - iii, ix, 5, 9, 16, 22-7, 36, 53-5, 62, 67-9, 71 73, 80, 82, 84, 89, 92, 99, 100-1, 110, 113, 122, 124, 126, 132, 134, 137, 147, 175-6, 179, 182, 201, 213, 215-6, 223, 235, 243, 268, 275, 286, 295-6, 298-9, 305, 309, 314, 321-2, 330, 346, 356, 369-74
Shiva Purana - 16, 22-4, 44

ABOUT THE AUTHOR

Radhe Shyam was born in Sioux City, Iowa, in 1928. He was christened Charles Swan. His father became a Presbyterian minister, so Charles went to school in four Iowa and Nebraska towns where his father was pastor. He received a B.A. in history and M.A. in political science from the University of Nebraska. He taught history and English in a Presbyterian mission school in Tehran, Iran, from 1950-1953. Upon graduation from the University of Michigan Law School in 1957, Radhe Shyam started a career of work in the Office of Foreign Buildings in the Department of State in Washington, D.C.

After 22 years in various positions in the Office of Foreign Buildings, Radhe Shyam retired in 1979. On a trip, early in 1980, intended to launch a consulting business, he met Haidakhan Baba - Babaji - in Vrindaban, India. Soon after, he abandoned the consulting career and his home in Washington, D.C., to live for five years in Babaji's ashram in the foothills of the Himalayas in northwestern India. Babaji gave Charles the name Radhe Shyam, one of the names of Lord Krishna.

"I Am Harmony" is the story of Radhe Shyam's and others' experiences of life and spiritual growth in the presence of this unique Himalayan Master.

In 1991, after publication of "I Am Harmony", Radhe Shyam went to Russia, where "I Am Harmony" was published in Russian. He lived five years in the city of Voronezh, south of Moscow, working with Association Peace Through Culture, U.S.A. to help create cultural, educational and business connections between Russia and the West. Since 1996, he has lived in Pittsburgh, Pennsylvania, with Sita Rami, who is now head of the Adoptions and Foster Care office at the Three Rivers American Indian Center, and practices law.

Radhe Shyam passed away in 2006. He was, the true eptiome of the selfless karma yogi generously giving of himself and working until the end on this new edition of "I Am Harmony" and serving as Board member of the American Haidakhan Samaj. It was his last wish to publish this new and revised edition. He lives on through the book, which has touched the hearts of so many people around the world. His presence, generous spirit, and guidance will always be with us through "I am Harmony".

ASHRAMS AND CENTERS AROUND THE WORLD

(Accessing any of the Web Sites will give you the most current contacts.)

AUSTRALIA
Gold Coast Shri Haidakhan Babaji Temple
http://www.babajiaustralia.com

AUSTRIA
Zentrum des Dienens
anamikabab@hotmail.com

BELGIUM
Ashram W.E.L.
http://www. ashram-wel.be

BULGARIA
raidass888@hotmail.com

CROATIA
http://www.haidakhan.net

CZECH REPUBLIC
Tel.: 011-420-7813114

ESTONIA
Haidakhandi Shiva Dham
http://www.lilleoru.ee

FRANCE
Le Samaj (French Samaj)
purnananda@free.fr

GERMANY
Bhole Baba Ashram, Rieferath
http://www. Bhole-Baba-Ashram.de

INDIA
Haidakhan Vishwa Mahadham
P.O. Haidakhan,
Dist. Nainital (U.A.) 263126

Anand Puri Ashram, Chilianaula
Raniket, Dist. Almora (U.A.)

INDONESIA
Anand Puri Ashram
aif@indo.net.id

IRELAND
Haidakhan Bhole Baba Centre Milmorane
ambai@circom.net

ITALY
Bhole Baba Ashram (Cisternino)
http://www.bholebaba.org
Centro di Pace Haidakhandi
falzoni@galactita.it

JAPAN
Babaji Centre
babaji@mv.0038.net

LATVIA
estere@latnet.lv

NETHERLANDS/HOLLAND
Sada Shiva Dham Ashram
http://www.Babaji.nl

POLAND
Shri Herakhandi Seva Dham Ashram
http://www.babaji.pl

RUSSIA
Omkar Shiva Dham Ashram (Siberia)
http://www.Babaji.ru
Mahaprabhuji Ashram
kumali@vmail.ru

SLOVENIA
http://www.SriBabaji.org

SOUTH KOREA
New Babaji Center (planned)
sukhdeva@hotmail.com

SWITZERLAND
Center of Unity Schweibenalp
http://www.schweibenalp.ch

UNITED KINGDOM
Haidakhan Samaj UK
http://www.Babaji.org.uk

UNITED STATES
Haidakhandi Universal Ashram
http://www.BabajiAshram.org

SWEDEN
Sambasadashiva Dham
intuition.bw@swipnet.se

TO ORDER THIS BOOK

GO TO:
www.babajiashram.org/mls/books/

OR EMAIL:
shop@BabajiAshram.org

OR CALL:
719-256-4108